Toward a New
CIVILIZATION

ARTHUR BLECH

Toward a New
CIVILIZATION
Why We Must Tame Our Instincts to Save Our World

59 John Glenn Drive
Amherst, New York 14228-2197

Published 2005 by Prometheus Books

Inquiries should be addressed to
Prometheus Books
59 John Glenn Drive
Amherst, New York 14228–2197
VOICE: 716–691–0133, ext. 207
FAX: 716–564–2711
WWW.PROMETHEUSBOOKS.COM

09 08 07 06 05   5 4 3 2 1

Library of Congress Cataloging-in-Publication Data

Blech, Arthur.
    Toward a new civilization : why we must tame our instincts to save our world /
Arthur Blech.
        p. cm.
    Includes bibliographical references and index.
    ISBN 1–59102–350–5 (hardcover : alk. paper)
    1. Civilization—Forecasting. 2. Religion and civilization. 3. Human beings—
Forecasting. I. Title.

CB161.B549 2005
303.49—dc22

2005014006

Printed in the United States of America on acid-free paper

Contents

Foreword

Arthur Blech's work will lead to much controversy. The intentionally nonacademic style of argumentation and citation, which has the advantage of penetrating, as it were, to the unvarnished "thing itself" (Edmund Husserl), heightens the seriousness with which the process of civilization is described. More importantly, it describes where this process will lead. What immediately stands out and often catches one's breath in reading the individual chapters—such as "Human Nature, the Greatest Threat to Its Own Survival," "The Opposition between Civilization and Nature," "The Effect of Judaism on Civilization"—is the rigor with which Arthur Blech describes the condition of the earth and humanity's situation. Under "civilization" is included all contexts and developments connected with the term since Cicero's influential definition. Cicero understood this concept to mean, as we do today, the condition and the process of humanity itself: to strive for ever better stages in general living conditions and also in morality, knowledge, the arts, and general capabilities.

Blech examines very closely this process and its current stage of development. He takes into consideration the heritage of religion and morality and of political and economic systems. The result is alarming. To sum it up in one sentence, the final conclusion of the author is: The path that was begun in Jewish, Greek, and Roman aniquity can no longer be continued. Only a profoundly new understanding of civilization can lead to a new, hopeful phase of human history; only in this way would the chance of survival be assured, along with a free and decent form of coexistence for all people.

The book is appearing simultaneously in Germany under the title *Für eine neue Zivilisation.* It will lead to animated discussions there as well as here. Before making judgments based on a 'purely academic standpoint,' I would recommend looking closely at the following: the condition of our civilization and culture, the condition of the earth and its future, and, above all, the contents of the unorthodox, yet exceptionally serious and careful argumentation of author Arthur Blech.

Prof. Dr. Bernhard Schäfers,
Dean of the Department of Sociology and Cultural Sciences,
Technical University of Karlsruhe, Germany

Introduction

Civilization is a term used by literary circles, historians, and publicists to describe a superior level of accomplishments of certain nations. Coined in mid-18th century France, it denoted initially good manners, a degree of civility, and possession of an elevated culture distinguished by artistic, scientific, and technological achievements to set the possessor-nations apart from others whose attainments signified nothing out of the ordinary. After many later attempts to refine the definition, the views of three men of letters deserve special attention.

(1) Civilization requires a modicum of material prosperity—enough to provide a little leisure, it requires confidence. (Kenneth Clark)

(2) The rise of civilization was a people's response to a challenge in a situation of special difficulty that rouses them to make an unprecedented effort; that Nature had to present itself as a difficulty to be overcome. (Arnold J. Toynbee)

(3) Civilization is the reformation of Nature. It depended upon the relationship of man and his environment, upon refashioning the natural environment to suit human uses, and upon the degree to which societies modify their natural environment. (Fernández-Armesto)

In other words, references are made to the difficulty posed by the physical environment and Nature's physical challenges which had to be overcome because they presented a danger to man.

Astonishingly, the three authors whose ideas about the nature of civilization represent the more advanced thinking on the subject ignored the importance of morality and the influence it exercises on the way man treats his fellowmen within the framework of a social setting. It should be evident that if men mistreat, oppress, and exploit their fellowmen (a violation of moral dictates), then material prosperity, the unprecedented effort made to overcome situations of special difficulty and the refashioning of the natural environment to suit man's uses would lack relevance in attaining a level of morality to serve as a foundation for civilization. For the actions of man, if unhindered in his struggle for self-preservation and seeking material prosperity to attain the desired level of creature comforts, bear the major responsibility in creating situations of special difficulty and give rise to self-made obstacles in his quest to defy the natural order. Man is the cause of hazards to his existence created by overpopulation, environmental degradation, and injecting various toxic substances into his food supply; he is the designer of an unbalanced economy whose stratification favors the well-to-do to the detriment of the disadvantaged, keeping most in a state of turmoil; he is the contriver of religious systems, some of which are responsible for the most unnatural crimes committed by humans against humans; last but not least, he is the sole instigator of murderous mass slaughters of humans resulting from wars fought in anger causing ever increasing casualties and destruction reaching totally destabilizing magnitudes. These acts bode ill for civilization.

Man, that flawed creation of a flawed Nature, in bondage to survival instincts and a virtual slave to circumstances beyond his control, nevertheless possesses the capacity to free himself from some of the burdens imposed by the natural order to rise above the gravitational pull confining all living species. He must discover that his welfare and that of society depend on the rejection of the natural order so as to be freed, however moderately, from Nature's evolutionary competition and the struggle for the survival of the fittest, an order totally in conflict with morality. For the aims of morality are antithetical to Nature's imposed scheme of things, reflecting the conflict between their aims and designs—stern stuff is needed to guide man's course.

To be moral means to oppose Nature's order. Morality is foundational for civilization to gain a foothold, for without morality there can only be pseudo-civilizations, a misnomer for impaired imitations, a flawed cultural milieu enabling the select few only to ease the burden of existence. The success or failure of man in his struggle to overcome the imperatives of the natural order and the causes which would persuade him to recognize the benefits morality and civilization have to offer depend on his reaction to the confluence of events and the interaction of forces embracing his effort to persevere in existence. Such events and forces are social, cultural, economic, and religious. It requires a redefinition of civilization, as well as morality, ethics, virtue, Nature, and the natural order; a new approach to the critique of monotheistic religions and of classical and conventional economics; an unhampered and bold insight into social and cultural anthropology. The problems man faces (social, religious, economic, scientific, and technological) are too complex and may defy complete resolution. But man must attempt to find fitting solutions, even though of limited applicability, to survive the consequences of his own creation. The existence of man-made problems, the required approach to resolve them and advance the cause of civilized man, civilized society, and a state of civilization are the subject matter of this book.

CHAPTER 1

MAN

The Greatest Threat to His Survival

(1) Nicolaus Copernicus (1473–1543), a Polish astronomer, was one of the seminal scientists who advanced the cause of astronomy at a time when a few courageous men, at great risk to their person, were beginning to cast off the theological shackles of the Catholic Church, which, in its limited wisdom, suppressed the awakening curiosity about the Universe. Those were exciting times, a complete break with the past (although Aristarchus, 3rd century B.C., one of those amazing Greeks, determined that the Earth moves and revolves about the sun in the circumference of a circle) geocentric Ptolemaic system, a steady erosion of the mythical cosmology of the Bible. He was able to let his thoughts soar because his post of canon ensured his lifelong financial security (his primary needs were satisfied). Tycho Brahe (1546–1601), a Danish astronomer, rejected the Copernican system and made his own contribution to the advance of astronomy. He also stated that the Universe is like a clockwork, ordered and precise. Although this fictive allegory can be excused in an age of emerging astronomy as a science, it has been subsequently reported often enough to grace the conventional thinking of the present, i.e., that the Universe represents perfection itself, ordered and precise. It is again the dramatic corruption of language which is one of the principal reasons for this misconception. For the term "perfect" is derived from the Latin "per-ficere", to finish, to complete. The intrinsic meaning of the word is that of something finished or completed (even though a clumsy product),

something static and changeless. But even the highly sophisticated modern astronomers with all their observatories and ever more giant telescopes, including those mounted on satellites, are unable to agree among themselves, nor assert scientific data with certainty and consistency, when contemplating the immensity of the Universe, though they progressed eons beyond Copernicus in knowledge of the Universe. (The distance from the planet Earth to the most remote Quasars is eight or more billion light years—one light year equals six trillion miles.) The newly born and dying stars; the billions of galaxies; some cluster of galaxies contain more than 10,000 galaxies; one of the largest clusters is more than 100 million light years away from Earth; some galaxies contain trillions of suns; immense galactic collisions, some in birth and some in decay; the mysteries of the black hole; the origin of Quasar explosions—possibly due to multiple collisions of millions of stars densely packed in the core of galaxies; continuous evolutionary sequences of exploding galaxies—fluid structures with 100 billion stellar components. We do know enough about the Universe to assert that it is not like a clockwork, ordered, precise. On the contrary. Most astronomers agree that the Universe is expanding in all directions at 90% the speed of light; talk is of infinite time and infinite space; new matter is continuously being created in an expanding Universe and becomes congregated into galaxies; some galaxies contain trillions of suns, with order and disorder equally evident, an immense variety of irregular galaxies with some blowing themselves up, a clear indication that something has gone mysteriously wrong. Do we need a new definition of "order"? Is the human understanding of "order" not applicable to the Universe? Is the Universe, in its inconceivable immensity, governed by different laws of physics and chemistry, unknown to us and not comprehensible by humans because it does not conform to human experience in physics, chemistry and mathematics? There is no order out there, no regularity, no correspondence, no conformity with anything the human neocortex is qualified to understand. We humans, inhabiting one of the planets of the solar system, located toward the edge of a peripheral spiral galaxy, which is itself located on the edge of a supercluster of galaxies, one such of a billion systems, will have to be reconciled to a given, namely, that the vast complexities of the Universe are beyond our understanding; that rather than have the collective intelligence of astronomers probe the origin of the Universe (a matter of dubious importance and value) in endless frustrating, costly and ever changing speculations, their scientific know-how be instead directed toward solving the problems here on Earth, such as understanding the fragility of Nature and devising a plan to save the human race from itself, from extinction. There is disharmony in the Cosmos, passed on to Nature, passed on to animal species, particularly to the human species. If the human eye were capable of observing an explosion in process for a fraction of a second, the observer would call the experience orderly, harmonious, precise and beautiful. Such a fraction is about all we have so far observed of the Universe. But we are most assuredly able to observe clearly the disharmony and chaotic conditions prevailing in objects much closer to us: the fractured Nature and fractured humans.

(2)   About 4.5 billion years ago, the planet Earth was formed in a process that involved trial and error, global magma oceans, the whole surface flooded with liquid rock, floods, tidal waves, volcanic eruptions, hot gases, oceans of lava cooling and solidifying. By the time the human species appeared, when conditions became propitious for human existence—and it was by a razor thin margin as if by accident—99.998% of the then formation of the Universe was over. The Earth was populated by animals that preceded man by hundreds of million years, when the evolutionary process was in full swing (it still is), with Nature discarding as useless and unfit most of the animal species it nurtured before man finally evolved in what appears a continuous process up to the present. We do not and cannot know, given the scientific techniques and know-how available at present, whether generations of humanity existed on Earth one or several times eons ago only to be wiped out by the changing hostile natural conditions, and close one chapter only to open a new one later, untraceably buried under mile-high lava. Archeologists may yet rue the day when they established, with pretended certainty, the Stone Age Palaeolithic period (circa 2.4 million years ago) as the inception of tool-making. If dinosaurs disappeared from the scene during the Mesozoic Era, why could not a species of man? Nature's fragility reflected in trial and error with the animal species could also have played havoc with the human species. Modern man faces possible extinction from environmental pollution and overpopulation which disasters, unlike convulsive eruptions of the past, are slowly and imperceptibly creeping up on him—could this be a repeat of some past similar experience? It is only reasonable to conclude from observation that man inherited the fragility of Nature, and his effort to tame and control his instincts and mend his structural disabilities may be doomed to failure on that account. A few thousand years in the Cosmic scheme of things, could that really be all the destiny of "civilized" man?

(3) Human life is possible on Earth by the narrowest of a thin margin, an environment basically hostile to man; the right temperature, adequate potable water and an oxygen atmosphere. All life on Earth is closely related, of common organic chemistry and evolutionary heritage. The domestication of animals by artificially inducing genetic changes has occurred within a span of less than 5,000 years. If so, can we comprehend the magnitude of changes induced by the natural order of things over millions, nay, billions of years? The struggle for existence, the adaptation to changed conditions had to have an explosive effect on the mutations and changes in the evolution of the animal species, including man. The structures of organisms are by necessity appropriate to their function. The simplest one-celled organism is a far more complex machine than the finest clockwork. The need of a Designer is a flawed but natural human explanation of the biological world. However, trial and error are evident from fossil records, an apparent inability to anticipate the future, a circumstance totally antithetical and fatal to the concept of a Designer. But the human mind, viewing natural phenomena in a finite and limited way, is incapable of grasping what wondrous changes a million, a hundred million years can effect. It compares its compressed experience in the time it took to craft a clockwork with the immensity of time encompassed in the humanly unfathomable epoch, of say, 300 million years, to work wonders with mutation, adaptability, variation and modification. Nor can there be any human comprehension or yardstick to grasp the utter immensity of the distance of an object a billion light years away. Human beings must be reconciled with the unknowability and ungraspability of much of the information about the Universe, the immensity of time and space, and confine their attention, at best, to their solar system, the planet Earth, the natural order of things, i.e. Nature, which is not in harmony with their interests, but on the contrary, hostile to their survival as "civilized" people.

(4) Let us look at those heavenly Greek thinkers of ancient times, between the 6th and 2nd century B.C., who without the benefit of any visual instruments but just relying on their common sense, reasoning power, and geometry, came to some startling conclusions which anticipated modern astronomers by almost 2,000 years. Pythagoras (6th century B.C.) was the first to call the Earth round; Anaxagoras (5th century B.C.) stated that the moon received its light from the sun; Aristarchus (3rd century B.C.) concluded that the stars and sun remain unmoved, that the Earth moves and revolves around the sun in the circumference of a circle, the

sun lying in the middle of the orbit; Hipparchus (2nd century B.C.) concluded that the solar year has 365 days, minus 4 minutes and 48 seconds,
an error of 6 minutes according to current calculations; the time for a
mean lunar month was 29 days, 12 hours, 44 minutes, 2 seconds—less
than a second away from the presently accepted figure; Erastothenes (3rd
century B.C.) calculated the Earth's circumference as 24,662 miles—the
current computation is 24,847 miles. This is breathtaking thinking. But
just as profound are their fellow thinkers' conclusions which anticipated
Darwin by over 2,000 years. For example, Empedocles (5th century B.C.)
expounded the theory of evolution of man from the lower forms of life
and described the slow advance of man from savagery to civilization; that
all higher forms of life developed from lower forms. Although these
Greeks were excellent thinkers—and were original in many other disciplines—they had no hint that man could ever be in opposition to Nature.
They admired Nature as something to be imitated. The Cynics (the
school founded in the 5th century B.C.) mounted the first major attack on
"civilized values", counseled that humans should study Nature not in
order to explain the world, which they insisted was impossible, but that
they could learn the wisdom of Nature as a guide to life; it was a reaction
to the vexing problems the then "complex" civilization posed. Zeno (4th
century B.C.) taught that the well-being of the individual is identical
with the law of Nature; that to live according to Nature is the purpose of
science and philosophy; made Nature the center of his ethics and took
Nature as a moral guide. Pyrrho (4th century B.C.), however, cautioned
that certainty of knowledge is unattainable and that all theories are probably false, so that one might as well accept the conventions of his time.
But what did the Greeks understand by the term "Nature"? That Nature
includes everything and that following Nature meant rejecting the institution of the city-state. Yet despite an unmatched capacity for intuitive
and insightful thinking, and despite the wisdom displayed in so many of
man's most esoteric disciplines, they did not confront the problems of the
natural order of things, i.e., Nature, because the social, population, environmental, economic, and political problems were superficial and incomparably less acute than at present on account of the technological
advances, population explosion, ecological degradation, economic
exploitation. Blinding political duplicity to the dangers threatening the
survival of the human species reached a level of intensity in the 20th century which could not have been foreseen, anticipated, imagined, and
comprehended in ancient times. When the ancient Greeks admired

Nature as something to be imitated, they were totally ignorant of the havoc caused by microbes, viruses and germs, organisms capable of causing various contagious diseases, many of them spread by airborne transmission, contagious illnesses spread by mosquitoes, immunodeficient conditions (just to name a few)—all adversely afflicting mankind by the grace of Nature. When they considered Nature as a moral guide they could not have known that 99% of the living species have died out; that countless species were brought forth only to be discarded; that more organisms are produced than grow to maturity; that thousands are born that one may live. When they identified the well-being of the individual with the law of Nature, they must have known that many children are born deformed, crippled, blind, whose lives have no purpose other than to be hopelessly wasted—causing great pain to their parents; that millions of human beings are indiscriminately destroyed. When they spoke approvingly of the law of Nature, they must have known that the strong rules and the weak obeys, that almost all animals (except those on top of the food chain and those that are domesticated) subsist by devouring other animals only to be devoured themselves; that the implacable struggle for existence is the rule of Nature and that any deviation from the rule is contrary to Nature and in opposition to it. The Cynics were wrong: to follow the wisdom of Nature as a guide to life is to descend to the level of savages, cannibals, lawlessness, total anarchy, primitive vulgarity, and dignify the law of the jungle—a course the Cynics could not have contemplated. The complexion of Nature in relation to man and his moral bearing was beyond the understanding of the ancient Greeks, those heavenly thinkers, because the interdependent components of the conflict and opposition have not coalesced till the most modern era when the population explosion and environmental degradation, those prime twin corroding and corrupting malefactors reached the flash point. But it was not only the resourceful Greeks who missed the conflict between Nature and man. From that time on till the middle of the 20th century, not one in the long parade of luminous thinkers, with the exception of the 19th century English biologist T. H. Huxley (who silently suffered the opprobrium of his colleagues on account of his views), was able to visualize the conflict and draw the inevitable conclusions. It did not require penetrating thinking (for the Greeks would have grasped it), nor scientific experiments, nor astronomy, mathematics or philosophy, but the simple expedient of observing the profound problems man has faced after the middle of the 20th century never faced by man before (what history is available to us), that presage his possible extinction. If man's interests are opposed to Nature, the consequences of this viewpoint are far-reaching. Gone is the unity of Nature; the basis for man's ever ascending destiny; the hollowness and futility of human progress; the footing of all mono-theistic religions which preach a Creation solely for the benefit of man.

(5) It is difficult to find an appropriate definition of Nature in the literature of the subject matter. Some examples are : Everything in the physical world of experience; everything that belongs to the world of Nature; Nature preserves spontaneity without incursions from outside by souls or spirit, divine or human; Nature is the world of organisms as the product of evolution, unseen vital process. There are two problems:

(1) Distinction must be made between Cosmic forces and Nature, by limiting the latter to the planet Earth, where it can be studied, measured, and compartmentalized for easier understanding.

(2) The creative and created aspects must be recognized as the vital functions of Nature.

The definition I consider most suitable: Nature is the sum total of the vital, life giving, and life sustaining forces, creative and created, material and other, that encompass all the phenomena in existence on the planet Earth.

It follows, therefore, that man is also part of Nature and his activities expressed in instincts and thoughts are governed by the natural order of things. Man is aware of Nature because he is a sentient being acquainted, in various degrees, with the inorganic objects and processes (physics) and the organic processes with the changing quality of life, evolution, growing awareness of his stewardship of the Earth, and the most recent penetration into the working of self-replicating molecules of DNA (Biology).

(6) If man is part of Nature, how can his thought be in opposition to it? How can man conclude that Nature is fractured, unable to control his instinct of procreation as it does very successfully that of other animal species, unable to control his thought processes which are developing the means of interfering with natural evolution, unable to halt his invasive steps to frustrate the effects of Nature's most fundamental instincts applicable to all organisms, namely, the struggle for self-preservation? Man developed beyond other members of the animal species because his erect posture freed his hands for making tools of ever greater complexity and variety to aid him in his struggle for self-preservation. With population growth, this struggle increased in intensity until the hunter-gatherer could not provide

adequately for his sustenance. His nomadic life changed to a settled communal status with the inception and growth of agriculture and communal pooling of resources, placing extreme demands on his thought processes, his inventiveness, his ingenuity in overcoming new impediments he never faced before. These all sharpened his intelligence, his neocortex, and together with the later development of language and writing, polished his thought process to the point where he could handle new experiences and overcome new obstacles which in turn improved his mind to face ever more complex problems. But his tool-making, agricultural pursuits to create a surplus, communal living to provide for common safety and a basic legal system, all these were acts in opposition to Nature since they subverted its primary axiom, namely, that only the strong and cunning survive and the weak and mediocre fall by the wayside. No room for honesty; decency; peaceable conduct; care for the frail, sick and old; safety from animal or human predators; in short, mitigating the struggle for existence and making life more bearable by attempting to alleviate pain and suffering—all these are acts in opposition to Nature, the natural order of things, and the natural evolutionary process. But Nature will exact a steep price for man's defiance. Yes, he will be able to overcome the constraints of natural evolution and selection by promoting medical science to level the field of diversity among humans; he will aptly make use of genetic engineering, biotechnology and reconstructive surgery—whose application will completely revolutionize the social and political future of mankind. Yes, man will be able to postpone the inevitable day when hunger, that primordial urge motivating all organisms to action, will exhaust his ability to frustrate the "Malthusian trap" and sadly concede his failure to supply adequate sustenance for all his fellowmen. For his uncontrollable natural instinct of procreation, that curse with its concomitant pollution of the environment and inevitable degradation of the ecosystem, will bring forth a modern version of the "Black Death", and at best, restore the population balance by decimating the excess, or, at worst, write a finish to the story of homo sapiens. Yet, considering the immensity of past ages, this may not be the first demise but probably one of the repeat performances of a fractured and fragile man.

(7)   The conditions for man's vulnerability are formidable, and getting more so with the passage of time. Most of the human race, uncluttered by doubt or hesitation, using pious disinformation, is unwilling and unable to grasp the seriousness that overpopulation poses to its well-being. The total population of the world at the time of Julius Caesar was 300 million,

compared with today's 6 billion, and growing by 100 million per annum. They require more land to live on and more food to sustain them, a contradiction that has been resolved in favor of population and against the wholesomeness of food. As more people need more land to live on and overcrowd cities, the crop-producing land is reduced and compensated by synthetic pesticide, herbicide, and fertilizer, more intensive farming with less available water, and genetically altered seeds and crops, all destructive to a well-balanced ecosystem necessary for the survival of man. But the sheer numbers of humanity cause more burning of fossil fuel (carbon dioxide); pollution caused by chemical fertilizers and automobile emissions (nitrous oxides); destructive and disabling carcinogens (CFC, PCB, DDT, dioxin) gutting the ecosystem and also the reproductive process of man and animal; the deforestation and burning of tropical forests harming the life-essential greenhouse effect; the global warming impact on seasonal crops, droughts, and climate; interference with the marginal (3%) water supply which must be constantly recycled; damage to ozone layer—all these increase what is bound to lead to destructive pollution wreaking havoc with the immune system of humans and animals. All these are man's doings, that structurally faulty being, which are irreversible unless a sustainable population balance is soon restored— this is not going to happen by man's thoughtful evaluation of the problem but will require drastic measures he would be loath to take. The peremptory actions necessary are not on the horizon. Man is pillaging the planet Earth, squandering valuable non-renewable resources, poisoning its rivers, lakes, and oceans, exhausting renewable resources faster than they can be replenished by Nature, burying the land in a cesspool of garbage (The United States alone generated a total of 200 million tons in 1998, a problem which will only get worse). But the problem is not difficult to understand and does not require exhaustive analyses. No need to delve into the esoteric aspects of chemistry and biology, macromolecules, algorithms, minimal self-reproducing mechanisms, synthetizing DNA fragments, building blocks of life, enzyme machines, solipsistic self-producers, one-dimensional protein strings, molecular design, and the like. The day must come when man will recognize that the key to his salvation is the simple application of controlled procreation; that the present population level must be reduced substantially to, and maintained at, ecologically sustainable levels; that his Nature-given instinct of procreation is flawed in that it recognizes no limits nor has Nature provided any constraints other than a slow process of measured degradation, which, in time, will erode man's vitality. Man's unlimited rate of procreation, which accords with the natural order of things, will, in time, nullify Nature's bountiful life-giving dispensations, a conflict and discordant note which is bound to occur by Nature's defective design to provide a milieu, a functionally efficient setting capable of accommodating the ever increasing masses of humanity. Man's concept of a global economy is just as faulted and contains within itself the seeds of its own undoing and demise. Global business depends on global consumers able to translate their needs into consumer demands; the latter depend on purchasing power, which is generally tied to gainful employment; consumer demand is increased by making the price of goods attractive, which encourages more efficient productivity; the latter is stimulated by cost-saving streamlining of production or service, which will most likely decrease employment, which reduces the purchasing power with the consequent reduction of demand—and so the cycle goes on. The ambition of global business is progressive and uninterrupted expansion that require an ever increasing cadre of consumers, promoting unlimited population growth as its badge and hope for success, ignorant and cynically uncaring for all the harm such enterprise causes to the environment specifically and to a large segment of the population generally. The business community and the Catholic Church—those strangest of bedfellows sharing some common aspirations (seeking prosperity and thriving on conflict)—are the worst offenders in scuttling isolated but determined efforts made by concerned and forward-looking environmentalists to control unbridled population growth, but the contest appears to be unequal for the present. The curse of homo sapiens is that the life-giving instinct of reproduction, Nature's magnificent gift ensuring the perpetuation of the species, if abused in the extreme, will cause his decimation or an imperceptibly slow-creeping demise of a flawed species.

(8) But Nature, magnificently endowed with awesome eye appealing beauty which excites the imagination and stirs the pulse of poets, painters, musicians and other artists, clasps within its powerful embrace all living creatures inhabiting the planet Earth, is flawed—conditions for life exhibit a pattern of design that has gone amiss or was structurally faulted from the outset. Man must be selfish enough to declare that if, on the one hand, Nature created conditions conducive to evolution of life and, on the other hand, simultaneously placed obstacles in the way which vitiate and corrupt that same effort to sustain life, placing endurance and extinction on the same footing, then the conclusion is inescapable and execrable:

Nature's plan for life is, from the human point of view, nothing but a sordid game of chance, a Russian roulette, without any taint of sustained order and regularity of design. When man follows his procreation instinct, urges implanted within his body by Nature without imposing any safeguards to limit an inevitable and predictable population explosion, and left it up to him to maintain a sustainable equilibrium, the antidote will not only be limited nourishment but also an energy-sapping environmental and nutritional degradation, a disorganization of society, a disruption of all accepted standards of conduct, a politically unacceptable growing chasm between the well-fed and starving nations, the expanding gap between the haves and the have-nots within nations, lawlessness, in short, inevitable tribulations and chaos disrupting everything civilized man stands for. The end is predictable—suffocation in a self-created environmental swamp. As for other animal species, Nature's response to excessive breeding is swift, orderly and successful: reducing the numbers by starvation, eliminating the weak and old, sickness, diseases, and epidemics induced by an impaired immune system, till a balance is restored between the available feed and the hungry mouths. Plentiful feed will encourage herbivores to proliferate excessively, which will have the same effect on carnivores that devour them. The restoration of the balance is orderly, planned and merciless. That is the natural order of things, Nature's way of ensuring the perpetuation of the species without disrupting the lives of survivors. On the contrary, the method employed brings about greater fitness of the survivors. The process is repeated, from time to time, with like results and no harm to the ecology or other unaffected species. Nature possesses the capacity to restore the status quo ante and the process can be repeated endlessly. With man, the orderly and natural restoration of population balance was employed up to a certain period in history, approximately until the 19th century, after which formidable man's forces intervened in Nature's scheme of things by infiltrating the order with revolutionary advances in medicine, techniques of surgery and all facets of technology to ease the burden of existence. Most importantly, however, it facilitated the beginning of a population explosion by drastically reducing the death-rate of infants, restoring the health of the previously discarded infirm, extending the life and usefulness of the elderly, providing greatly improved habitation to withstand the elements, more adequate and healthful hygienic conditions, but primarily, supplying an abundance of nutritious food to feed the growing human population, however unevenly allocated, as time would show. But all these prolific innovations and making life a bearable experience had one particular fault. The intelligence of man, even though a part of Nature, has exceeded Nature's built-in mechanism to control the harmful and escalating population increases by thwarting Nature's restoration of a suitable population balance (as in the case of animal species), and in the process causing irreversible harm to the ecosystem, causing harm not only to the human species but to all the animal species inhabiting the Earth, as described above. The result will not be a restoration of the status quo ante but the progressive and incremental poisoning of the environment and the ensuing injury to all living creatures, including man, the most structurally fragile, in particular. This result would accord with the natural order of things.

(9)   Man perceives the Universe and Nature through his senses and inevitably judges everything connected with them from the egocentric point of view: what advantage, benefit, and profit he can derive from them. Just like most religions ascribe anthropomorphic attributes to their God in spite of defining the Deity as infinite, invisible and unknowable, so do scientists ascribe attributes to the Universe and Nature despite their pious claim to secularity. When speaking of the Universe and Nature, they use terms such as the beginning; the birth of stars; the big bang; the age of the Universe, stars and planets; death of stars; black holes swallowing stars; expansions; contractions; loss of energy. But man must acknowledge that the Universe and Nature do not exist for his benefit and that he will remain forever ignorant for what purpose they do exist and for what purpose he exists. He must also accept that the Universe is infinite in space and time, that most likely other Universes exist and that life on Earth did not necessarily have the putative beginning calculated by man, but could be the succession of numerous birth-death cycles preceding the present (and therefore such terms as beginning, age, expansions, contractions, etc., are not appropriate). These are all interesting portrayals to keep the scientists occupied. There is no purpose served by constantly revising the probable age of the Universe, or the planet Earth, or the date of appearance of the first complex life (as recently—August 1999—pushed back by 500 million to 1 billion years from previous estimates). Will the probable age of the Universe expedite a cure for cancer? Will one hungry or homeless child find comfort in knowing that some stars are dying? What difference does it make to the magnitude of environmental pollution that the black hole is swallowing stars? Man is facing real survival problems on this Earth which cannot be counted in billions,

millions, thousands of years, nay, probably not even in the hundreds. Yet scientists of various disciplines eagerly strive to satisfy their curiosity concerning knowledge that is "sub specie eternitatis" instead of pursuing the more essential and indispensable solutions "sub specie humanis".

(10) Man must humbly admit that his presence on Earth is not beneficial to the survival of Nature, animal life, the ecosystem, and that except for domesticated animals, things would be more in harmony if he were to disappear from the scene. But man is on the scene, and as long as his presence is sustainable, he will view his interests "sub specie humanis". Since Nature is indifferent to man's existence, no more and no less than to thousands of species that have disappeared from the scene, the question is not whether some events were brought into being which enabled homo sapiens to appear, but rather whether the laws of Nature are structurally faulted so as to frustrate man's development of a civilization consistent with his increasing numbers and evolving intelligence, or whether man should have never advanced from the primitive conditions of the Stone Age, when the population was numbered only several millions and was in harmony with Nature. The densely populated Earth is becoming increasingly vulnerable to ever more destructive natural forces, disrupting and frustrating the lives of humanity by totally arbitrary and random shocks which can only be described in human terms as the "Wrath of Nature". The consequences of catastrophic natural disasters are the more pronounced the greater the density of population directly affected by the calamity, the disruption and disorder caused to their lives, the pain, suffering, hardship, and financial losses endured by the people affected. The suddenness of the tragedies, the complete innocence of the people affected, the extent of the damage sometimes setting back progress by the life of a generation, the rebuilding and restoration costs mostly funded by governments because they are beyond the means of the victims—all these constitute an ever increasing drain and depletion of natural and financial resources. Instead of being spent on progressive improvements benefiting all people, they have to be applied to cover losses of the affected minority.

(11) How does Nature manifest its "wrath"? Even with the sophisticated advance warning systems of impending disasters, lives might be saved but properties destroyed. Since most of Nature's catastrophes are either repeat events in the same locality as in prior years or new ones occurring for the first time, man, in his wisdom, could avoid placing his property in harms way. The same applies to improvements built by governmental

entities, such as highways, bridges, dams. In such cases losses from catastrophes could be greatly minimized or even avoided. The result would be a substantial reduction in livable space, increased density in the populated remaining space and a continuous decrease of safe areas to choose from. But the financial dislocation, which would be immense, would pose hardships of catastrophic proportions, doable if there is sufficient resolve, but the resultant disorder would present massive problems and no government could risk such steps. It is taken for granted that most people live in areas because of their choice and those very few unwilling to suffer repeat natural disasters (named for some peculiar reason "Acts of God") would relocate on their own to safer locales. It would not only be a financial hardship to do so, but a social one as well involving disruption of community, friends, church and school attachments. For it is one of those curious phenomena of humans that those who escaped with their lives but suffered loss of property, even a complete wipe-out, would stubbornly defy Nature in the future and risk repeat disasters rather than admit defeat and surrender. But most people have no choice in the matter and return to the scene of disaster to rebuild bravely and start all over again. If, however, there were a decision to abandon the affected areas forever, and thus frustrate the adversity caused by the forces of Nature, the consequent overpopulation in the safe areas would most assuredly cause—because of the excessive overcrowded conditions—a near cessation of population explosion by government fiat and provide for an orderly transition to a sustainable population balance in accord with available resources and living space. If surging gale-force winds and tidal waves of a potent hurricane cause storm losses of devastating proportions to coastal lands, ruining homes, bridges, farms and cities, then the answer is not more government subsidy to rebuild, but total evacuation and abandonment of the affected areas and resettlement in safer regions. To rebuild and raise the fist in defiance against the forces of Nature only to be exposed to similar disasters and suffer similar losses in the future, is not a compliment to man's resourcefulness or intelligence, but is not even on par with animal instincts, which, once injured or abused, would steer clear of the place. But then animals have much more superior instincts of survival than man because they have been here longer and experienced more. The same argument applies to monster earthquakes, cyclones, tornadoes, volcanic eruptions, floods, avalanches, recurrent fires caused by lightning, rock and mud slides, and ruptured dams. The distressing thought comes to mind that if man is unwilling to be concerned enough about his and his family's safety by relocating to areas not exposed to the hazards of natural disasters, then what hope is there that he would be willing to voluntarily curb his reproduction instincts and share his contribution with others in curbing overpopulation and the resultant environmental degradation? A man once bitten by a poisonous snake would not seek shelter among them. What lessons can be learned from the "Wrath of Nature"? That not only the destruction of property but also the loss of lives are colossal and that man's survival instinct, unlike that of animals, is not sufficiently fine-tuned to refrain from returning to the place of disaster. Even though maps depicting earthquake fault lines and earthquake zones are readily available to scientists and updated frequently, the human (and property) losses from some of the worst earthquakes are mind-boggling:

(a) July 28, 1976, Tangahan, China   —240,000 deaths
(b) September 1, 1923, Yokohama, Japan —200,000 deaths
(c) December 16, 1920, Gansu, China   —100,000 deaths
(d) May 31, 1970, Northern Peru   —70,000 deaths

All these occurred in areas mapped as earthquake zones. But no matter, people were in seismic denial, buried the dead and rebuilt the destroyed properties because there was no other choice. Governments provided subsidies; charities and neighbors helped in alleviating the pain; the rebuilding commenced and the will to live made its mark again. Similarly, a violent hurricane catastrophe in Bangladesh (1970) caused the death of 300,000 coastal inhabitants. But no matter, people rebuilt and resettled the land because there was no other choice. And so in some parts of the world, catastrophic natural disasters are the order of the day, causing massive destruction of property and immense losses of lives. But the losses are "acceptable" because the alternative is deemed much worse, unacceptable from the practical and financial point of view. What would it entail? Relocating people inland to higher ground from coastal areas; from all earthquake-prone zones; from all river or dam overflow areas; from all land recurrently exposed to tornadoes, avalanches, mud-slides and hill slides. But much more must be done. Whole cities, farms, industries would have to be abandoned and relocated elsewhere to safer zones. For safety reasons, employees would refuse to work in high-rise office buildings and refuse to occupy high-rise apartments. We have the know-how to build three story commercial and residential structures to withstand almost all known earthquakes. Most bridges and roads would have to be rebuilt using material and engineering techniques considered too costly before and unaffordable (learn from the Romans). To do so would entail radical changes, a restructuring of society, a transformation of capital markets, and an end of the free-market economy as we know it—all these are barriers too radical for the present mode of thinking. There just is not enough disposable wealth in the whole world to fund such changes; there are no world leaders with the kind of courage, new thinking, dedication, and will to see this through. So man will have to muddle through, periodically spending billions and more billions in relief of increasing property losses, ignoring the tragedy of lost lives until the ultimate dilemma will confront him: the cost of funding disaster relief versus the morally unacceptable tragic loss of life with all the pain and tears. So for now, millions upon millions will be exposed to the hazards of recurrent natural disasters and suffer the consequences. However, the ever growing population and the consequent climate warming will, in time, melt enough polar icebergs to cause a rise in sea levels and the resulting permanent flooding of low-lying coastal areas around the globe will, by itself, bring about massive evacuation and relocation of population centers (cities, industry, farms, roads) with man having no choice in the matter. There will be no talk of unacceptable and unaffordable costs—funds will have to be found. It will be the most expensive undertaking ever faced by man and concerns a disaster that will most assuredly happen—it is only a question of time.

(12) The rules of Nature demand conformity with its most fundamental imperatives applicable to living species—from microorganisms to man—that existence has two designs only: self-preservation and propagation of the species. Everything else is peripheral and of secondary consequence. Since the extent of breeding depends on the duration of existence, anything which promotes that design is in conformity with Nature; anything which hinders or frustrates that design opposes Nature and such acts are deemed to be in conflict with Nature. Self-preservation and propagation are instinctive responses, i.e., inborn behavioral propensities common to all organisms. Health, physical strength, cunning gained from experience, and determination are the prime attributes, the sole required criteria calculated to advance success or failure. Any acts which promote these attributes are in conformity with the rules of Nature (Nature, as defined above, briefly, the sum total of vital, life giving, and life sustaining forces which are in balance, etc.). There are no acts, however devious, crafty, insidious, dishonest, cruel, scheming, and perfidious that are precluded or barred from application which further the interest of self-preservation and prop-

agation of the species. Man's rules of morality and ethical conduct find no resonance with Nature and are opposed to the natural scheme of things; such rules would assist the unsuccessful and hinder the successful. Prehistoric man was unrestricted in his competition for existence and propagation of species by any artificial, unnatural obstacles and was therefore in harmony with Nature. The same applies to all other past and present free-roaming animal species whose breeding is controlled by the stabilizing forces of Nature; their numbers are kept within sustainable limits by an abounding and harmonious ecosystem. But man has disrupted that harmony. By creating artificial political societies which restricted his natural activities for the benefit of the many, establishing laws which nullified the advantage of the strong, healing the ailing and caring for the old, punishing the dishonest, cruel, and perfidious, man has transformed his existence from one in harmony with Nature to one in opposition to Nature. Additionally, by removing all self-regulating obstacles which place limits to his procreation, the only species able to do so, man has not only succeeded in unbalancing the razor-thin symmetry of Nature but his unparalleled escalating numbers and insatiable needs, detrimental to all aspects of the environment, guarantee an ecological disaster in the making. How does Nature manifest its wrath? By inflicting catastrophic natural disasters? Man can learn to elude the harm. By inflicting viral epidemics, infectious diseases, plagues, pestilence, and deformed children upon unsuspecting parents? Man is constantly improving his knowledge of vanquishing these curses. By opposing the natural order of things? Man will learn to adjust to such impediments and survive. By giving free rein to his instinct of procreation, overpopulating the planet Earth, exhausting and poisoning its limited resources required to sustain life and in the process destabilize and devastate the ecosystem? Once irreversible contamination is inflicted upon the environment, man will be unable to find countermeasures despite his vaunted intelligence and resourcefulness. In the end, man, this fragile and fractured creature of the most recent evolutionary process, this self-proclaimed apex of the natural order, will be guilty of ecocide—the consequences of this man-made disaster will be the equivalent of ecoterror. The self-preservation rules also apply to Nature; it will employ its natural mechanism to extirpate any species bent on unbalancing its ecosystem—probably one of many prior uprootings of eons ago. The "Wrath of Nature" will be upon man for not heeding its warnings. There is still time to reverse the process, but it is doubtful that mankind will find the resolve to change the course, given the history of man.

(13) Man's effort to control the world population growth is of doubtful success as differences of policy have evolved between the developed and
developing countries, between the haves and have nots, but mainly
between the secular factions and conservative religious forces opposed to
any and all reasonable efforts of concerned nations to set up programs
educating the public, the younger generations in particular, as a first step
in a very belated effort. Stealthily, in the background of all opposition
groups which constitute a mere minority but vociferous enough to thwart
the will of the majority, stands the Vatican, that devious logic chopping
group of priests, who in the sole furtherance of their special interests and
uncluttered by doubt, have defied throughout history all progressive
efforts of man. World population growth, the result of man's natural
instinct of unlimited procreation implanted by Nature, will in due time
cause dramatic adverse changes in the environment endangering the survival of man. This is Nature's way of restoring and stabilizing the mechanism that has served it well over billions of years by providing environmental changes conducive to the evolution and demise of millions of
species. The survival of most was foiled by environmental conditions
(although modern man has also helped), a stark reminder of what is in
store for man whose brief sojourn and possible disappearance from the
scene would constitute just one of millions of episodes played out in the
long unfolding of evolution.

(14) Any vital force which continuously causes its creatures to evolve and
then disappear within the dynamics of the evolutionary process and
which advances as its foundational principle an unremitting and merciless conflict of each against all, whose design enables a thousand to be
born so that one may survive, can be said to be fragile, fractured, and
without any vestiges of constructive design. Man, who prides himself to
be the apex of Nature's evolutionary process, but who is on the way of
unwittingly succeeding in degrading the very environment that gave him
life and may now cause his demise, is not only fragile and fractured but
in addition also fractious, an impediment totally absent from all other
animal species—a characteristic prominently exhibited throughout his
bloody history. But despite man's successful efforts of possibly reversing
the forces that could cause his demise from the scene, and despite the billions upon billions of years during which Nature successfully maintained
the appearance of symmetry between its life-giving and life-destructive
forces, there are powerful cosmic forces to be reckoned with, invariably
hostile and destructive, purposeless and without any semblance of order

that could purely fortuitously, in a matter of time too short to estimate, disrupt, devastate, and destroy Nature's capacity of providing a life-giving and life-sustaining environment for all species, man in particular. These cosmic forces manifesting cosmic supremacy are the destructive asteroids, one of nearly 14,000 unnumbered small planets (many hundreds of thousands whirl about), each having a diameter of a few hundred kilometers or less. There are as many asteroid orbits as there are asteroids. The largest asteroid, Ceres, is about 945 kilometers across. Now and then a big one crosses the Earth's orbit, such as Eros, which came within 23 million kilometers; another, Apollo, within about 4 million kilometers of the Earth. Approximately every million years, three or four of the asteroids ram into the Earth and blast out craters many kilometers across. If a giant asteroid should strike the Earth, it could result in an explosion equivalent to 20,000 megaton hydrogen bombs. It is believed that just such an impact 65 million years ago led to the extinction of the dinosaurs. Scientists recently approved a method of calculating, on a scale of 1 to 10, the probability of an asteroid collision with the Earth. The scale is called the "Torino Impact Hazard Scale", whose scales 8, 9, and 10 are classified as "Certain collisions", which assess the risk posed to Earth from local, to regional, to global destruction. However, scientists have determined that all asteroids that have been found so far are assigned zero ratings, i.e., no chance of collision, or the object is too small to cause damage, although they insist it is not a question of if, but when, one of them collides with the Earth.

It would seem, therefore, that in the near foreseeable future the greatest threat to man's existence and survival on this planet Earth is not Nature, or cosmic forces, but man himself.

CHAPTER 2

MAN IN BONDAGE TO HIS SURVIVAL INSTINCTS

(1) In the distant prehistoric Middle Palaeolithic period, when humans first congregated in social groups for reasons of security and food gathering, when adequate food and safe shelter were rewards of the successful in the struggle for survival, some in the group rose to pre-eminence and leadership by virtue of their strength, cunning and organizing talent. They were a minority who, in time, became the leaders, and the rest, the majority, the followers. It was incumbent upon the leaders to plan for the well-being of the group, became quasi-functionaries, gained in importance to the social group and, as such, were not required to perform the everyday menial tasks demanded of others, the majority. These leaders gained in power and influence, allocated duties and benefits, demanded preferences for their kind to which they claimed entitlement by virtue of their higher standing, and sought to make their advantage permanent and hereditary. This brought about the first division of labor—the governing group were the administrators and the working group were the hunters, food-gatherers and foot soldiers.

(2) It was inevitable that the administrators gained in freedom of action, were spared the confining burden of menial labor necessary for the functioning of the social group, and arranged for themselves a framework of an aristocracy of common interest. They issued orders to others—they were free men. The majority, the working group, were carrying out orders of the administrators, their time occupied with physical labor nec-

essary for the functioning of the social group, had no freedom of action as their work was all-consuming and never-ending. They formed the framework of an institutionalized bondage who, in time, became unrecognizable from slaves.

(3)   The foundation of all living things is the effort of self-preservation which involves the struggle for existence. It is Nature in its most fundamental, raw and unburnished, favoring none except the strong, cunning and enterprising. The most important components in the struggle are the steady procurement of food and shelter to protect against the elements (to those were added, at a much later date, healthcare and provisions for old age). These components comprise the primary needs. All other needs, such as enjoyment of creature comforts above those necessary to persevere in existence are secondary needs. Pursuit of any secondary needs implies that primary needs were satisfied to a degree sufficient to the individual. Before the creation of an adequate food surplus this applied to all individuals, i.e., they were fully engaged in satisfying their primary needs. It must, therefore, be taken for granted that an individual's time was formerly fully occupied in satisfying primary needs. There was no freedom of choice not to pursue this gratification of primary needs to the fullest extent—man was in bondage to his survival instincts, a slave to circumstances beyond his control, all in accordance with the natural order of things. For the definition of "slave" is someone who has no freedom of action because he is completely dominated by the necessity to satisfy his primary needs essential for his survival. Taking the term at the above defined meaning, all men were at one time or another slaves, and the contrary is not free man but freedman, used in the conventional sense of the word. This concept better expresses the circumstances in which a freedman was an ex-slave and could revert to that status, as described later in this chapter. There were no free individuals, only ex-slaves, i.e., freedmen, who managed to extricate themselves from the bondage of their primary needs and gain some freedom of choice, i.e., freedom of action to pursue secondary needs.

(4)   Civilization has been variously defined as an advanced state of human society, urbanized with an orderly government, some scientific thought and practice, some accomplishments in various forms of art. This was conditioned upon adequate food supplies, shelter and an abundance of free time for certain privileged segments of the population to pursue secondary interests—the opposite of barbarism (this conventional meaning of the latter term will be criticized in a later chapter). Since the greater

part of the human race has always been tied to burdensome economic conditions beyond control and therefore possessed no freedom of action, but was fully absorbed in satisfying their primary needs of self-preservation, all civilizations have at all times depended on the existence of human slavery. The well-being of some depended on the privation of many. So also on the international scene with nation-States: the well-being of some States requires an underclass of economically subordinate States—this has been the situation from the beginning of history and nothing appears on the horizon to alter this condition. If man had time to spare to let his imagination soar in pursuit of nobler aspirations, it meant there was an adequate supply of necessities brought forth by the toil and sweat of a restrained underclass.

(5) For the able, efficient, talented, skilled and educated—the horizon of advancement is unlimited; for the one not so endowed, the possibilities of economic advance much beyond the basic procurement of self-preservation primary needs are minimal. This applies universally, Nature's way of sorting things, one of the many disorders which afflict mankind without the possibility of radical change.

(6) To lighten the load of existence, to ease the harsh and demanding struggle for self-preservation (conatus), to advance the state of society, to create a surplus that would satisfy more than life's necessities, to engage in activities not tied to the conatus, to enable as many members of society as possible to have the time to engage in activities which lighten the burdens of existence—that would come much closer to the definition of civilization. But not quite yet. For the conventional term is also tied to "urbanization", the interplay of humanity in tight-knit areas—made originally possible by an agricultural surplus—the first overcrowding which was to create nowadays conditions of overpopulation. The very opposite effect, namely scarcities of nourishment, diminish the discretionary free time by making the struggle for the conatus more difficult, the added burden culminating in misery, starvation, and disease. One can see, therefore, that the conventional term "civilization" has acquired a totally different meaning and is a classical case of subversion and corruption of language.

(7) Slavery and serfdom have been known to us since antiquity, since the first clay tablets, epigraphs, and papyri became known to archeologists. In those days they were an essential part of organized society and remained as such until the 19th century when the United States, Europe, and South America abolished the slave trade, slavery and serfdom. It lasted that long

despite its despicable nature, abuse of man, degradation, and palpable
injustice because the perpetrators of this tyranny found it economically
profitable and indispensable for the preservation of their standard of
living and because they had the power to enforce it. Besides, all three
monotheistic religions, despite their sanctimonious claims to preach justice and goodwill toward fellowmen, sponsored and approved it in their
holy writings—God sanctified greed and oppression. Historians are wont
to make a big to do about the Babylonian, Egyptian, Minoan, Roman, and
Greek civilizations, but are quick to admit that it was made possible by
the institution of slavery. In other words, as we are enraptured and spell-
bound nowadays in contemplating the masterpieces of the Ancients—
their architecture, poetry, philosophy, prose and sculpture—little do we
realize that it was made possible by the great masses of humanity toiling
under the most inhumane conditions, spilling blood and sweat, suffering
the agony of the most savage maltreatment, and as slaves, entitled to, and
expecting, nothing better from their masters. In those days their total
economic exploitation was the common practice, the supply of slaves was
inexhaustible to successful military powers which initiated wars of conquest for booty and the enslavement of captured enemy soldiers and
civilians. Success bred more success. Slaves were considered chattels, to
whom special property laws applied, some were freed by their masters in
an act of manumission and as freedmen were able to better their economic conditions—but this privilege and dispensation applied only to
the lucky few. Serfs bound to their feudal masters had to wait for State
laws abolishing their servitude or to the reprieve by their masters,
whichever occurred sooner.

(8)   A slave can be defined as someone compelled to render involuntary labor,
which, by definition, reduces him to an inferior status by decreasing his
freedom of action. His pay, if any on rare occasions, equaled his upkeep,
or else his minimum upkeep and shelter provided were his compensation.
In either case, his resultant economic benefit beyond bare existence was
zero. Some of the slave-prisoners of war or captured enemy civilians
were highly educated and under the Roman legal system of antiquity
allowed to own property or other slaves. Thus they could aspire to buy
their freedom legally and progress to the status of freedman, which, however, did not enable them to escape all disabilities except for a time in
ancient Athens where they suffered no disparagement or stigma. The
value of a slave mattered only to his master; his day to day existence
involved the crudest of creature comforts necessary to sustain his utility

and even that dispensation depended on the supply and cost of replacements. Typically, he did not rise above his station and endured the degradation and privation till redeemed by fatal sickness or old age. The transition from legalized slavery to a new kind of socially acceptable slavery has been determined by the social structure of organized society, as defined in this chapter. The all-pervading, driving, and energizing force actuating man is, for all the times of his existence, the effort of self-preservation and struggle for existence, his conatus. Those who by stint of ability, hard work, and good fortune manage to free themselves and break loose from the gravitational pull of bare existence can be said to have achieved the status of freedmen. Those who, on the other hand, remain indentured to the struggle for existence, whose total effort and activity are directed toward that pursuit are truly said to be in a state of slavery, slaves to an economy which, as if by design, makes the demand for their labor essential for the orderly working of any society, and who, by virtue of their preoccupation with the conatus, are unable to escape the confines of their existence. The conclusion to be drawn from this is apparent. Adhering to the definition of slavery and freedman, without being overly concerned by unessential nuances, it is apparent that in all civilized societies and others, two categories of individuals emerge: the one who is eking out his existence and bound by necessity to continue to do so without ever having any choice in the matter; the other who has overcome the gravitational pull of the conatus tied to necessities of survival and has some freedom to choose the direction of his activities. The former can be depicted as a slave, the latter as a freedman. All humanity consists of slaves and freedmen in varying stages of their accomplishments, an unavoidable necessity for all, civilized or savage, and a requisite link that holds any society together. The existence of freedmen is only characteristic of homo sapiens—in the animal kingdom, from the highest mammals to the lowest microorganism, all are slaves and determined by their instincts and Nature to remain so. Just like in ancient times when a slave could become a freedman and a freedman a slave, nowadays in all societies a slave could manage to advance to the status of freedman, similarly a freedman, who experienced financial reverses or other misfortunes, could be reduced to the status of a slave, to recover in the future or remain condemned to the chains of the conatus. The meek will never inherit the Earth, and yes, mankind will have to worry about tomorrow because tomorrow will not take care of itself.

(9) I have analyzed the reasoning process of the human mind in my book

entitled "Contra Naturam"; suffice it to say here that the reasoning
process is not a separate function of the human mind (all other animals
possess that ability to the extent of their basic needs and experiences) but
the power to organize ideas which the cognitive process obtained from
sense perceptions and the mind converted into conceptions, i.e., ideas.
The reasoning process is affected by the conatus to the extent of human
need (the same with survival needs of the animal species) and is completely enveloped by man's survival instinct and the instinct of self-
preservation, since it must be taken as axiomatic that a man, in command
of all his senses, will not choose a lesser good over a better good or a
greater evil over a lesser evil. The reasoning process and the working of
the mind are one and the same and not a faculty peculiar to humans but
to all living species. The reasoning process of humans is the most developed because their needs are the greatest and the competition the most
intense. The greater the competition for survival and the maintenance
and improvement essential to creature comforts, the greater the need of
bringing into focus all ideas to the necessities, with the exclusion of discordant ideas. It is the narrowing and bending the horizon of ideas that
necessarily misconstrues and distorts the understanding of reality with
its limitless gradations of error. The greater the role of the instinct of
self-preservation, the more biased and prejudiced man's ideas become.
The more focused the mind is on self-preservation to the exclusion of
other aspirations and striving, the more it is in harmony with Nature,
whose essence requires the continuous struggle for survival of the human
and animal species (and all other organisms). Nature has endowed all
living creatures with the essential instinct of self-preservation resulting
in the consequent "bellum omnium contra omnes"; the war of each
against all is its design to keep all creatures in conflict with one another,
i.e., in slavery. Man is the only living species who can incrementally overcome the gravitational attraction of the instinct in the struggle of self-
preservation, an unnatural act in opposition to Nature, elevate his status
above slavery and become a freedman. As such, it implies the potential
for widening the horizon of his ideas not directly connected and tied to
the instinct of self-preservation. A man who is truly triumphant and has
overcome, even for a limited time, Nature's scheme of things can hope,
and has the potential, to generate and appreciate ideas not tied to the
instinct of self-preservation, i.e., ideas which are less discordant, less distorted and less misconstrued. His introspection and grasp of the nature
of events would be greatly expanded.

(10) Man's struggle of self-preservation and preservation of creature comforts, i.e., his conatus, depend on the degree of his needs and how successful his is in their satisfaction. Such needs are diverse. In distinction
with other animal species, he has primary and secondary needs, whereas
the animals have only primary needs, i.e., those essential for basic survival. Secondary needs are those which the mind perceives as essential of
attainment but are not indispensable for survival. Human primary needs
are nutrition, adequate housing, healthcare and provision for old age. 50
million people die each year from starvation, 12 million children die each
year from poverty-associated causes, and over 100 million children are
homeless—totally failing to satisfy their primary needs. Man's fertile
mind succeeded in creating primary needs out of a multiplicity of secondary needs not essential to his physical survival, but perceived by him
as necessary for his preservation of creature comforts, essential to his
perception of an acceptable lifestyle and peace of mind, some reaching
beyond the luxurious. It is the identification of some secondary needs
with primary needs that gives rise to event-driven conflict within man
and society, and collectively among nation-States. By promoting the pursuit of some secondary needs man rises above the natural order of things;
it is the fractious nature of man living within a hostile environment of a
fractured Nature that has caused unspeakable suffering and degradation
to his fellowman. It is his arrogant profligacy, his rapacity, his cupidity, his
perverse zeal for sordid aggrandizement that have resulted in practically
perpetual enslavement of the majority of the human race throughout history, the progressive destruction of the environment, the recurring economic crises that threaten the stability of nations. The horrors of the
Roman gladiatorial games which arouse so much revulsion and righteous
outrage among the refined segments of society rate as trifling compared,
for example, with the vulgarity and insatiable hunger for gold of the
Spanish Conquistadors of the early 16th century (a period when the
Renaissance was in full bloom, but so was the Inquisition), whose secondary needs knew no bounds and who, accompanied by the ever present
ambitious priests and professing the utmost devotion to the Catholic
faith, managed to destroy within a few decades the Aztec and Inca nations
and causing the death of over 100 million of their people in the process.

(11) But then in the history of man most of the wars were fought for conquest,
rapacity, theft, and aggrandizement. Some, however, were fought to satisfy primary needs, such as hunger and adequate pasturage for grazing
herds, as in the cataclysmic changes which occurred as a result of migra-

tion of the Visigoths, Ostrogoths, Vandals, and Franks, whose masses were driven westward from eastern Europe and beyond by the primary survival urges. They were successful in settling in the areas of Spain, Italy, France and North Africa. The Huns, on the other hand, who thirsted for exploitation and plunder of Roman wealth, were thwarted in their attempt because their effort was directed toward purely secondary needs and the slightest setbacks caused disenchantment and discouragement of their warriors. The conquest of hunger has always been the strongest impetus in Nature, just as Nature favors the strong over the weak. Any other result would be unnatural, opposed to Nature's scheme of things, the work of man in opposing the forces of Nature, combating the restraining conditions of slavery and alleviating, however minimally, the burdens of existence.

(12) The pursuit and satisfaction of some secondary needs, which assume the successful fulfillment of essential primary survival needs, elevate the condition of man above slavery and thus upgrade his status to that of a freedman. There could come a time, however, when the pursuit of too many secondary needs revert man to the condition of slavery (particularly if secondary needs assume a significant importance and are identified with primary needs); secondary needs assume the cloak of necessities because freedom of action becomes restricted, and, as such, result in onerous burdens of an oppressive existence. A man on either extreme side of the spectrum could maintain an existence which, at times, becomes onerous—one, with no or minimal freedom of choice because of circumstances beyond his control, the other, with freedom of choice curtailed because of circumstances within his control, a condition that could be minimized with some self-control.

(13) Self-control is the forbearance of acts which appear to be superficially beneficial, but avoided and judged to be an impediment to some aspect of the self-preservation effort. It is the most praiseworthy quality of man because it involves (a) reflection of an intense mind (b) recognition of the importance of peace of mind (c) satisfaction in overcoming and frustrating Nature's scheme of things (d) resignation to conditions beyond control (e) acceptance of limitations of the ability to overcome all obstacles (f) perception that by reducing avoidable needs, freedom of actions is enhanced. The latter perception is the most significant. By tilting the scale in his favor, eliminating unessential and burdensome needs, man can affect the course of his life by foiling Nature's foreordained design to keep him entangled with necessities. The prudent man, exercising self-

control, can therefore (a) reduce some of his primary needs and thereby gain some freedom of choice (b) reduce some of his secondary needs and enhance his status of freedman.

(14) The primary needs, among others, include food, shelter, healthcare, and old age security. Anyone of these can be modified to fit within the affordable capacity and stabilized lifestyle. Most people are unable, for one reason or another, to provide adequately for all the four stated needs to the detriment of one or two or all. This is the cause of anxiety, fear, insecurity, compulsion and apprehension. All of these adversely affect the thinking process and disposition only to place more urgency upon the self-preservation effort. The result is a vicious cycle, a self-perpetuating process which most are unable to escape. Anyone, for example, who is overwhelmed by concern for his subsistence or shelter is not likely to give much thought to the problems of overpopulation or degradation of the environment; anyone suffering from ill-health is not likely to be concerned about exploitation of child labor. Without elaborating further, the reader will get the point: the mind is programmed to focus on the conatus to the proportional exclusion of unrelated matters of less immediate importance by a proclivity toward narrowness, egocentric and arbitrary ideas. The situation can be compounded by adding to the concern over primary needs problems common to most individuals, such as regard for children, parents, friends, marriage, divorce, and so on; the list is practically endless. The conclusion is clear: in the limited span of life available to man affected with the pursuit of primary needs and the concomitant problems common to most, the time available for most to impede Nature's preordained design and escape from the clutches of bondage is likewise limited and the solution thus more difficult to achieve. The importance of self-control is apparent.

The man fortunate to pursue the fulfillment of secondary needs after succeeding in overcoming primary necessities is truly a freedman. But he too could jeopardize the loss of this standing by compounding his needs with too many ill-chosen and frivolous obligations. For example, the temptation to follow too many seemingly profitable pursuits which strain his resources could prove irresistible; living luxuriously beyond affordable means; too many foolish divorces and resultant oppressive alimony payments; the list is long. It could beset the previously favored freedman with burdensome obligations beyond his control; the freedom of action becomes so restricted as to reduce him to the condition of slavery.

(15) How does the pressure of the conatus affect the thinking process of man,

one burdened by primary needs? How about the one responding to the call of secondary needs? Nature endowed man with survival instincts (an instinct is a faculty that requires no learning process) which dominate the reasoning process, focus ideas on necessities such as satisfying the demands of hunger, thirst and shelter, and by embracing discordant ideas narrow his understanding of purpose. The resultant reasoning develops ideas which are the more biased, prejudiced, confused, self-centered, and egotistic the more difficult the process in meeting the needs of the conatus. The consequent self-gratification is in accord with Nature's scheme of things, an unavoidable behavior that would ordinarily result in anti-social conduct but for the instinctive tendency to join forces with neighbors and fellowmen to face potential hardships in common in the hope of mitigating the burden of existence. But what of the true freedman who possesses some freedom of action, not burdened by the weight existence imposes? Is his reasoning process less distorted? Since man's reasoning process receives its stimulation from sensory perception, which are unreliable, the adequacy of ideas suffers on that account except for mathematics, logic and experimental sciences. In other disciplines, all of man's ideas are slanted, biased and distorted—it is only a question of degree and approximation to seeming reality, a narrowing of the gap between reality and imagination that man can hope to achieve. There is no anchor except the opinions of the majority and that carries little assurance of reliability. Be it ever so seeming and biased, it suffices. The man not weighed down by the demands of his conatus, who preserves some freedom of action in satisfying his secondary needs and is not driven by the perverse zeal for power and wealth can, if so minded, contribute in alleviating the economic and cultural problems of society. From that group have come forth the movers and shakers who have placed in the forefront of innovative ideas and lightened the burden of existence of their fellowmen. Some of them contributed selflessly toward the betterment of human conditions and made true civilization possible. A social action that tends to ease the burden of existence of humanity carries within it the proof of its own realism and necessity and requires no reasoning process or chain of ideas, however simple, to give it logical sanction. For when Neolithic man successfully gained a surplus in agricultural food stuffs and therefore required a social hierarchy to administer the distribution and also elementary writing symbols to provide for some form of accounting, a privileged and dominant class of overseers (freedmen) was established which made the first modicum of civilization possible. But even such initial easing of the burdens of existence was contrary to the natural order of things which requires a rigorous struggle for existence. The reaction was quick in coming. The dominant class of overseers, i.e., administrators, gave birth to an abusive autocratic and tyrannical elite of rulers, kings, princes, emperors and High Priests. The latter, with the aid of the ubiquitous priestly order, symbolized a class system that has lasted ever since in one form or another, made a travesty of man's secondary needs by enabling the haves to live a life of luxury, superabundance, and self-indulgence at the expense, and on the shoulders, of the great majority of mankind who were, on that account, reduced to a condition of bondage, to the status of slavery. But the privileges gained by the freedmen, who have always constituted a minority, had to be perpetuated by stealth, cunning, subterfuge, mystique, and an aura of the supernatural, for their dominance hung by the thinnest of threads and would have easily ruptured by the sustained drive of the majority, had it been minded to do so. It would be an exhausting and time-consuming endeavor—the majority had to keep its noses to the grindstone in the all-consuming effort to earn a decent livelihood and take care of family responsibilities. It left very little stamina for the level of thinking required to gain a clear understanding of the foundation upon which the system of privileges is based. Fear of losing some of these privileges and doubts about their endurance caused some of the brighter freedmen of old (and not so old) to invent a panoply of artificial props of seeming gravity, complex and abstruse on the surface, but shallow and simple beneath, to remove their activities as far as possible from the understanding of the uninitiated and tilt the playing field in their favor. To that scheme belong, but not limited in this outline, the following: (1) The concept of gold as a store of value (compounded foolishness, a carryover from ancient mentalities). (2) The economic theory of capitalism (still the only workable economic system which, in its pure and unmodified form, has never existed in practice). (3) The rules of ethical conduct (made the functioning and tranquillity of the State possible, as opposed to universal moral conduct). (4) The establishment of revealed religious systems with all the mythical rituals (the greatest and most lasting deception ever perpetrated).

(16) The freedman, customarily identified with the haves (a variant is not precluded, as stated elsewhere), does not need a clear understanding of his privileged position—he already gained it and is enjoying the benefits— only an awareness of his achievement, gained lawfully or otherwise, and

the need for its preservation. There have always been slaves throughout history who succeeded in reaching the status of freedmen by the exercise of self-discipline, self-control, schooling, political change, and sometimes by the throw of dice. Likewise, freedmen lost their status and were denigrated to slavery by neglect, ignorance, inattention, dissipation, change of political conditions, and sometimes by adversity. The typical freedman is incapable and unwilling to be overly sympathetic to the predicament and distress of slaves, in particular if his privilege is inherited or held for some time. He would treat as a threat any advantage gained by slaves, an encroachment and potential usurpation of part or all of his privileges. This sort of attitude and motivation cannot lead to sound pursuits because, by the nature of things, most changes are precluded. This is the way of Nature, for man's self-preservation instincts impede the voluntary alienation of benefits unless confronted by a more powerful or resourceful adversary. Therefore, the freedman will only relinquish any of his benefits if forced to do so, or with his consent and understanding that his self-preservation and enjoyment of desired comforts would not be materially affected. Such interplay between haves and have-nots, sometimes conciliatory and sometimes hostile, has been going on, in one form or another, since Neolithic man succeeded in creating an agricultural surplus which needed competent administrators as overseers who, in time, became privileged. It led to constant discords within society and became more confrontational with the growth of its complexity. And so later on with nation-States as harsh circumstances encouraged usurpation of privileges and rationalized their legitimacy. This interplay of opposing interests is the stuff of human history, sanctified by the natural order of things, Nature.

CHAPTER 3

THE OPPOSITION OF CIVILIZATION TO NATURE

(1)   In Chapter 2, Par. 4, the conventional outline of civilization was defined as encompassing an urbanized state of society with an orderly government, some accomplishments in various forms of art and some scientific thought and practice. Expanding the conventional understanding, it also includes respect for authority, the common heritage of humanity, human achievements involving challenges and responses, a vigorous respect for law and discipline. The term also invariably means the opposite of savagery. All these descriptions appear superficial and with little cohesion. There is, however, some consensus among historians that "civilization" is the opposite of "barbarism". But how do they define "barbarism"? Very few make an attempt, taking it for granted that the reader would understand the meaning of evil, cruelty, uncultured, unrefined, primitive, vulgar, savage, etc. The Greeks and Romans had a very simple definition of "barbarism": anyone foreign, alien, who did not speak their language, i.e., Greek or Latin. The Romans, bruised and defeated in battles against Vandals, Huns and Goths, had good reason to denigrate, vilify and deride their enemies as "barbarians", from the Greek "barbaros", meaning foreign, ignorant. But what about the present-day consensus? If "civilized" is the root of civil, civility, as for example, the civilizing influence of cities, urban life, the meaning becomes clearer, namely, that life in the city (community, society) tames and disciplines man, teaches him respect for laws and further, for his fellowman, fellow citizen. Further, we can say

that the civilized man is one who has polite manners, good conversation, an adequate education, fulfills his duties as a member of the community, is considerate to members of other communities. Then, to be civilized means to spread the value of civility, to temper the primitive nature of man and teach him principles that will accommodate and prepare him for a useful and productive life in a society, city and State. When this concept applies to a society, nation, or a segment of humanity located in a specific geographic area enjoying some permanence, it can be said that it is civilized and part of a civilization. But few individuals can claim to have reached such pinnacles of ethics and morality, and most certainly a people as a whole, or nation, have never come even close to qualifying. Man's fragile and fractured nature inhibits him from total compliance. As for the so-called barbarians, they were fierce fighters and ruthless when dealing with enemies, speaking a language and following customs the "civilized" could not understand and made no effort to do so. Since their tribes consisted of great masses of people, they must have had some form of organization, capable leaders, a well functioning infrastructure, civil laws, rules of obedience, and punishment for violators, their disposition tamed sufficiently to preserve internal order and "civility" within their tribes. It is a corruption of language for historians to describe their culture as barbaric and the opposite of civilization. True, they did not build roads or bridges, but they did not have to. The "civilized" did, but with only negligible effect upon their conduct. Perhaps a new definition would be in order, as might also well be for the term "civilized".

(2) The term "civilization" has acquired trappings embellished by connoisseurs who consider art, in whatever form, the highest achievement of man. As such, they take for granted that an efflorescence of a galaxy of artists, confined within a time frame and geographic area, are sufficient to counterbalance any deficiency and shortcoming of man. The magnificent architecture and sculptures of the ancient Greeks; the unsurpassed engineering achievements of the ancient Romans; the plays of Euripides and Sophocles; the poetry of Virgil, Horace, Homer; the philosophy of Socrates, Plato, Aristotle, Lucretius, Epictetus—all these grand achievements, which excited wonder and pride throughout subsequent history, were made possible by merciless and rapacious wars of conquest, the systematic exaction of oppressive tributes from conquered nations, by the institution of the most inhumane slavery and abuse of fellow human beings. The radiance of ancient Greeks and Romans was more than overshadowed by the price paid by the forgotten, nameless, untold millions of

voiceless, exploited and abused humanity ignored by posterity. The magnificent artistry of a Titian, Raphael, Hals, Ruebens, Velazquez, and Michelangelo, whose works continue to amaze and inspire millions of an admiring public, illuminated man's ignorance and gloom during the Renaissance (1450–1620), that proud period of human history called the rebirth and liberation of man's spirit from the darkness of superstition, and considered by historians as the noble beginning presaging changes for the better. But that was also the period when the Spanish and Roman Inquisitions were in full bloom, pitilessly burning or incarcerating men and women whose opinions deviated ever so slightly from the established religious dogma of the times. That was also the period in history when the Inquisition burned about 300,000 "witches"—a construct of man's perverse reptilian complex—mostly women and children, completely innocent of any wrongdoing, but satisfying the bloodlust of totally perverted men, who viewed the Renaissance period as the work of the devil. That was also the period of the Thirty Year's War (1618–1648), a primarily religious war (Protestants against Catholics) that extended across almost all of the continent of Europe, known for wanton pillaging, raping and killing, a most brutal and destructive conflict that, among other horrors, left much of Germany in ruins. The sculptors sculpted, the painters painted, the playwrights wrote their plays, the poets their poetry, and the philosophers their philosophy, but blood flowed as profusely as before on the battlefields and off; the torture and denigration of man continued unabated and the exploitation by man of his fellowmen reached ever greater intensity.

(3) This could not be the behavior of a civilized people. Their ruthless conduct of wars of conquest, taking no military prisoners and exploiting the civil survivors, razing cities (Carthago deleta), plundering and devastating everything in sight to punish the vanquished and serve as warning to others, all these were acts of a people devoid of any restraints, following their raw untamed natural instincts, yielding to the same crude behavior attributed to the much maligned barbarians, those foreigners. It is totally absurd to speak of them as a civilized people; these were bestialities inflicted by savages. Likewise, the burning of dissenters and nonconformists to keep the people in line were acts of monsters, a conduct devoid of any vestiges of humanity. Recital of poetry, a classical education, good behavior, obedience to law, all these recede into the background and are of little use when man is confronted by the struggle of self-preservation and pushed to the edge, that leveler and equalizer of all his natural

instincts of survival, bringing forth an almost universal reaction in human
beings, educated or not, civilized or uncivilized, caring or uncaring. This
reaction is instinctive, driven by the natural order of things, applicable to
all living creatures including man, prevalent throughout the whole history
of man and nations from antiquity up to the present. The Golden Age of
Greece, the Renaissance, the Age of Enlightenment, the Industrial Revolution, the Age of Technology, computers, atomic energy, and ballistic
missiles, all these did not, and will not, play any role when men's conflicts
are reduced to a do or die struggle for existence. These armed conflicts are
only getting progressively more vicious, brutal and destructive to all, as
ever more developing technology and resources are devoted to holo-
causts; instead of killing thousands, the talk is now of millions. The
playing field is level, all men and nations are guided by the same natural
instinct of survival. This "no holds barred" reaction precludes any
rounding of edges, any appeal to religious faith, to decency or humanitarian considerations. For it is the first and primary duty of man and
nations to spare no effort, of whatever nature, to persevere in existence.

(4) Culture is behavior peculiar to man; it consists of language, beliefs, customs, institutions, tools, techniques, works of art, rituals, ceremonies,
morals and law. It is a movement in the direction of making human life
more secure and enduring, following life-sustaining and avoiding life-
destroying conduct. Given the same requisites, conventional wisdom
identified culture with civilization—a neologism which emerged in 18th
century France—but separated the two, although they were for a long
time synonymous by associating culture with primitive societies and civilization with developed communities. But culture and civilization have
different foundations. The former is dependent upon a general improvement of the mind and behavior; the latter's benefits are conditioned upon
a division of society into the haves and have-nots, i.e., freedmen and
slaves. Civilization can be said to depend on the existence of a discretionary economic surplus and the use to which such unfettered surplus is
put, whereas primitive societies spend their energies in taking care of
their primary necessities and are forced to allocate any surplus to the
basic needs of an essential infrastructure. This distinction is critical. For,
as outlined in Chapter 2, all civilizations depend on the existence of
slavery for their support, the literal or virtual kind, which enables certain
advantaged segments of the population to satisfy their secondary needs
(which by definition are discretionary) and become not only consumers
of nonessentials (defined above as secondary needs), i.e., luxuries, but

also participants in the enlightened fields of human activities which are the preserve of those freed from the survival necessities. On the other side of the spectrum is the husband and father, who keeps his nose to the grindstone by striving as well as he can to keep body and soul together and that of his family, have a comfortable home, and take his family on annual vacations; relying on a pension and some savings for his old age retirement and that of his wife. He does well to satisfy his primary needs without creating much of a discretionary surplus. Exceptions always prove the rule, but this individual will not likely become a participant in the enlightened field of human endeavor, having neither the time, inclination, interest, or ability to do so. These fields are left to people who enjoy some leisure, freedom of action to engage in activities not tied to necessities, time to meditate, respite to admire, inclination to read, desire to travel, and uplift the mind by learning about the achievements of prior civilizations. But these two kinds of individuals, deprived of food and water and the customary creature comforts, even if only for the brief period of a few days, would descend to the level of savages, their conduct indistinguishable from each other. These same two individuals, exposed to the danger threatening the preservation of their existence, would react with like vehemence and tenacity that would make their responses parallel by using any and all means available, bar none, to restore their prior circumstances. What is the lesson of this exercise? That the margin between the advantaged and disadvantaged is razor-thin; that both will strive to persevere in existence with vehemence and tenacity equal and commensurate with their ability, leaving nothing undone, however harmful to their fellowmen; that though the path to financial independence and achievement of a desired level of creature comforts may be difficult and require time-consuming effort, the loss of these hard-earned benefits may be swift and pervasive; that the loss of these benefits is due, in most cases, to forces beyond the control of the beneficiaries; that if anything can be learned from the colorful history of man it is that his tenure of permanent status is far from secure, passing and transitory; that all of his hard-won achievements may prove to be ephemeral and evanescent. It is this awareness of the impermanence of benefits, which accords with the natural order of things, that propels man to such inflexible determination to persevere in his never ending struggle for existence against all odds and continue to do so without moderating his efforts. If the term "civilization" has any meaning at all, if it can be said to have any practical application in the field of human endeavor, it is that it imparts some justifiable feeling of permanence to man and his society, some sense of purpose and direction, some design of progression in the scheme of things, minimizing not only the vicissitudes of unkind fortune and the fear of an unknown fate, but gives him encouragement in overcoming his fragility and fractiousness, these curses of Nature, the "Wrath of Nature".

(5)   Whatever state of civilization man has attained, however it has been compromised and abased by savage wars of conquest, however fragile it has become, worn down and tarnished by innumerable conflicts and hostilities among humans, civilization, and Nature are in increasing opposition with each other. To counter the natural order of things; to overcome obstacles Nature placed in his path in the attempt to rise above primitive conditions and attain a feeling of permanence which would make his achievements more secure; to promote his most praiseworthy and revolutionary attempt to remove his species from the process of natural evolution and replace it with one based upon genetic engineering, i.e., subject to his control, that extraordinary tool of late 20th century science, man must make it his mission to abort Nature's foreordained design to keep him entangled in turmoil and with necessities. For if man labors constantly to satisfy solely his necessities, i.e., his primary needs, and particularly if there is a certain unpredictability about it, the creation of a discretionary surplus will constantly elude his grasp. It is the existence of a discretionary surplus that frees a segment of society from the entanglements with necessities and partake in the more elevated forms of existence, variously described as civilization. But speaking from the global point of view, no matter how advanced man's state of civilization, no matter how large the discretionary surplus, no matter how compelling his drive to retain the advantages civilization has to offer, there has never been a time in the known history of man, and not likely ever to be in the future, when he was totally free from entanglements, turmoil, and friction that resulted from his disputatious and discordant nature. It is this quality in man that will never be satisfied with results achieved; cease resentment of his exclusion from participating in another's advantage or preferment; constantly strive to improve, enlarge, and augment his surplus to the detriment of others and thus create conflicts with his fellowmen. For it must be taken for granted that the Nature-given instinct of self-preservation coexists with innate impulses such as greed, envy, jealousy, avarice, rapacity, cupidity, all of which are not only essential to his efforts but also the cause of interminable turmoil and friction within humankind, societies, among nations and States. Human aspirations are never harmonious

or balanced but constantly in search for advantages or lessening disadvantages, betterment and superiority at the expense of competitors or adversaries. All these activities are in pursuit of natural instincts, keep humans, societies, and States in intermittent unrest and agitation (including military actions, armed uprisings or civil disorder) which erode the hard won surplus of some and promote it for others in constantly shifting balances. Man must always strive to overcome obstacles placed in his path by the natural order of things; to the extent he has succeeded and profited from the experience he can be said to have laid the foundation of a civilization, which is never constant but always changing. A well developed and mature civilization will be more resistant to the corroding effects of man's turmoil and friction which might diminish a weaker one. No civilization is possible without some permanence, order and stability, some wealth to free segments of society from the pursuit of primary necessities—to build towns and cities, universities and libraries, museums, theatres and music halls, hospitals and rest homes for the elderly, an adequate transportation system, and many other cultural and useful facilities, to not only tame and discipline man but to place at his disposal benefits that would teach him the value of civilization and lighten the burdens of existence. These are the brighter sides of opposing the natural order.

But there is also a dark side. Man's constant striving to improve his well-being at the expense of his neighbors, the achievement of benefits and procurement of knowledge which made his kind of civilization possible are dependent upon conditions of a system of slavery and a system of economic exploitation of other societies, nations, States, which participate unequally in the benefits civilization has to offer. For them civilization is defined differently. In the extreme, it is a condition of political and economic weakness, stress and distress, fear and insecurity, of privation and hardships; of feeling exploited and disadvantaged. It is a condition in which the effort to persevere in basic existence is ongoing, pervasive, without respite. It is a civilization of a more modest kind. They possess an orderly government; a society in part urbanized; their citizens mandated to respect law and order; unable to provide for orphans, the elderly and the infirm, for they lack sufficient discretionary surplus. They bear the mantle of civilization nevertheless, because they are opposed to the natural order of things which demand a merciless competition for survival, where hunger is the prime mover; no consideration for the weak, infirm or aged and the loser is discarded; where the strong and cunning rule, the weak obey. Their subordinate condition may be due to criteria of size and population, lack of material resources or infertility of soil, geographic location adversely affected by inclement weather conditions, domineering neighbors or simply the chance of history. They must suffer the supremacy of political and economic influence of more developed neighbors, absorb it into their system and turn the handicap to their advantage. For the attainment of a civilization is that much more to be admired if possessed by those who had to overcome more oppressive obstacles not of their making; the sense of purpose and direction would be more valued by those who at one time did labor to possess it; the preservation of even modest benefits would be the more treasured by those who have the most to lose by the void left.

(6)   The outline of civilization in the preceding paragraphs is of the industrial developed and the underdeveloped countries. They differ in degree of maturity, the latter are less mature but catching up in this age of instant communication. Even though the latter are dominated and economically exploited by the former, their civilizations share certain fundamental traits:

(a) They depend on a system of virtual slavery.

(b) They constantly strive to augment their surplus.

(c) They are never free from turmoil and friction.

(d) Greed, avarice, and rapacity are paramount in their economic endeavors.

(e) They are inhabited by individuals whose disposition is by nature fragile and fractured, easily provoked to anger and strong reaction if their vital interests are threatened.

(f) The well-being of some depends on the privation of many.

(g) The economic interests of their people are never in harmony but in constant shift of gains and losses proportionate to the circumstances.

(h) They are fundamentally opposed to the natural order of things, Nature.

Any reference to individuals applies also by extension to societies, nations and States.

The effort to persevere in existence is the strongest natural instinct of man which prompts him to action. The consummation of this effort, which is the most basic of Nature's instincts, overrides any forbearance on account of educational or cultural restraints interposed by moral or ethical considerations. Man justified the use of any force as necessary under the circumstances to gain and advance his interest; any wars or armed conflicts in which his side participated throughout mankind's turbulent history, however brutal, savage, and cold-blooded and however great the devastation and depredation suffered by antagonists. Such conduct and result did not contravene or compromise his vaunted concept of civilization, nor inhibit his profiting from it. The same man can witness, or be aware of, violent or cruel incidents in which he is not a participant but only an observer, interested or not, for he can divert his eyes and mind and with equanimity reconcile the event with his understanding of justifiable conduct. But this is exactly the flaw in the presumed civilized man, that fragile and fractured being, for these last related events are in conformity with Nature, a contradiction which man is unable to resolve because his self-preservation instinct is paramount, whereas the cloak of civilization is an acquired artificial shield to protect him from the stronger and more cunning in the preservation of his existence and creature comforts. This contradiction between Nature and civilization cannot be reconciled; the preponderance shifts between the two depending upon the degree and urgency of man's self-interest. Except for the natural right to follow survival instincts, there are no natural rights, only civil rights, and any claim justifying an action under the guise of natural rights is pure fiction, a sham and self-delusion.

The 20th century presents a great number of examples of presumed civilized nations descending to the level of savages, finding no inconsistency between their murderous conduct and sermonizing about their high state of civilization. They brazenly went about their business and showed not the slightest scruples or hesitation. Some of the more outrageous conflicts:

(a) World War I, the German invasion of Belgium, the level of trench warfare in France, particularly the battle of Verdun, where one million men (on both sides) were sacrificed on the altar of stupidity and criminal misconduct by the military High Command of all belligerents.

(b) The 1917 Russian revolution.

(c) Japan's invasion of Manchuria and China.

(d) The Spanish civil war.

(e) Fascist Italy's invasion of Abyssinia.

(f) Nazi Germany's conduct in World War II, the most outrageous of all.

(g) The Soviet Union under the Stalinist hegemony, within and without.

(h) The Catholic and Protestant conflict in Northern Ireland.

(i) Ustashi Croatia treatment of the Serbs.

(j) Treatment of Croats, Bosnians, and Kosovars by Serbia.

(k) Treatment of Kurds by Turkey.

The list of horrors is endless. Civilized man's savagery against his fellowmen occurred throughout history, but the 20th century is unique in its concentrated ferocity, bloodlust and casualties. This, notwithstanding the claims voiced by the culprits of attaining the pinnacle of civilization with the help of scientific and technological disciplines. The more adept the killing machine, the more likely its use and the greater the casualties. None of those nations cared a whit about observing the rules of civilized conduct; they were driven by considerations of pure selfish interest and thus guided by the natural order of things, the "law" of Nature, under which each is its own master and observes no rules but those which profit its advantage. This dualism has always served the aggressor who invoked the claim of natural right. But when the tables were turned, out went the natural right and in came the hasty appeal for respect of civilized conduct.

This brings us back full circle. When the struggle to persevere in existence concerns primary needs essential for survival, appeal is made instinctively to the natural order of things; when the primary needs are satisfied, secondary needs and discretionary creature comforts above those considered essential are pursued, the call is made for law and order, protection for property and civil rights, a degree of security and permanence, civilized conduct, i.e., civilization. Any man who disposes of a discretionary surplus is well aware of the impermanence of his good fortune, how transitory and ephemeral the conditions are which brought it about and the danger that conditions beyond his control, natural, political, or economic, may rupture the bonds which keep his estate under control. An earthquake, hurricane, flood, or tornado could endanger his estate. He could be too discouraged, too old, or in poor health to rebuild or restart. Losses from economic downturn, or in the extreme, wartime activities, could all adversely affect his estate in a relatively short period, sometimes with no time to spare. All these named adversities are sudden and caused by circumstances beyond anyone's control. If he was pursuing the satisfaction of discretionary creature comforts before, he may be forced to concentrate on his primary needs after the reverses, which could not help but negatively affect his previously held views on civilized conduct—such is the unpredictable play of fortune, such is the razor-thin margin of civilization which, like any human achievement, is on no solid foundation.

(7) An individual's surplus can be defined as the discretionary excess left over after satisfying primary needs, measured chiefly in monetary units (or any other unit of wealth). It can be saved, spent on secondary needs,

invested, or disposed as an individual saw fit in any combination. Such individuals are commonly referred to as the "haves". The surplus of a State can be defined as the excess of revenues over budgeted mandatory expenditures measured in monetary units. It can be spent on improving the infrastructure and on socially necessary programs, part can be returned to taxpayers as a rebate on taxes and a reduction of future budgeted expenditures. But unlike in the case of individuals, the law and good government usually mandate that it must be spent. All civilizations depend on the existence of a surplus, both in the State budget and in the finances of a significant segment of society.

The "haves" were formerly the landed gentry, the patricians, the elite, the upper classes, the aristocracy; they were replaced as the elite by the entrepreneurs following the Industrial Revolution when production, investments, and commerce became the new source of wealth and the pursuit of a new "aristocracy". They shared common interest in preserving complete freedom of action, complete freedom to dispose of their discretionary surplus as they saw fit, in a society oriented toward free enterprise capitalism in which the pursuit of profit and a market economy predominate. They were understandably intolerant of any governmental interference. In due course, on account of their contribution to the success of the economy, they began to exercise an influence on the direction of government policies totally out of proportion to their numbers. They were the major producers of wealth, the major employers, the major hope of the State in achieving and maintaining the desired budgetary surplus, which was not only an indicator of a sound fiscal policy but of a growing economy—the badge of achievement and pride of elected government representatives. Free enterprise capitalism has always been expansionary, seeking new markets and new methods of production to maximize profits and minimize competition, until the accumulation of wealth proceeded well beyond the economically justifiable needs; it became, of necessity, politically involved and exercised undue influence upon national and foreign policy. The business establishment thrives in a climate of unmolested freedom of action for themselves, and consider governmental furtherance of social programs and legislation benefiting their employees as undesirable interference, even though they benefit indirectly from the influence of the impact. The business establishments further their interests by promoting a self-indulgent materialistic consumerism to induce excessive spending and debt by the majority. The object is to turn secondary into primary needs in the mind of consumers, not only to advance their revenues, but to have most consumers exhaust their discretionary surplus and motivate them to work that much harder to replenish the coffers. For if, hypothetically, the surplus were evenly distributed among consumer-employees, there would be less incentive to work for their employers who would end up the losers. Abstinence is discouraged and immediate gratification encouraged. The propagation of this culture leads a substantial segment of consumers, with limited or no discretionary surplus, to seek relief by borrowing funds and or explore avenues for quick gain by gambling, or plunge into speculative ventures. Such attempted solutions only increase the awareness of their insecurity, the entanglements with necessities, the burden of their circumstances—all criteria of a condition of servitude as desires always exceed affordable demands. This cannot but adversely affect their morality, their civilized conduct, for, as stated previously, the effort to persevere in existence and enjoy basic creature comforts is to follow the natural order of things, to improve well-being at the expense of others, if necessary, which gives free reign to avarice and cupidity—so fragile and impermanent is the foundation of civilized conduct.

The enlargement of profitable operations is the magnet that energizes the business establishments to ever greater expansion and reach for new markets. If the domestic markets become temporarily or otherwise saturated, expansion across the borders is pursued until, with increased competition and ever more lucrative opportunities, the markets become global. For some the free-market economy, the freedom of action unhindered by governmental interference so fully embraced originally by the business establishment, is now ever more transformed with requests for government protection in foreign markets, government subsidies and guarantees of foreign debt repayment and against expropriation, stabilization of currency and foreign exchange rates, demand for low interest loans to foreign governments or outright subsidies to create a market for exports. With competition for markets getting ever more costly and discordant, the higher the risks the lower the morality. Business efforts begin to be drawn toward the politics of bringing about accommodation among the few and powerful, the creation of trust agreements to eliminate competition, yearning for the calm waters of oligopolies and monopolies. But this course is only open to the few privileged and powerful. They seek freedom and order for themselves only to create tumult and disorder for others. For the attraction of high-stake entrepreneurs is the creation of instability in the markets, gyrations in prices and production, controlled business cycles of scarcity and plenty in order to disrupt the planning of their smaller competitors, most of whom would be adversely affected by the climate of unscrupulous competition and unsettled markets. In the struggle for commercial supremacy there are no rules, no stability, no rest for the sated, no future for the losers—all these demonstrate the fragility and impermanence of a man-made system which permits no one to stand still in the world of competition. This accords with the natural order of things; civilized conduct takes second place to unrestricted competition and the resultant instability of economic conditions. The availability of a discretionary surplus should create stability and harmony, an equilibrium, conditions conducive to civilized conduct but for the fragility of man who is unable to keep free from entanglements and turmoil.

For the enterprising and ambitious are, in general, tone-deaf to economic stability (there is too little profit in that), are exhilarated by the potential for large profits created in the seesaw of the economic pendulum and the related instability in the markets. When things go well most humans proclaim the virtues of civilization. But at the first sign of a disequilibrium, when competition becomes undisciplined and exploitative, the natural combative instincts gain the upper hand, undeterred by any restraints civilized conduct might impose. Man accepts as just the use of any means, without any inhibitions, as long as they serve him in his quest for survival and the preservation of the desired level of creature comforts. Such conduct is far removed from civilization. But this has been the lot of man that throughout history, the civilized and savage conduct and responses have existed in a matched relationship, their distinction blurred and obscured by ever changing needs. Man has never managed to set himself free from this burden, by doing one without perpetrating the other.

CHAPTER 4, PART ONE

EVOLUTION OF RELIGIOUS IDEAS

(1)   Prehistoric humans formed communities for their mutual benefit, such as protection from enemies, coordinating forage for food, security of barter, and other advantages man finds in belonging to a social group. His fear of harm from visible external dangers was reduced only to be replaced, in due time, by a new kind of fear of invisible danger concealed everywhere outside his closely guarded compound. Typically, he was convinced that evil spirits walked abroad whose chief aim was to cause harm and disruption to a seemingly orderly existence, and had to be pacified by various incantations, sacrifices of something valued by the individual or community, all with the aid of sorcerers (later priests) exclusively selected for their claimed possession of mystic powers to shield him and the community from abuse and harm. Because knowledge about the working of Nature and natural phenomena was most primitive, anything not understood was attributed to some supernatural source as the cause, such as drought, rain, thunder and lightning, diseases, death, dreams, victory, or defeat in battles. This gradually evolved in Nature worship, the belief that spirits animated everything from ordinary inanimate objects (trees, stones, rivers, etc.) to all the inexplicable powers and natural phenomena in the world. They classified the spirits into good and evil, favorable and malignant. The evil and malignant spirits had to be propitiated by offerings and worship; it was generally believed that such conduct could have the desired influence and results. Certain spirits were deemed

to favor a particular community of worshippers, with the result that some of them gained preeminence to the exclusion of others. Anthropomorphic qualities were attributed to those considered most powerful. It was not long before the idea of a Deity was identified with the most powerful spirits, with many sub-Deities associated with other spirits, accompanied with complex and mystic rituals to gratify the spiritual hunger of the community. Idolatry led to polytheism, which in a few instances culminated in monotheism. Basically, the foregoing has been the origin of all religions from primitive animism to revealed monotheism.

(2) Anthropomorphism, derived from Greek words which mean "in the form of man", in religion means the attribution of human qualities to God or Gods; any reference to the divine as having a human body, manlike mental aspects, or performing the actions of man fall under this definition. But how else could it be? It is impossible for man to conceive God or Gods except through human faculties, i.e., sense perception, leading to ideas of the perception which constitute the human mind. For the attribute of religion is that of an attitude of awe towards God or Gods, a system of doctrine and worship regarded as having divine authority. But awe and worship, if not devoid of any meaning, must have an object susceptible to human senses; man prays to evoke some responses from God or Gods, i.e., there are communications and expected responses which can be understood only in human terms. By attributing qualities such as infinity and invisibility to the Deity is to remove the concept from any possibility of human understanding. Some form of anthropomorphic religious belief has existed since man could communicate his thoughts to his neighbor. It fills a void in the fragile mental constitution of man, who needs to be constantly reassured that his conduct does not displease the imagined all-powerful father-figure, i.e., Deity; that he does not incur his wrath with all the consequent punishments in this life and hereafter. Man's fear of the unknown, standing alone facing an uncertain future and assaulted by a variety of potential adversities confronting him all the time and everywhere, a condition applicable in some measure to all human beings, finds a release from this predicament in concentrated efforts of propitiation of his particular Deity by offering sacrifices, prayers, fasts, penances, eulogies, flattery, entreaties—all to obtain some token of absolution of his real or imagined misdeeds. For in his struggle for self-preservation, man is bound to violate some community rule or moral taboo in besting his fellowmen without considering the repercussions, only to seek absolution as presented by communal sorcerers or priests, in

prayer and sacrifices shrouded in sacramental mysteries in order to restore his peace of mind and equanimity.

(3) The fear of the unknown and anxiety about helplessness is implanted in childhood when the mind is most susceptible to influences and impressions of such emotions. Most people do not lose this dread in adulthood when the mind acquires some stamina and understanding enriched by experiences gained in confronting the problems of living. For many less fortunate adults the dread even increases as a result of a multiplicity of mind-warping experiences. It is during childhood when the mind is most impressionable, uncritical and passive, that the idea of a caring and forgiving Deity is implanted to serve as a comforting and calming antidote to help overcome life's anxieties. It cannot usually be completely eradicated but is retained and augmented by more complex accretions during adulthood, so deeply is the implant rooted during childhood. The idea of a stern but caring Deity, meting out punishment to those who commit misdeeds but absolving those who ask for forgiveness, should be beneficial to mankind and supportive of civilized conduct. As is, however, evident from history, most human beings behave like semi-savages when pressed to the limit. One would expect, mistakenly though as will be shown, that the belief in a Deity should help modify for the better, however imperceptibly, such semi-savage conduct of man. But in the struggle for self-preservation, the believing man will rationalize as just any conduct, however damaging to others, which is of desired benefit to him, as long as he is assured of absolution of his misdeeds by priestly prescribed remedies. However deeply the idea of a Deity is implanted, the effort to persevere in existence takes priority. Man's natural instincts commanding survival are stronger than fear of a punishing Deity, because the effects of survival are immediate, whereas the punishment anything but certain. The idea of a Deity gave rise to various religions which were further divided into as many sects as there were nuances of belief. It is not a unifying force but, on the contrary, a divisive stimulus setting man against his neighbor, at times because of hardly recognizable gradations of different beliefs, most of which would evaporate on close inspection. Present-day protagonists of religions claim that their kind of particular religious beliefs are indispensable for society to function as a civilized community; that but for the practice of their teaching family units would disconnect, children would grow up as blameworthy delinquents, and that all sorts of crimes and immoral behavior would flood society to the detriment of civilized behavior. It is undisputed that religious beliefs could have a sta-

bilizing influence upon society. It is equally undisputed that the same beliefs had a destabilizing influence upon society throughout history by causing divisiveness, separatism, exclusions, pitting man against man in fatuous religious conflicts, politicized to serve as a pretext for the basest of human criminalities, with all antagonists calling on the exclusive support of their Deity to sanction the deeds perpetrated. This contradiction of effects is further proof of the fragility of man in that his fertile imagination structured beliefs as justifiable self-defense to counteract the dread of the unknown only to cause unintended harmful consequences to others. His particular beliefs were meant to erect useful defensive barriers against disunity only to be neutralized by causing harmful intolerance and discordant schisms, with the result that his well intentioned efforts proved to have the opposite effect.

(4) A religion is said to be divinely revealed if its laws, commandments, ordinances, rituals, and morals were communicated to man directly by the Deity. Such claimed revelations are so unique and compressed within such a narrow historical period (compared with the length of human existence) that they must conform to certain standards in order to meet the credibility test of the most sympathetic and impressionable believer. Revelation does not include inspiration, which is quite common and is the result of a visionary mind contemplating the Divine Presence. Divine revelations were unnatural occurrences, outside the natural order, and therefore supernatural, i.e., miracles. An event which is beyond the purview of the natural order is beyond the scope of human understanding. Divine revelations as recorded in the Scriptures and other sacred texts imply a dialogue between a Deity and humans, and in order for the subject to be discussed at all, must conform to certain criteria intelligible to humans. Just like the intelligent mind is capable of understanding most natural phenomena, the incomprehensible mysteries of the past are gradually subjected to critical analysis and giving way to explanations comprehensible in human terms. Considering the unique and momentous significance of such events, it can be stated that:

(a) Divine revelations cannot contain errors, anachronisms or contradictions.

(b) Divine revelation has to be original. Something preexisting and known to others cannot be the subject of revelation.

(c) Divine revelations cannot contain human corruptions, i.e., interpolations, or material from non-revealed religions.

(d) Divine revelations must be direct. Third-party quotations of the original interlocutor cannot be treated as revelations.

It would be a grievous error to suppose that revealed religion, as it appears today, is not the result of substantial modifications and development of the original, as it would be to suppose that revealed religion, as it appeared at inception, was not itself a modification and development of more ancient preexisting beliefs. All religions, in so far as they have affected the moral conduct of man, are part of the sum and substance of civilization. The moral teachings they propound are either the result of divine revelation or inspiration.

Any reference to God will be spelled with a capital "G", to avoid any inference of advancing a particular view. Since some adherents of a particular revealed religion claim superiority over other religions (revealed or other), it will be shown that such claims are unwarranted and without basis. Further:

(a) All religions are equal which effectively teach a universal morality and conduct conducive to a fraternity of mankind.

(b) No religion can claim originality in all its aspects.

(c) There is a thread running through all religions which aims at calming the fear of the unknown and that some good shall be the final goal of suffering.

(d) All religions espouse a belief in a supernatural being, a God or Gods.

(5) The major present-day religions are (in order of their founding): Judaism, Hinduism, Buddhism, Confucianism, Christianity and Islam. Of these only Judaism and Christianity can put forth a claim of divine revelation, i.e., direct communication with God.

Judaism. Moses received the Torah (the Pentateuch, which contains the law, commandments and rituals), the basis of Judaism, directly from God on Mt. Sinai after the Exodus from Egypt.

Christianity. The case is slim since during his recorded lifetime the putative founder Jesus never conversed with God but was identified as the Son of God in Christian dogma, part of the Trinity (Father, Son and Holy Ghost), the union of Three Divine Persons in one Godhead. His life and teachings are related in the four Gospels (Mark, Matthew, Luke and John).

In Hinduism, Buddhism and Confucianism, no claim is asserted of direct revelation. The Koran, the holy book of Islam, was revealed to Mohammed by the angel Gabriel.

The following will clearly demonstrate that neither Judaism nor Christianity can put forth a claim of divine revelation since their core Scriptures (Torah, Gospels) contain basic information that is not original:

- The ancient Egyptians tried to promote health by circumcision of males. There are records of circumcisions before 2500 B.C. The rite was common to most Semites. Non-Semitic peoples, such as the Phoenicians and the Syrians in Palestine, practiced it and acknowledged that they learned it from the Egyptians. Edomites, Moabites, Ammonites, and Canaanites used it. Circumcision was not original with the Hebrews.
- The Egyptian sun-God Rah, the father of the earliest men and women, had destroyed a large part of the human race when they took to evil ways.
- Osiris was the Egyptian God of the Nile. His death and resurrection were celebrated yearly, ruled benevolently and ascended to heaven to reign there as a God.
- The Egyptian Isis, Mother of God, with her divine infant Horus nursed the child in a stable.
- The Egyptian priestly class was hereditary. Their skill was indispensable in approaching the Gods. The sacrifices offered to the Gods supplied them with food and the temple buildings gave them homes.
- The Egyptian king Amenhotep IV (1380–1362 B.C.) was the first known to history who proclaimed there was but one God and condemned the existing ceremonies as vulgar idolatry.
- The Sumerians, who reached a high state of culture by 4500 B.C., had legends of creation, Paradise, a flood that destroyed the sinful.
- Sargon I (2637–2582 B.C.), the king of Akkad, had a Mosaic beginning in that his mother (unknown), after his birth, placed him in a basket-boat of rushes on a river, was rescued and became the cup-bearer to the king, rebelled, displaced his master.
- In ancient Babylonia, the law of "lex talionis" was established, i.e., an eye for an eye, which also became the law in the Torah at least 600 years later.
- In ancient Babylonia, the king was an agent of the city God, his power was limited by the priesthood and the proceeds of taxation were deposited in the temple.
- Hammurabi (c.1955–1913 B.C.), the greatest king of the first dynasty of Babylon, received a set of laws as a gift from the God Shamash standing on a mountain, who promised to establish Babylon as an everlasting kingdom.
- The Babylonian priesthood became the greatest center of wealth and also the greatest merchants and financiers. The temples grew in wealth and the treasures deposited in them were considered sacred and jealously guarded against unauthorized use by secular authorities.

- Most of the Babylonian Gods lived in temples and ate the sacrifices with a hearty appetite.
- The Goddess Ishtar (the Egyptian Isis, the Greek Astarte, the Jewish Ashtoreth) was addressed by her worshippers as "The Virgin", "The Holy Virgin", and "The Virgin Mother".

Other Sumerian and Babylonian religious concepts which influenced Hebrew and Christian writers:

(a) In the beginning was chaos (before Creation).

(b) Man was fashioned by the Gods from a lump of clay.

(c) The Gods became dissatisfied with the men they created and sent a great flood to destroy them. But one man and his wife, who built an ark, were saved. When the flood receded, the ark landed on the mountain Nisir and the man released a dove to make sure the flood was over. Then in gratitude he offered sacrifices to the Gods.

(d) The story of Creation consists of seven tablets, one for each day of Creation.

(e) Tammuz, the son of the Goddess Ishtar and the God Ea, the God of fertility (legend from about 2000 B.C.), associated with the power in the grain, dying when the grain was milled (annually), commemorated in a day of mourning and followed by rejoicing over his resurrection. (See the Jewish fast of Tammuz, inaugurating three weeks of mourning that culminate with the fast of Tisha be-Av).

(f) They had no idea of personal immortality (the Torah is silent on immortality). God inflicted punishments upon wicked people during their lifetime.

(g) Animal sacrifices were complex and required the expert services of priests. A frequent sacrifice was the lamb, which was considered a substitute for man.

(h) Religion meant correct ritual to appease the Gods. A good life was not a substitute. Gods demanded proper ritual sacrifices of the prescribed animals in the temples.

(i) Sickness was considered possession of the body by a demon which had to be exorcised by magic ritual.

(j) The Ebla and Mari tablets (approx. 2500 B.C.) refer to people with names like Abram, Jacob, Leah, Laban, Ishmael.

(k) Temples set on platforms were found as early as 5000 B.C., which subsequently gave rise to the story of Babel (18th century B.C.), described as the temples of foundation of heaven and earth.

(l) The burnt offerings were pleasing to the Gods.

(m) Religious processions in which the Gods were carried in arks.

(n) A Sabbath was observed for the purpose of easing the wrath of the Gods so that their hearts might rest.

(o) The king, God's representative, goes forth to conquer under his command.

(p) The year began with the month of Nisan (March–April).

(q) The king himself was not above the law.

(r) Mandatory tithes supported the temples and priesthood.

(s) Ritual calendars were carefully compiled for the priests and worshippers.

(t) Priests wore special dresses; ablution was strongly insisted upon.

(u) Clean and unclean animals were carefully distinguished.

(v) In the temple there was no statue of any kind set up in the place.

(w) Their Gods were represented as standing on a mountain.

(x) The plans and materials to be used in the building of their temples was communicated to them by their Gods.

(y) Eve fashioned from the rib of Adam.

(z) The Cain-Abel rivalry.

- The Messiah in Enoch (a Jewish noncanonical pseudepigraphic work, variously dated around 200 B.C.) is called the Righteous One, and the Son of Man. Depicted as a preexistent heavenly being who sits on the throne of glory, passing judgment on all mortal and spiritual beings. He writes about a messianic kingdom, resurrection and final judgment. He writes further that Satan, the demons and evil spirits (the fallen angels) are responsible for sin (in addition to Adam's transgression), which continue to lead man astray, causing moral ruin on Earth.

- In the mysteries of Mithras (pre-Christian), the worshippers were offered consecrated bread and water. The Spanish conquistadors were shocked to find such rites among the Indians of Mexico and Peru.

- Gnosticism antedated Christianity and had proclaimed a Soter, or Savior, before Jesus was born.

- The central theme in Jesus' teaching—the coming Judgment and Kingdom—was already a century old among Jews. Christianity did not destroy paganism—it adopted it.

- From ancient Egypt came the idea of a divine Trinity, the Last Judgment, personal immortality, reward and punishment, the adoration of Mother and child, monasticism.

- From ancient Syria came the idea of the resurrection drama.

- From ancient Persia came the dualism of Satan and God.

- From the Jewish Book of Wisdom and other apocalyptic Jewish books (pre-Christian): The reign of evil will be brought to an end either by direct intervention of God himself or the earthly coming of his son or representative, the Messiah or Anointed One. Enoch and Daniel called him the Son of Man and pictured him as coming down from heaven. The author saw him (the Messiah) as incarnate Wisdom, the first-begotten of God.

- The Roman general Pompey's (106–48 B.C.) soldiers brought the religion of Mithraism from Cappadocia (Asia Minor) to Europe. The 7th day of each week was held sacred to the Sun-God; towards the end of December his followers celebrated the birthday of Mithras, "the invincible Sun". The priesthood had a high Pontiff. Daily sacrifices were offered at the altar of Mithras. Worshippers partook of consecrated bread and wine. It so closely resembled the Eucharist sacrifice of the Mass that Mithras priests were accused by Christian fathers of plagiarizing these similarities.

- The Romans, who under Emperor Claudius (41–54 A.D.) worshipped the Great Mother, had as chief rival the Egyptian goddess of motherhood, Isis.

- In Greek Asia, the Roman emperor Augustus (31 B.C.–14 A.D.) was hailed as "Savior" and as "God the Son of God"; some have referred to him as the long-awaited Messiah, bringing peace and happiness to mankind.

- In ancient Greek religions, the precinct of the temple was sacred and inviolable, it was God's home. Dionysus, son of Zeus, was killed and mutilated into fourteen separate pieces, resurrected and worshipped; he changed water into wine. All sickness meant possession of alien spirits. To touch a sick person was to become unclean; dead persons were unclean; sexual intercourse rendered a person unclean, so did childbirth. Madness was possession of an alien spirit. The priest was an expert in purification—he could exorcise by magic and prayer. Salvation depended on ritual purification rather than nobility of life.

- The idea of a slain and resurrected God is pre-Christian; Dionysus, Adonis, Attis, Mithras, and Osiris were part of the legend of dying and resurrected Gods. So were the legends of a Virgin Mother and her Dying Son.

Finally, one of the most astonishing verses from the Book of Wisdom 2:10–20, written by a hellenized Jew in the 1st century B.C., written in Greek:

"As for the virtuous man who is poor, let us oppress him; ... let our strength be the yardstick of virtue, ... let us lie in wait for the virtuous man, since he annoys us and opposes our way of life, reproaches us for our breaches of the law ... he claims to have knowledge of God and calls himself a son of the Lord ... the very sight of him weighs our spirits down; his way of life is not like other men's, ... in his opinion we are counterfeit; he holds aloof from our doings as though from filth; ... and boasts of having God for his father, let us see if what he says is true, let us observe what kind of end he himself will have. If the virtuous man is God's son, God will take his part and rescue him from the clutches of his enemies. Let us test him with cruelty and with torture, ... and put his endurance to the proof. Let us condemn him to a shameful death since he will be looked after—we have his word for it."

(6)   Even for the reader who only possesses a working knowledge of the Bible (The Old and New Testaments), the above paragraph must contain amazing information. The similarities, nay the outright appropriations of central themes and other relevant accounts lead one to the inevitable conclusion that the writers of the Torah (redacted in Babylon between the 6th and 5th centuries B.C. during and after the Exile and finally completed by about 300 B.C.) and the Gospels (written in Greek in the latter part of the 1st and 2nd century A.D.) freely and selectively copied from existing available sources without fear of detection, considering the cumbersome process of manuscript compilations prevailing in those days. They did it brazenly, massively, surreptitiously, and without the slightest intent of admitting attribution. But perhaps this was the custom of the time, before the art of printing and before copyright laws were instituted (and before commercial exploitation of authors' works) which frowned on such flagrant plagiarisms. The written word can still be a source of profound inspiration even though copied and collated from existing sources. But when such writers claim to be in possession of knowledge of first impression; when they claim exclusive access to information about events which are bound to affect the beliefs and conduct of the human race; when they lay claim that their written works contain the imprimatur of exclusive divine revelation; when they claim for themselves and their followers privileged access to a Deity to the exclusion of all others; when they claim their belief to be superior, on that account, to all others and to be in possession of the only truth which can bring salvation to mankind and damnation for the recusants—then one is forced to call them to account. In their wildest dreams they never imagined a time in the future

when research—historical, literary and archaeological—would be guided by standards that would expose their bold deceptions, fraudulent claims of originality and scuttle their temple of beliefs built on crumbling foundations. For all their claims to be recipients of divine revelation are bogus, of no validity, and subject to critical analysis applicable to all man-created literary works. Based on the foregoing, the following conclusions can be drawn:

(a) The Torah was not divinely revealed to Moses but written by scribes and priests who freely appropriated material from Egyptian, Sumerian and Babylonian sources. It contains contradictions, emendations, subsequent corruptions of text, anachronisms and errors. The other works of the Old Testament were, by admission, authored by profane men. The Old Testament cannot claim divine revelation for any of its 24 books.

(b) The first original New Testament writings were the epistles of Paul, 14 in number, of which only 5, possibly 7 are authentic, the rest are forgeries. Paul did not know Jesus personally although he was his contemporary, did not know the Gospel writers or any of the Gospels. He was an ordinary man who had access to the Septuagint, a Greek translation of the Old Testament, and freely borrowed from it. He is regarded as the founder of a theology (Christology) which later developed into Christianity. The named Gospel scribes were unknown and were not the real authors (2nd century tradition assigns these respectively to Mark, Matthew, Luke and John). They did not know Jesus, relied on the original Gospel of Mark for source material, who himself relied on writings identified as the Q text, author unknown, time of composition unknown, the written text never found. The Gospel of John also drew heavily from the Old Testament Book of Wisdom. The rest of the New Testament consists of the Acts of Apostles, various other epistles, and The Book of Revelation—all written by profane men without claiming any divine revelation. The authors of the New Testament books and epistles borrowed extensively from Old Testament and various pagan religious sources, which they appropriated as their own. Their writings contradict each other, bear the corrections of later times and extensive interpolations. Nowhere do they cite first person direct divine revelation and massively quote from non-revealed sources. The New Testament cannot claim divine revelation for any of its books or epistles.

(7) From the amalgam of these writings, from this melange of pseudo-historical accounts, from these sanctimonious, self-assured, self-righteous, and simplistically crafted factitious accounts bordering on puerile superstitions, written by men who believed the Earth to be flat, to have four corners, that diseases were caused by evil spirits inhabiting the body and could be exorcised by mysterious incantations, that the moon was the size of a silver dollar, came forth doctrines of religious beliefs which with uncommon anthropocentric certitude proclaimed a new message, which, reduced to bare bones, proclaimed to all who wanted to hear that mankind is doomed to perdition, the wrath of God aroused, and reprieve secured only if divine absolution is sought in accordance with priestly prescribed rules.

   In the case of Judaism:

(a) Daily ritual animal sacrifices consecrated in the Temple by the divinely chosen priesthood (which requirement was thankfully abrogated by Rabbi Johanan ben Zakkai after the destruction of the Jerusalem Temple by the Romans in 70 A.D.) as commanded in the Torah.

(b) Observance of all other Torah laws, commandments, and ordinances.

   In the case of Christianity:

(a) Belief in the divine Jesus Christ (Christ-Chrystos, Greek for "anointed"), the Messiah of Davidic descent, who shed his blood on the Cross for the sins of mankind, so that in believing in him mankind can be saved.

(b) Belief in Jesus Christ's Second Coming to establish the Kingdom of God on Earth and confront all humanity in Final Judgment.

(8) In this Chapter I have tried to present man's beliefs in the supernatural from inception up to the conceptual founding of the Judeo-Christian religions. I have tried to show that no established religion can claim an instantaneous breakthrough in systematizing its beliefs, but that instead all of them borrowed extensively from older preexisting sources and evolved additions and deletions by human hands over a period of time. Accordingly, as defined in Par. 4 of this Chapter, none of them can claim divine revelation. The designing and systematizing was painstakingly performed by profane hands of men who followed their self-serving agenda. I have intentionally avoided engaging in any critical examination of the theological context of religious beliefs in arriving at my conclusions. Nor did I engage in an exegesis of the Bible—such an effort would require an examination from within and not from without. My interest is

to analyze what impact man-made established religions had upon civilization (and vice-versa) and what influence, if any, they exerted upon the conduct of man. For all religions, stripped of their divine revelation impediments and claim of exclusive possession of keys to salvation, must promote peace and amity among neighbors, communities, and nations to justify their usefulness. The final judgment will be rendered by the part they played in the history of civilization and whether they promoted or impeded the most important moral categorical imperative—the control and blunting of greed, avarice and cupidity, man's most pernicious tools of self-preservation, instincts implanted by Nature to assure his survival in a competitive natural order.

CHAPTER 4, PART TWO

THE EFFECT OF JUDAISM ON CIVILIZATION

(1)   Almost from inception, Judaism and Christianity had to offer an answer to the question so well articulated by the biblical Job: If God cares for man and governs with justice, why is there so much pain and suffering? Why do the upright and God-fearing suffer while the evildoers and idolaters prosper and flaunt their good fortune? They had no answer because the timeless problem is inexplicable and unanswerable. Instead, a priesthood (Bishops for the later emerging Jesus faith, i.e., Christianity) was established to act as intermediary between the Deity and man, to exercise exclusive prerogatives of seeking divine oracles and communicate them to for his worldly guidance, in addition to providing him with divinations, signs and omens. To fortify the priestly permanence and make their services indispensable, they devised all sorts of rituals, taboos, proscriptions, bans, ceremonies, sacraments, and most importantly, sin-offerings, all attributed to divine commands, to entangle man with obligatory acts of contrition, penitence, and repentance as his only hope of assuaging the anger of the Deity and obtain grace and salvation. Thus, the inexplicable and unanswerable were partially made plain to the layman that his only hope of mitigating, perhaps even avoiding, pain and suffering was complete reliance on priestly mediation and fully complying with their ordinances. The priests became an order, a special sect, a class governed by divine, i.e., their own, laws subject to no secular interference or direction, permanent, exclusive, with succession either hered-

itary or chosen from specially designated candidates. But all this cost money, and lots of it. The Old Testament divinely prescribed tithes became the rule, imposed on the laity as a form of taxation to keep the divinely appointed intercessors in comfort and well provided (without pain and suffering). The priesthood grew in wealth and in time better than equaled the riches of most monarchs. And with wealth came superior power, which could not help but corrupt the priesthood who, as ordinary men, were subject to ordinary human frailties of arrogance, greed and venality.

How did the Judeo-Christian religions contribute to civilization? At this stage the two religions must be separated since their contribution and development followed along different routes.

JUDAISM

(2) The priesthood was abolished with the destruction of the Jerusalem Temple in 70 A.D., never to appear again. Except during the Hasmonean period of kingship (2nd and 1st century B.C.) when the offices of king and High Priest were combined (to the great detriment of both), the office of High Priest exercised a negligible restraint upon the rulers whose conduct resembled that of oriental despots. On the contrary, the High Priest became an appendage in their service. The function of social critics was taken up by the Hebrew prophets; their confrontations with the rulers are legendary. They preached the highest form of morality, extolling the virtues of social justice and righteousness as the guiding principles, more attuned to exhortation than to the exigencies of practical living. But no matter, their writings not part of the Torah do uplift the mood of man and excoriate the evildoer. They reserved the harshest criticism for the priests whose actions they denounced in language of unvarnished condemnation and disapproval. They spoke out vehemently for the fair treatment of the widow and orphan, against oppression of the poor, for aid to the ailing and helpless, exhorted the strong to alleviate their suffering, to walk humbly and control their pride. They were active from about the 8th century to the 5th century B.C. (unfortunately many of their writings were lost or intentionally omitted from the Old Testament canon), most of them suffered the burden of their convictions. The writings of the prophets had a most profound and lasting effect upon civilization, giving man pause in his quiet and pensive moments to reflect

upon, and question, the mode of his conduct; this could not help but have some stabilizing influence.

The Torah instructed the Jews to become familiar with the commandments, laws, and ordinances and made it binding on all male Jews to devote as much time as feasible to the study of its content. Hence the Jews had to be literate, not as a choice but as a religious duty. This not only contributed to their state of edification but also to their substantial educational and commercial advantage in dealing with their neighbors and nations at large, particularly during the Diaspora, the expulsion and dispersion from Judea in 135 A.D., and after, when up to the late 16th century most of the Europeans lived in the darkness of illiteracy. The study of the Torah, which in the days of the darkest period of oppression and persecution (during the Diaspora), was the most cohesive force in holding the Jewish people together and assured the survival of the remnant as Jews. But the study of the Torah brought to their attention as well verses which had a ruinous and devastating effect upon their destiny as a nation and State (prior to their dispersion), namely Deuteronomy 17:14–15, "If you appoint a king to rule over you … it must be one from among your brothers … you are not to give yourself a foreign king who is no brother of yours", together with verses reciting the promise that God would raise up a liberator-king of the Jewish people during their darkest hour and establish the rule of God on Earth. This was enough to set the radicals and fundamentalists (Zealots, Sicarii, and Pharisees) on a fatal course of suicidal rebellions against the militarily superior might of the Roman Empire. In three major ill-advised and ill-thought uprisings against Rome (66 A.D., 115 A.D., 132 A.D.), instigated primarily by the reading of claimed divine revelations in the Torah and the exhortations of some zealous Rabbis, successors to priests, spurred on by frivolous and foolhardy messianic expectations, the Jewish nation in Judea was decimated, almost exterminated. For those who survived the bloodbaths, the Roman victors mercilessly decreed slavery and expulsion from their homeland to suffer the indignities of living in foreign countries and under foreign rulers. Thus, a strange union of the sublime (the moral teaching of prophets), the crude mandated rituals (priestly animal sacrifices), the monotheism (a stern and jealous God who will not forget his people in their darkest hour), the exclusive religion (chosen People of Israel), and the messianic fever (God will send a Redeemer), all combined to pervert the mind of Jews in causing them to choose the wrong options and made them blindly obsequious to their religion. It caused them also to be con-

temptuous of others, i.e., non-Jews, disdainful to the need of following
their self-preservation instincts as a basic rule of survival, lacking purpose
and direction. After the defeat of the Bar Kokhba rebellion (135 A.D.),
most having been expelled from their homeland, the Jews were forced to
seek tolerance among Gentiles, practicing a religion which had to be modified to suit the new circumstances. It was only much later, when the Gentiles relaxed, or even in some cases eliminated, the confining restrictions
which precluded the Jews from fully participating in the social, economic,
and cultural activities of their neighbors, that they experienced a worldly
Enlightenment in the early 19th century, resulting in the split of their religion into three distinct groups: the established orthodox, the new conservative, and the new reform. The latter two shed some of the retarding and
confining tribalism and their adherents were able to absorb the prevailing
milieu of culture (the orthodox consider them beyond the pale). The
Torah religion, designed by parochial and unworldly priests who totally
lacked any ability of governance and serving their own special interests,
dominated the adherents with the claim of divine revelation, whose doctrine preached exclusivity, separateness and intolerance, predictably and
inevitably caused the downfall of the 2nd Jewish Commonwealth and
almost the ruin of the Jewish people in other parts of the Roman Empire.
It was the abolition of the priesthood and the purifying effect of exposure
to hostile and confining domination of a Gentile majority that saved
Judaism from extinction and the Jewish people from absorption by their
neighbors. As soon as Gentile hostility abated, Jews felt free to apostatize
from the beliefs of their ancestors but most remained within the camp out
of pride and prospect of economic benefits. The conservative and particularly the reform segments of Judaism absorbed and made a contribution,
completely out of proportion to their numbers, to the more uplifting
branches of civilization in the fields of science and research, philosophy,
medicine, and humanism in general. The fundamentalist orthodox segment, on the other hand, retained its traditional aloofness, exclusivity and
intolerance, disdained differing opinions and freedom of speech, condemned their coreligionists of different persuasion and denounced them
as blasphemers. They enjoy their isolation, ignore the opprobrium they
arose on account of contempt for others, which they consider God's test
of their devotion and await a Redeemer, a heavenly sent Messiah, who will
lead them to the Promised Land (they consider the secular State of Israel
not a stroke of fortune but misfortune). The orthodox were unaffected by
the influence of culture except for their insistence on literacy, proscribed

all intellectual contact with classical literature or any philosophy not consistent with their kind of orthodoxy. They consider themselves the only true Jews, sole heirs to the divinely revealed Torah, their religion and views the only criteria of Judaism. Their kind of Judaism, even though only a small minority of the total, unaffected by spiritual forces or the civilizing influence they exercised on man's conduct, is guided by their own religious laws and traditions unaffected by the swirl of changes around them. Their fundamentalist intolerant religion, with an orthodoxy representing the Judaism of the Bible, keeping their isolation from the rest by design of divine command, does not portray a civilizing force and made itself intentionally immune to the influence acculturation brought to mankind, albeit a merely superficial influence. One of the properties of acculturation is its universal application, it must be contagious, sink its tender roots in receptive soil, and demand unconditional reciprocity. Judged by this yardstick, their kind of religion has failed the test.

But in speaking of the morality of all Jews practicing Judaism intensely, sparingly or not at all, it can be stated without reservation, whether exposed to the uplifting impact worldliness exercised upon their conduct or not, that except for periods of unmitigated tragedies of monstrous proportions (such as the calamities of lost wars against the Roman Empire and the Nazi era), they have always managed to take care of their poor, hungry and ailing, provided orphanages and retirement homes, comforted the dying and accorded them a decent funeral—none was ever buried in a pauper's grave—provided needy women with dowries, and purchased the freedom of slaves who were their brethren. They consider such acts not as charity but a compelling religious duty imposed upon all Jews able to provide help. The charitable gifts of Jews are ecumenical; their funded humanitarian facilities open to all people regardless of faith, belief or ability to pay. This represents the highest form of civilized conduct worthy of the name, truly a light unto nations.

(3) It has already been shown that biblical Judaism is not a revealed religion but a composition by profane hands. Biblical Judaism as represented by the orthodox segment of Jewry is its only representation. The Conservative and Reform segments (the latter in particular) are artificial offshoots of the original base and are rightly designated as blasphemous by the Orthodox. They chose which parts to believe and which to discard, and since they are a moving target removed themselves from criticism. What matters to them are their beliefs, however artificial and without any pretense of foundation, which give them solace and comfort, a clouded

vision and understanding of purpose, a protection against fear of the unknown; most importantly, a willingness to adjust to changing circumstances of time. They view with sympathy the plight not only of their own but also that of others. They exemplify the weakness and fragility of man in that they consider all man-originated knowledge doubtful and refutable, but are content to accept beliefs in a mythical supernatural Deity, secure and irrefutable, because they provide the most cherished and prized possessions—peace of mind and conviction that man's existence is purposeful.

The Orthodox accept the Torah as the word of God, unchangeable and timeless: not a word can be added or deleted, as divinely commanded. They came to view the study of the Torah as the fundamental purpose of their worldly existence and pass the knowledge gained to their sons and future generations in an unbroken sequence, to earn God's promise "to be a people all his own". But they are mistaken. In addition to the reformation by Rabbi Johanan ben Zakkai, as related above, the Torah laws and commandments were changed and they know it. The Torah, the word of God, which prohibited any charging of interest "to your brother" (Deut. 23:19) was countermanded by Rabbi Hillel (30 B.C.–9 A.D.), who permitted the charging of interest to all for purely practical reasons. The third change is major and fundamental and goes to the roots of Judaism: the belief in the immortality of the soul. The Torah is completely silent on the subject. God promised his people prosperity on Earth for keeping his commandments; it was the prophets (Ezekiel and Daniel) who spoke of God raising his people from the graves at some unspecified time in the future and lead them back to the soil of Israel. Except for the above references to the resurrection of the dead, there is no dogma elaborating further on the subject—total silence. And the prophetic writings are not part of the Torah. The Orthodox, therefore, entertain certain fundamental beliefs which are plainly the invention of rabbinic Judaism in the post 1st century A.D. era. The conservative and reform Jews also accepted this belief in the immortality of the soul. The Rabbis knew exactly what they were doing—the changes were necessary to keep a firm hold on their adherents and prevent massive apostasy to religions such as Christianity and (later) Islam, which preached a more comforting faith. The need to believe in the immortality of the soul, the reward and punishment for earthly deeds in a future life beyond the grave give a clear purpose to an otherwise inexplicable human existence; such a belief completes the circle of understanding the divine design and makes the vicissitudes of life bearable and comprehensible for the greater part of humanity. The idea of future life beyond the grave, once implanted and absorbed in childhood, almost always endures as a necessary prop in maturity. It causes no harm, unless the believer is possessed of an oppressive proselytizing zeal and seeks to accomplish his evangelizing by forcible means. This has been regretfully, as will be shown, the history of all monotheistic religions and hindered, nay retarded and obstructed, the propagation of an otherwise civilizing influence of certain uplifting moral religious precepts. But the Orthodox Jews nowadays are not seeking converts to their kind. They desire more than anything:

(a) To be ruled by a theocratic government. A democracy, as generally understood, is considered not consistent with the Torah.
(b) The Torah must be the law of the land.
(c) No freedom of speech or expression of opinions not consistent with their teaching.
(d) To be a people separate and apart from other people; no community of interest with others.
(e) The Conservative, Reform or secular Jews are not to be admitted to their assembly.
(f) Not to force God's hand but wait for the promised Redeemer to lead them back to their homeland, Israel.
(g) Only their prayers are acceptable to God.
(h) Rabbinic courts to be the only courts of justice.
(i) Restoration of the Temple in Jerusalem.
(j) Restoration of the Temple priesthood and the ritual of animal sacrifices.

After almost 1900 years of dispersion in Gentile lands, after suffering the brunt of repressions, discriminations, isolation, forced conversion and martyrdom, nursing an understandable hostility toward their tormentors, the Orthodox stand today where they stood throughout almost 19 centuries: defiant, isolated, confident, unchanged in their basic beliefs save for the noted modifications (which were merged into their faith), untouched by cultural changes, and content in their apartness. They have remained unaffected by the progressive cultural transformation and are offended by the reproach; nor did they make, or are capable of making, any contribution to civilization. The aforementioned morality is based on religious and not human commandments and applicable only to their own congregation. They are extraneous to the process, uncaring about the fraternity of man, consider contact with outsiders undesirable for fear of encouraging apostasy. They are the ultimate survivors, convinced that their cause and practice are the only ones acceptable to God and see no reason to change. They prefer to be ignored by the rest of humanity and the latter should accommodate them—the progress of civilization would be better served if they did.

CHAPTER 4, PART THREE

THE EFFECTS
OF CHRISTIANITY
ON CIVILIZATION

(1)   When examining the origin of Christianity it is most difficult to separate
      fact from fiction. The fictional aspects of the beginning mirror those of
      all religions since we are obliged to consider any assertion of divine rev-
      elation and transcendental (supernatural) communication as beyond the
      realm of human understanding. We are, however, capable of examining
      the factual, i.e., historical foundation of Christianity, dealing with histor-
      ical events, conditions and personalities to the extent that their contribu-
      tions were essential to its development, propagation, and cohesion of
      written texts. But we know that certain deeds and activities of admittedly
      historical personalities and description of events were embellished, the
      text corrupted by interpolations, some letters or writings forged in order
      to present a more palliative sequence of events and one corresponding
      with the tendentious agenda of its authors. The intentional corruption of
      texts, the selective fictional additions of events in the lives of real persons,
      the accretion of fictional episodes with the passage of time, all point to
      perpetrators not satisfied with the impact, cohesion, and congruity of
      writings, freely added or deleted passages to give a firmer and more dra-
      matic effect and compatibility to the creed of their choice. For it must be
      remembered that none of the writings were concurrent with the histor-
      ical narrative but were written and collated long after the events; that no
      original texts are available but only reproductions by scribes who are sus-
      pected of altering the text to conform with the then developing dogma of

81

the Catholic Church. That evidence was intentionally destroyed can be gathered, for example, by the selection of the four New Testament Gospels when more than forty were once in existence, the others expunged from the record, condemned as heretical by orthodox Christianity in the middle of the second century and burned. Bishop Irenaeus (ca 180), who supervised the Church in Lyons, declared the other Gospels to be "blasphemy against Christ", even though some of them can be dated earlier than the canonical Gospels. Why the vehemence, venom, animus, rancor of the Bishop? Because he recognized the danger to clerical authority and that some of the offending Gospels offered theological justification for refusing to obey the Bishops of the Church, who already in those early times led a life of comfort and abundance. The passion which accompanied the early formation of the Church, the excommunications, banishments, and murders perpetrated in the first few centuries in pursuit of the "truth" of a creed in the formulation stage can be better understood if we take into account the financial benefits accruing to the prevailing and dominant exponents of the new faith. It was a power struggle in its crudest form and the teachings of Jesus merely secondary. That is why it is so difficult to separate fact from fiction in the early formation period of the Church, the Catholic Church, orthodox as it was called, because there was an incentive, not merely theological but foremost economic, to prevail victorious in the struggle by any means available, not excluding forgeries, lies, corruption of texts and simply burning the offending works. For it must be remembered that the effort to persevere in existence applicable to man is equally applicable to the institution of the Church, the Roman Catholic Church.

(2)   The story of Jesus' life and ministry are outlined in the four canonical Gospels. They are depicted against a background of calm, order, serenity, peace, a society seemingly in harmony, without turmoil. We get the impression of an almost pastoral setting in which the drama of Jesus' ministry was the central theme. Pontius Pilate was described as a decent, understanding, and magnanimous Procurator who found no fault with Jesus even though, as the Gospels relate, his accusers charged him with claiming to be the "King of the Jews". The Pharisees, as portrayed in the story, were persons of evil disposition who had nothing better to do than harass Jesus, argue with him, and try to trick him into saying something blasphemous. The Sanhedrin, composed of Pharisees and Sadducees (who were at each other's throat on account of theological differences basic to Judaism), preoccupied with serious affairs of governance (how-

ever limited by the Romans), were said to be aghast and bewildered and acted totally irrationally when the High Priest asked Jesus whether he was the Christ (Messiah), Son of the Blessed One.

The narratives related above are so seriously flawed that one must conclude that they were written by authors who were not acquainted with the subject matter and were far removed from the scene, both in time and place. They had a theological agenda in mind and were anxious to place the Jews in the worst light possible. They were mistaken and could not have written as they did had they known that:

(a) *Political conditions*

If Jesus was crucified between 30–32 A.D., the periods preceding and immediately following were a veritable cauldron of plots and counterplots instigated by opposing messianic aspirants seeking to overthrow Roman domination by force of arms and restore the Davidic Kingdom. Those were turbulent times, a ceaseless class struggle between the aristocratic and wealthy Jews (largely Hellenized) and the impoverished who were swayed by the promises of every militant demagogue bent on stirring up violence and rebellion. Bandits swarmed all over the country, robbing, pillaging, murdering the wealthy, and setting villages on fire. The agitation was viewed by the radical segments as the precursor of the apocalyptic period fulfilling the prophecies and that God was putting the Jewish people to the final test to establish his rule on this Earth. Simon, a former servant of Herod, rebelled in 4 B.C., proclaimed "King" by his followers; in the beginning he defeated an entire Roman army unit; was finally defeated, and 2,000 of his followers were crucified by the Romans as a warning to others. Athronges, a shepherd, designated "King" by his followers, defeated several Roman army units in 4 B.C., feared no bloodshed, and engaged in successful guerrilla warfare. Judas of Galilee led a revolutionary movement against the Romans in 6 A.D., urged his countrymen to resistance, founded the movement of Zealots, the ultra-radical revolutionaries. In 44 A.D., Theudas rebelled against Rome, was considered the Messiah by his followers; he promised to imitate the miracles of Moses.

The bloody turmoils during the lifetime of Jesus and immediately after were ongoing, the explosions taking place only after lengthy simmering of animosity, unrest and bitterness. Without exception, all rebellions went down to defeat only to encourage others in the never-ending quest to rid Judea of foreign rule.

(b) *Pontius Pilate*

He was Procurator (governor) of Judea (in fact, he was only Prefect) from 26–36 A.D. He subjected the Jews to never-ending humiliation, constantly sought bribes to ease their burden (he was appointed by Sejanus, chief aid of Tiberius, one criminal appointing another) and oppression, commanded that Jews must worship the imperial emblems and insignia superimposed upon the Roman army standards, which inflamed the passion and agitation of Jews who refused to comply. Pilate, like most of the Roman governors of Judea, constantly overstepped his authority, excelled in acts of wickedness and cruelty. Finally, in an act provoking the wrath of the Jews and High Priest, plundered the treasures of the Jerusalem Temple and had his soldiers massacre a great number of people who responded with outrage at this desecration. Emperor Tiberius finally had enough. Upon learning of his flagrant misdeeds, he had Pilate recalled to Rome in 36 A.D. to stand trial for cruelty and oppression. To claim that such a scoundrel, upon hearing the accusation that Jesus claimed to be "King of the Jews", was willing to release him and incur the wrath of the Emperor who would have charged him with high treason (followed by swift execution)—and to give up his ongoing gains from lucrative bribes—is to display total ignorance of the political climate of those days. The episode, as related in the Gospels, just could not have occurred. Pontius Pilate had a good thing going and was cunning enough not to throw it away.

(c) *Pharisees*

Far from exhibiting rigidity in interpreting religious laws, the Pharisees were known to be flexible in their application of biblical commandments to everyday circumstances. They were in constant opposition to the fundamentalist Sadducees, the biblical literalists, and were even expelled from membership in the Sanhedrin during the reign of John Hyrcanus (135–104 B.C.) for opposing the inflexible views of Sadducees. The Pharisees, followers of the humanitarian and compassionate Rabbis Hillel and Shammai, believed in the resurrection of the dead, the Day of Judgment, reward and retribution in the life after death, the coming of the Messiah, and the existence of angels—views and beliefs preached by Jesus. They interpreted the Mosaic law of "an eye for an eye" to refer to monetary compensation and not retaliation; rejected any appeal to force and violence; devoted much of their time to education, since they regarded learning as the basis of all useful and virtuous living. They believed in the "Kingdom of God", an apocalyptic expression, part of Pharisaic phraseology and not first coined by Jesus. The Pharisees did not view anyone's claim to be the Messiah as blasphemous; that title carried no connotation of Deity or divinity and had many claimants, none of whom was ever accused of blasphemy. "The sabbath is made for the sake of man and not man for sabbath" is a Pharisaic maxim; their law books taught than the saving of life is more important that the sacredness of the Sabbath.

The Gospel authors, writing after the destruction of Jerusalem (including the Temple) by the Romans, aimed at depicting Jesus and the subsequent Christian movement as not opposed to Roman rule but hostile to the Jews, the singular rebels against the Roman Empire, so as not to draw unfavorable attention and arouse the antipathy and suspicion of the dominant power.

(d) *Sanhedrin and the High Priest*

The Messiah in Enoch is, among others, called the "Son of Man", a preexisting heavenly being who sits on the throne of glory. In Samuel 7:14, God speaking of King David, "I will be a father to him and he a son to me." The first reference is an elevated and noble title of "Man"; Jesus spoke Aramaic and such an expression did not exist in that language. There were many claimants (who led armed rebellions against Rome) to the title "Messiah" before Jesus and none of them was charged with blasphemy; it carried no connotation of divinity. The second reference was spoken by God about David to signify his intent, among others, to make his royal house secure for ever and to treat him like a son—pure allegory. The trial before the Sanhedrin was not witnessed by anyone who made a record of the proceedings for history and we have to take the dubious Gospel story as our guideline. The members of the Sanhedrin (Sadducees and Pharisees) and the High Priest were sufficiently well versed in the laws of the Torah to know:

(i) That there is no connection between a Messiah and the Blessed One.

(ii) That the Blessed One (God) had no son (all Israel were his children and he a father to them).

(iii) That the title "Messiah" carried no connotation of divinity.

To conclude, as the synoptic Gospel writers did (Mark, Matthew, Luke, John ignored the story), that members of the Sanhedrin and the High Priest, all educated men of experience and well grounded in the Torah, upon hearing Jesus accused of the claim of being the Messiah and the Son of the Blessed One (Jesus' non-response was taken as a sign of affirmation), should be seized by apoplectic fits and pious consternation, is monstrously absurd since all of them would have to be guilty of devout imbecility and incomprehensible fatuity. But this famous episode is fiction, it did not happen for all the above stated reasons and the authors should have been laughed into silence. Unfortunately, their long-nursed hostile agenda left its indelible corrosive mark upon future generations of Jews.

(3) About 200 Christian scholars from all over the United States conducted a study of the sayings of Jesus as related in the Gospels with a view of establishing, to their satisfaction, which sayings they considered authentic. Called the "Jesus Seminar", it was based in Sonoma, California. After six years of intensive effort ending in 1991, they reached the following conclusions:

(a) They rejected the authenticity of all the sayings of Jesus in the Gospel of John, except 4:44.

(b) In the synoptic Gospels they accepted as authentic 20% of the sayings; 30% were termed doubtful and 50% were rejected outright.

This study was performed by men sympathetic to the cause, painfully aware of the impact their conclusions could have not only on the devout, but biblical scholars as well. The study was conducted for obvious reasons. The Gospels are so full of contradictions, inconsistencies, anachronisms, errors, and interpolations as to bring into question the authenticity of the narratives. Some of the sayings put into the mouth of Jesus, whose divinity they accepted without any scruples, are absurd, irrational, ill-suited, mistaken, and demonstrate the confusion and ignorance of the authors. The choice of four Gospels (three synoptic) instead of collating the narratives into one is itself ill-conceived and more a reflection of the times in which they were written, since they were never meant to be read together but were prepared for geographically widely separated audiences. These distances disappeared, however, with the passage of time. The very fact that a great number of passages in the synoptic Gospels are literally, word for word, identical means that the authors not only copied from each other (Mark was the original of the three) but were writing for different audiences. But apparently embarrassed by the suspect textual similarities, the authors embellished their work with a personal touch by adding, or deleting, episodes and vignettes to enliven their version. How else can one explain the contradictions; just a few are cited by way of illustration:

(a) Only Matthew and Luke trace the ancestry of Jesus. Merely a few ancestors are identical out of a completely differing genealogy (going back to Abraham in one case and to Adam in the other), and both end with Joseph as the father of Jesus even though the authors elsewhere are most careful to point out that Jesus had no natural father.

(b) Jesus was born in Bethlehem (Matthew, Luke), Nazareth (Mark).

(c) Virgin birth not mentioned by Matthew.

(d) Jesus death sentence carried out by Jews (Luke, John), by Romans (Mark, Matthew).

(e) The resurrected Jesus appeared in Galilee (Matthew), in Emmaus (Luke), none named (Mark).

(f) Ascension not mentioned by Matthew.

The above mentioned contradictions are not minor blips. A lot of arduous work by experts has gone into reconciling the many discrepancies, but the results are not convincing. Solving such intriguing problems may be amusing when dealing with literary trifles, but pietistically proclaimed divine revelations? What about the following mental lapses of the authors placed in the mouth of Jesus:

(a) He mistakenly thought circumcision was first instituted by the Covenant with Abraham (the custom long preceded Abraham and practiced first by the Egyptians).

(b) He mistakenly advised a Palestinian Jewish audience that a wife should not seek divorce (only husbands could).

(c) He mistakenly believed the world would end in his lifetime (Christianity arose as a response to this failure).

(d) He never mentioned his virgin birth (Jewish audiences would not have understood that concept).

(e) He believed that evil spirits caused sickness and could be exorcised by his command (a false contemporary belief; the discovery of the true causes had to await research in the distant future).

(f) He believed in sorcery and efficacy of witchcraft (a totally false belief which was ultimately eradicated by science, but not until hundreds of thousands of innocent victims were sacrificed on the altar of this madness).

(g) He mistakenly believed that the Torah was authored by Moses (written by profane hands and redacted during the Babylonian Exile).

Thanks to the movies produced by Hollywood depicting biblical stories, the viewing public has been exposed not only to vivid and colorful representations of the life and suffering of Jesus, but also to the added touch of realism sprinkled with liberal accretions and artistic privileges smoothing over an otherwise implausible story. The intense scenes have become calcified in the mind of viewers, most of whom construe and visualize biblical events not from reading of the Gospels but from viewing the movies. It makes for good pictures, but this is not history. A religion which claims to be in possession of the exclusive "truth", which is aggressively promoting conversions to its faith offering the only salvation available to man to the exclusion of all other creeds, has justifiable reasons to be humble and contrite about its inauspicious beginnings, which, though shrouded in mystery like the origin and source of all other religions, could not withstand a critical examination.

(4) Paul, an unquestionably historical figure, born about 10 A.D. in Tarsus (now Turkey), died in Rome between 62–68 A.D., considered the founder of Christian theology. He had a penetrating mind but often given to casuistic reasoning, at times approaching sophistry. The New Testament contains 14 Epistles attributed to him, but only 5, possibly 7, are authentic (Romans, 1 Corinthians, 2 Corinthians, Galatians, 1 Thessalonians, possibly Colossians, Phillipians). The authentic Epistles contain many later interpolations to conform the text to the new Christian dogma. Though he claimed to be a Pharisee and to have studied under Rabbi Gamaliel, he used only the Septuagint (a Greek translation of the Old Testament) as a guide in citing biblical references.

Paul never met Jesus although he was his contemporary, was never mentioned by name in the Gospels although the Epistles predate them, knew nothing of Jesus' actual earthly existence or any of his activities or his teachings, his miracles, virgin birth, nothing of the empty tomb, or the circumstances of his death, or his admonition to his disciples to preach only to Jews. Paul did say that Jesus was a descendant of David, born a Jew "according to the flesh" (Rom. 9:5), but nothing of his trial or Pontius Pilate, that he lived on Earth in some distant unknown past and was crucified at the instigation of wicked angels (1 Cor. 2:8), that he existed as a supernatural personage before God sent him into the world to redeem it by shedding his blood on the cross (suggestive of a sacrificial death) so that those who believed in him would have salvation and eternal life.

It took Paul sometime to reach his new theology. The process was expedited by him receiving the "Good News" (which initiated Christianity) in a series of revelations of the post-resurrection Jesus (Gal. 1:13). Additionally, he drew heavily on the Old Testament Wisdom literature and the mystery religions of his birthplace. His conversion took place about 36 A.D. and his Epistles were written between 55–60 A.D. The Greek population of Tarsus, his birthplace, had many followers of the Orphic and other mystery religions, who believed and worshipped a God Soter (Savior) who died for them, was resurrected, and would grant them salvation and eternal life if propitiated by faith and ritual. But there were many other prevalent mystery religions depicting a dying and resurrected Deity, such as Attis, Dionysus, Adonis, Mithras, Apollo, Asclepius. To the inhabitants of the 1st century Greco-Roman world, the new religious group called Christian seemed merely like a new mystery cult, not much different from the existing cults with which they were familiar. Paul had many existing models to guide his thoughts; there was not much new in his design but he was more resourceful, imaginative, sharp-witted and determined. Paul, like Jesus, had no interest in founding a new religion because he was sure that the end of time would come in his lifetime, "… the Lord is coming …" (1 Cor. 16:22), never used the term "Christian" in any of his authentic letters, and his Epistles, though only an outline of his myth, make a vain effort in reconciling his doctrines with Greek philosophy. So much for the ideas of Paul. He gave later Christianity a theological foundation and prepared the way for a nascent Catholic hierarchy, powerful and wealthy, to articulate and promulgate its articles of faith, its dogma, which affected and transformed the concept of civilization for millennia to come. Implausible ideas do not gain credibility by amalgamation—the chain, however fancy, is not stronger than its weakest link. The Catholic Church still had to establish its primacy and the Bishop of Rome his legitimacy. This legitimization was achieved by the questionable doctrine of apostolic succession, a doctrine which did not detract from the purely abstract idea of the Catholic Church but added another weak link to the weak chain.

(5) It seems to be one of the idiosyncrasies of Christianity, with its belief in a God of love and mercy, that early on when practically going through its birth pains, it was already ruptured by theological schisms and this propensity stayed with it almost throughout its bloodstained history. The postapostolic age required a nexus, a continuity of the apostolic succession centered in the primacy of the Bishop of Rome, subsequently referred as the Supreme Pontiff, head of the College of Bishops. Early in the 2nd century, with the Christian communities spreading rapidly

throughout the Roman Empire, each supervised and ruled by a Bishop who interpreted the "Good News" variously according to his own understanding. Centralization of authority and the systematization of the Christian creed were essential if the disparate religious communities were to survive the heretical trends and innovations. For the challenges to the orthodox creed so early in the postapostolic period boded ill for the message of Jesus. The doctrine of apostolic succession was the means whereby the mission which Jesus conferred on his Apostles was transferred to, and perpetuated in, the Church's College of Bishops, who in turn passed on this prerogative to their specially selected successors. It was necessary to establish the agents and the means which conferred the legitimation upon the Bishop of Rome and the preeminence of Rome as the seat of apostolic authority. That agent was the Apostle Peter and the means the Gospel of Matthew (Christianity also accords Paul the title of Apostle, but that appellation is without authority since he appropriated that title simply by self-appointment on account of the claimed several visions of the post-resurrected Jesus. He was not an Apostle of Jesus and no amount of theological quibbling can change this).

The legitimation required the Christianization of the Old Testament, which was the only biblical canon possessed by the Church authorities in the early 2nd century. Marcion, a Christian Gnostic, active in Rome ca 139, maintained that the Church had been mistaken in retaining the Old Testament and regarding Jesus as the Messiah foretold by the Old Testament prophets. Asserting that the Mosaic law was the cause of sin (he agreed with Paul's view), he concluded that it could not be the work of the Christian God, and that the absolutely perfect God, the God of pure love and mercy, was embodied in Jesus; he was new because he was revealed only in Jesus. Marcion concluded that the Jesus creed must be dissociated from Jewish apocalyptic eschatology (obviously because the prediction of a second coming proved to be false) and the Jewish Jesus excluded from authentic Christianity because, in his view, Jewish preconceptions had contaminated Jesus' message. He was promptly excommunicated by the orthodox Christians for his heretical views since, according to Marcion, the concept of apostolic succession was false and invalid.

How do the sayings of Jesus in the Gospels justify the concept of apostolic succession? There is nothing in the Gospels to indicate that Jesus made any reference to the handing on of the apostolic mandate. The total weight of evidence relied upon is Matthew 16:18 and 28:19-20.

In the first citation, Jesus speaking to Peter: "You are Peter and on this rock I will build my Church" (Church, translated from the Hebrew "Kahal", the community of the Chosen People). Several chapters before, the author quotes Jesus, speaking to his Apostles about proclaiming that the Kingdom of Heaven was close at hand: "Do not turn your steps to pagan territory ... go rather to the lost sheep of the House of Israel" (Matthew 10:5-6). These verses are contradictory, for if the Kingdom of Heaven was close at hand then why the instruction to Peter that through him he "will" build his Church, the sense being sometime in the future. The second citation (Matthew 28:19-20) is obviously a later interpolation, since the verses include Jesus' instructions to his disciples to "Go ... make disciples of all the nations, baptize them in the name of *the Father and of the Son and of the Holy Spirit, ...*" (emphasis added) which is a Trinitarian expression, a liturgical usage established at a much later date. Furthermore, considering the importance of the future propagation of Jesus' message of the quoted verse, Matthew is the only Gospel writer to insert this episode in his text. The other three Gospels are silent on the subject, except for an admittedly fraudulent interpolation in Mark 16:16, the resurrected Jesus instructing his Apostles: "Go out to the whole world; proclaim the Good News to all creation." The Gospel of Mark ends with verse 16:8; the addition of verses 16:9-20, the so-called "long ending" of Mark, is included in the canonically accepted body of inspired Scripture, but it suited later compilers of the canon to do so even though they knew it to be a forgery. For verses 16:9-20 are not included in the Vatican Codex, nor in the Codex Sinaiticus, the oldest extant Greek manuscript of the New Testament Bible, said to date from the 4th century. So much for the "means".

As far as the "agents" are concerned, the picture is just as dismal and dispiriting for the Catholic Church. There are no words of Jesus in the New Testament indicating how the apostolic mandate was to be handed on. The Church relied on Peter and Paul as the agents of this mandate. As already noted above, Paul is excluded; he was not one of Jesus' Apostles, he did not know Jesus, his views contradicted Jesus in the most fundamental aspects (preaching to the Gentiles, doing away with the law of Moses), and for the Church to assert that Paul conferred on two of his fellow workers (Timothy and Titus) the mandate to exercise the apostolic ministry is absurd and a total invention. As for Peter, there are difficulties of a different kind. With reference to the two letters included in the canon and attributed to his authorship (1 Peter and 2 Peter), the latter is admitted by biblical scholars as not authored by him. As to the former, the Jerusalem Bible (1966) commentator states that, "… though Peter's Greek is unsophisticated it is too accurate and unforced for a fisherman from Galilee." Another biblical commentator (G. A. Wells) asserts that, "A Galilean fisherman could hardly have been capable of the scholarly correct Greek." Furthermore, the author of 1 Peter seems never to have heard of the Sermon on the Mount, does not know Jesus' manner of life, and figures only as a preexistent supernatural personage; when he quotes authorities he uses passages from the Old Testament and not words of Jesus; the letter contains no hint of an acquaintance with the earthly Jesus.

The Catholic Church needs the story of Peter as the first Bishop of Rome to justify its doctrine of apostolic succession and the primacy of Popes. The New Testament does not refer to, or mentions, the apostolic succession of Peter nor to the Roman community as leaders of all Churches. Peter was never Bishop of Rome (Irenaeus, Bishop of Lyons in the latter part of the 2nd century, compiled in 180–185 a list of the Bishops of Rome; Peter's name is not on the list. It was not till Eusebius, the 4th century Church historian, who stated that Peter was Bishop of Rome for 25 years). It is not even certain that Peter was ever in Rome; his sojourn in Rome has not been established to this day. The Roman Christian community was not founded by Peter (nor Paul) but by unknown Jewish Christians. Emperor Claudius (41–54), because of disturbances between Jews and Jewish Christians, expelled them both from Rome; the Emperor did not distinguish between the two. Peter is said to have been martyred between 62–64. Paul, in his last letters from Rome (he was in jail at the time) knew nothing of Peter's martyrdom, nor is there any mention in the synoptic Gospels, not a word in the 1st century Christian letters. Clement, who was supposed to have headed the Roman Church from 88 to 97 (and would have followed Peter by about 25 years), had no knowledge of the manner of Peter's death or the location of his grave. Ignatius, early 2nd century Bishop of Antioch, one of the Fathers of the Church, knew nothing of Peter's martyrdom. Eusebius (4th century) mentioned for the first time Peter's place of martyrdom (in the Vatican). Peter's grave is said to be located on Via Appia or under St. Peter's Church in Rome. The search for his grave has continued to this day but the results are not encouraging for the Church. So much for the "agents".

The Roman Pontiff as successor to Peter, and the Bishops as the successors of the Apostles, exercised the supreme authority (power) over the Catholic Church, and until Luther's Reformation, their authority extended over all Christendom. In the Roman Catholic belief the College of Bishops, as successor to the College of Apostles, succeeded to the apostolic power to govern the Church. But the primacy of the Pontiff and the legitimacy of the Bishops are an illusion, a monumental and brazen fraud perpetrated by some clever men who, operating in the vacuum of the postapostolic period, arrogated to themselves the perquisites, prestige and security by means of bluff and deception. They succeeded by the thinnest of margins and fortuitous circumstances to prevail over dissenters and nonconformists by declaring them heretics, eliminating all opposition by excommunication, expulsion, banishment, expropriation and murder, in the crudest of power struggles so well learned from the pagan and ruthless Romans. As they grew in power and influence, they struck the coarsest blows at the already enfeebled civilized values and continued to defy gravity by spreading pious disinformation; they plunged mankind into the darkest period of its short history by enforcing its creed, dogma and belief in a loving and merciful God by the practice of bluster, cunning, sophistry, guile, duplicity, lies, fraud and forgeries, all applied in an unprincipled and reprehensible struggle of self-preservation and perseverance in expansion of power and wealth. It was only thanks to the indomitable spirit of some men, commencing in the 16th century and increasingly beyond, that the theological and political influence of the Church and man's primal fear of sin so well exploited by it began to be circumscribed by emerging new powerful and secular dissenting forces. But the damage inflicted upon man's mind can never be totally eradicated.

The Catholic Church is not the legitimate successor to the College of Apostles; that phantom concept was the product of phantom minds. It served as a portent of other frauds to come. The most ambitious and rapacious of them all, the "Donation of Constantine", will be treated next.

(6) Constantine, and his fellow Emperor Licinius, issued in 313 the Edict of Milan, which stated that Christianity and other religions would be tolerated throughout the Roman Empire. This in effect made Christianity a lawful State religion (religio licita) although it did not make it the official State religion; this was a most auspicious turn of events for Christians and their leaders most adroitly managed, in due time, not only to make Christianity the predominant religion to the exclusion of all others but to suppress any heretical divergences from the Orthodox faith. Little did Constantine anticipate that his exhortations to the convocation of Bishops for unity, peace, and tolerance of divergent religious views would give birth

to the most arrogant, intolerant, and tyrannical system of ecclesiastical domination which brooked no interference, made its own laws and ordinances to serve self-seeking interests; that it was only a question of time before the Church sought temporal powers coequal with that of the Emperor and, in time, attempt to usurp even his authority by invoking the spurious doctrine of divine right. To make sure that such claims would not be resisted or questioned, the Church resorted to crude and unsubtle forging of documents. Had such documents been forged by men with some degree of sophistication, as assuredly happened with the earliest writings, the frauds would not have been detected. Thankfully for the course of subsequent history, some important forgeries were committed by men lacking sufficient worldly polish, and their efforts involved not simple but multifaceted documents of a broad scope which would have daunted even the most intelligent of forgers. One such forgery was the Donation of Constantine.

In the 9th century the Roman Church was confronted with two problems, which threatened its well-being, possibly its survival: (a) The Lombards militarily in the west, (b) in the east, the refusal by the Byzantine Empire to acknowledge the primacy of the Pope in Rome.

(a) Shortly after the accession of Pope Steven II (752–757), Rome was militarily threatened by the Lombard King Aistulf, who regarded the duchy of Rome as his fief and proceeded to levy taxes from every inhabitant, to the obvious detriment of the Church. The Pope turned to Pepin III, King of the Franks (751–768), for help in delivering the Roman people from the Lombards and restoring the Church ownership of Rome and other parts of Italy. Pepin not only agreed to give military assistance to protect the Roman Church but also promised in writing to guarantee the Church's rightful possession of the duchy of Rome and other various cities, including Ravenna and other extensive areas in northern and central Italy, which were previously held by the Lombards. Pope Steven II was thus responsible for the formation of the Papal State. As a legal basis of his claim, the Pope produced an instrument called "Donation of Constantine", under which the Emperor Constantine (Roman Emperor 306–337) handed over to Pope Silvester I (314–335) the imperial power, dignity, and emblems, the Lateran Palace and rulership over Rome, and all provinces, localities, and towns in Italy and the Western hemisphere. As justification for the grant, the instrument cited Constantine's intention to reward the Pope for his miraculous recovery from leprosy and for the gift of baptism. Because the Emperor considered it inappropriate (so the document reads) to reside in the same city with the successor of St. Peter, he removed his residence to Constantinople, which thereby became the urbs regia (royal city).

(b) At the time of the composition of the Donation grant, relations between the Papacy and the Byzantine Empire had reached the breaking point. Byzantine officials protested to Pepin that the territories given to the Roman Church legally belonged to the Byzantine Emperor and that since the ecclesiastical status of a city is determined by its civil status, Constantinople was the urbs regia and therefore the primacy of the Roman Pope was not acknowledged. But according to the Donation, Constantine offered the imperial crown to Pope Silvester I, who refused to wear it. The implication was that if he had so wished, Silvester could have worn it, and therefore Constantinople had become the urbs regia through the acquiescence of the Pope himself. Therefore, the Pope could withdraw his permission at any time and retransfer the crown from Constantinople to Rome, which he did by accepting the return of the territories from Pepin. This incident was a significant episode in the disagreements which were to increase between Rome and Constantinople in the following centuries, until a complete rupture occurred in 1054, when the Patriarch of Constantinople was excommunicated by the papal legate. The seat of the imperial government was where the imperial crown was kept. The Donation supplied the Papacy with the right to exercise governmental functions (e.g., to collect taxes) and made the Pope a true king and legal ruler of the West. The Donation established the legitimate rulership in the Christian world, i.e., the Roman Empire.

Lorenzo Valla (1407–1457), a humanist of the Italian Renaissance (ultimately protégé of Pope Nicholas V and his papal secretary in 1448), was asked by his then patron, King Alphonso of Naples, to write some article against Pope Eugenius IV (1431–1447) with whom he was at war. Valla obliged by examining a document called "Donation of Constantine", drafted in the papal chancery, most likely in the middle of the 8th century, probably by its head Christophorus, in which Emperor Constantine made certain grants, as described above, to Pope Silvester I, dated March 30, 315. These grants were very influential throughout the medieval period; permitted the Popes, as Bishops of Rome, to step into the position of the vanished emperors; served the Papacy as a basis for a number of its claims, in particular, to make legitimate the newly gained ecclesiastical and political position of the Popes after the extinction of the Western Roman imperial region and the development of the political ideology of the Papacy. The document had been used by the Popes from the middle of the 8th century as justification for their claim of being the supreme temporal rulers in Italy and Western Europe. The effect was to make the Popes feudal lords placing great financial value on their office and holding the keys to many revenue-producing cities in Italy.

Valla, expertly versed in Latin, made short shrift of the document called "Donation of Constantine". He declared it to be an outright forgery, written by someone in crude and bad Latin (he maintained that on this account alone it could not have been written in the 4th century when good Latin was in vogue) and who was unfamiliar with contemporary history. The forger referred to Silvester, Bishop of Rome, as "Pope Silvester", nearly two hundred years before the title was limited to his office and made Constantine refer to himself as the "conqueror of the Huns", nearly fifty years before they made an appearance in Europe. It is a reflection on the state of poor scholarship that the forgery remained undetected for so long. The fraudulent grant was influential throughout the medieval period and served the Papacy as a basis for more spurious claims asserted with impunity. But the damage was done. There is no question but that the forger was in cahoots with Pope Steven II in concocting this fraudulent document, but history has a way of compensating for such fabrications which led to unlawful usurpation of temporal power bordering on the criminal. For the abuse of temporal power corrupted the Papacy, led to incessant turmoil and armed conflicts with much bloodshed for territorial aggrandizement, in order that more exactions might flow into papal coffers to support the Vatican hierarchy in a sumptuous style. In time, this aroused the resentment and contempt of the devout and led to schisms, to pitiless and ferocious suppression of critics, apostates, the non-orthodox and the perplexed. It caused John Hus (1373–1415), one of the courageous critics and dissenters, to state in a sermon (delivered in Prague): "Our Popes and successors of Peter have turned themselves into hangmen and executioners; they call faithful Christians heretics and burn them." Martin Luther (1483–1546), a vehement denouncer of papal morality, assaulted the primacy and powers of the Popes, declaring in 1520, "... If we strike thieves with the gallows, robbers with the sword, heretics with fire, why do we not much more attack these masters of perdition, these Cardinals, these Popes, and all this sink of the Roman Sodom which has ... corrupted the Church of God, ...?"

There has never been unity in Christendom. From the early beginnings up to the present time Christianity has been beset, nay overwhelmed, with schismatics who put their own interpretation on the meaning of the divine message, unmolested by authoritarian interpretations, and clearly unable to distinguish fact from fiction and authenticity from forgery. A religion whose highest representatives and protagonists conducted a murderous and criminal policy throughout much of its existence based on fraud and forged documents, particularly between the 9th and 11th century, when in a period of 155 years there were 35 Popes, of whom 18 were murdered in office by rivals and / or their accomplices who then usurped the office of Pope; the Crusades, the Inquisitions, the murdering of about 300,000 totally innocent people accused of witchcraft, the massacre of the Albigensians, forced conversions under penalty of death or expulsion. For from the mythical foundation of Christianity, mostly administered by an arrogant clergy, lacking in competence, with no tolerance for dissent, buttressed in their domain and lifestyle by many writings of questionable authenticity and outright forgery, it was inevitable, as effect follows cause, that their presence on this planet embroiled humanity in innumerable bloody conflicts over minutiae of theological nuances. The consequence of all these misdeeds was not only loss of prestige and respect but the undermining of faith in their teaching and loss of temporal power which caused the furor and insanity in the first place. The damage inflicted on the dignity of man is without equal in the annals of human history.

CHAPTER 4, PART FOUR

A FAITH SUITED FOR THE DARK AGES

(1)   As the old order faded away, a new order made its appearance intending, not by force of arms but by a newly designed creed, to re-establish harmony and accord a new orientation among a multiplicity of uprooted nations seeking stability. This new order was claimed by Christianity represented by the Roman Church, aspiring to instil its authority by a complex ecclesiastical hierarchy of Bishops, priests, and in due time, by Cardinals and a Pope, as Vicar of Christ, the apostolic successor to St. Peter. Led by an ambitious clergy who stealthily schemed to reach the heights of temporal power not only coequal with that of kings and emperors, but surpassing their authority by having recourse to the most impenetrable, esoteric and mystical construction of divine sanction. With astounding ease and daring, the Church theologians dulled the senses of the literate and illiterate alike by dispensing knowledge of the transcendental with self-assurance befitting the elect given the power of divine insight. They inverted the simple and upbeat message of the Gospels and Epistles about the Kingdom of God on Earth and substituted the natural sinfulness of man exposed to the dread of everlasting hellfire, a fire burning without consuming and agony without let up, to subdue any hesitancy of the adherents to strict obedience to the clergy and reinforce the terror of excommunication, interdict, anathema, blasphemy and heresy. A small group of men, however intelligent, could only prevail and maintain their position of power by trading on the primal fear of man of the unknown

and perpetuate the myth of salvation exclusively dispensed by the clergy. The life of faithful Christians during the Dark Ages and many centuries after was one of painstakingly avoiding the pitfalls of sin and eternal damnation, attending Church services and Mass regularly as required, seeking forgiveness, grace and absolution of sins known and unknown. At every turn the fatherly figure of the Church priest made his presence felt involving himself and the Church in the major events of life with appropriate rituals: birth, marriage, death, and burial. Christianity became a religion of fear, hate, revenge, accusations of heresy for ever so slight deviations of belief; frowned upon and condemned freedom of speech and thought; feared and denounced progress and anything that questioned or criticized ecclesiastical authority; showed little mercy for apostates for fear of disrupting the status quo; forged, corrupted, altered, and concealed the interpolation of documents with changes helpful to its creed and dogma. Finally, the Church considered itself the sole dispenser of the true faith, consigning all others to the heap of blasphemy (in this respect it did not differ materially from other religions). It was truly a faith ideally suited for the Dark Ages and the few centuries following, until the depravity of its clergy and the unstoppable progress of spiritual enlightenment affected the views of enough men to open the gateway to radical dissent, to positivism and humanism, culminating in agnosticism and various forms of atheism.

(2) But the small group of self-appointed men prevailed by other means. The few people who held spiritual power in the Roman Church corresponded to the few people of nobility who held secular power in the State. From the time of Constantine until the French Revolution, the interests of Church and State coincided in Christian countries, the spiritual and secular joined forces to hold sway over masses of slaves and former slaves, the underprivileged, the illiterate people close to or crossing the borderline of poverty, who eked out a daily existence without assurance of tomorrow, fearful in their insecurity but encouraged by the promise of a blissful afterlife if they dutifully obeyed the rules of the Church and the laws of the State. The Church soon gained primacy in this alliance which lasted until the secular rulers also claimed their status by divine right (which circumstance they learned from the Church) and regained their predominance. But until that time, the Church felt all-powerful and exercised its authority with a degree of profligacy, self-indulgence, malice, and calculated cruelty unique in the annals of history. Nothing was too vile, too scandalous, too savage, or ruthless if such actions gained the

Church an advantage. Even if the Roman Church could claim validity based on the doctrine of apostolic succession (which claim is a total invention, as shown above), its subsequent conduct during the centuries of arrogance and crude domination would have assuredly repudiated and rendered null and void any claims to divine blessing, and the institution should have been consigned to everlasting torment in hell as it imperiously promised would happen to any sinner not even remotely guilty of such misconduct. But then all powerful secular rulers and priesthoods of old (and not so old) ever commanding similar authority and operating in similar fluid and unstable circumstances would have likewise crossed the line and been guilty of such villainous conduct.

(3)   The Roman Church was plagued by what it considered heresies throughout its existence. In the early period Gnosticism, Arianism, Montanism, and Marcionism tormented the Church Fathers in their attempts to modify and preempt the loose orthodox creed; such deviations were combated with uncommon resoluteness and brutality, most often involving violence and bloodshed of Christians opposing Christians; the Roman Church learned early the art of protecting and maintaining its primacy through thick and thin; that the lesson was well learned is clearly evident from its subsequent history and the continuity of its survival that would have daunted most institutions. If we could understand the Roman Church (the later Roman Catholic Church) and the ecclesiastical hierarchy to be a monopolistic commercial institution dispensing faith and salvation instead of manufactured products, we should then understand that anything interfering or disturbing that monopoly, and thus undermine their privileged status by subverting the faith it dispenses and the benefices it enjoys, would necessarily be resisted and condemned with all the means at its disposal, as would be the case with any commercial monopoly. But as soon as the Roman Church (and certain other Christian sects) lost its power, prestige, and influence (after the French Revolution of the 18th century), it relented in its hatred and antagonism to social forces and devoted whatever prestige and influence it could muster to social and moral causes, becoming an advocate of the poor and ailing, expending considerable efforts to relieve their suffering, implementing a strict code of priestly conduct to avoid the scandals which plagued it in the past (It could not, however, shake off some of its affected concerns for abortion and euthanasia, the marriage of priests, the ordination of women, and that intractable mother of all inventions: deicide). Gone were the forced confessions under torture; the prison dungeons and fiery

stakes; the Crusades and Inquisitions; the burning of witches; the placing of papal interdicts on whole communities; the sale of indulgences to raise funds for worldly papal extravagances; the papal chess game switching kings, bishops, and knights to serve papal interests; instigating murderous wars to settle perceived theological quarrels and disputes; the arbitrary condemnation of man's conduct as sinful, deserving punishment in the afterlife or denial of rewards in heaven; placing certain authors' works on the index of prohibited books the reading and possession of which incurred mortal sin and the burning of such books; declaring secular learning harmful to morality; promising the faithful heavenly rewards for fighting and dying in battles for the Church; preaching and declaring Holy Wars against recusant rulers; impeding scientific progress by threats to haul scientists before the Holy Office to answer trivial and frivolous charges formulated by ignorant men with power of life and death; and finally, the Church instigated and organized persecutions of Jews and their forced conversion, justified on spurious theological and historical grounds, causing unspeakable suffering, privation and bloodshed to innocent Jewish men, women and children.

(4)   The Roman and later Catholic Church and Christianity, in general, have maintained a world outlook that was hostile to the progress of civilization, to the spirit of the Renaissance, to basic democratic ideals and aims, to freedom of expression. It could not be different for it is based, like most other religions, on intolerance of dissent, on doctrines of myths and the improbable, praising the value of faith but discounting the worth of understanding as useless for salvation, since the divine mysteries require unquestioning acceptance by the faithful. They know nothing, nor do they care to know anything, nor are they capable of assimilating the knowledge of the dangers to the ecology by unrestricted population growth and the pollution such growth causes to the environment and its adverse effects on the survival of the human species. They are totally oblivious of man's Nature-given instincts of self-preservation which coexist with innate life-sustaining attributes, such as greed, envy, jealousy, avarice and rapacity, all of which are considered sinful by the Church if committed by the laity but not so if practiced by the clergy. It is all very well to preach not to worry about nourishment or how to clothe the body; not to worry about tomorrow because tomorrow will take care of itself; to bless those who curse you; not to ask for return of stolen property; to lend money without hope of return and to love one's enemies—could anyone contrive more absurd and irresponsible preach-

ments that are totally contrary to human nature and social order, totally outside the realm of morality, and can, therefore, never govern human conduct? These sayings of Jesus, quoted in the Gospels, could not have been expounded by rational men but instead sound like the absent-minded daydreamings of some cloistered monks, living in seclusion in some monastery and totally separated from, and ignorant of, the humdrum existence of humans struggling to keep body and soul together—they are totally amoral. Anyone studying the history of the Papacy and supporting clergy during the early centuries and up to the French Revolution, must be completely dumbfounded upon learning of the clergy's criminal conduct; accumulation of wealth through fraud, extortion and murder; the sexual depravity of the Popes, Cardinals, Bishops and priests; the quest for political and military power; the excommunication, imprisonment, and murder of Pope by Popes; the violation and debasement of every norm of accepted civilized conduct, the total absence of decency and morality, the treachery, corruption, mendacity, and venality bordering on the insane; the maintenance of brothels in the Vatican; the dabbling in witchcraft and Satanism; the prevalence of fornication and sodomy; the liberal use of poison to dispose of enemies—all these charges can be laid at the doorstep of the Vicars of Christ (there were notable exceptions), these corrupt representatives on Earth, who disgraced their calling and deserve nothing but contempt, loathing and scorn. What teaching did they follow? Not the New Testament. We see very little concern for the hungry, poor, disabled, orphan, or widow during the period under discussion. Their reprehensible and outrageous conduct constitutes a cancer on the body of Christianity that cannot be expunged, purged or erased. Yet these men tainted by guilt made sanctimonious pronouncements, convened numerous conciliar meetings dealing with Church doctrines, creed and dogma, hairsplitting rules of theological discernment for which they claimed an ecumenical status in the Western world. To these belong the various Lateran Councils, briefly described in order of their date sequence.

First Lateran Council (1123)

Attended by 300 Bishops and about 600 Abbots, dealt with episcopal control of granting the cure for souls; cohabitation of clerks with women; clerical concubinage and marriage; safeguards for Church property; protection of Church goods; alienation of Church property by intruders; indulgences for Crusaders; matters generally dealing with the establishment of order and discipline within the Church.

Second Lateran Council (1139)

Attended by between 500 and 1,000 Archbishops, Bishops and Abbots, dealt with rights of Bishops and clerks; sanctions against those condemning the Eucharist; prohibition of payment for Confirmation, Extreme Unction and burials; clerical dress and behavior; married clerks and those with concubines; marriage after solemn vows of chastity; the prohibition of study of civil law and medicine by the religious; protection of monks, pilgrims and merchants; nuns failing to live by their rules; the prohibition of usury; false penitence.

Third Lateran Council (1179)

Attended by about 300 Bishops, dealt with ruling that required a two-thirds majority of the Cardinals in all future papal elections; occupations forbidden to clerks; clerical and Church immunities; clerical vices; regulations concerning the Templars; sanctions against cooperating with the Saracens.

Fourth Lateran Council (1215) Attended by more than 400 Archbishops and Bishops, dealt with the promotion of a new Crusade; the obligation of preaching and supporting the Crusade; condemnation of the heresy of the Cathari and Waldenses; procedural rules for the repression of heresy; the confirmation of Pope Innocent III earlier rejection of Magna Carta, judged to have been extorted from King John and therefore invalid; neglect by clerks of their spiritual duties; on privileges enjoyed during interdict; the prohibition of blessing of the hot iron and hot water for judicial ordeals; no Christian was to have commerce with usurious Jews; Jews and Saracens were to wear distinctive dress to mark them off Christians; Jews were forbidden to appear in public in Holy Week to avoid the risk of insult to Christians.

Fifth Lateran Council (1512–1517)

Attended by 150 Cardinals, Archbishops, Bishops, Abbots and Prelates, dealt with condemnation of the Pragmatic Sanction of Bourges; declared papal elections null and void if tainted with simony; regulations regarding the Curia's taxation system; definition of the individuality of the human soul; the censorship of books; decision for a Crusade against the Turks; imposition of a 3 year tax on all benefices.

What conclusion can be drawn from these deliberations of so many assembled dignitaries? Not one single word was expressed by those well-fed and well-provided clergy on behalf of the poor, hungry, aged, widows, orphans; no funds for orphanages or hospices for the dying; no protection for the virgins; no alleviation of the plight of the incarcerated fellow Christians or others; no condemnation of the abuse of power and immorality of the clergy. But Pope Innocent III (1198–1216) condemned the English barons for improperly extorting from King John a document known as Magna Carta (1215), and declared invalid on that account, a document of monumental politico-historical importance, which limited the power of the king by guaranteeing certain civil and political liberties, the first such concessions by any monarch. The same Pope, however, did not invalidate the forced confessions extracted from poor wretches under torture, victimized for their perceived heretical views, and consigned to the flames for admitting guilt. That same Pope not only made current the title of Vicar of Christ but claimed the right to govern the whole world by virtue of that cognomen. The Lateran Councils also gained notoriety for instigating the murderous Crusades not only against infidels but also against Christian sectarians (the Albigenses), the censorship of books, and ordering Jews and Saracens to wear a distinctive dress to make them easily recognizable by Christians.

Although Christianity was born when men's ignorance was overwhelming and its faith manifested intolerance and aggression, it nevertheless performed an essential historical function: After the destruction of the Western Roman Empire it saved Europe from total chaos, disorder and lawlessness. The Church was the only unifying authority in Europe capable of functioning as a government. It would be idle to speculate whether the price paid was worth the cost. It is highly unlikely that other secular competing forces would not have found a solution and filled the void without the benefit of Christianity. For we learn from history that the bloody conflicts of the human race have never halted but have continued unabated and unaffected by any moral or religious scruples, considerations or influences. It is undisputed that Christianity was solely responsible for instigating religious wars, Crusades, religious persecutions and massacres, tortures, inquisitorial burnings, and other criminal acts, which, but for Christianity, would not be part of history. What a depressing record. What a debasement of human worthiness. It is hard to think of any institution created by humans which would retard more that spark of spiritual dignity that resides within man than the confabulations of this blood-stained clergy, and all this in the name of a religion that preaches the nobility of resplendent love.

The Goths sacked Rome in 410 A.D. under Alaric. In 476 the Ostrogoths completed the destruction of the Roman Empire under King Odovaker, ruling until 526. In 415 Attila the Hun invaded Italy but died before sacking Rome, and his army had to retreat. This enabled Christianity to seize political control and shape European life for more than a 1,000 years. The ensuing theological disputes became contests for worldly gains rather than efforts to settle differences over theological principles. Throughout all the initial turmoil, the Roman Church managed to hold two councils to resolve what it considered "urgent issues".

Council of Ephesus (431)

Attended by about 150 Bishops. After several strange excommunications, it decided on the personage of Christ, stating that his natures must be distinguished but must be united and assigned to one sole person, the two natures constitute one Christ and the one Son, the difference in natures is not suppressed by the union but the indescribable meeting of divinity and humanity produces one sole Christ.

Council of Chalcedon (451)

Defined one Christ, perfect God and man, consubstantial with the Father and consubstantial with man, one sole being with two natures, without division and separation and without confusion or change. The union does not suppress the difference in natures; however, their properties remain untouched and are joined together in one Person.

In case one wonders how the Bishops could find time to meditate upon such refinements of dogma in the face of the ongoing pillage and plunder by invaders, suffice it to say that Chalcedon marked an important step in the development of Roman primacy, as opposed to a "Church of the Empire" held by the emperors of Constantinople, which ultimately led to the schism in 1054 between the Christian Churches of East and West. Rome held the belief in the twofold nature of Christ which the East rejected. But nobody really believes that was the real motif. The reason for the split was more mundane: the ascendancy of political influence and economic wealth of Rome and the corresponding decline of Constantinople.

CHAPTER 4, PART FIVE

THE CIVILIZING INFLUENCE OF MONOTHEISMS QUESTIONED

(1)   About 350 years after Galileo (1564–1642), one of the greatest scientists of the 17th century was summoned to Rome during the Papacy of Pope Urban VIII (1623–1644), tried by the Inquisition, and under threat of torture forced to abjure belief in the Copernican system (1633), the Catholic Church admitted its error. Pope Urban's reign coincided with the period of Church's decline as political manipulators in Europe (the Thirty Years War 1618–1648 between Catholics and Protestants, and the rapid growth of Protestantism in Germany) and tried, unsuccessfully as was inevitable, to prolong the myth that the Earth was the center of the Universe (which was essential to the Church to maintain its primacy in accordance with the Creation story, as related in the Bible). In 1996, Pope John Paul II put the teaching authority of the Roman Catholic Church firmly behind the view that the human body may not have been the immediate creation of God but the product of a gradual process of evolution. Yet only a few years before (1950), Pope Pius XII (1939–1958), that infamous Pope of World War II, in his encyclical letter "Humani Generis", strongly condemned evolution as playing into the hands of naturalists and atheists, who, the Pope declared, sought to remove the hand of God from the act of Creation. In May 1995, Pope John Paul II, in a visit to the Czech Republic declared, "Today I, the Pope of the Church of Rome, in the name of all Catholics, ask forgiveness for the wrongs inflicted on non-Catholics during the turbulent history of these peoples … We forgive

and ask for forgiveness." This kindly Pope should have been reminded to also ask forgiveness for the wrongs inflicted on the many saintly Catholic martyrs and innocent Catholic men and women burned at the stake, accused of witchcraft by the Church. The reasonableness and moderation displayed by Pope John Paul II (and a few of his immediate predecessors) reflect a pragmatic and judicious attitude of the Catholic Church to the changed circumstances—loss of political influence. The bloody civil war in Northern Ireland pitting Protestants against Catholics; the murder of Catholic nuns in Central America; the persecution of Catholic clergy in the former Soviet Union and present-day China; the persecution of Catholic clergy in India; all happening in the last quarter of the 20th century, took their course unaffected by the concerns of the Vatican. It is true that Pope John Paul II rallied the spirit and resistance of the Catholic Polish nation to overthrow the Communist regime, but the Pope's Polish origin must be recognized as one of the factors. The Polish people, throughout recent history and past centuries, have been vehemently patriotic and always motivated by a remarkable nationalistic fervor. But Poland was an exception, for it must be remembered that not so long ago (1939) the Polish foreign minister (Beck) condemned the Vatican (Pope Pius XII) in the most vehement terms for betraying the Polish people in favor of Nazi Germany.

(2) It would be a mistake to feel complacent about the present moderation of Christianity and the unaccustomed restraint shown. For not deep beneath the calm facade, a new species of intolerant and evangelizing fundamentalist forces are raising their voice preaching a literal interpretation of the Bible, dispensing with, and mostly ignorant of, the turbulent and belligerent past 2,000 years history of Christianity. Concentrated mostly in the United States, sermonizing their newborn Christian message all over the media, this new Christianity of charismatic messengers, mostly ignorant of the true contents of the Bible (which is itself the bedrock of intolerance and exclusivity), preach their kind of radical vision for regulating the private behavior of law-abiding citizens. Their plan is for schoolchildren as well as adults of all faiths—or no faith—to become captive audiences to religious displays, denominational prayer, and other religious observances. This new religious activism by certain Protestant factions, in the United States in particular, brims with boldness and self-righteousness, does not seek the social remedies mandated by the Bible nor searches for alternatives to the failed social policies but declaims against their perception of the current state of immorality and

low state of family values, which, they assure us, will be remedied by a return to what they obscurely refer to as, "religious values". But they aspire for much more. Their accustomed religious critique of secular power has been replaced with the erstwhile and long past religious quest for power; besides aspiring for a return to the old morality (whatever that means), they now inveigh against "the new world order", "the international bankers", "radical feminists", "militant homosexuals", and other satanic scapegoats. We recognize the symptoms and we have been there before. No concern for the homeless, ailing, widow, orphan or aged; no funds for orphanages or hospices; no provisions to feed the starving children, but an unshakable faith in the efficacy of school prayers and prayers in other public areas, the posting of the "Ten Commandments" in schools and public places. Their intentions are quite transparent: the transformation of secular society and government into an orientation which conforms to their understanding of formerly practiced Christian values. This kind of religious fundamentalism, affecting also other faiths, a criterion of the latter part of the 20th century, is also being propagated in other parts of the world.

(3)   The adherents of Islam, residing in mostly developing countries, almost all militants whose acceptance of the Sharia (the religious law of Islam, which makes no distinction between religion and secular government) as the supreme law affecting everyday conduct permeates their existence, whose mistrustful and hostile attitude toward other religions (the Western in particular) has not advanced beyond the primitive conditions of the Middle Ages, is the next potent religious force to be reckoned with. Brimming with confidence in the justice of their cause, accustomed to be ruled by autocratic and theocratic regimes strongly influenced by their Mullahs (religious teachers), resentful of Western influences, and over one billion strong, believe they hold the key to the future of the human race and are determined to attain their rightful place in the sun by peaceful or militant means, if necessary.

(4)   Jews are scattered all over the world, are minorities (except those living in Israel), eager to practice undisturbed whatever form of Judaism appeals to them and are therefore moderate in the attitudes and exercise of their influence. In Israel the situation is different. Jews constitute the majority and contain certain religious sects which long for conditions prevailing during the Second Commonwealth (about 2,000 years ago). The ultra-Orthodox, also known as Haredim, exhibit the intolerance and dogmatism of the biblical injunctions; do not recognize democratic political institu-

tions nor secular judicial systems but insist to be governed by the laws of the Torah and their own judges. Their attitude toward other religions, as well as secular coreligionists, is one of hostility and bigotry, a trait shared by all fundamentalist sects. The Haredim, like the Christian and Islamic fundamentalists, do not care to belong to the community of nations but intend to go their separate ways, convinced that their exclusive religion is the only true one and which could bring salvation. They disdain any civilizing concepts and treat any overtures for tolerance as satanic.

(5) Christian leaders boldly assert that Christianity is not only fundamental to civilization but has contributed a major share to its perpetuation. This claim is based on these basic foundations:

(a) Belief in the saving power of the God of Christianity.

(b) The teaching of morality, as described in the sayings of Jesus related in the Gospels.

(c) The Greco-Roman literary classics were preserved for posterity by the Christian monasteries.

(a) Christian monotheism (one has to be broad-minded to make this assertion) is no different than that of Judaism or Islam, i.e., the belief in one supernatural Supreme Being. Whereas both Judaism and Islam had the idea of God well defined at inception, Christianity had no clear idea of the nature of God in the early centuries of its existence, but progressively defined and redefined the relationship between God and Jesus over several centuries, selectively refining the concept by majority vote of clerical conciliar assemblies until Jesus, the man, became consubstantial with God, one perfect union and one perfect meeting of divinity and humanity. It is unclear whether the promulgators of this new and unique theology ever formulated a distinct concept in their mind of this eclectic Deity or whether the confounding mystique of language got the better of them, but the ordinary Christian has seldom given "consubstantiality" a second thought and conceived God as Jesus Christ crucified, who was resurrected and ascended to heaven, who preached the golden rule and the Sermon on the Mount (both taken from Hebrew Scripture and therefore not Christian) during his brief sojourn on Earth. The typical Christian believer's life was one of man-made suffering and primitive superstition, and could therefore easily identify, and find solace, with a suffering Deity, who, as the creed taught him, died for his sins. Man can love someone who suffered and sacrificed his life for his sins and who offers everlasting salvation in the afterlife for following the prescribed faith, but it encourages unthinking obedience, conformity, and constant fear of transgression, attitudes not conducive to civilized behavior. To live a life of pious resignation in order to gain salvation in heaven may lead to uplifting spirituality and godliness but is prone to self-seeking, submission, orthodoxy, and distrust of dissent, qualities which do not foster a morality applicable to the generality of mankind. It is no wonder that such people are easily provoked to defend their faith by any means necessary, however violent, to persecute and punish those who strayed from orthodoxy or are foreign to the practiced religion, and whose influence is viewed as a danger to their salvation. The herd instinct brings forth an evangelizing fervor to assimilate others to the established faith, conform to the rule or, failing that, appease God's anger by eliminating their presence from divine sight. Such attitudes and temperament can explain the drastic religious and bloody upheavals of past centuries which, regrettably, despite all the progress in science and secular education of the majority, are reappearing with a strain of vehemence reminiscent of past passions. There is enough historical literature on the subject of prior religious excesses to warn the wary and concerned not to permit a return to the abominations of the past without exerting every effort to deflect the intended course and to preserve the freedom of conscience and thought for those anxious to exercise it, for which freedom so much was sacrificed. But this trend toward a modern version of religious fundamentalism is also evident in the religious movement of Judaism and Islam and the above analysis is applicable, almost verbatim, to them as well (the followers of Reform Judaism or Unitarianism and several other similar offshoots of mainstream religions are not likely to be influenced by the rising fervor of fundamentalism). Any form of faith that preaches exclusivity, preeminence of its doctrines, salvation limited to the elect and damnation for others, intolerance of dissent, demands conformity and unquestioning obedience to its teaching, demands bigotry as a religious duty, and ostracizes or punishes the skeptic—such a faith is antithetical to the concept of civilization and radically opposed to what it stands for (but this is exactly what the Bible teaches). To the previously defined aspects of civilization must be added freedom of speech and thought, the right to hold differing views without fear of repercussions, the right of privacy, and freedom to choose, the discretion to read or publish any books, study or teach any subject—all these proud achievements of civilized man gained at such great cost, are all anathema to any religious faith inclined toward fundamentalism. There is no compatibility or affinity between civilization and religions tinged with fundamentalist proclivities. The claim of Christianity that its teachings and practical application are fundamental to civilization is false and without basis. Likewise false and without basis would be such claims asserted on behalf of Judaism and Islam, and for the same reasons. These three religions and the potential for passions and violence they arouse are incompatible with the concepts civilization stands for.

(b) Of the three monotheistic religions reviewed above, Christianity is the only one which claims preeminence of its moral teaching and asserts that its moral code, based upon the sayings of Jesus as related in the Gospels, is the foundation of civilized conduct. This claim is false and contradicts all credible historical and religious evidence: there is little connection between morality and Christian imposed conduct; it is tenuous at best.

In the struggle for self-preservation, when satisfaction of primary needs are at stake, all means at man's disposal are applied to gain the desired ends, and no methods, however injurious and unfavorable to others, are precluded out of consideration for morality. The application of moral codes in situations threatening survival or the well-being are luxuries a man can ill afford and would do so at his own peril. For the prudent man will not treat the preservation of his basic interests as a sport which is the domain of fair play and gentlemanly conduct. It is virtuous for man to strive for perseverance in existence and maintenance of primary creature comforts and to do so with all means at his disposal—regard for morality, religiously induced or otherwise, never played a conclusive role in such efforts, although there have been cases of intentional self-destruction (in whatever form), but such acts, by definition, served the perpetrator's interests.

It is well to define the concept of morality, as distinguished from ethics. Ethics is a code of conduct conducive to an atmosphere of social tranquillity, the compliance of which can be enforced by penal provisions. Such a code is typically mandated by an institution of authority, i.e., a government, to promote harmony and facilitate untroubled and peaceful intercourse among its inhabitants. The prudent government leaders will only seek laws to promote such conduct which can be enforced and provide appropriate sanctions for violators. Ethics is only a small part of morality. That part of morality which does not embrace ethics deals with conduct conducive to the promotion of compatibility and amity among men, which cannot be enforced by sanctions and which elicit approbation, admiration, and esteem of humanity in general. Transgressors face censure and opprobrium by the offended or harmed. Examples of the former are: laws against perjury, theft, murder, polygamy, prostitution, libel; bearing false witness; abuse of children, etc. Examples of the latter are: charity toward poor and weak, orphans; and infirm; care of others' needs; kindness to animals; respect for parents; helping a neighbor or friend; tolerating dissent; kindness to children; keeping one's promise; tolerance of other religions or views; etc. Ethics and morality can never be in conflict. The degree of morality is the measure of civilization; the control of the savage instincts of man by civilizing, i.e., moralizing, his conduct, and making him fit for a harmonious community life.

What are the sayings of Jesus as reflected in the Gospels which support Christianity's claim of indispensability to civilization? Almost all of the moral preachings of Jesus are taken from the Old Testament and are of Hebrew not Christian origin; so is the golden rule and the Sermon on the Mount, pointed to with pride by Christians as the sublime crowning essence of their morality. As for the other sayings not of Hebrew origin, to turn the other cheek, to give to anyone who asks, not to turn anyone away who wants to borrow, not to worry about tomorrow for tomorrow will take care of itself, anyone who humbles himself will be exalted, sell everything and give your money to the poor, bless those who curse you, do not ask for your property back from the man who robs you, to lend without any hope of return, to love one's enemies, to do good to those who hate you—can anyone really believe that such totally absurd, impractical, visionary, and imprudent advice, standing morality on its head, wholly incompatible with human nature, and going against all conventions, could be offered by a divine personage possessing the wisdom of heaven? Or that the suggested conduct could have any influence on the civilized conduct of man, on civilization? Or will such counsel confuse, demoralize, and frustrate anyone wishing to follow the divine precepts? Elsewhere, what are the well-to-do to think of Matthew 19:23-24, "… it will be hard for the rich man to enter the Kingdom of Heaven"? Matthew did not enlighten the reader about the definition of "rich man". It was the wealthy, those extremely wealthy Christians, who contributed lavishly toward the building of Churches, to the financial support of the Roman Church and the Papacy during the Dark Ages (for a time the wealthy Jewish Pierleoni banking family was the sole support of the Church), when such support saved the Roman Church from financial disaster. The funds were gratefully accepted and the donor graced with the most lavish papal blessings. And it was the faithful rich who were the most prolific purchasers of papal indulgences and thus bribed their entry into heaven. Pope Alexander VI (1492–1503) amassed a great fortune as Cardinal Rodrigo Borgia; Pope Leo X (1513–1521), son of Lorenzo the Magnificent, the wealthy Florentine banker, both, as Vicars of Christ, had no difficulty dealing with their or other people's riches. What is one to think of John 8:7-8, "If there is one of you who has not sinned, let him cast the first stone at her"? There are no perfect humans, everyone has sinned at one time or another; does that mean that no one should ever accuse another of any misdeeds, however outrageous? No judicial administration would be possible. What about all the accusations of ritual murder, image desecration, and desecration of the consecrated host invented by the clergy? All these were later admitted by the Church to have been false and the Jews unjustly vilified.

But even some of the objectionable moral teaching of Jesus which are wholly impractical and unsuited as guides for moral conduct (such as to love one's enemies, to bless those who curse you), which Christianity claims as its own by virtue of original revelations in the Gospels, were propounded over 2,000 years before Christianity in a collection of Babylonian precepts in a more literate and discreet version:

"Do not do evil to one who has a dispute with you;
Return good to one who does evil to you.
Maintain justice for one who is bad to you;
Be pleasant to your enemy ..."

Needless to say, none of the above precepts for moral conduct were taken seriously by the Babylonians.

In a direct challenge to man's earthly desires based on envy, hate and pride, and in response to his limited intellectual adequacy, a religion arose on the Indian subcontinent possessing sufficient lucidity to stand well above past and present religions in its pragmatic approach to life. For it held that, among other original beliefs, the religion of an experienced man cannot be the same as the one taught to a child; that what was meant to satisfy a child's need for security would not be adequate to nourish the mind of a grown man; that mystic rituals so pleasing to an impressionable young mind would discourage a grown man wisened by experience. It admonishes man to follow such moral precepts, among others:

(i)   Subdue the passions of the senses.
(ii) Be charitable to your neighbor.
(iii) Have pity on those who deserve pity.

It condemned any effort to seek salvation by sacrificial or ritual acts; that a state of happiness is attainable in this life through the complete elimination of selfish desires; that we possess everything within us to find ourselves richer if we just shut our eyes and our hearts against the illusion of the world. It admonishes man to follow certain fundamental moral precepts: generosity, benevolence, cooperation, service, courtesy, sympathy and honesty. But what is most important, it taught tolerance of other religions and beliefs; that meditation alone can secure salvation; that the human mind cannot conceive God except behind the veil of human language; it did not claim to possess exclusivity or preeminence. This is an eternity removed from the crude anthropomorphism of monotheistic religions, which falsely took credit for a morality they did not originate. What a breath of fresh air. What a nobility of spirit. What a present to the dignity of man and contribution to civilized conduct—no supernatural revelations, no divine punishment for transgressions, no miracles or colloquy with a Deity needed to teach man the obvious: the importance of moral conduct and getting on with his fellowmen based on common sense. All this was part of the religious teachings of the Upanishads, a segment of literature of the Veda, the Bible of the Brahmans, which came into existence about a thousand years before Christianity. It influenced Gautama Buddha (563 B.C.–483 B.C.), the founder of Buddhism.

(c) It must be granted without any hesitation that the Greco-Roman literary classics, such as the works of Socrates, Plato and Aristotle, were preserved for posterity by Christian monasteries, the dwellings of monks and clerics living a communal life separated from the rest of society. One cannot help but recall the Essenes of the Qumran community, members of a small Jewish religious order, living in a highly organized monastic fraternity, originating in the 2nd century B.C., and who lived apart from the rest of the Judean population. They held possessions in common, led a life dedicated to piety and ritual purity, and refused to immerse themselves in public life. But most importantly, they were responsible for preserving for posterity that treasure of biblical writings referred to as the "Dead Sea Scrolls". Their order of lifestyle and organization must have served as a prototype to the founders of Christian monasteries and monastic orders.

Members of the Christian monastic orders had occasion to transcribe, among many others, some of the works of the Greco-Roman classical literature and thus preserve them for posterity in their libraries, handed down from generation to generation. Thanks to their efforts, the scholars of the Middle Ages (until the invention of the printing press in the 15th century) were able to study some of the preserved ancient literature. Their thoughts, discussions, and writings made a valuable contribution to the gradual development of civilization.

CHAPTER 4, PART SIX

DISCLOSURES ABOUT RELIGION WHICH SHOULD DISCOMFIT THE FAITHFUL

(1) It is wholly understandable why religion, of whatever stripe, should be so prevalent among humankind. The child's mind, incapable of grasping the relationship of life and death events, curious in seeking an explanation, will easily assimilate the idea of a supernatural Father-figure overseeing all events in minute details. Such an idea is implanted and strengthened by observing the solemn and impressive rituals conducted by grave-looking and unsmiling agents of the divine who chant their prayers in mystical language, which only adds an aura of dignified majesty to the ceremony. The child's idea of a caring but stern Father-figure is gradually strengthened in the process of growing to maturity as an indispensable comforter in overcoming stress experienced in typical episodes of everyday living, such as joy, grief, illness, death in the family, the sight of a suffering friend or family member, and, in ancient times, the desire to communicate with the departed. The comforting and caring Father-figure who hears the prayers of the believer watches and takes notes, observes all comings and goings, is pleased or angered by the conduct or misconduct, rewards or punishes according to a set of rules laid down in his revealed message—such a Father-figure identified with God becomes, in due time, an indispensable silent partner of the faithful bringing meaning to an otherwise inexplicable life filled with cares, decisions and options. The typical man, whose faith is unhampered by conflicting views and immune to its flagrant contradictions, whose inquisi-

117

tive mind is stifled and fearful of tempting vacillations, will remain faithful to his God and religious attachment throughout his life and make sure to pass on this persuasion to his progeny.

(2) It is incomprehensible to the typical religionist that there are men and women who despise the idea of immortality, who do not wish to spend the afterlife in eternal bliss, and who happily anticipate earthly death to be the end of all forms of existence. Such people find the idea of reward and punishment absurd; that man's character, i.e., which motivates him to action, is shaped by the environment, nourishment, education, and genetic make-up over which there is but little control; that responsibility for one's actions would require the existence of free will, with the intelligent better qualified to choose than an illiterate and therefore can be held more reprovable for his conduct; that free will would involve uncaused choices exempt from causality—a logical impossibility; that since humans cannot be held responsible for their good and bad actions, reward and punishment would be as justifiable as the religious doctrine of predestination, repugnant to human sensibilities and meaning of justice. But the good or bad actions are themselves relative terms: what aids one's effort of self-preservation is called "good" and what hinders that same effort is called "bad". Or, for the religious, good and bad can simply be defined as acts in conformity with, or in opposition to, biblical commandments and ordinances. This concept would have a meaning, at least for the religious, if such biblical commandments and ordinances were precise and clearly stated and guide an anxious believer with a sense of certainty. But the opposite is the case. Such biblical injunctions are ambiguous, contradictory, vague, replete with exceptions and exculpations, mistranslated in critical parts, corrupted by scribal errors and negligent redactors so that biblical sages were kept busy writing volumes of interpretations and commentaries in an attempt to clarify the meaning, and scholars were kept busy reconciling the differing interpretations of the sages. The anxious believer not only required the guidance of a teacher to simplify the various interpretations for him, but had to make sure that the teacher was competent and that he was familiar with the authoritative version, for otherwise all the believer's efforts come to naught.

(3) Some of the religious, brought up since childhood in the faith of their fathers, endowed with an inquisitive mind thirsting for new knowledge and experience, may, in time, ask questions which could lead to a path of no return. Typically, some questions would depend on the intelligence of the inquirer, but generally, the common sense line followed would be:

(a) God made his revelations within a particular historical time frame to benefit the contemporary and future generations. How did the preceding generations, unaware of the revelations, benefit? How were the subsequent generations affected who were ignorant of the revelations?

(b) Multiple religions and sects each fervently claim to hold the sole key to divine truth. Only one can be true and the rest false or, applying the same standards to them, all could be false.

(c) Nothing is more perceptible in the world of human relationship than that many of the believers suffer and many of the unbelievers prosper.

(d) Acts of God, such as tornadoes, hurricanes, volcanic eruptions, floods, etc., harm believers and non-believers alike.

(e) Many children die in childhood without ever reaching the age of belief or disbelief. What purpose did their life serve?

(f) Certain believers are totally imbued with the spirit of God, yet capable of committing the most heinous crimes against humanity without affecting their faith. Certain unbelievers are capable of the most charitable and unselfish acts toward man without expecting anything in return.

(g) It must be God's flawed design of man that since recorded history there has practically never been a year without wars, massacres, man-caused destruction and misery, regardless whether all belligerents were devout believers in the Divine Presence.

(h) In contemplating the immensity of the Universe, the innumerable number of galaxies and the insignificance of the planet Earth in the cosmic scheme of things, is it reasonable to conclude that the existence of the human race was the central theme of Creation?

The above common sense approach, intentionally excluding any theological or biblical considerations, should raise sufficient doubts to open a small crack in the solid veneer of faith even of an ardent religionist.

(4) Let us suppose that the believer, endowed with an inquisitive mind, who has grasped the significance of the above recited common sense approach, is prompted to delve deeper into the problems religion poses, without excluding any phase of inquiry.

(a) The idea that God, the Creator of this immense Universe, needed animal blood sacrifices as offerings of propitiation is absurd—it points to priests who benefited the most from this ritual, as the originators of this purely self-serving public worship.

(b) Neither monotheism, nor henotheism, polytheism, or any other pantheon of Gods, including idolatry, can claim, historically speaking, superiority in bringing about moral behavior among the faithful.

(c) The idea that a God of the Universe would arbitrarily select one people as his own out of a multiplicity of peoples has the earmarks of priestly machination.

(d) God is the God of all people and justice would require that all, regardless of race or color, would be treated equally with preferences, if any, based on individual merit.

(e) Any claims to know the nature of God are the inventions of man and priests. His nature is incomprehensible and none of his attributes are knowable.

(f) Man attributes existence to finite objects, i.e., those that have a limited life, a beginning and an end. It is the limitation of language which precludes the attribution of existence to God, who has neither beginning nor end. Another term, peculiar and applicable to God, must be contrived. We cannot circumscribe the idea of God by imprisonment in the limitations of language.

(g) Any system which commands conformity and prohibits dissent is suspect; it betrays weakness and insecurity.

(h) Why are there diseases which strike humans indiscriminately in the bloom of life? Why are there natural disasters which kill many thousands of people every year? Is this by divine design, default or scorn?

(i) An impartial observer cataloguing the frequent natural and man-caused disasters could only conclude that the Earth and natural order of things are designed and directed with unconcern for the interests of man.

(j) The human species is not energized by divine faith but by fundamental natural forces—hunger and efforts of self-preservation.

(5) Let us suppose that the believer has absorbed the preceding information and, troubled by what he learned, decides to turn to the source, the Bible and history of Christianity. Even a superficial perusal would reveal that, apart from what was already noted in this Chapter, the disclosures would discomfit most self-possessed minds.

(a) The early religion of Israel was polytheistic and not monotheistic and did not differ materially from that of its neighbors.

(b) The sacrifices of children was part of the early ritual of Israel (as commanded by the Deity) as well as the worship of pillars of stone.

(c) The animal sacrifices described in the Book of Leviticus were no different than those of Israel's neighbors. Anyone sacrificing to other Gods was to be put to death.

(d) Death was also commanded by God for the following offenses:
Acts of necromancy, sorcery or magic.
Anyone who profanes the Sabbath.
Anyone who curses or blasphemes God.
Anyone who disobeys the priest.
Any prophet who speaks in the name of other Gods.
Anyone who serves or worships other Gods.
Any bride who cannot prove her virginity.
Anyone who will not listen to the voice of his father or mother.
Anyone who strikes down a human being.

(e) God set Israel apart from other peoples and commanded that they not mix with them for fear of defilement; they were not to make any covenant with them nor show them any friendship.

(f) The prophets of Israel were adamantly opposed to animal sacrifices (and the sacrifices of children) and the institution of priesthood. Yet both spoke in the name of God who commanded sacrifices.

(g) The laws of Moses and Sinaitic Covenant were unknown to the Israelites until the late 7th century B.C.

(h) The Bible refers to God in anthropomorphic terms.

(i) It was the Prophet Isaiah (Second Isaiah—there were four authors who used that name) who gave the world the idea of a universal God, a God to all the nations, which idea took permanent roots. (The Egyptian King Amenhotep IV, 1380–1362 B.C., was the first to announce that there was but one invisible God who belongs to all the nations. His idea was far ahead of its time and he paid the price of all radical reformers throughout history—vilification by the Establishment, the priesthood, and his idea faded quickly).

(j) The Prophet Habakkuk, a Hebrew prophet around 600 B.C., whose writings were included in the Hebrew canon despite their defiant message, remonstrated with God, referring to the prevalence of evil committed against just men, "Why do you look on when men are treacherous, and stay silent while evil man swallows a better man than he?" (Habakkuk. 1:13)

(k) Jesus instructed his Apostles to bring his message to Jews only, directing them that the children (Israel) should be fed first and not to throw children's food "to the house-dogs", i.e., Gentiles. Yet Paul, Jesus' contemporary, who knew hardly anything about his teachings, claimed that he was commissioned (by Jesus' voice from heaven) to preach the Good News to the uncircumcised, i.e., the Gentiles.

(l) The Christian Church that followed the time of Jesus is the best proof that his prophecy about the coming of the Kingdom of God was a failure.

(m) The Catholic Church forbade for a time the possession of the Bible by the laity for fear that its reading would lead to heresy.

(n) Certain Vicars of Christ were deposed from papal office for heresy and excommunicated.

(o) Over 200 million Christians died in inter-religious wars since the dawn of Christianity, all of them devout believers.

(p) Jesus never publicly claimed to be the Messiah.

(q) Jesus admitted that he did not know when the Kingdom of God would come, although he predicted that its coming was imminent.

(r) Jesus is quoted in the Gospels, "he who is not with me is against me"; "Do not suppose that I have come to bring peace to the earth ... but a sword. For I have come to set man against his father, a daughter against her mother"; "I have come to bring fire to the earth ..."; "Do you suppose that I am here to bring peace on earth? No, I tell you, but rather division"; "If any man comes to me without hating his father, mother, wife, children, brothers, sisters, yes and his own life too, he cannot be my disciple."

(s) Anyone who refuses to believe in Jesus "will never see life, the anger of God stays on him."

(6) The putative believer has by now been exposed to a cursory and common sense approach as well as to a superficial biblical and historical presentation of religious significance. If his curiosity and doubts are satisfied, he would be advised to go no further. But if he still has reservations, is perturbed and baffled by the ease with which contradictory statements are ignored or smoothed over and simple statements made contradictory or not easily comprehended, he should be told that the hand of a self-appointed and self-anointed priesthood can be detected raising the inevitable deceits and deceptions with the sole design to make themselves indispensable and serve their own interests. They interposed their fabrications between man's simple faith in a God (like today's Deists) and his susceptibility to ritual pomp and quest for an assured afterlife to appoint themselves essential intermediaries between God and man and in the process devise a whole array of divine attributes, rules, commandments, ordinances, to enmesh man in guilt and sin, for which they possess

the sole key of absolution. It manifests clearly the fragility and weakness of man that he required an impressive priesthood to give meaning and purpose to his existence and permit them to foist supernatural myths upon him in the guise of revealed religion, in order to restore and maintain his composure. It can be taken as a given that most men will never discard their childhood religious grounding and will cling to their beliefs throughout mature life, if only to place immortality on the safe side of doubt. For in their quest for a sense of certainty, they could miscalculate about afterlife and never know the difference, but they could blunder in their unbelief and suffer the pangs of error. But all this comes at a steep price. The ardent believer in a supernatural Deity who calms his anxious moments, forgives his sins, knows his innermost desires, and expects grateful acknowledgment of his achievements in life demands lifelong humble homage without relapse, reminiscent of the relationship between master and slave. Such a believer will be unable to understand the feeling of independence and pride of achievement of an unbeliever, or a Deist or Agnostic, who tolerates no restrictions on his activities, thoughts and views; counts on self-control, self-discipline, and self-reliance to avoid the inevitable pitfalls in life; who views the ups and downs of life with knowing resignation that there is nothing beyond the grave and views the frequent natural disasters not as divine punishment for misdeeds but as accidents of the moment, the result of natural causes. Unlike the ardent believer, he owes no apology for the religious misdeeds inflicted upon mankind throughout history, for he is well aware and can grasp clearly the identity of the malefactors, and point his finger at the criminal and abominable suffering visited upon the innocents. The non-religious find it preposterous that a Deity would create man so defective and inferior as to require him to spend much of his life paying servile and obsequious obeisance to his Creator, praising him and giving thanks for his promised benedictions. The priests and the religionists make a mockery of whatever language they use when referring to the Deity, standing the meaning of words on their head; doing violence to man's credibility and capacity to absorb the unintelligible, fully expecting to have their pronouncements taken on faith alone and, in the process, mocking man's trust in his reasoning ability; crossing the line between the mundane and divine with the facility of demigods; using terms like transcendent, immanent, infinite, omniscient, omnipotent, and omnibenevolent to prop up their esoteric religious message when such terms are beyond the comprehension of the human mind, however well endowed. The effort of self-preservation generates its own behavior and, if in conflict, assumes primacy over any other morality, especially the religious.

(7) The inquisitive believer, who has gone so far down the road of inquiry, should have enough determination and intellectual curiosity left to examine the theoretical aspects of theistic pronouncements and, perhaps, discover whether the human mind has the wherewithal to delve into the esoteric aspects of theology, or whether priests and religionists engaged in nothing more than tortured reasoning and mysterious empty verbiage. Briefly put, the human mind derives its ideas from sensory perceptions external to the mind, subject to the laws of causality, within the scope of natural law and therefore within the scope of human understanding—the knowable. The mind forms ideas of ideas called conceptions. Reasoning is the power to organize conceptions and the better the memory of ideas the greater the inventory of conceptions to be organized. The preceding is the foundation of human knowledge. Faith, on the other hand, is believing something without rational inquiry on the authority of another. Divine, that is, supernatural, revelations are based on faith, i.e., on the authority of another. All human knowledge, other than faith, is founded upon natural laws and the consistency and regularity of cause and effect, i.e., causality. All existence that can be known and understandable by the mind is based upon natural laws. Anything that exists beyond the sphere of natural laws exists beyond the sphere of human knowledge, i.e., it is unknowable. The quality, the distinctive feature or characteristic mark of an object is called an attribute, i.e., we know objects through attributes. Attributes are used in definitions, which are limitations by negations, i.e., they define what the object is and, by implication, exclude all other attributes. To define any knowledge is to subject it to limitations. The concept of "infinite" is beyond the understanding of the mind since it is not subject to natural laws which deal only with finite objects. Any object whose attributes are beyond the understanding of the mind is indefinable and unknowable. Anything designated as supernatural is, by definition, not subject to natural laws and therefore unknowable.

Applying the above information to a Deity, it can be stated that:

(a) The terms "supernatural", "transcendent", or any other attributes cannot be applied to a Deity since they involve limitations.

(b) The term "infinite" can be applied to a Deity (this is the only term applicable) only as a negation of "finite", and is therefore incomprehensible and cannot be used as a basis of knowledge or as a foundation from which to draw any deductions.

(c) The terms "omniscient", "omnipresent" and "omnipotent" imply a negation of the finite, and are therefore incomprehensible.

(d) A Deity cannot be defined since this would involve limitations, and is therefore unknowable.

(e) Attributes of a Deity cannot be named since they would involve limitations, and are therefore inapplicable.

(f) Any object that cannot be defined and has no attributes is beyond the scope of human knowledge.

(g) The terms "incomprehensible", "unknowable", and "beyond the scope of human knowledge" mean one and the same thing.

(h) The human mind can only comprehend knowledge which is finite, subject to natural laws, laws of causality and qualifying attributes.

(i) The term "infinite" transcends natural law and is therefore incomprehensible.

(j) There is no evidence that natural laws known to man and applicable to the sun and planets of the solar system are also applicable to the rest of the Universe. This lack of evidence alone regarding the visible Universe should humble man's assertive claim to speak of an invisible God in the finite and inadequate language of humans.

(8) All the conventional and theological discussions concerning the nature and attributes of God are the inventive imagination of fertile minds suffering from no greater delusions than, and not much above the level of, the animistic visions of ancient and contemporary crude savages. Theology, a discipline which attempts to talk rationally about the divine and the relation between God and mankind, is dealing with a subject matter that is beyond the sphere of comprehension to the human mind and an idle exercise serving a totally different purpose: the subjugation and bondage of the mind to the self-serving designs of the priestly orders (or their equivalents) to place themselves as intermediaries between their mythical concept of Deity and the believer and vouchsafe for themselves a level of comforts of their choosing, skirting the edges of pride and indolence; it is the same for all priesthoods of all religions, from ancient times to the present—it will never change. Nevertheless, the priestly religions have managed to attract immense followings of adherents throughout their history, many of whom were sufficiently motivated to do any of the priestly biddings, even if not quite in line with the preached faith or contrary to conventional morality. For the multitude of adherents needed assurance of divine grace to give meaning and direction to their lives and the priesthood was there to fill the void by counseling and inter-

ceding on their behalf with the Deity. Many dedicated faithful were so convinced of the veracity of the revealed message that they preferred to suffer martyrdom rather than be guilty of apostasy; by their display of dedication they added a veneer of solemnity and sublimity to a speculative theology not far removed from mythology.

(9) We are today far removed from those terrible days when the fagots and instruments of torture symbolized priestly power, although we are witnessing nowadays ominous signs of a resurgence of religious fundamentalism, pitting the religious against the secular in opposition to toleration of pluralistic societies, that proud and costly achievement of civilization. The revival of religious radicalism and their dark designs upon our freedom of expression together with their obsession to foist their beliefs onto others to achieve a tranquilizing conformity bode ill for the rights enjoyed by the secular and nonviolent religious-minded citizens. History teaches that in every case where radical fundamentalist religio-political forces gained the upper hand in the political process, coercion, persecution, tyranny, and fear ruled the day (and night) resulting in murder, massacres, incessant savagery, and religious wars. The forces of civilization were in retreat and stagnation and retrogression of cultural values the result. A bad tree will bear bad fruits. If religious intolerance with all the attendant evils are the fruit, what are we to think of the foundation of the divine religious genesis, the tree, which bore and thrust such abominations and plagues upon mankind?

The Founding Fathers of the United States, those inspired creators of the Declaration of Independence and the Constitution, political documents which should be placed, considering the century in which they were written, at the apex of rational, innovative, noble, and groundbreaking literary masterpieces, guided by an uncommon sense of justice, did not limit their opinions to political matters but also volunteered their views on religion. A couple of views are cited as an illustration.

John Adams: "This would be the best of all possible Worlds, if there were no Religion in it."

James Madison: "Religious bondage shackles and debilitates the mind and unfits it for every noble enterprise, ... What have been its fruits? ... pride and indolence in the Clergy, ignorance and servility in the laity; in lofty superstition, bigotry and persecution."

(10) Religions must preach the existence of God. The existence or non-existence of God cannot be established (the term "existence" is used in its conventional sense, even though its use is precluded for it implies a

beginning and an end—not applicable to a Deity). Such a conclusion is not demonstrable because of limitations of human faculties. Further, the existence of God involves knowledge of the supernatural, which is unknowable and forever closed to human understanding. Therefore silence is the only wisdom. This is the view held by Agnostics to indicate that knowledge is impossible in many of the matters covered by religious doctrines. This point of view differs from Deism, which professes a belief that God exists but has not revealed himself except in the normal course of Nature. Deism differs from Agnosticism in that it postulates the existence of God. Opposed to the Deists are the Atheists, who not only hold the opinion that there is no God but deny the possibility that a God could exist. But Atheists are no more rational in their views than Deists, and all opinions holding that God does or does not exist are unsupportable and untenable. The prudent man will keep an open mind on the subject and the views of Agnostics appear to be the only rational persuasion of minds guided by common sense.

Religion has always aroused the most ardent emotions and will continue to do so. Even though relying on the authority of others, religious faith is the greatest equalizer of emotional involvement, since it is within reach of all people without reference to any effort of reasoning and regardless of age, ability, profession, and financial standing. It binds believers together in a fraternity of common persuasion and the resulting community of interests, so easily gained and so easily validated, fills the void created by fear of the unknown and encourages them to face the uncertainties of fate together. This void burdens the nature of all men. The need to find purpose and meaning in life including the assurance of afterlife is the most forceful justification of the belief in a Deity and explains the emotional attachment to a faith which defies rational explanation. As long as belief in a Deity is not forced on others and as long as the emotional attachments are confined within the professing community and abstain from radicalism and fundamentalism, a pluralistic society, that proud achievement of civilization with room for all, is the best result to be hoped for. But what about the others, those unaffected by the temptation of salvation and disdainful of the thoughts of afterlife? The secular and Agnostics, content to fill the void by absorbing the literary, artistic, and other cultural treasures produced by humanity past and present, or the absorbing activities of sports and entertainment, reconciled with the incomprehensibility and unknowability of some aspects of life, Nature and the Universe, observing civilized conduct and demanding the same from others, are fully committed to respect the rights of their fellowmen of whatever faiths, beliefs or inclinations, to build together and form the foundation of a truly civilized society, an achievement which has eluded mankind to this date and, from all appearances, will continue to do so. The blame for this failure can be placed at the doorstep of men, religious in particular, who obsessed with hatred and hostility, subservient to the dictates of their faith and in response to primal impulses of their reptilian complex, religious bigotry and irrational fundamentalism, may yet manage to overwhelm and eradicate the benefits civilizing forces brought to mankind over thousands of years. For the burden of overcoming the malevolence and truculence of religious radical fundamentalists will not be eased by prayer or expectation of divine intervention, but by the conscious realization of all that these latter-day crusaders, these unreconstructed fanatics, may yet succeed in destroying their Nemesis, the trappings of civilization, and contemptuous of all cultures except their own, succeed in bringing down upon themselves and the many lethargic bystanders the sanctuary of a Stone Age.

CHAPTER 5

THE REQUIRED MODIFICATION OF THE PRIMITIVE NATURE OF MAN

(1) Civilization and Nature, the natural order of things, have always been in conflict. What promotes civilization, that proud achievement of man, are the challenges and contraventions of some particular laws of Nature, that sum total of unseen vital forces, creative and created, which favor the relentless and merciless struggle for existence of all living species, advancing the cause of the strong, ruthless, cunning, and providing no respite for the weak, ailing, dim-witted, irresolute and compassionate. For as far as the interests of civilized man are concerned, there is no order or harmony out there and Nature does not favor his survival; it is his mission and task to frustrate Nature in its efforts to maintain him at the level of animal species, to entangle him with necessities in order to make his survival an obstacle course. Nature exercises control over living organisms which engage in continuous hostile struggles of self-preservation and self-advancement. As far as man is concerned, all the instincts which aid his survival, such as greed, envy, cunning, jealousy, avarice, rapacity, cupidity, hatred, hostility—all these are Nature-endowed to promote incessant conflict and are common to all living species in various degrees of development. Any efforts to blunt those aggressive instincts to which one can add, in the case of man, murder, killing, robbery, stealing, rape, mistreatment of women and children, oppression, suppression of free speech and thought—just to name the more obvious—are acts against the natural order of things, against Nature, and such efforts can be identified as acts of civilizing influence.

129

(2)   Man's journey through known history has been arduous and blood-stained. Progress did not come in a straight ascending line but through peaks and valleys in a slightly rising scale. There were many focal points which contributed, directly or indirectly, to the advances of civilization, but restricting the outline to the most cardinal events and episodes which exercised the greatest impact on society and man: The Greece of Pericles, the Roman Empire under Julius Caesar, Augustus and Marcus Aurelius, the birth of Christianity, the Black Death, the Renaissance, Guttenberg's printing press, the birth of Protestantism under Martin Luther, the American Revolution and Declaration of Independence, the French Revolution, the Napoleonic period, the Industrial Revolution, the Second World War. Of the documents produced by these extraordinary events the most noteworthy were: The Declaration of Independence (1776) and the Declaration of the Rights of Man (1789).

(3)   To be civilized means to temper the primitive nature of man; to make life more secure and enduring and thus lighten the burden of existence; to enjoy the availability of a surplus that provides adequate food supplies and essentials in order to escape the confining constraints of primary needs, enable the satisfactions of secondary needs, and provide sufficient time to pursue interests not tied to the primary instincts of self-preservation, such as spiritually uplifting music, art, poetry and literature; to treat his fellowmen and strangers fairly; to have tolerance for a diversity of opinions, beliefs and religions; to abjure settling of differences or arguments by force; to be sufficiently involved in community affairs to insist on the fair treatment of the poor, weak, helpless, ailing, widows, orphans and aged; to treat children with consideration and understanding; not to be unmoved by the suffering of humanity be it from hunger, diseases, or catastrophic acts of Nature; firmly demand and take the necessary action to be ruled by an orderly government subject to just laws and an independent judiciary. This is the meaning of civilization, civilized conduct, civility. The required modification of the primitive human nature can only be achieved by degrees. A residue will always remain only to explode with primal violence if man's existence or his basic interests are threatened.

(4)   There is nothing in the natural order of things that can be said to promote civilized man's perseverance; on the contrary, Nature is hostile to his survival. The greater the impact of the instinct of self-preservation, the more biased, convoluted, confused become man's ideas and morality. For man cannot long remain civilized if his existence is continuously endangered or his primary needs unsatisfied; he is sucked into the vortex

of Nature's primitive design, which is contrary to his creation of civilized conduct. But the greatest threat to man's perseverance on this planet Earth are the activities of the imprudent man who, like all humans, being in bondage to survival instincts and slave to natural circumstances beyond his control, and unable to extricate himself from this curse, continues to overpopulate this planet and cause environmental degradation which will, in time, make life on this Earth impossible. Nature's design is to keep the population of man's species in check: conflicts, hardships, diseases, epidemics, starvation, and other attritions would keep human, like animal, populations stable. As long as man satisfies primary needs only, human population would stabilize and the environment remain sustainable. But the activities and efforts of man to produce an ever greater food surplus and surplus of other life-sustaining necessities cannot help but encourage an ever greater human population (the present increase is 100 million per annum, net of deaths) in developed but mainly in undeveloped countries, which, of necessity, causes environmental pollution and degradation injurious to man. Civilized man could find a solution to both problems (which are symbiotic) and succeed in saving the world's human population from misfortune, but the resistance is overwhelming. Not only Nature, natural instincts, and bondage of the majority of the human race to their Nature-given procreation urges, but the opposition from religious sectarians and the prevailing laissez-faire philosophy of multinational business corporations present insurmountable obstacles frustrating the efforts of well-meaning activists (a mere minority) determined to sound warnings of impending disasters.

(5)   In paragraph 3 above, the attributes of civilized man were catalogued from which any religious persuasion or reference was omitted. The monotheistic religions, whose adherents constitute almost 40% of the world's population, are based on the Bible and Koran, both of which preach intolerance and hatred of differing creeds, frown on freedom of speech and thought, and foster separateness and exclusivity. Throughout history they frustrated, at most times forcefully and with bloodshed, man's aspirations to attain independence and dignity and in so doing meant to thwart his progress toward a civilized existence. In Chapter 4, their claimed exclusive divine imprimatur of morality was forcefully disputed. The moral attributes which differentiate civilized conduct from the rest require no affirmation of divine origin. In both instances they were man-made and in the case of civilized man are free from tainted religious bias and obsessions—the criteria of civilized conduct.

(6)   The achievements of a free enterprise economy, in addition to causing
       overpopulation and unacceptable pollution of the environment, two
       defects which are the direct consequence of that condition, also made
       possible man's and society's most denigrating and humiliating concomi-
       tants: the condition of slavery, bondage, serfdom—literal or virtual—of
       the majority of the unprosperous working population. For it must be
       taken for granted that a worker who manages to earn just enough to keep
       body and soul together, able to merely satisfy primary needs, and dispose
       of savings sufficient to maintain him for no more than a few months if
       unemployed, without adequate possibility of advancement or betterment
       of his status, is a wage-slave tied to his condition by the inexorable forces
       of economic necessity: there just is not more expected from him than his
       actual contribution to the aggregate economic output and his potential
       excess productivity—whether skilled or unskilled—is just not needed
       nor will it be compensated—there is no market for it. The mainstream
       economists, who managed to do well for themselves under the capitalist
       system, will vehemently criticize the foregoing characterization. But the
       facts are against them. Just to manage to make ends meet and to keep
       one's head above water is the mark of a level of privation, however
       defined, and tantamount to poverty no matter how elevated the primary
       needs. To exert the necessary daily effort or else some basic primary need
       would not be met is the mark of indigence equivalent to slavery, no
       matter what euphemisms are used to embellish the circumstances. The
       division of labor which exists in the free-market economy—unskilled,
       semi-skilled, skilled and highly skilled—not only ensures a disparate
       compensation for the various skills, but also presupposes the need for
       such services. No economy could function without the lowest paid
       unskilled labor nor could it function without any other category of skills.
       The lowest paid skills are just as necessary as any of the other. If an
       economy had only skilled and highly skilled labor, it could not function.
       The skilled and highly skilled labor are usually identified with the
       "haves", and the unskilled and semi-skilled with the "have-nots" or poor.
       The existence of a great majority of the latter have made free enterprise
       possible. The conduct of the "haves" minority is preeminent in setting
       the standards of morality and affects the behavior of the other segments
       of population. It is the treatment of the majority of the poor by the
       minority of "haves" that elevated or denigrated the standards of morality,
       which in turn depended on the level of intensity of the minority's efforts
       of self-preservation. The greater the intensity of such efforts, the lower

the acceptable standards of morality. As has been said before, in the intense struggle for existence morality, or civilized conduct, is pushed into the background and assumes a subordinate role. A high level of morality is most profitable to the successful who enjoy the fruits of secondary needs which also afford them sufficient time and leisure to pursue activities not directly connected with their effort of self-preservation. The standards of morality are defined by these privileged, which have always been their domain, for they have the most to lose by their absence.

Man must face a difficult choice:

(a) Oppose the natural order of things, promote the advantages and benefits in which surpluses of whatever kind mitigate the struggle of self-preservation and make existence tolerable; militate against destructive wars of all against all; be uneasy to satisfy primary needs only; encourage medical and other scientific experiments and treat the science of medicine with approval for it helps the ailing and disabled and keeps them in the fold; do not favor the strong and cunning for they must not inherit the Earth. Maintain a stable and sustainable human population and an ecosystem benefiting man, whose continued life on Earth would not be endangered. Such an equilibrium would result in harsh and painful measures, but man would not overpopulate the planet and would be forced to maintain a stable population level. A stable population growth within determined limits, an ecosystem functioning at sustainable levels—although achieved with much sacrifice—would ease the self-preservation effort and elevate the standard of morality.

(b) Follow the natural order of things; believe in the magic of the marketplace; promote the technology-driven advantages and benefits which surpluses bestow; seek salary and profit maximization as a response to the self-regulating market mechanism; find the idea of a constant population growth attractive as do megacorporations which sponsor corporate colonialism; consider any criticism of environmental pollution, at best, as unproven science and, at worst, as obtrusive market interference, ideological baggage and doomsday prophecy. Seek unlimited economic growth as a universal principle; deride the idea that the Earth's shrinking resources could not be overcome, that population growth could ever become unmanageable, and that the ecosystem equilibrium would suffer permanent damage. The consequence would be a more exacting self-preservation effort and a lower standard of morality.

But this would be a fool's paradise. At the present rate of population growth and with no mitigation in the planning stage, the present population numbers (6 billion) are already overtaxing the available living space, which will only further decrease as the warming effect takes its toll by raising the sea level and inundates the low-lying coastal areas. The environmental degradation is already with us. The greenhouse effect, aquifer salinization, carbon dioxide, nitrous oxides, PCB, DDT, dioxin, CFC—all these are already visibly affecting the human (and animal) habitat. Humans are slowly poisoning themselves, their health infected with all kinds of diseases of seemingly mysterious origin, and their thinking process exposed to adverse toxic effects, especially the children. And humans are drowning in their own garbage with no solution in sight which would alleviate the problem. All these are the results of man following Nature, the natural order. All these repugnant consequences could be mostly alleviated if man opposed the natural order, maintained the dignity and distinction of homo sapiens as separate from the animal species, refused to submit to the natural evolutionary process (the survival of the fittest) by inventing a morality and civilized conduct that would lighten the burden of existence and make his brief sojourn on Earth a worthy experience.

(7) Man must acknowledge that Nature's design eludes his understanding; that his diligent and arduous effort to thwart Nature's natural selection and survival of the fittest and thus create a culture and morality that distinguish his species from that of other animals nevertheless failed to control his instinct of procreation and curb his appetite for a limitless variety of consumer goods, the procurement of which not only exhaust renewable and non-renewable resources but degrade the ecosystem in the process. The conclusion is inescapable: Unless man manages to mitigate the population explosion and learns to control the abuse of the ecological balance, his existence, despite the achievement of a unique culture, will in time approach that of savages. This would accord with Nature's scheme of things.

(8) If man is unable to control overpopulation, it is mainly due to his procreation instinct being stronger than his reasoning power, i.e., the ability to evaluate the consequences of the failure to plan ahead. He may not be a profound thinker or his conclusions could be mistaken, but he bears the sole responsibility for his conduct and no sinister undercurrents conspired to influence his views. But there are two organized special interest groups which pursue their particular agenda with uncommon zeal in

claiming to know more about population problems than demographic specialists and, besides, consider the latter to be pseudo-science, leading to false conclusions. The two groups are:

(a) Those who adhere to monotheistic beliefs.

(b) Those who favor the free-market economic system.

> (a) The proposition that overpopulation with the attendant environmental pollution of the Earth, that creation attributed to a Deity, could make human life unsustainable at some future date unless procreation is strictly controlled, is anathema to believers. It would be an admission that God's creation is flawed, inadequate and improperly planned, an admission which no self-respecting theist could ever endorse. The same imperfection can be attributed to man, God's creation. In addition, God promised Abraham: "I will make your descendants as many as the stars of heaven and the grains of sand on the seashore" (Gen. 23:17), i.e., billions of billions, not an invitation for population control. This is not an idle promise to one for whom the Bible is the result of divine revelation. One can only say that if their concern for the suffering of an unborn fetus was matched by the same spirited attention to the millions of starving, homeless, abandoned, and, yes, enslaved children whose predicament clamors for redress, then even an unsympathetic observer of their religious views would be moved by their consistency and denunciation of the torment of innocents.

> (b) That part of human activity which deals with man's efforts to provide for his self-preservation is the subject of economics, the ability to satisfy a need, his willingness and capacity to pay for a commodity. The subject of economics will be examined in future Chapters. It should suffice to say for now that production and distribution of goods, but mainly the earning of profit by the producers, give rise to various economic theories reaching disparate conclusions. The common denominator, however, is growth. Continuous growth, maximizing of profits and minimizing of costs, and a market economy are the lifeblood of any economic system worthy of that name. Complete freedom of action without any restraints imposed by governmental interference is the ideal desired forum in which enterprising entrepreneurs prefer to compete for market advantage and achievement of growth. Briefly, the criteria of growth are increased sales, adding

to production facilities, larger control of the market, and decreasing the influence of competitors. But the most important factor of growth is an increase in the number of consumers, i.e., population growth. The industrious entrepreneur knows the importance of population growth, which he interprets as a greater potential market for consumer goods and an increased supply of labor, with all the attendant results of greater profit adding to a climate of optimism. His self-preservation instincts will downplay as "tortured reasoning" the environmentalist's warnings about the dangers of population explosion and damage to the ecosystem as so much interference with the market and as so much spouting by doomsday environmentalists. All warnings are set aside and ignored, the reasoning of necessity becomes forced and blurred and the goals short-sighted: the greater the population growth, the greater the consumer demand, and the greater the potential for profits.

CHAPTER 6

TAMING THE INSTINCT OF SELF-PRESERVATION

(1) A slave, in the original and historical connotation of the term, meant a human being, owned as chattel by his master, forced to perform usually onerous involuntary labor for his master, generally without pay and time limit, supplied only with the barest of necessities (food, shelter, and clothing) to sustain life and good physical condition. This was profitable to his master both for output of labor and the maintenance of resale value. He possessed no freedom to choose his activities, no right to voice grievances, no standing before a court of law, required by law to follow strictly his master's orders. Slavery, in other words, was total subjugation by another for the purpose of economic exploitation. That kind of slavery has been proscribed by most countries and expunged from all the corners of the Earth, except it still persists in isolated and modified form in India, Pakistan, Thailand (prostitution), and Brazil, where slaves are procured by entrapment. Disconnected from its crudities implying open servitude and separated from the primitive and blunt physical power and constraints man exercised over his fellowmen, there exists another kind of slavery not achieved by force or superior power of one over another but by an unseen, covert, and intangible dragnet which envelopes all the being, activities, and thoughts of man. He feels physically free and not subjugated, retains freedom to express grievances, and has recourse to courts of law, freedom of movement and choice, and all other criteria of social unfettered contacts such as belonging to a community of equals.

But beneath the seeming patina of freedom, stealthily constricting his thoughts and desires, without being aware of the causes or circumstances, man is prompted to action by a condition of slavery created by the natural order of things, Nature, possessed by all men of whatever cultural standing, i.e., their inherent subjugation to the instinct of self-preservation and, to a lesser extent, the instinct of procreation of his species.

(2)   Man's status of slavery is directly tied to his economic circumstances. If he barely manages to satisfy his need for food, clothing and shelter (with later additions of healthcare and provisions for old age), defined as his primary needs, without disposing of a discretionary surplus to gain some freedom in his choice of secondary needs, such a man can be said to be entangled with necessities connected with the instinct of self-preservation and truly a slave to that instinct. This definition is to be taken literally and not as a metaphor or analogy. A man capable of satisfying solely his primary needs will remain subject in thought and deed to Nature's evolutionary process and the natural order of things.

A man who disposes of a discretionary surplus and has the freedom to elect to satisfy any number of secondary needs can be said to have escaped the gravitational pull of Nature's evolutionary process. He is a freedman and not a slave to his economic necessities. As freedman, he has truly exceeded the restrictions applicable to the animal species, his struggle for preservation no longer consumes all his efforts, giving him some free time to contemplate man's dignity and need for morality and thus partake in, and contribute to, the advancement of civilization. It can be taken as axiomatic that civilization, that apex of human achievement, has been created by freedman and not by slaves, even though existence of slavery made that achievement possible. With very few exceptions, which only prove the rule, all progressive ideas, works of art, and scientific inventions were accomplished by freedmen or those who had the support of wealthy patrons, which amounts to the same thing—they were assured in having their primary needs taken care of and were able to devote their spare time to spiritually uplifting activities.

(3)   There are humans whose ambitions get the better of them, who will attribute importance and necessity to secondary needs as if they were quasi-primary needs. Some do it out of conviction but mostly to enhance the quality of existence. The man who converts secondary into primary needs, and thus increases the needs to be satisfied as if they were necessary to his self-preservation, decreases his status of freedman and correspondingly increases his condition of slavery. He is, therefore, saddled

(burdened) with more primary needs to the detriment of his discretionary surplus and the reduction of freedom of action. A secondary need is strictly relative and would enhance the existence of some as it could diminish it for others. It all depends on the size of the available discretionary surplus and the relative security of its possessor. For the exhaustion or diminution of a discretionary surplus together with the transitory nature of its existence are bound to decrease the security of possession, expand the effort and intensity of self-preservation because more needs would have to be satisfied. It is a mark of insecurity of possession of a discretionary surplus that causes the otherwise well-to-do to engage in impassionate and cutthroat competition to uphold and augment its safety. For it is this kind of competition of the "haves", and not the "have-nots", which causes disruption and turmoil of the economy endangering the financial safety-net and well-being of all participants except of those who, by applying energetic management or possession of an excessively large discretionary surplus (referred to later as disposing of tertiary needs, the super-haves) or both, remain barely affected by the financial convulsions swirling around them even though they are influential participants in the marketplace. The "haves", who expand their needs right up to the margin of their capacity to handle, will continue to do so impulsively because their increased potential will only ensnare them in confronting an ever widening circle of needs—success breeds risk taking, risk taking pushes the envelope and that risks failure. It is this tension of avoiding failure by the "haves" and the pressure of succeeding that define the conflicts of the marketplace. In doing so, the freedmen have become unwitting slaves bound to Nature's design giving free reign to greed and ambition, haunted by fear of failure, their conduct becoming amoral by necessity, making a sham of any pretense of civilized comportment. In pursuing boundless needs straining the capacity to perform, the "haves" as well as the "have-nots" become fractured pawns of a fractured Nature, corrupting the direction of "the invisible hand", unable to escape the all-consuming instinct of self-preservation. Pressured by such compulsions, population control and the preservation of ecological balance become irrelevant.

(4) Above the din and chaos of everyday life, distanced from the effects of market mechanisms, immune to the rule of consumption spending, enjoying an autonomy reserved for the financially elect, and living in a surrounding of their own making are a variant of freedmen, an elite class of their own who managed to defy gravity. They are the super-haves, who

made it on their own or by generous inheritance, or both. They are capable of satisfying any need including purely unimpeded, spontaneous, and whimsical desires traditionally labeled as "conspicuous consumption", supporting numerous industries which compete to tailor their products to such special needs. Price is not a factor and competition is directed to the pomposity and affectation of the demanding patrons. Such demands will be referred to as "tertiary needs".

(5) They are not impelled to act by necessity of circumstances unless they are self-created. They do act to protect their self-interest, and although greed and ambition are common to all humans as well as the instinct of self-preservation, the struggle for existence of the super-haves cannot be reduced to financial terms since there is no fear of falling through the cracks of any safety-net. They dispose of an excessively large discretionary surplus sufficient to handle all practical contingencies. They do engage in business activities mostly for the sport of it, the desire and pride of winning, the bustle of business competition excites their acquisitive instincts; mainly, it is the desire to be occupied and escape from one of their own worst nemesis: boredom. Any gain achieved is pleasing and makes for good party conversation, and losses—they do occur—just do not matter much. They are the movers and shakers of the business community and their wealth gives them real power to exert influence, if not outright participation—overt or covert—in the political and economic affairs of their government and country. Their expensive tastes and accumulation of great wealth, commented upon almost daily by admiring business journals, are the envy of lesser equals, attracted as if by a magnet to imitate in some measure society's free enterprise paragons of success. But it has always been so. Throughout known history, self-made riches commanded admiration except that in pre-modern autocratic institutions the continued possession was fragile and exposed to arbitrary expropriation by the ruling monarch. The rule of law, reliance on the marketplace and the inviolability of property rights were essential criteria of the emerging capitalist system of the late 18th century.

(6) The super-haves constitute a small minority (1%–2%) of modern society. Yet by exercising their vast financial powers they succeeded in inducing the governing chieftains to bend many of the economic rules in their favor. Such rules, while clearly beneficial to them, are of questionable benefits to the rest of the population—the haves and the have-nots. In the intense interplay of the various economic groups comprising modern society, the interests of the have-nots, the haves, and the super-

haves are on a collision course. The latter could concede a great deal without making as much as a dent in their status quo; the have-nots are always in an acquisitive and non-yielding mood, and the haves, pushed to the margin, are dedicated to resist giving up any of their discretionary benefits. The varying disposable incomes, the diverse consumption spending, the greatly differing capacity to sustain losses, and the contrasting modes and responses to weathering a downturn in the economy all point to a necessarily flawed marketplace due to far-ranging contrary interests. The existence of a self-regulating market mechanism as an inhibitor and reconciler of contradictory self-interests is an exercise in illusion, the invention of intelligent minds sequestered from the drama of reality. The magic of the complex marketplace applicable to all the disparate segments of the economy acting as the final arbiter of values just does not exist. Just like the mysteries attached to priestly incantations of old and dispelled by iconoclasts of modern times, just like the aura surrounding the claim of divine rights of kings totally demolished by the American and French revolutions, so the vaunted efficiencies of the unregulated free-market system, operative in the 20th century, were rendered ineffectual by the centrifugal forces generated by the opposing and growing irreconcilable needs of the three principal segments of society. The effects of this diversity of interests (explored in later chapters) will have far-reaching consequences in the 21st century.

(7)   The economic eminence of the super-haves, a minority, is dependent upon the continued vigorous existence of the have-nots, the wage-slaves, by far the greater majority. The continued well-being of the majority should, therefore, be a matter of unceasing self-interest of the super-haves, yet they have acted unreasonably, considered any gain achieved by the have-nots as an unwelcome intrusion into their own prosperity. Medical insurance and provisions for old age, for example, came to be regarded as survival necessities by the majority and included among the essential primary needs, including the continued pressure for higher compensation. Yet progressive gains achieved over many decades were not realized, in most cases, by sweet reasonableness but had to be, as if by design, wrested from reluctant and unwilling super-haves and / or their representatives so as to keep advancements at a minimum. This led, of necessity, to adversary interdependence when the opposite should have been the case, since the super-haves did not suffer any measurable adverse consequences by conceding the demanded adjustments. Beginning in the 19th century, another division of labor took place creating two new busi-

ness endeavors of the highly-skilled: management and entrepreneurs. Due to rapid corporate expansion approaching in size that of megacorporations, teams of management technocrats, more suited for the task than the original owner-operators or their heirs, assumed the operational functions; the world of commerce and high finance have been guided ever since by a new technocratic elite, the new super-haves, answerable no longer to themselves for their actions—like the owner-operators of old— but to a Board of Directors, another collection of technocrats, a body of stockholder-elected officials charged with protecting the interests of a class of owners: the stockholders, a mix comprising all segments of society. The main change in direction occurred in the measurement of gains. No longer were investments guided by long-term trends or long-term profit potentials but by short-term gains wrested from the competitive economy made less so by a wave of mergers and acquisitions. Management is judged by the continuous achievement of profitable results from year to year, nay, from quarter to quarter, in order to retain their job security, their job-preservation dependent upon corporate performance. For over a period of time, particularly in the last few decades, the gains achieved by the super-haves have by far outstripped those of their production employees. When a super-have's annual income reaches the rate of 300 to 400 times that of a worker, a have-not, a wage-slave, there is no mutuality of interests and any pretense to share a common goal is a sham. And when in the name of global economy production facilities are moved to other countries in order to take advantage of cheaper and more docile labor, or less hostile environmental regulations, the income spread increased even more and caused havoc with the old social order: Resultant unemployment and underemployment of the vulnerable labor force whose fortunes were changed for the worse so that the fortunes of their superiors might change for the better. The reduction of the employability of former workers made it necessary, in many cases, that wives enter the labor market in order to help make ends meet of the family unit. The clamor for larger short-term profits demanded of management brought on the inevitable disruption of the family unit, the mainstay of a healthy society, reduction in total family income and aggregate demand, an impediment to social order, a disruption of long established social expectations—developments with long-term damaging effects which should give pause to corporate technocrats and their planners.

(8)   Even if transnational corporations are here to stay (there is no guaranty that host countries would not assert their independence and react

adversely to the arrangement), the gains are purely temporary since saturation of the market would be reached sooner or later; capital investments could be blocked and not repatriable to preserve the soundness of the local currency; the profit margin could narrow to remove the advantage of the original relocation; there could be a change of government or policy demanding profit or ownership participation; but most importantly, the growing political chaos in host countries due to interference with their system of government and the proclaiming of laws favoring multinational corporations to the detriment of local interests.

The super-haves pursuing the rewarding spell of tertiary needs not only disrupted the orderly governmental process of host countries by insisting on special expanded monopoly powers but interrupted the orderly working of the home economy by demanding, and obtaining, globalization privileges for their transnational corporations. In the indefatigable drive for ever greater profits and in complete disregard of the methods used, the multinationals are in the forefront of disrupting the orderly economic process by setting the clock back more than a 100 years and nullifying the hard-won social gains achieved by fair-minded reformers seeking to improve the conduct of expanding modern business enterprises. And the clock has been set back. The multinationals, managed by the elite super-haves, no longer care whether they market merchandise produced in host countries—in more cases than one cares to chronicle—by indentured slaves, exploitation of child labor or prisoners, all working excessive hours under conditions totally disregarding safety measures—conditions which would subject employers to punitive fines or incarceration in the home country. To demand, for example, as a condition of globalization particularly in developing countries, the removal of controls on foreign investments, elimination of price controls, imposition of wage controls, reduction of social and health services, and minimal, if any, rules protecting the environment, thereby causing growing unemployment and lower standards of living, all this in order to increase profits and be more competitive (or so it seems) in the home market is not amoral but immoral—a retreat to the days of Charles Dickens—a cynical regard for self-interest to the detriment of others, a denial of progress, a decline of decades of uplifting efforts wasted in the cause of tertiary needs. The sellers as well as the purchasers of such merchandise, even if they knew or were told about the source of labor and other regrettable conditions, would not be deflected from their delight—the joy of paying slightly less for their purchases.

But multinationals managed by super-haves also turned their back on the domestic labor force in order to gain benefits for their companies by practicing global corporate colonialism. They paid no attention to the disruption of families and communities by peremptorily shutting down productive plants for removal to foreign countries, they abandoned the labor force which played an indispensable part in bringing about their corporate success, they turned their back on the home country whose laws and protection of the free enterprise system made their prosperity possible. There surely must be something wrong with an economic design which permits the strangulation of the domestic labor force, lowering the material standard of living, and causing related havoc in order to summarily remove production facilities to foreign countries in search for higher profits and causing similar mischief abroad.

(9) The super-have managers of global investments pursue the only policy with which they are familiar: expansion, growth, new markets and greater profits. If the domestic business climate was not conducive to such promotions, then ways were found to secure not only worldwide markets for the products, but profit maximization and cost minimization by transferring domestic production to foreign countries receptive to a new type of commercial colonialism. Are there no limits to economic growth? Can growth continue indefinitely even if it causes social disharmony, involuntary unemployment, and regressive shifts in income? The answer must be in the negative. Continuous growth which will, in due course, radically lower the standard of living—despite the sophistries of inveterate optimists—is based on continuous expansion of markets, i.e., population increase, which in turn is unquestionably limited by progressively diminishing living space and exhaustion of non-renewable resources. Man must accept the limits of Nature's gifts and adjust the direction of his progress accordingly. It would certainly be in line with the fractured man's disposition if the pursuit of tertiary needs, far in excess of what is necessary or indispensable for a comfortable and pleasurable existence, should, by an irony of fate, cause substantial restrictions to a free-market economy and reach a point at which the privilege of globalization would self-destruct.

Globalization, of necessity, must exercise an adverse influence on civilization. To make life less secure and enduring; to be unconcerned about the treatment of the poor, helpless and weak; to be unaffected and aloof to the plight of children; to mistreat fellowmen with equanimity are all acts of uncivilized conduct perpetrated by colonialists at home and abroad in the pursuit of unrestrained greed and rapacity. The search for growth and profits without limits is unsparing and coercive; no customs, however long and acceptable their usage as a cultural underpinning of civilized behavior, can stand in the path without being swept away relentlessly in search of tertiary self-seeking by corporate and banking managers whose misdeeds may yet endanger the capitalist system by their colonialist adventures.

(10) As was repeatedly pointed out before, uncivilized conduct is following the natural order of things, whereas man can take pride in his effort of partially breaking away from Nature's evolutionary process by not willing to participate in the natural laws governing the animal kingdom. Only by opposing the natural order of things can man hope to civilize his conduct and practice some morality in dealing with fellowmen. Implacable struggle for existence is the rule of Nature. The super-haves are engaged in pursuit of tertiary interests, freed from the burdens imposed by that struggle, whereas the have-nots are fully immersed in Nature's preordained design to keep men entangled with necessities; the haves, i.e., the freedmen, not weighed down by the demands of the conatus, enjoy some freedom of choice by virtue of disposing of a discretionary surplus sufficient to satisfy secondary needs. Many managed to promote a standard of morality which serves as the foundation of civilized conduct, the pre-condition of civilization. What did the super-haves contribute? Without attempting to lump them together since there are the usual exceptions, the majority successfully exploited the opportunities offered by the free enterprise economy to amass large fortunes invested in production, trading, construction, insurance, and banking institutions which formed the substratum of modern capitalism.

The term "greed" is typically defined as excessive desire for possessions—it is uncomplimentary in its implications. For the have-nots, struggling for their existence possessing no discretionary surplus, no conduct is too greedy in furthering their interests, no desire is too excessive because their possessions are few. For them greed is justified in pursuit of survival and as to them, greed is a virtue. The haves, who dispose of a discretionary surplus, successfully preserved some freedom of action in satisfying secondary needs, a sign of superior achievement. Although some may have many possessions, their conduct is dominated by a persistent fear of failure. From their ranks, nevertheless, arose the worthier few to whom moral conduct is a way of life. Even so, since their self-preservation efforts may, at times, approach the margin of have-nots, they too survive by greed as a necessary tool of self-interest. Consequently, as applied to them, greed is a virtue. The haves and have-nots are too preoccupied with common ordinary and everyday problems to contemplate harmful combinations to exploit economic opportunities beyond the borders. They lack the means, the inclination, the need, and self-assurance (which is based on possessing great wealth) to engage in such adventures.

The super-haves who possess great wealth, on the other hand, have the capacity, inclination, and the means to give free reign to their predatory instincts participating in the pursuit of domestic and international business ventures. In doing so, those capable of satisfying tertiary needs, those who exhibit the desire and urge to pile possession upon possession without limits or pause, are guilty of excessive greed. As to them greed is a vice, a defect. The possession of great wealth demands intensive investment in profitable enterprises, many of global proportions disregarding national borders, demands interference with, and contempt of, national rights and interests of others, causing volatility in markets at home and global instability. Their movements in the world's capital markets, rapid and massive investments, withdrawals and transfers, precipitate global maldistribution and contraction. It is the nature of such business activities to avoid stability, order, harmony and equilibrium, but precipitate crises and disorders in world markets, whether consequential or instigated, to profit from marginal gains derived from substantial investments and inevitable price movements. They are not the harbingers of stability but disorder. The super-haves' constant striving to augment wealth at the expense of others is based on exploitation of others by design and cannot help but dispense with civilized conduct, creating self-serving rules and ad hockery to benefit the advantaged. It is a road back to Nature and the natural order of survival of the fittest, despite their own non-involvement in the struggle for existence. It is a struggle on a higher plain, a world apart from the haves and have-nots. They cause and gain from local and global economic instability and, by doing so, adversely affect the well-being of the haves and have-nots without impacting negatively upon their own well-being.

CHAPTER 7

THE FAULTS AND FLAWS OF CONVENTIONAL ECONOMICS

(1) Throughout history man pursued the satisfaction of his wants which were most closely conjoined with his survival instinct. Such faculties driven by innate urges defined the utility of necessary choices determined without the benefit of prudence, since needs were few and choices limited. As choices began to multiply and his wants increased, the economic man emerged relying on his intelligence to satisfy needs based upon his limited physical strength and upon the limited means at his disposal. Self-preservation became the necessity of selective choices due to limitation of means and to instincts to make the necessary choices. Superior mental alertness and diligence possessed by some men began to differentiate them from those not similarly endowed, with the result that division in society assumed the character of permanence; with the passage of time the segmentation stabilized. Based upon the capability of satisfying needs, three classes of humans emerged in organized society, defined by their means: the have-nots, the haves and the super-haves. Economic progress has depended on the manner of harmonious interaction of these divisions of society (the term "class" is used for convenience and has nothing to do with any Marxist connotation).

(2) Although the division of society into classes is not sufficiently delineated to forestall overlapping and permit the ascent or descent of any particular member of a class, nevertheless the division is real, serves the indispensable function of division of labor to enable society to operate as an

organic whole and economic aggregate. For the contribution of the classes to the growth (or decline) and well-being of society was always unequal and the allocation of benefits disproportionate. As each class pursued its material self-interest, all in accordance with the natural order of things, competition between and within classes spawned economic disharmony. It is as much in the interest of the super-haves to engage in a frenzy of accumulations as it is in their interest to spread a culture of insecurity among the have-nots and the haves—the more they squabble among themselves the weaker they are politically. For the super-haves are a small minority controlling disproportionally a greater part of wealth, whereas the other two classes, by far the greater majority, are wholly dependent upon the whim and mood of the entrepreneurial class to keep the wheels of production turning and procure the maximum share of the distribution of wealth for themselves. It is fundamental human nature, which also accords with the natural order, that every man claims the right to enjoy the products of his exertion to the maximum exclusion of others; that stable prices are not the desired aim of producers; that buyers seek the cheapest market and sellers the high-priced; that every producer publicly praises the efficacy of competition but privately espouses a monopoly for his product; that there could be no market and price disorder without human design and machinations; that producers favor a free-market only when it benefits their interests; that effective competition is impossible since it would be based on complete market information, which is never available equally to all participants; and finally, it can be taken as axiomatic that although consumption is the sole end of production, man must first produce in order to consume.

(3) It was the priests in antiquity whose function, among others, was to communicate divine oracles to their community to serve as reliable guide in making decisions of consequence, such as declaring war, seeking peace, selection of a ruler, or predicting times of prosperity. In modern times, the successful struggle for existence, a fact of life about which the ancients were totally ignorant, assumed the quality of virtue and this recognition deepened not only with the substantial population increase but also with the division of labor and the escalating interdependence and integration of the factors of production. When money (gold and silver coins) became the medium of exchange, divers business activities became possible with the market facilitating commercial intercourse. With the rise of secularism, priestly oracles lost their efficacy in predicting times of prosperity or famine to the commercial classes. As pros-

perity was the cornerstone of an invigorating societal compact, the feeling was abroad that unlike the mysteries of religion, which were beyond man's capacity to unravel, it was thought possible, in light of many other ongoing revolutionary scientific break-throughs, to unravel the mystique surrounding the predictability of commerce and reduce it to comprehensible essentials. A few 18th century French physiocrats attempted to decipher the mysteries of *économiques* by designating land and its products as the only true source of wealth and the only basis of revenue (understandably, since France is primarily an agricultural country). An Englishman, Adam Smith (1723–1790), a professor of moral philosophy, held that not land but labor was the source of value; that division of labor led to specialization which was most beneficial to the prosperity of society, and preached an optimism so wonderful for its day as it was simplistic: that the world is capable of unlimited improvement. Smith was followed by an army of economists, each of whom presented slightly to radically divergent views on the subject. So many brilliant thinkers reaching so many varied, nay sometimes contradictory, conclusions so that one could not help but wonder which views were well-grounded and which were false, or perhaps whether or not all were false since they set aside, as if to discount, the influence of the most important component: the unpredictable and impulsive human behavior and responses.

(4) The thinkers who chose the subject of economics as their field of specialty were impressed with the scientific achievements of physics or chemistry, both experimental sciences which required the application of mathematics and logic in arriving at conclusions. They took pride in treating the subject of their inquiry as if it were a science based upon universally well-founded laws grounded in observation but not experiments, methodically arriving at their conclusions, their propositions, principles, and theorems as if they paralleled in efficacy the established sciences. It is well settled that scientific law is deterministic and that everything, every event, is subject to inflexible laws of causality. Economics is mainly an observational discipline, like history, and cannot be laced in the straightjacket of mathematics and logic, which are not concerned with facts but with valid deductions and easily become the playground for sophists. To reach a desired conclusion the economist could choose any number of assumptions and still insist on the validity of his conclusion. For it must be taken as axiomatic that a true or false theory equally affects man's conduct and that a valid conclusion based upon an erroneous premise is always false. In the final analysis, the test of the soundness of

economic theories is the ability of its champions to predict the impact upon the economy, for example, of specific fiscal or monetary policies, or the impact on investments of a currency devaluation. By that standard, economics is a failure since its forecasts scored worse than the unscientific flip of a coin. To prognosticate, for example, that long periods of prosperity encourage confidence in the market is to engage in psychology and not economics, which can be said of many of its propositions. The failure of economics as a tool of successfully predicting economic trends or the long-term results of some of its established propositions is due to:

(a) Ignoring psychological ingredients which affect all human behavior and cannot be measured with objectivity.

(b) Misunderstanding the laws of causality. There are a great number of antecedent conditions to any effect, and the economist selects one particular condition as the cause which satisfies his agenda. But each effect has multiple causes, all of which are essential and the choice of any one particular cause is a fallacy.

(5) An economist would be much happier as a philosopher than a scientist. His field of expertise is more aptly classified as a discipline, a branch of learning which follows certain rules, or as technicians like accountants or attorneys. For the inductive method of social science theories, which is the most that economists can claim, can never be accorded more than provisional acceptance since all universal statements, though unprovable, remain disprovable upon the finding of a single exception. Obsessed with certainty that the universal magic of mathematics and logic bestow on observations, though not on solid foundation, economists dabbled with statistical significance and economic models in a determined attempt to force predictions, describing in mathematical terms the relationship of key economic forces, such as labor, capital, interest rate and government policies. How far into the future, if at all, and with what degree of reliability can any model predict economic scenarios? Relevant statistics may be unavailable or improperly recorded, deliberately repressing some features and emphasizing others, imposing order on a world that appears disorderly, manipulating models by a process of claimed logical deductions, and arriving eventually at some prediction of general significance. But economists must begin and end with observable events, and those that are typically observed never exhaust the aggregate of such events— they are merely representations of it. Yet what is wrong with such predictions based on economic models is that human beings are unpredictable, their responses incalculable and their economic behavior lacks

any degree of expected probability. Who are these economists who propound such theories detached from the humdrum and clatter of everyday life? Most of them have never met a payroll or had to make decisions in which their financial net worth was at stake because of losses caused by their advice. Safely sheltered by favorable tenure in the world of academia, think-tank organizations, or advisors to major corporations, light years removed from the insecurity of the have-nots, never required to dig into their own pockets to pay for their flawed forecasts, couching their language in obscure acadamese, these professional economists addressed their ponderous tomes to members of their fraternity, to the cognoscenti and to the initiated. Some of the sharpest criticism originated from other economists—there are some intellectually honest enough to care—as for example: "...anyone who has seen how economic statistics are constructed knows they are really a subgenre of science fiction ... actual estimates of economic growth are based on a good deal of fudging ... describing the growth of national income ... (they) ... collected only about a dozen actual statistics and based the rest on fairly casual guesswork" (28:25-26). A more incisive critique attacks the present methodology: "Economics as a field of study has a problem nowadays. The problem is that its methods are wrong, and produce wrong results ... most of the allegedly 'scientific' economics have to be redone with another method before anyone should believe them ..." (6:13-14). Or hear it from the mouth of Charles Partee, after he retired form the Federal Reserve Board: "As someone who has been doing this for thirty-five years, it's a very humbling experience. I can't maintain any theory. All I can say is that I have a pretty good sense of the economy. That's all ... Any economist who's going to be honest ought to say just the same thing" (21:702). Another economist painfully admitted, "... in recent times economists have been so seldom correct that the suspicion is abroad in the land that something must be seriously awry with economics itself" (8:XI). Stripped of its unnecessarily esoteric language, its misleading statistics, weighty mathematical equations, and pretentious unreliable predictions, there could emerge an observational discipline that deals with various aspects of the most important activity, namely, man's efforts in earning a living within a civilized society. But the mainstream economists have little reason to write for the general public, most of whom are satisfied with shorthand and cursory statements and possess only a nodding acquaintance with a subject considered by most as perplexing and studiously mysterious. Yet there is nothing impenetrable about economics.

It is logical and requires some abstract reasoning, but the basic principles and theories can be presented in readily understandable language and would be intelligible by readers possessing some college education. Such as that a clever currency speculator can profit from devaluations which cause affected nations to raise interest rates to defend their currency (against flight), which in turn results in higher unemployment, so pleasing to stock market speculators; that the largest corporations, contrary to the laws of supply and demand, are strong enough to raise their prices during both recessions and booms, if it suits their self-interest. This should question the necessary connection between prices and demand; that recessions and high unemployment are most welcome news to bondholders who thrive on the instability of the markets and therefore their interests are antithetical to an orderly society; that free markets are not compatible with free societies since some activities must be regulated to work more efficiently to maintain proportionality and a level playing field; that global financial markets, by design, have no supervision and are therefore the playground of freebooters; that central bankers, whose raison d'être is to maintain a stable economy for all participants in the process, are in fact most concerned with the welfare of bondholders by advocating less spending, less demand, tighter credit, and less prosperity so that inflation can be kept to a minimum; that financial markets prosper during times of instability and, lacking that, will induce volatility in price movements to generate greater profits; that social values are inconsistent with, and contrary to, market behavior which disregard moral values and civilized conduct; that it is totally illusory to believe that the level of stock market indices and activity have any relation with the health of the economy, and that trading in existing stocks does not produce wealth for the economy; that it is likewise illusory to maintain that growth of the economy will diminish poverty because a certain amount of poverty is necessary for the economic process to function; that the larger the bank or business corporation the more the likelihood of government intervention in case of threatened failure because the domino effect is larger; that huge currency trades do not necessarily have anything to do with normal business transactions because currency trading has become an independent business activity; that some level of unemployment, however induced, will decrease inflation because it lowers aggregate demand for goods; that an increase in the quantity of money raises prices and a decrease lowers them; that contrary to common beliefs, private business does not remove inefficiency and corruption which is to be found in all human activities, public or private; that the foundation stones of economies are affordable wants and scarcity because they constitute the basic elements of demand; that trading in stock futures is pure gambling and profits in commodity trading require equivalent losses for the opposite trade; that slumps follow booms because booms cause slumps; that capitalism cannot long endure stable prices because it would eliminate competition and profitable speculation; that if constant equilibrium of money is maintained, it would lead to stagnation because price fluctuations would be eliminated as well as incentives for investment.

(6) All the foregoing divers fragments drawn from economics are expressed in language which should create no difficulties for the average reader. These statements are concise and could be expanded to become the subject matter of essays; they are integrated and form interrelated segments of economics. The claim that economic models are simplified representations of reality is false, for reality is always presented by economists with the conditional qualifier "other things being equal". This is nothing but wishful thinking because other things are never equal and can never be equal. The problem with economics is that is has for too long eluded serious criticism the way models are structured, but it has also revealed many other shortcomings. Economics cannot endure for much longer concerned mainly with factors of production, setting price levels and equilibrium of the market. It cannot endure for much longer ignoring morality, corporate greed and value preferences; the high level of unemployment and underemployment, poverty and hunger affecting to some degree a greater part of the world population; the problems entropy poses; environmental degradation and global warming; rampant infectious diseases in developing countries; and finally, the unstoppable population growth—economics has steadfastly ignored these problems. The 21st century will demand that an effort be made to rectify these shortcomings and take corrective steps to ease the plight of the less fortunate, especially by those countries that can afford it. This would apply, without exception, to all developed countries. Universal health insurance, adequate child-care, senior care and retirement benefits, adequate education facilities for all children, unemployment insurance above poverty level, clean air and water, elimination of harmful chemicals from food, provision of shelter for the homeless—all such benefits must become minimum standards for capitalism and civilization to endure. Economics can no longer afford to be an amoral discipline because economists do not only play with models or analyze statistical data and make predictions,

but are more often called to advise governments and businesses on the most prudent course of economic action, i.e., they become the unseen and unnamed economic collaborators in the process. They resisted vehemently any changes required, especially the followers of the avant-garde Austrian School of libertarian economics, much in vogue nowadays and commanding the greatest respect among present-day economists. One of its founders, Ludwig von Mises (1881–1973), viewed with disfavor any government intervention in the market; expressed the view that "compulsory social insurance, unemployment insurance ... labor legislation favoring unions or controlling the conditions and hours of work ... are the types of policies that slowly eat at the moral and economic fiber of society. Through them individuals lose their sense of self-responsibility ..." (22:156). One wonders what economic models was he structuring? Unemployment insurance causes loss of sense of self-responsibility? What choice does the unemployed have? One would have thought that such Neanderthal views were long passé. Does the fire insurance policy on the entrepreneur's factory building affect his moral fiber and cause him to lose his sense of self-responsibility? Spoken from the safety of a tenured professorship with all the attendant benefits, von Mises abhorred government interference in the free-market, describing his reaction: "It is important to remember that government interference *always means either violent action or the threat of such action* ... Government is in the last resort the employment of armed men, of policemen, ... and *hangmen*. The essential feature of government is the enforcement of its decrees by *beating, killing* and imprisoning ..." (Emphasis added) (22:98-99). This could only have been written by someone totally detached from Western thinking, totally unacquainted with the stark realities of commercial corporate misconduct under rigorous competition. It is a sad commentary on the provincial thinking of a prominent school of economists, totally obsessed with the idea of government interference as the destroyer of the free-market, a concept which has no regard for the government's role in securing basic social benefits for the majority.

Obsessed with the predominant importance of the bottom line, rigorous competition becomes nothing less than a struggle for survival, discarding all non-profit related considerations. If businesses do create toxic waste dumps, pollute potable water, cause environmental pollution, are responsible for global warming, create unsafe consumer products, and generate all sorts of health hazards, then reasonable people must conclude that businessmen are not only incapable but unwilling to act responsibly and monitor their activities and that government must step in to assert its regulatory authority for the health and safety of all citizens.

(7)   The 21st century will require that economics becomes more than a discipline dealing with stable money and prices, satisfaction of human wants, and how the forces of supply and demand allocate scarce products. Today, there are environmental problems which were never faced before. But of more importance is that we have entered the information age with global computer-satellite link up when news, economic data, and science know-how travel instantaneously within a matter of seconds all around the world, with knowledge and information carried to the most distant and least accessible corners of the world. Information about the business behavior of economic man will, sooner than later, become common knowledge. The consequence may very well be a reexamination by the average consumer of what are referred to as the inevitable results of man's efforts to make a living within a society which give him freedom to pursue his self-interest. He may disdain, reject, abhor, or find tolerable some of the below listed results of such efforts, a cross-section of the free enterprise system taken at random, warts and all: Government subsidies for research selectively granted to private business without seeking restitution; subsidies for giant corporate agribusiness originally designed for the support and benefit of small (family) farmers earning a living as farmers; foreign emergency loans, which are in reality bail outs for domestic high-stake risk takers acting irresponsibly, who really do not risk anything, assured of a financial rescue; the mistaken belief that Wall Street is an investment market accessible to serious-minded profit seekers, instead of being a cosmopolitan gambling casino where insiders and friends of top traders reap the largest profits; falling wages are considered good for the economy by the stock market and bondholders because, in their judgment, they are anti-inflationary and reduce costs, therefore raise profitability of employers; many businessmen who embrace the efficacy of competition seek government protection when the competition becomes intense, such as laws against dumping (importers selling their wares at a loss) or the imposition of tariffs on imports to make them less competitive; devaluation of currency constitutes a partial repudiation of debt obligations since repayment is in cheaper currency, but the debt was incurred in hard currency; corporate globalization lowers the standard of living for most people in the developed and developing world and causes growing unemployment worldwide due to downsizing of the labor force and lowering of wages; the

well-being of a nation cannot be measured on the basis of volume of production and consumption—a myth perpetuated by most economists because it fits neatly the concept of models, who also mistakenly consider the level of production of a country to be its measure of civilization, a totally myopic understanding of the term; foreign aid is not quite the selfless charity that it appears to be because most of the aid requires donees to purchase goods from donor countries which would, in fact, make it equivalent to financial assistance to donor's domestic commerce; global financial markets are, by definition, unstable and lack continuity since anyone wishing to transfer funds by means of secret electronic device can order wire transfers across the globe and escape the watchful eyes of regulators; multinational corporations and international banks, those two ambassadors of democratic capitalism, prefer to deal with authoritarian regimes because their principles and demands are authoritarian and use their power and prestige to the point of abuse; financial markets are not amoral, they are immoral—speculators push up interest rates to the detriment of capital investments, consumers, and employment—they are one of the causes of disorder. It is tortured reasoning and demagogy to liken unbalanced budgets of countries with the conduct of family finances—the latter invites insolvency and the former monetize the debt, i.e., pay the debt by printing money and in the process cause inflationary pressure; predictions in economics—always to be taken with a grain of salt—tend to be self-fulfilling. Guided by the proverbial herd instinct, optimistic predictions cause increase in productive investments and expand facilities; gloomy predictions cause business contractions and liquidation of investments.

(8) The inadequacy of the present-day economic system to provide life-sustaining employment for the greater majority of mankind and eliminate the gnawing poverty stalking over 50% of the world population may, one day, reach the breaking point. The feeding frenzy of commercialism, the trampling and treading on each other's heels in order to make ends meet, the great excess of wants over effective demand all point to a depressing social system which phlegmatically and with equanimity countenances a state of affairs that will prove to be unacceptable to the have-nots as well as to the haves. The latter are bound to become aware that the burden imposed on the have-nots could grow intolerable and the resulting tension—because of the great majority of the financially impaired—would make the coming social and economic order a difficult and vexatious experience. The super-haves, economically untouchable and enjoying

the lavish bounties life has to offer, would not wish to stumble into a frivolous and debilitating confrontation with the great majority, which would, to say the least, cast a pall of misgivings on the stability of their exclusive prerogatives. This should not be viewed as an act of generosity or philanthropy, but as a pragmatic acknowledgment of a potential shift in the rising new social forces whose confounding and suppression could, unlike in the bygone days, undermine the enfeebled economic structure and bring it tumbling down. Such a culmination could not serve the interests of the super-haves, nor accord with their self-preservation instinct. The super-haves, the dominant class, cannot engage in rhetorical contortions and affect pronouncements hedged with dangling qualifiers when set face to face with the disaster of 12 million children dying each year from poverty-associated causes; the homelessness of 100 million children, with one billion people suffering from hunger most of the time, and 50 million people dying each year from starvation. On the watch of the dominant class things are getting worse, not better.

As for the economists, who take pride in grasping the meaning of financially gainful human activities, they must cease simplifying their economic models by the expedient of ignoring 50% of the human race and cease engaging in fancy speculations disconnected from reality. The neat, orderly, and symmetrical world of their fancy just does not exist and no construct of models will make it so. The time has come when economists will have to work with a system of values that are all-inclusive and recognize poverty, unemployment, and underemployment as dangerous depressants of the economy, to be taken into account when formulating propositions and theories of future economic systems. Only in this manner will a semblance of realism be restored. Adam Smith never faced such problems and could afford to ignore them. But that was over 200 years ago.

CHAPTER 8

THE PROBLEMS ECONOMICS FACES

(1) The subject of economics is variously defined. It is essential, therefore, to know what some of these definitions connote and whether the subject and all that it encompasses under its name lends itself to a single and clear definition. There are certain basic rules to follow. In order to arrive at a distinct idea about the subject defined, a definition should not contain the term to be defined, it should state the essential qualities (attributes) of the term defined, it must not be too broad or too narrow so as not to include non-essential or extraneous matter nor exclude basic criteria. It must be expressed in language that is clear and concise rather than obscure and ambiguous. It must not be negative, for a negative definition depicts what the term is not and not what it is. A good definition isolates a subject and clearly distinguishes it from others in that it invokes the idea only of the subject defined.

(2) Some definitions of economics gathered from various textbooks on the subject:

    (a) The study of empirical data by statistical methods, the purpose of which is the testing of hypotheses.

    (b) Concerned with that aspect of behavior which arises from the scarcity of means to achieve a given end.

    (c) Encompasses social laws governing the production and distribution of the material means of satisfying human needs.

    (d) Assumes that everybody in this universe is rational and makes rational decisions, value neutrality, natural equilibria, maximum efficiency, freedom of choice.

(e) Deals with that portion of human activity which is concerned with man's effort in securing a living.

(f) The study of allocation of scarce means of production toward satisfaction of human wants.

(g) The study of scarce resources and how they should be allocated.

(h) The study of how the forces of supply and demand allocate scarce products and service resources.

(i) The science of human nature in that man is guided by principles and human nature becomes the focal point of every economic theory.

(j) The study of man who carefully calculates the consequences of his acts in selling at the highest possible price and buying at the lowest possible price.

(k) The science of scarcity.

(l) The study of the creation and distribution of wealth, of the behavior of prices and of the forces that determine national income and employment.

The more clearly a definition is expressed, the more the mind can deduce from it. This is fundamental, for from a confused or unclear definition no reliable deductions can be derived. One term is most common in the above cited definitions, namely scarcity, scarce means, scarce resources and scarce products. The term "scarce" signifies limited and not free for the asking and therefore scarce products command a price which must be paid to satisfy human needs. But the consumer must first have sufficient means to pay the price for scarce products to satisfy his needs. When he can afford to pay the price, i.e., acquires economic resources, his needs become effective demands. To secure the means to pay, the consumer must engage in an activity of earning an income.

(3) A clear and concise definition of economics can be stated as follows: The study of the process of earning an income—which is the same thing as the effort in securing a living—the allocation of scarce means, products, and resources and the behavior of prices in relation to supply and demand of anything required to satisfy needs. Most of the propositions, principles, and theories of traditional economics can be deduced from an expanded version of this definition, including the availability of the means at the disposal of consumers, the affordable standard of living and the pursuit of self-interest.

(4) The concept of market can be deduced from the expanded version of this

definition. It is the aggregate of people with the ability to purchase or sell a product or service, where the supply and demand factors determine prices and quantities to be traded. The inference can be drawn that in the case of demand, prices and quantities bought are in inverse relation; in case of supply, quantity and prices are directly related. When supply exceeds demand and demand exceeds supply, a market disorder is said to prevail. In the former, supply prices are reduced. In the latter, supply prices tend to increase. Each participant in the economic process should do what is monetarily most advantageous. But this is predicated on certain basic assumptions:

(a) *Effective competition*

It would depend on complete market information available equally to all participants. Considering the number of participants, knowledge of market conditions can never be equally shared and therefore effective competition is impossible to achieve.

(b) *Discretionary surplus*

A participant lacking discretionary surplus cannot effectively compete with those who possess a limited or a superior discretionary surplus. The former can participate in the bidding and compete until the price demanded would exhaust his surplus, if any. The latter can participate in the bidding to the extent of his limited discretionary surplus, and the one who disposes of a superior discretionary surplus can participate in the bidding regardless of price demanded. Effective competition is not possible.

(c) *Perishable or durable goods*

A supplier of perishable goods must submit to price competition or suffer a total loss. A supplier of durable goods can choose whether to sell at prices offered depending on his discretionary surplus, whether the price offered covers his cost (at least his fixed costs), or the need to dispose of inventory to make room for replacements of merchandise that is not selling well. Effective competition is difficult to achieve.

(d) *Life sustaining necessities*

The have-nots are hard-pressed to satisfy all the basic needs. If the price of one or the other is increased, selective choices have to be made in accordance with the means. The surplus possessed by the haves require minimal choosing since only secondary needs are involved; the super-haves are never confronted with the need to choose, no matter how much the price increases even of tertiary needs. There is no effective competition.

(e) *Economic downturn due to recession*

The have-nots would experience an almost immediate impact from the effects of recession due to loss of income, having to reduce or even give up some of their primary needs. The haves would need to reduce expenditure for secondary needs before cutting primary needs, or cushion the shortfall by borrowing or pledging their assets. The super-haves, whose virtues are said to have been rewarded by the beneficence of wealth, are so well protected by the size of their surplus that not even tertiary needs would be affected and there would be no impact on the standard of living. There could be no effective competition.

(f) *Luxury items*

Such items are referred to as secondary or tertiary needs and are available exclusively to the haves and super-haves. In case of limited supply there would be no price competition since the super-haves could pay any price demanded. There could be no effective competition.

(5) It is a fact of economic life that society consists of three classes of consumers whose income and wealth are highly disproportionate. In the effort of self-preservation all three classes are guided by material self-interest. Of these only the have-nots, the great majority, are limited by Nature's primitive design to be entangled with necessities and the confining restraint of primary needs. The haves and especially the super-haves managed to be free from Nature's gravitational pull of survival necessities and afford the satisfaction of secondary and tertiary needs to gain singular freedom of choice, the reward of achievers to pursue a variety of interests not directly connected with self-preservation instincts. The super-haves, the greatest achievers constituting about 1% of mankind, skillfully maintain their dominant influence against all encroachers, not making too much noise about their favored circumstances. They share no mutuality of interest with the other classes, especially with the have-nots, whose constant turmoil and insecurity (loss of employment, reduction of wages, energy expended to keep body and soul together) are treated as necessary stratagems in order to secure for themselves the maximum share of income distribution. The haves, mostly consisting of medium size shopkeepers, well-established tradesmen, professionals such as attorneys, accountants, engineers, and medical doctors of average success, gained some freedom in affording secondary needs and participate, even if moderately, in the blessings life has to offer. Yet

their economic success is seldom so well-established but that a shadow of uncertainty burdens their achievements—the self-preservation effort is still all-consuming and ever present in their thoughts. They are far removed from the super-haves with whom they share but a superficial community of interests to the extent that one of the haves could advance to the more affluent class.

(6)   In an economy where there are many sellers who sell the same product and outsiders have free entry into the industry, a state of perfect competition can be said to exist. Such conditions are seldom encountered. Effective demand, the driving force of the economy, is a term depicting what consumers are willing and able to buy, i.e., the ability to pay for a commodity. Such a demand determines individual consumption. The total money available to people who could afford to buy things is referred to as consumer demand or purchasing power. A society's standard of living depends on the division of total income among the various individual consumers. Amounts which are offered at different prices constitute aggregate supply that requires the existence of competition for the effective operation of supply and demand, i.e., the market. Suppliers cannot do well if consumers are few and purchasing power does not sustain consumer demands. Competition between buyers and between sellers tends to adjust prices to a level where the maximum amount of commodities are traded. When prices are stabilized at levels at which total quantity supplied equals total quantity demanded, a state of equilibrium is said to exist. But this is purely a figment of abstraction, an ideological jargon, since a state of equilibrium never exists but only an approximation towards that target where the market price is said to be either above or below the equilibrium price.

The economic concept of perfect competition, effective competition, stabilization of prices (supply and demand), equilibrium price, and community of interest between consumers and producers are artificial props designed by economists to aid them in the formulation of principles and theories and altogether without pragmatic foundation. These concepts have no independent existence outside the mind of economists. The above concepts do not follow from the definition of economics as related in Paragraph 3. Instead, as recounted in Paragraph 4, the concept of market, the availability of purchasing power, an affordable standard of living, the behavior of prices in relation to supply and demand, can be deduced from the expanded version of the definition, subject, however, to certain assumptions (six in number) as outlined in Paragraph 4. The concordance of these assumptions is the division of consumers into three classes according to the division of income and possession and size of a discretionary surplus, namely, the have-nots, the haves and the super-haves. The outlined assumptions preclude these consumers from treatment as an aggregate group, but as divers separate interests, all of which are essential to the functioning of a viable economy, yet aligned at opposing ends, claiming adversary rights to enjoy the products of their exertion and manifesting no community of interest. Therefore, when speaking of consumers, there is not a single effective demand, a single purchasing power, and a single consumption but three of each, corresponding to the three economic classes, competing not in a single market but each class competing in its own separate market corresponding to the division of income among the classes. There is competition within each class but not among classes. For the have-nots could no more compete in the super-haves' market than the latter would choose to compete in the former's market. Demand is the driving force of the economy; competition is the central mechanism of the market system; the market system requires that each should do what is to his best monetary advantage—as long as it is understood that there are three classes of demands and three classes of markets serving three classes of consumers, regardless of the degree of affluence of the society.

(7)   In Paragraph 3 a concise definition of economics was submitted encompassing the core of conventional economic theory. It was susceptible and lent itself to manifold deductions, which is the nature of clear and concise definitions. It was shown in prior paragraphs that the scope of economic propositions and theories would have to be modified to allow for the existence of three separate classes of demands and three separate classes of markets as opposed to the traditional single demand and single market. Conventional practice can no longer count on the harmonious interaction of the three classes. But economics must also change a part of its direction and contents. It can no longer remain an amoral discipline, value-neutral, ignoring the effects of continuous technological and scientific changes and the destabilizing effects such changes worked upon humans and society. As quoted above: "Economics ... has a problem nowadays ... (it) ... produces wrong results" (6:13-14). It can no longer ignore 50% of the human race (the structurally unemployed, underemployed, the indigent, and those continually undernourished) and consider them expendable, standing in the way, a nuisance. It can no longer proclaim the foundation of a stable economy to be its grand design without

considering the destabilizing effects upon the economy caused by out-of-control forces of Nature, be they natural disasters (so-called Acts of God), environmental degradation or overpopulation—although the last two are more the malfunction of humans than Nature. It can no longer expect production managers to foresee the desires of consumers without taking account of psychologically driven wants and preferences. Nor can it any longer take for granted that in the present-day complex interaction of economic forces consumers and producers are necessarily guided by rational decisions when, more often than not, other aspects far removed from prudence affect the patterns of wants. Economics, as taught presently, has become wedded to mathematics and statistics, where abstract differential calculus and selective data of probability create a make-believe atmosphere of illusory harmony and order, where all things must balance because that is the nature of equations, far removed from the humdrum and sweat of humanity toiling in pursuit of self-interest in a competitive world. No wonder serious modern students of human and societal self-preservation problems have become enstranged from economics (econometrics in particular), viewing it as a field of dilettante pursuits, who rate as the "producers of wrong results". Economics must make major adjustments and embrace in its research the answers to newly encountered problems, many of them disorderly and unpleasant, which will burden and hinder man's economic progress in the 21st century. Economics must abandon the claim that it can find the solution to every problem and admit that it has no answers to some problems. It must discard the notion that economic growth is possible without end and repudiate the belief it made common that more is always better and most is best and that all progress can be achieved painlessly and without cost.

(8) The major adjustments which must be made to economics to bring it within the range of realism of the 21st century concern the inclusion and absorption of the following spheres of activities and problems:

(a) The degradation of the ecosystem.

(b) Unchecked population growth.

(c) Behavioral irregularities of humans.

(d) Rational economic decisions are the exceptions.

(e) Natural and man-caused disasters.

(f) The dark side of competition.

CHAPTER 9, PART ONE

THE DEGRADATION OF THE ECOSYSTEM

(1)   A system formed by the interaction of all living organisms, plants, animals, and bacteria with the physical and chemical factors of their environment is called the ecosystem. The interaction of the component parts have reached a steady balance after eons of attrition, but the finely tuned ecosystem has developed cracks, structural flaws, which portent ominous changes for the human race. In pursuit of material self-interest, man has been increasingly, wittingly and unwittingly, abusing and overexploiting the gifts of Nature, causing environmental degradation, damage to the biosphere and adverse climatic changes. Man is facing, above all else, a moral problem. Does he have the moral right to pass on to his children and future generations a diseased and fractured environment unsuited for a healthy and enjoyable lifestyle, which was available to, and enjoyed by, ancient and preceding generations, because of his insatiable wants and effort to maintain a standard of living selfishly devastating the environment? Like the bubonic plague of the 14th century, the coming affliction recognizes no national borders, developed or developing countries, the poor or the affluent. No trading in environmental permits or carbon rights, a subterfuge so dishonestly proposed by the wealthy polluters to indigent sellers of developing countries, will mitigate the damage inflicted in the long run. All the manipulators whose thinking made the design of the IMF an acceptable solution for financially strapped developing countries will grasp at any straw rather than face the world pollu-

tion problem head-on and reduce pro-rata the allocable percentage of emissions proposed by the Convention on Global Warming. The manufacturing industries, churning out more and more merchandise and profits in complete disregard of other than internal costs are knowingly causing irreversible damage to the environment and in the process contributing to an ever worsening contamination and pollution. One thing is perfectly clear: the unfettered market is incapable and unwilling, without external constraints and controls, to take corrective steps to improve the condition of the environment.

(2)   One would assume that reasonable people, listening to environmental scientists, would ponder the problems facing all living species, man in particular, if the scientists' warnings are not heeded. It is further assumed that man, guided by his strongest instinct, that of survival, would not voluntarily and without the strongest countermeasures countenance the slow and gradual deterioration of his physical well-being even if it meant the sacrifice of some of his creature comforts. It is these expansive demands for creature comforts, demanded by all and at an inordinate extravagance never even closely achieved by previous generations, which are at the root of the problem. The meaning for the economy is clear: Less discharging of liquid waste pollutants and effluents into rivers and lakes, less dumping of wastes into oceans, less burning of coal, oil and gas, less use of chemical fertilizers, less cutting down of forest, tropical forests in particular. What used to be considered external costs and disregarded by manufacturers in unit cost computation and leaving the problem of pollution control to society will have to be internalized, and the cost of mitigating or eliminating the environmental damage considered part of the true cost of a product. In other words, polluters will be required to pay for the clean-up costs or for the technological development preventing pollution and providing for efficient waste disposal. The net result will be higher cost of products, less output due to downsizing of demand, less efficient production, lower standard of living due to lesser selection and variety of goods and smaller GDP, increasingly more government regulations, less freedom of choice, less economic freedom due to prohibition of some industries or their production methods, less political freedom due to policing and enforcing corrective regulations, and finally, if enforcement or public cooperation becomes a problem, the possible institution of an authoritarian regime to save society from itself. But the problem will not stop at the country's borders. Since the damage to the environment will transgress all political boundaries, conflicts among

countries will require compliance enforcement power of some mutually appointed supervisory institution, or at worst, the supervision of a self-appointed supra-national State dictating environmental policy to intractable and recalcitrant States. If individual States are unable or unwilling to enforce damage control, and what is required by consensus of major powers to save mankind from catastrophic environmental degradation, the only option left open is a world government to rule by decree. It is a foregone conclusion that protagonists of the unfettered market economy would not be in the forefront of those who preach tolerance for downward transformation of expectations, nor would they disavow growth in favor of exalting stable and sustainable economic development to save the environment and manage to bring about a natural equilibrium. Such talk is cynically labeled as bad science. Unlike control of nuclear arsenals of various nations that achieved nuclear capability, though even there are many fatuous skeptics, which invokes compelling reasons for caution to avoid a chain-reaction of deadly fall-out, the minuscule but regressive and detrimental changes in the ecosystem due to pollution cause no alarm to the cosmopolitan bon vivants and their ilk who take the inviolability and eternity of Nature for granted. Much of this is due to the religious belief that God could not be the creator of a global system so deficient that it would not endure human mismanagement. There is only slim hope that enough rational men will band together and, possessing ample foresight, will halt the downward spiral of debasing human living conditions as life becomes unlivable on this planet. For there is no question but if the present rate of contamination progresses without let-up for several decades, the damage will become irreversible and environmental stability an elusive expectancy. To give the reader some understanding of what problems humanity faces if matters are left alone to their own devices and continue unabated, as there is no genuine expectation to the contrary, a brief outline of the abominations will be presented. This may yet turn out to be more than just the "cry of Cassandra".

(3) It is obvious that Nature is unable to absorb all the shocks created by man in pursuit of natural self-interest, ever higher production and growth. The Earth is the only planet in the solar system that supports life as we know it. The light and heat generated by the sun reach the Earth and create climatic zones which determine and limit the variety of organisms and vegetation. Life can exist only in the lower atmosphere, on the surface and in oceans. Only about 3% of the water supply is fit for human

consumption and soil irrigation and must be regularly recycled by natural processes. The balance of 97% is too salty and unfit for human uses.
Carbon, a gas originally released from the interior of the Earth, is essential in insulating the Earth's atmosphere and making life possible by
retaining the right amount of the sun's heat to enable life to exist. But for
the protective ring of the atmosphere, the average temperature on the
Earth's surface would be about minus 19° Celsius. This blanket of
retained heat creates the life-essential greenhouse effect. Light, heat,
water, carbon (carbon dioxide), oxygen, vegetation, soil with sufficient
nutrients, enough light for photosynthesis to occur, nitrogen, are all
essential for the maintenance of life on Earth within the limits of the carrying capacity of the environment. But they must be in the right proportions, and any imbalance would cause self-adjusting environmental resistance and restore the equilibrium within the ecosystem. The equilibrium
is so razor-thin that man has managed to cause major ecological disruptions within just the 20th century. Sulfur and nitrogen oxides cause acid
rain as a result of too many automobiles and smokestacks spewing fumes
into the atmosphere. The ravages include polluted and lifeless lakes,
ruined fisheries and dying forests. Annually, in excess of 50 million acres
of lush tropical forests are destroyed with dramatic effect upon climate
changes, contributing to global warming. Scientists predict that average
world temperatures will increase up to 6° F over this century. The Earth
has only warmed $1\frac{1}{10}$° F so far but polar ice sheets are already melting, sea
levels will rise by up to three feet within the century, flooding coastal
populated areas and farmland worldwide. Millions upon millions of flood
refugees will have to be resettled inland to higher ground, causing permanent dislocation of community centers and business facilities. The
problem can only get worse as we burn more fossil fuels—coal, oil, gas—
and pump more carbon dioxide into the atmosphere; the result is carbon
dioxide overload in the atmosphere and trapping of solar heat. Violent
storms and hurricanes will become more frequent and severely flood
entire regions; global overheating will cause droughts, famine, and disease to inland communities; disease carrying mosquitoes are moving
north; vector-borne diseases, such as malaria, dengue fever, yellow fever
will expand and shift their ranges. Farmers will have to grow more food
for an additional 100 million people each year, on less land with 24 billion tons of less topsoil, counting on adequate rains and irrigation water,
no plagues of pests, no dramatic weather changes and no crop fungus.
Without topsoil, there is no food. Every inch of good topsoil—the thin

surface layer of nutritionally rich soil—takes 500 to 1,000 years to create. Agriculture cannot be sustained without adequate irrigation of clean water, supplies which are increasingly being contaminated by excessive use of chemical fertilizer and salinization; 95% of the world's urban areas dump raw sewage into rivers, lakes and oceans. Contaminated water is killing in excess of 10 million people every year. Desertification is a process whereby formerly fertile land is turned into barren wasteland, degraded by overuse, water shortage, soil erosion, overgrazing by cattle and adverse climatic changes. Soil nutrients can be restored by massive doses of chemical fertilizers, but this process interferes with the survival of essential pests which help maintain the ecosystem equilibrium. Air pollution, referred to as smog, that dense layer of contaminated air hanging over industrial cities and megacities, particularly in warm weather, causes all kinds of respiratory health hazards, especially for the elderly and children. The microscopic particles considered to be the deadliest air pollutants are discharged from diesel trucks, automobiles and power plants. Tropical forests recycle the harmful carbon dioxide, Nature's own filtering process, and their destruction by deforestation contributes to the greenhouse effect, warming the Earth, creating a hot and dry climate that would seriously threaten mankind's way of life. Global ozone is declining on the average by about 4% per decade, caused by carbon dioxide and nitrous oxide. Depletion of the Earth's protective ozone layer causes skin cancer, cataracts, and damages the immune system, making man more susceptible to infectious diseases.

(4)   Pollution is wreaking havoc with wild animals' immune systems. Sewage is biodegradable and breaks down naturally, but pollution due to raw sewage and other chemicals is despoiling the oceans. The vast oceans are becoming overloaded with sewage and garbage from surrounding countries; oceans, rivers, lakes, and aquifers are also polluted from runoffs of chemical fertilizers and pesticides; oceans are further polluted by oil spills, refineries, and rinsing of oil tankers, all affecting the nourishment for nearly one half of the world's population. The direct consequence of this contamination is the destruction of European seals, Canadian whales, Maryland Oysters, California sea lions, sea otters, oysters, striped dolphins, and many other marine animals.

The deadly toll of man's misdeeds sacrifices unsuspecting animal species on the altar of his limitless greed and lack of foresight; contaminated water, food, and air suppress man's immune system, lower his resistance to deadly viruses and bacteria. Man's welfare, health, and survival are threatened by causing pollution of every primitive phase of life-sustaining forces. The most polluting poisons—PCB, DDT and dioxin—are already carried in the bodies of every living organism, resulting in previously unknown viruses. Damage from polluting agents is permanent; it cannot be excreted but accumulates with each additional exposure. Man is not only gutting the ecosystem but also disrupting his reproductive capability. Countless millions of humans are condemned to a life of poverty and starvation, to be rejected as so much debris. The synthetic chemical pollutants cause the births of deformed, mentally impaired and neurologically damaged children, born to a useless life and dependency on subsidized support, to be sacrificed on the altar of man's stupidity. All this is symptomatic of a total ongoing and growing collapse of man's stewardship of this planet Earth and makes a mockery of his vaunted cognomen to be the most intelligent of the living species.

(5) Productivity depends on a healthy, capable and intelligent labor force. Absenteeism due to environmentally caused illnesses will lessen productivity, raise unit cost of production and adversely affect demand. Human well-being is essential to achieving a sustainable economic development which involves interference with free-market allocation of resources. Present consumer demand cannot be sustained nor can interminable population growth be absorbed by society or the economy. Market-based incentives to control pollution limited to waste assimilation and recycling policies will not significantly reduce national output, a necessary precondition of any effective pollution control policy. Economists must realize that unceasing economic growth is not consistent with the ecosystem equilibrium and a healthy environment, which is essential not only for the preservation of civilization but of the human race itself. Pollution control policies and regulatory oversight, however strictly enforced in a democratic society, will not forestall irreversible consequences. Economists can speculate about ways to increase production and distribution efficiency; about the efficacy of competition and its benefits; about the need of thrift to finance more investments to produce more goods; whether business cycles are caused by a sort of mass nervous disorder or whether Central Banks, against all showing to the contrary, are really capable of controlling the economy. But any economy which is said to "flourish" where unemployment is on the rise; where minimum wages are kept well below the recognized poverty levels; where adequate healthcare is available only to those who can well afford it; when millions of senior citizens waste away in retirement homes receiving medical

attention unworthy of that name—an economy which tolerates and ignores such aberrations and distortions is sick to the core and no amount of spouting about the merits and achievements of free-market capitalism will save the day. An economy which nonchalantly countenances the progressive deterioration of the environment and the vital forces sustaining necessary living conditions is moribund. But then no economy, free or totally regulated is, historically speaking, capable of controlling the totally negative influences of pollution and environmental degradation, which is bound in time to devour the discretionary surplus, a part foundation of civilization, of humanity itself. In every direction we look, we observe too much of everything. First of all there are too many people, a subject dealt with later. Every mile goods travel has serious environmental consequences: increased air and water pollution; increased need for roads, bridges, tunnels, waterways, airports, seaports; increased use of packaging (made from wood products); increased need for energy-consuming refrigeration; increase of greenhouse gasses from fossil fuel used to power transports; increase in global trade and the collateral global transport, which have become the largest single source of greenhouse gas emission. There are just too many people driving too many cars on too many freeways; too many real farmers driven off their land by absentee owners using technology in place of experience; too many large-scale industrial-agricultural companies which specialize in export-oriented monocultures—luxury items that bring higher profits: flowers, ornamental plants, cotton, exotic coffees, exotic fruits; too much consumption of electricity with rationing a real possibility, but a substantial increase in price to user a certainty.

Does anybody who is preoccupied in making a living really care that the market-driven economy will ultimately bring on us global warming? People will not care enough to voluntarily change their standard of living, but they will get the message when the cost of pollution control and waste management is reflected in the price of consumer goods; when allocation of scarce resources will be mandated by regulatory government agencies and consumer goods will not be available in the desired abundance or expected quality; when the health of parents and children will be adversely affected by diseases caused by ingesting contaminated food previously considered safe, such as pesticide residues, classified as carcinogenic presently found in over 35% of the food, such as apples, grapes, green beans, peaches, pears, spinach and winter squash; when the toxicity found in water will unalterably damage the brains of children and retard their learning potential; when healthy mothers give birth to deformed children all due to ingesting chemically contaminated foods; when food-borne pathogens (such as Salmonella and E. coli) due to antibiotics in animal feed and injections with growth-inducing hormones could ultimately produce an uncontrollable "supergerm", even a global pandemic, that will make life of humans a woeful and wretched experience. All this because most animal products now come from animals jammed together in tiny cages or on floors poorly ventilated, covered with each other's excrement, gone crazy from crowding instead of freely grazing and being raised in open spaces, as on farmland. If we can borrow an episode from Exodus, the time of the biblical Moses, when only after the ten plagues were inflicted did Pharaoh finally relent and free the Hebrews from bondage, similarly will it take several plague-like calamities for people to react forcefully to the disasters caused by global warming still in time to be reversible? But by then conditions may not be reversible. It is one of the characteristics of man to put off facing problems that will not become a burden until some time in the distant future, particularly if it requires a cost that does not produce income and the effort must be collective. The most discouraging aspect is the unlimited population growth that would frustrate efforts for corrective action. Why reduce air pollution, carbon dioxide emissions, improve technology including hydrogen power, develop renewable energy sources, reduce the gas-guzzling automobiles, increase efficiency of waste management, which entail sacrifices, if such efforts are neutralized and canceled out by new hordes of people whose presence would nullify any and all corrective efforts, with the result that a sustainable ecosystem proves to be that much more elusive? Three preconditions are indispensable for the achievement of the desired results:

(a) Control of population growth.

(b) Attainment of a sustainable ecosystem must be a global effort.

(c) Achieving and sustaining the above two aims will require selection of a committee of major powers to rule by decree until the emergency is terminated. Use of democratic methods will not achieve the necessary compliance but endless meetings and debates.

CHAPTER 9, PART TWO

UNCHECKED POPULATION GROWTH

(1)   Land is limited on this Earth and any population growth raises the density of habitation on this planet. There is not the slightest doubt that population growth is a real phenomenon and expert demographers indicate an annual 100 million net after deaths increase of global population. It occurs mostly in developing countries, but no developed country has as yet reached a condition of zero-population growth. Had it been reached, it most likely would have a prosperous economy where workers achieved a respectable employment status, but such a well-being is bound to attract immigrants (legal and illegal) from impoverished undeveloped countries, and in the end would reflect an annual growth. This seems to be the fate of most developed countries, for we are witnessing a global migration of major proportions, mostly indigents in search of a better life, a migration of a size probably not experienced since the wanderings and resettlements of Vandals, Visigoths, and others in the 6th century A.D. The presently ongoing migration has greatly impacted the countries of their destination since the immigrants are mostly unskilled and of a lower education, causing assimilation problems, but mainly an initial more extended financial burden upon the host country. Welfare, costly job training, and language barriers have to be overcome, all of which require budget expenditures which would else be devoted for the originally intended purposes. The unskilled newcomers compete for jobs with unskilled or semi-skilled domestic labor, filling jobs that are the least desirable, in the process

depressing wages and causing domestic labor to seek skills to prepare them for better jobs and compensation. Immigration of women suited for work as domestics is a boon to middle-class and wealthy families, for although wages paid are not a problem, the willingness of native-born employees to take menial jobs with no future has been an obstacle. Competition among newcomers invites cost-cutting measures by employers who are not above taking advantage of such opportunities.

(2) But population growth and massive immigration have their dark side. About 80% of the world's population standard of living is impaired and those people are not benefiting from bounties the improved economic systems have to offer; about 25%, or a billion and a half, live in dire poverty, and a billion suffer from hunger most of the time; twenty million are at the point of starvation. Population growth in poor developing countries will only make these conditions worse. An increase in population would not only require an increase in nourishment but a greater exploitation of agricultural resources, which requires farming of ever less productive farmland, fully utilizing chemical fertilizers, and increased dosages of herbicides and pesticides, all agents which tend to contribute to environmental degradation and injury to the ecosystem. Overworked land will lose its yield only to restart the cycle of artificial fertilization. More people will require more space for habitation, which means less land for farming. Less land will be available for living accommodation, which will not only become more expensive for the average family or the less well-to-do, but the tendency will be to migrate to cities, causing widespread urbanization with all the attendant crowding, diseases, unemployment, and substandard living conditions in inhospitable urban surroundings. The overworked facilities will be sewage disposal, garbage collection, treatment plants, sanitary housing, air-pollution, safe drinking water and control of crowded city streets. About 500 million urban people are either homeless or live in housing unfit for human habitation. By the end of this year (2000), 50% of the world's population will crowd the inhospitable urban areas, giving rise to megacities, some of the largest of which (Bogota, Calcutta, Mexico City, Jakarta) cannot afford sanitary housing even for its present inhabitants. Humanity squeezed into megacities is exceeding the population of many developed countries and will experience newly emerging bacterial and parasitic diseases due to unsanitary living conditions caused by the density of people living too close together, density-caused stresses and mental disorders, social disruption. Any attempt at remedial measures, even though modest in scope, would

strain city finances to the point of exhaustion. Those who can afford it will relocate to the suburbs or smaller towns to escape from the stressful and unsanitary crowded environment, but this relief is only temporary. The passage of time will bring new surplus humanity to the cities and will be forced to move to the suburbs, if not on their own then at government's direction. An exodus to greater distances from the city core area would have adverse cultural and social repercussions since universities, theaters, museums, concert halls, other entertainment centers, and sport events are located closer to the city core area and distances will make transportation a daunting experience.

(3) With population growth steadily expanding the total numbers, the quality of life will take an emphatic turn for the worse. The available land habitat of humans will steadily decrease, with the land prices increasing substantially; as a consequence of the cost and scarcity of space, the living areas of homes and apartments will have to be considerably reduced to accommodate the population growth. The same would apply to commercial stores and offices. There is little incentive on the part of the business community to slow or halt the trend toward overpopulation since, as the term implies, an ever greater number of customers is good for business, both retail and housing. This, however, is not the long-term view which holds that overpopulation beyond optimum levels means an unstable economy with the gap between the wealthy and the poor ever widening, the latter continuously increasing and the former decreasing in numbers as a percentage of the total. More needy will require a growing bureaucracy to administer the welfare support apparatus and income distribution payments with the always present wastes and frauds. But the latter two, although unhappy concomitants, are always present when large sums of money are disbursed, and the sums will grow with greater need. Since overpopulation will lower the standard of living, with necessities becoming scarcer and therefore increasingly more expensive (food, transportation, utilities, housing, medical), the disposable income will not suffice to support the great number of non-essential commodities which are the staples of a variety of retail stores and production facilities; their profit margin will be squeezed ever harder, competition will drive many of the production facilities overseas to save on labor costs or force many of the retail outlets out of business. Overpopulation will witness a radical income redistribution with the greatest share allocated to necessities (primary needs) at the expense of non-essentials (secondary needs). Food, shelter, utilities, and healthcare will see the largest price increases

not only due to greater consumer demand but because of intrinsic cost increases.

(4) With overpopulation growth rampant, it will be a cruder and a crueler world where the worth of an able-bodied man to society will cheapen and the lives of the handicapped, retired elderly, and permanently ill becoming an impediment, unwillingly tolerated at best, quietly dismissed at worst. With shortages of food and shelter, there will be little tolerance for the non-contributor to society's well-being, more likely treated as a burden to be fed and housed without getting anything in return. The extension of this attitude could have far-reaching consequences upon the anti-humanitarian perception of able-bodied and efficient survivors, the creators of a new morality, harsh in its design and not consonant with civilized conduct, as the term is commonly understood. It will not only be a question of food and shelter but scarce medicine and shortage of health-care that would augment the torment of the unwanted and those unable to earn their keep. For the instinct of self-preservation, if sufficiently tested, would preempt any inclination toward morality. A new era will come into existence where the act of abortion, in whatever form, is welcome; euthanasia is generally practiced; fatal epidemics are treated as Nature's relief; starvation is mostly ignored and only marginally relieved; terminally ill or incurable patients denied treatment as medical facilities are inadequate to handle the load; the mentally ill viewed as so many undesirable mouths to feed with no benefits received in return; and finally, the unemployed and unemployable treated as so much permanently useless accumulation of humanity, who are not needed and for whom the social order and economy provides no part to play. Such a new morality would only be fitting in times of stresses and strains which the burden of overpopulation will foist on humans.

(5) The urge to procreate the species is a basic natural instinct. In other than humans, Nature provided nourishment as a self-limiting factor keeping a check on propagation and ecological balance, in addition to diseases and epidemics. But for the intervention of man, Nature's system is efficient, however harsh and pitiless it may appear to man's morality, and keeps the proliferation at sustainable levels. Man feels he has somehow bested Nature and keeps propagating his species well beyond optimum levels and well beyond achieving population stability applicable to non-human species. But Nature has its weapons to force population growth at stabilized levels and restore population to optimum levels with, or without, man's cooperation. Degradation of the ecosystem, ecological catastro-

phes, epidemics, air pollution, and exhaustion of potable ground water will frustrate unlimited growth and achieve a restoration of the natural sustainable ecological equilibrium. The only difference between the two is that whereas animal population is kept in check permanently and an occasional breach is quickly repaired to a sustainable equilibrium, man will exceed all limits and barriers, suffering the increasing discomforts and torments brought on by conditions of overpopulation until the congestion becomes intolerable and man is forced to take measures into his hands to reverse the unchecked population explosion and restore the sustainable population stability. For if man lacks the fortitude and stamina to intervene and restore the natural life-sustaining forces providing for a stable population within limitations of the environment, then Nature would assuredly do it for him, using forceful and draconian measures to restore the symmetry. No reliance can be placed on voluntary cooperation to restrict excessive procreation, and individual freedom of choice would no longer be acceptable. An authoritarian rule mandating selective coercions is inevitable to enforce conformity. Persuasion will not be effective to counteract this aberration, especially since the prohibition against birth control derives from religious sources, Catholic in particular.

(6)　What kind of a world will man live in when the time comes and he is forced to take measures into his hand in an attempt to restore sanity? Because of the harsh prevailing conditions we know that cultural development will be moribund; there will be hardly any trace left. What took a thousand years of painstaking effort to accomplish would be immersed in a morass of man's doings. A global 100 million annual population increase would double the population in 50 years to 12 billion. But the increase would not be evenly spread and must be calculated on a regional basis. Whereas developed countries in Europe would experience about a 25% population increase in 50 years (this does not agree with the World Almanac 2000, which assumes that population control in Europe is achievable in the near future with the result that countries like France, Italy, Poland, Germany and Spain will actually experience a decline. This view is overly optimistic, except for Germany). By the year 2050, the Islamic block in the Near East (Iran, Iraq, Egypt, Syria, Pakistan) with a present population of 309 million would increase to 627 million; India's population from 900 million to 1.7 billion. These are conservative figures. Africa's population is projected from the present 778 million to over 2 billion (All figures taken from the World Almanac 2000). The population of Mexico has increased by 10 million to 91 million between 1990 and 1995 and will double in 40 years.

The human body is about 70% water; man cannot survive dehydration if he loses as much as 12% of his body water. "The next war will be about water" (The World Bank). At the present trends global consumption of water will double every 20 years. Of all water only 3% constitutes fresh water supply and only 0.5% is readily available from rivers and lakes. 65% of the world's fresh water goes to industrial agriculture; human beings use 10%, the rest is used by other industries like high-tech and computer manufacturing. Silicon chips require massive supplies of pure water. More than one billion people already lack access to clean fresh drinking water, and more than 3 billion, one half of the world's population, live in water-stressed regions. Water may soon be more valuable than oil. The Arabian Peninsula groundwater use is three times greater than its recharge. Saudi Arabia's fresh water supply may be completely depleted in 50 years. Israel's extraction exceeds replacement. In Africa, the aquifers barely recharge at all. Cities and industrial zones are now in direct competition for water with industrial agriculture. Some countries are near war over water. Namibia and Botswana are arguing about diversion of the Okavango river; Israel, Jordan, and other mid-East countries are arguing about diversion of water from the river Jordan; Malaysia has threatened to cut off Singapore's water supply. In India, low income families pay 25% of their income for drinking water. Poor residents of Lima, Peru, pay $3.00 for a cubic meter of often contaminated water. In England, 30% of the rivers are down to one third their average depth. 75% of Poland's rivers are so contaminated that their water is unfit even for industrial use. What will the fresh water conditions be like in 25 to 50 years? How many humans will be there to drink it? How much will be available for agriculture, how much for industry?

(7) Overpopulation serves no purpose except to harm the survival of the human species by placing a strain on every facility designed to serve man and give free reign to his reproduction instinct. Man is not prescient enough to calculate with any degree of likelihood the inevitable hindrances Nature will place in his path of overcrowding the Earth with more people than can be safely accommodated. Man's genius has created biotechnology and genetic engineering, sciences, even though in the early stages of development, show the greatest promise of truly elevating him above the impediments of human frailty. He is now able to contemplate the conquest of almost all diseases which have pained and shortened his existence in the past. Likewise, with the application of this technology, man will be able to provide adequate and healthy nourishment

for the existing human population of the Earth in the right quantities and at affordable prices. All that is required is sufficient time for research, testing and application. Man's obstinacy in freely overpopulating the planet will manage to create, by his irresponsibility, global and natural disorder bound to hinder, if not frustrate, the determined efforts of scientists to ease the burden of his creature discomforts. Overpopulation will interfere with the research of scientists who will be unable to cope with the multitude of complications confronted and who are bound to create problems faster than scientists can find solutions: the task will overwhelm them. Preferential treatment and discrimination would be the result since scientists will be forced to concentrate the major part of their work on scientific research and laboratory experimentation. While the new biotechnology will appreciably lengthen the life span of people in well-to-do developed countries who would receive the most attention and real benefits from the new science, those in poorer developing countries would face the ordeal, privation, and new diseases brought on by never before experienced dimensions of population density.

(8)   How do populations of the rich developed countries countenance with equanimity the conditions of 3 billion people who live on $2.00 a day, or the 1.2 billion who live on less than $1.00 a day? Is there any foreboding that to this mass of dispossessed most of the 100 million are added annually? Do the traditional economists show any concern for reality when speaking of disposable incomes or aggregate demand? The character of humans never changes but their morality does. We have reached a stage of morality which permits us to calmly contemplate the wretched lives of about one half of the world's human population without grasping that some of our major technological advances may not turn out to be user-friendly. Is it possible that it has not occurred to a single well-fed mortal that some of these hopelessly deprived unfortunates would not forever silently bear their deprivation? That their misfortune cannot assume the air of permanence? Nothing economists have written so far should embolden the Western economic powers in the belief that they will always manage to keep their economic superiority. The contented well-off should not look with studied contempt at the ease with which radical elements of the impoverished are recruited by revolutionary nationalist movements, fully convinced in the cause of their ascendancy and that the sun is slowly setting on the present-day economic powers. In the Middle East, presently the primary energy source, the oil-wealth will allow the region to resist reform. With the population projected to expand and the

masses becoming poorer and more frustrated about their future, the resulting inequities may bring Islamic fundamentalist movements to power. The industrial nations can only hope that scientists will discover a substitute for oil by the time power shifts in the Middle East. Based on sheer numbers, the result of steady population increases, and the aptitude of its peoples, China and India are bound to become the world's new military powers; based on their technological capabilities and determined effort, they will challenge the current powers for economic superiority in their regions of influence in South Asia and the Far East.

(9) The gravity of the overpopulation problem will not be appreciated by those unwilling to keep an open mind. The growth is gradual and hardly perceptible, but the historical figures are convincing. The global population was 3 billion in 1960, by 1970 it reached over 3.75 billion; 4.5 billion by 1980; it passed 5 billion by 1987; 5.3 billion by 1990; 5.7 billion by 1995; and 6 billion by 2000. In other words, the world population doubled in the last 40 years. We do know that conditions are not favorable to permit the same level of growth in the next 40–50 years, and we have reason to know that this planet could not accommodate such a multitude. We do know that man is reaching the zenith of his production capacity only to be burdened by new surpluses: a surplus of people, surplus of starvation, surplus of poverty and surplus of hunger. We know that resources previously taken for granted and free to all, such as fresh air, fresh drinking water, adequate living space are becoming the domain of those who can afford to pay the price. The able and enterprising will not pay the heavy price overpopulation is bound to exact from those not so endowed, whose misfortunes will inevitably lead to more poverty and lower standard of living and who will have little choice but to suffer their adversity silently, without hope. We do know that man is responsible for this proliferation and possesses the know-how to prevent its occurrence. But that would take long-term foresight and careful design for the future several generations removed, and dealing with distant circumstances not of immediate concern to man. It is the growing economy, profitable allocation of resources for some and stable employment for others, that are of immediate concern. It is man's short-sighted expectation that the natural order would preclude population growth from ever reaching cataclysmic levels. This confidence, bordering on the religious, is symbolic of his survival instinct getting the better of his common sense and will not preclude Nature from exacting the inevitable retribution.

CHAPTER 9, PART THREE

BEHAVIORAL IRREGULARITIES OF HUMANS

(1)   The problem with economists is that they can structure their models only with the caveat "other things being equal". Of course, other things are never equal. The sun cannot stand still while economic models are put to the test, nor can a situation occur where common circumstances remain unchanged at different times for different models. It is also apparent that economists, deeply committed to their special theories, become convinced of their veracity and expect universal application as the reward of such endeavors. In that sense, it can be said that economists are the prisoners of their own theories; eventually, the more reliable ones evolve into economic laws. Let us take the economic law that customers always seek the lowest price of products of equal quality. The behavior of customers would be considered irregular if they deviated from this course. But what is the basis for this conclusion? The economic model structured by economists to demonstrate their theories? Why is there even consideration of regular and irregular behavior? Behavior which is not consistent with prognostications based upon economic models is termed irregular. If regular behavior follows a particular causation, why is it assumed that irregular behavior does not follow causation? One must accept as axiomatic that all human behavior, regular and irregular, prudent or foolish, considered or arbitrary, are all actuated by proper causes and could not be otherwise, since no human action is uncaused, hanging in the air, so to speak. It is much more accurate to say that irregular behavior has its

causes just as regular behavior except that we are ignorant of the causes of the former and treat them as random uncaused actions. But Nature is uniform in this: there are no uncaused actions and to contemplate their possibility is a sign of ignorance. To come back to the above illustration of a customer always seeking the lowest price of commodities of equal value, his decision to purchase a commodity not of the lowest price is a decision for which causes exist that may not be clear to the observer, who in his ignorance considers the customer actions irregular. It must be further taken for granted that no two people are motivated equally by the same causes, or to put it in another way, the same causes would, or could, arouse different reactions in humans. In the course of human affairs, man is prone to choose a better good over a lesser good, or a lesser bad over a worse bad. Yet two men could react differently to the choices, given their different education and life experiences, but in each instance, both men would be motivated by causes which they follow in their own fashion. If the reactions were different, neither could be called worse or irregular, but each was regular, i.e., followed antecedent causes.

(2)   The view that every effect has a single cause and every cause a single effect is not valid. Everything which exists must have a cause, an origin, a source which gave rise to the idea. The attribution of causality to events is natural to the mind. Where the mind errs is in selecting a particular antecedent, out of a great number of antecedents, and treat such a condition as cause. Every phenomenon has many antecedents and many consequents. The same conjunction of antecedents would always give rise to the same consequent (or consequents), but the mind mistakenly selects one antecedent and assigns to it the quality of cause. But the mind really knows only subsequent events, one event following another, and by habit refers to one event as the cause and to another event as the effect. If an effect had only a single cause they would be identical. An effect must, by definition, have two or more causes or antecedents, and the mind in its simplicity selects the one it deems most important and mistakenly attributes to it the quality of single cause. For man to understand Nature and explore its secrets, the sequence of events had to be fragmented into single causes and single effects, a purely artificial prop that has nothing corresponding outside of the mind. When analyzing the causes and effects of economic events, man must be mindful of these limitations and abstain from propounding theories based on simplistic causation of events when choosing to deal with single causes and single effects, artificial choices which have nothing corresponding to them outside of the economist's mind.

All laws of Nature are permanent and follow the same sequence of antecedents and consequents, predictable, regular, uniform and invariable. There is no chance or coincidence, no consequents without antecedents, no effect with but a single cause and no cause with a single effect. An observer, who witnesses a chain of events, focusing on a particular consequent and selects a particular cause out of a multiplicity of causes as the single cause of that consequent, is just as mistaken as the next observer who focuses on the identical consequent and selects a different cause. It is impossible for man to select all the antecedents of effects and all effects of antecedents, because Nature, in endowing man with a survival instinct, fashioned his mind to superficially identify only single causes of an effect and assign to it the attribute of cause. Whereas in experimental sciences it is possible to isolate sufficiently, but never absolutely, an event and call for conclusions on the assumption of "other things being equal", however, such assumptions cannot be made when dealing with events of social sciences whose main concern is the study of human activities as related to a particular field of interest of which economics is a part. Realizing these limitations, economists have good reasons to be most humble in asserting universal application of their theories deduced from their "models", or for that matter for any of their theories, however obtained. To select a single antecedent out of many (even though the mind is not aware of the many) and ascribe to it the function of cause of an event under investigation makes for good mathematics or logic, but not for realism.

When referring to certain human behavior as irregular, we must be mindful of the ignorance of the observer, whose critique is aimed at those whose behavior reflects a different result than expected by the observer from his "single cause, single effect" theory. Economics assumes that everybody is rational and makes rational decisions. This is another way of stating that the observer's assumptions derived from his single cause theory were contrived. Humans must be content to know only sequences of events and observe one event following another in a chain of succession. When one particular event has always been followed by an identical other event in a regular chain of succession, the human mind is so constituted as to determine a cause / effect relationship between the two events. Even though this determination is, at best, superficial, it sufficed to serve as the foundation of man's knowledge of the many disciplines which aided his survival and overcame most of the obstacles placed in his path by the natural order of things. A creature from another planet, exposed to a different causal relationship of events, could duplicate our body of knowledge by assimilating our process of reasoning and using a different set of cause / effect relationships.

(3) Economic behavior is determined, to a large extent, by psychological factors of man interacting with his social and physical environment. His effort of self-preservation is basic to the understanding of his economic choices and reaction to economic challenges encountered in everyday living experiences. Such effort is predictable when satisfying basic needs, i.e., primary needs, such as food, shelter, clothing, and security, but beyond basic needs his reaction to challenges involving secondary needs is diverse and no regularity or consistency can be determined—such reaction cannot be predicted. Even when speaking of his primary needs, we can only state with assurance derived from experience that man will do his utmost to the extent of his abilities to satisfy such essentials. The primary needs were stated in generic terms, such as food or shelter, but such categories contain innumerable particular varieties, any of which could serve the intended purpose. But the choice of specific varieties would involve a process of specific selection, the very process which is not subject to economic predictions. We can predict with certainty that man must eat to survive. We cannot predict what kind of food man will choose. When dealing with secondary needs (which comprise other than primary needs), i.e., needs not essential for self-preservation, the resultant choices could be subject to other than economic predictions. It is said that humans are too unpredictable to suit the purposes of economic models—that statement is correct. It is said that humans are essentially incalculable—that statement is incorrect.

(4) The discipline of economics has been structured by fallible humans and since not limited by the strictures of scientific experiments, it is no less fallible than its architects. Many economic theories and systems have been propounded, some profound and some superficial, most are inconsistent with the others, many contradict the fundamental conclusions of others. It is rare to find two economic schools but that they differ on some essential points even though they all deal with the same reality and claim prestige based upon reputation and scholarship. Yet they all fall into the single-causation trap in assigning but a single cause as the central issue to phases of their economic theories. They rely on simplistic conclusions that complex economic outcomes are the result of a single antecedent only to be replaced by another antecedent propounded by some other school. This may have given rise to the perception that instability of eco-

nomics is equaled only by the instability of economists. However events turn out, economists often speak in language intentionally obscure to justify any outcome of their predictions.

(5) A few examples of common errors, past and present, will be discussed. The statement that prosperity has fixed limits is in error. No human endeavor has fixed limits. The effort to achieve permanence of any desired aspiration has always eluded man who instead spent most of his exertions climbing steps to greater success or resisted descent to lesser standards of comfort. Permanence looked attractive from a distance, but once achieved in part it was identified with "standing still", a sign of backsliding, and the human spirit reasserted itself in seeking upward movement, i.e., ever greater prosperity. But this is both his strength and weakness. The striving for ever greater success is his strength, and having achieved success, i.e., prosperity, the tendency to take unnecessary risks is his weakness. For this steady and ceaseless climbing not only encourages dishonesty, friction, and selfishness, the baser traits of humans, but also leads to over-optimism, taking reckless chances, and to possible miscalculations. It is said that prosperity breeds recession. It would be more appropriate to say that too much prosperity breeds failure and blunders. Too rapid plant expansion and overproduction lead to decreasing profit margins; too much build-up of inventory in expectation of a price increase; too great demands for increase in wages and benefits; too many speculative ventures and investments by people in the stock market who are beginners and most likely losers; too much speculation of all kinds including gambling; too much spending on discretionary personal items and incurring large debts to pay for them—the feeling is abroad that no one wants to miss out on enjoying the fruits of prosperous times and the herd frenzy takes over. The feeling of optimism is contagious, it sweeps the land and affects all commerce and consumption. Too much optimism, in time, leads to recklessness and at the first sign of increasing doubts that what started as an economic slowdown could turn to pessimism and outright recession. A deep and prolonged recession could bring on a depression, but the economic infrastructure of the modern State should have enough built-in stabilizers to prevent deep depressions from occurring and the negative slide should halt with the onset of a deep recession before recovery and optimism reappear. A positive or negative assessment from a respected business leader; some index of economic activity, however artlessly compiled and showing a current upswing or downswing in the economy; stock market gurus expressing some bearish or bullish

comments, or some gloomy or cheerful forecasts, and all these purely superficial and insignificant signals could well result in the bursting of the speculative bubble and economic slowdown or spur a return of optimism. Swings between prosperity and recession have a regularity about them and give them an aura of inevitability. But nowadays, we know somewhat more about the causes to reduce the swings from cataclysmic proportions to milder and more acceptable cycles between prosperity and economic slowdown, possibly turning into a mild or longer lasting recession. Crises marking booms and severe busts will not be 21st century phenomena because when they occurred in the past (especially in the 18th and 19th centuries) they were mostly precipitated by speculators and financial manipulators plying their own self-seeking agenda, and the public was damned. This sort of predatory conduct would no longer be acceptable. It would trigger a chain reaction that could not be controlled and in case of a lasting deep depression—with millions thrown out of work and hunger stalking the land, countless businesses declaring bankruptcy, and residential mortgages foreclosed—the minority of propertied haves risk losing all in a blind vendetta inflicted upon them by the despairing multitude of the dispossessed. All would be losers.

A recession is indicated when a downturn in economic activity occurs in at least two consecutive quarters of a country's gross domestic product (GDP). The GDP is basically the market value of goods and services produced. To counteract the economic slowdown (or keep it from sinking further) a central bank's usual remedy is to cut short-term interest rates in the expectation that such a move would reinvigorate growth. But such a step is merely symbolic. Any possible optimism aroused by such a move is meant more as a psychological boost to the mood of consumers and producers than as a stimulating impetus to increased activities affecting the GDP. The reduced interest rate will not encourage personal savings, a necessary corollary to boost investments. It will benefit bondholders whose increased trading does not add anything to the GDP. It will restart frenzied stock market trading of great benefit to major traders and speculators who speechify for all to hear that their repeated bullish predictions will now come to pass. But the trading of issued stocks does not add anything to the GDP. Consumers, who are homeowners and mortgagors, are urged to refinance and achieve some savings in servicing their mortgages. Billions worth of mortgages will be rewritten. But mortgage refinancing does not add anything to the GDP. Consumers will not purchase additional cars, TV sets, computers, or

house appliances just because financing costs have dropped imperceptibly but will refrain from doing so because the market is saturated with
the same technology that has spurred sales in the past, and consumers
must be attracted with new products using more advanced technology.
More money may change hands, but this does not necessarily mean that
the economy is improving. One would expect that common sense would
dictate to lower prices and shave profit margins during recessions in the
hope that such moves would encourage reluctant customers to maintain
consumer demand. Food chain supermarkets are continually boosting
their prices, however imperceptibly; property taxes are raised annually
ever so slightly; apartment rents are inching up because new construction
cannot keep up with population growth; utilities are steadily drifting
higher, deaf to consumer protests and insensitive to the hardships caused
by doing with less. Finally, medical bills and hospital costs are totally
impervious to maintaining price stability during recessionary periods,
continually raising fees mainly due to research and need for ever
improved diagnostic equipment. All dominant corporations, no matter
what their field of activity, raise prices regardless of recession or prosperity to keep the stockholders happy and the positions of chief executives protected. Most businesses engaged in the above cited fields of
endeavor behave the way they do fully confident the demand for their
product is inelastic and if they encounter consumer resistance, there is
always the unfailing standby: maintain the profit level by cost-cutting
measures, such as lowering employee wages and / or downsizing, i.e.,
reducing the payroll. Consumers affected by the stress of recessions are
restricted in their options: eliminate or reduce expenditures for secondary needs and downsize outlays for primary needs by making hard
choices. Market volatility and manipulation, man's herd responses, the
psychological momentum of economic expectations, the concept of the
consumer as a calculating individual are all behavioral criteria sometimes
harmonious, at other times pulling in opposite directions, and contribute
to economic instability. Behavioral irregularity, if such a term can be
applied, should be laid at the doorstep of capitalism because it does not
endure stable prices or tranquillity but thrives on instability, turmoil,
crises, irregularity, and upheavals of the market system. Many corporate
businesses have done well, both in recessions and prosperity, because the
ignorance and lethargy of the public have made corporate greed and
crude acquisitiveness acceptable. It is the perceived irregularity and
unpredictability of humans that make economics an interesting field of

endeavor for risk capital and risk takers who think they can outsmart the volatility of the markets and profit handsomely from it. There is almost no interest rate increase at which an enterprising businessman will not borrow if he knows how to profit from the market volatility. To say that productivity slowed because interest rates were raised, by say 100–300 basis-points, is to engage in the unreal. If higher costs can be passed on to consumers and sales are only moderately affected, then most interest cost can be absorbed. In some countries the bank rate for borrowing is 7%, in others 18%, but the level of production and consumer price acceptance have adjusted to the rates and the pace of business activity absorbed the cost: it is all relative and the price levels of other goods and services have adjusted to it. How can an item sell at different prices in the same locality? Is it solely because of consumer ignorance or alleged behavioral irregularity? This is the best example of consumer preference, partiality for custom and appreciation of service. The store of choice may have better parking facilities, more courteous clerks, better credit terms, less time waiting in line for service, free delivery, better advertising, or more convenient access to neutralize the price differential. So much for the unchangeable economic law that the customer always seeks the lowest prices. But then all laws of economics are suspect. This may offer a facile explanation why many corporations in France seek the advice of astrologers to help with market prospects.

(6) Monetary policy seeks to control the level of economic activity by raising or lowering the supply of money. Monetarists believe that money supply is the key to the ups and downs of the economy. Simply put, if the money supply is raised by 10% then prices will rise by 10%. This is a very simplistic theory and fails in two respects:

(a) It ignores the velocity of turnover of money.

(b) It makes measurement almost impossible; certainly its accuracy is not credible. It states that if the economy is below full employment, an increase in the money supply would lead to an increase in production. If the economy is close to full employment, an increase in the money supply would lead to an increase in prices, i.e., inflation. These are all tidy mathematical calculations but are practically useless if the measurements are faulty or inadequate.

The velocity rate of money turnover is the Achilles heel of the monetarist theory. If money supply should double and velocity of turnover decline by 50%, it would have no effect on prices. If money supply increases by 10% and velocity is ignored or stays the same, then prices would rise 10%. But velocity of turnover like "other things being equal" is never constant, never the same, and the measurements amount to pure guesswork. It can be said, however, that the velocity of money turnover affects the amount of economic activity generated by a given money supply. The unpredictable human behavior, as it affects economic activity, makes the measurement of velocity and money supply impractical. The former chief of the Federal Reserve Bank of New York, in a speech (Alfred Hayes, 1975) stated that the quantity of money (money supply) cannot be determined and its short-run movements (velocity) cannot be controlled and have no material economic effect. This is a devastating revelation by someone who should know. Nor can government statistics and indices published periodically to measure economic activity be determined with any degree of reliability, although, considering the source, they exert a significant economic effect. One has to express the greatest astonishment at the credibility and reliance accorded such government figures, which are, to say the least, speciously compiled by certain government bureaus in some murky offices, inaccessible to the public or any other scrutiny or confirmation, incredibly reducing complex aggregate measurements to within one-tenth of 1% accuracy even though these calculations are admittedly taken from some random surveys. One further wonders with what unquestioned trust and ready acceptance such figures are received and acted upon by other departments of government, the business and financial community, and the public. No allowance is made for factors of error as would become discretion. Furthermore, these figures have every appearance of being tendentious since they are never shockingly revealing, never militate aggressively against expectations, nor ruffle too many feathers. Surprisingly, as if by prearranged consensus, they are never seriously disputed. One is reminded of the priestly oracles of antiquity which were given total credence by the faithful, even though we know assuredly today that such oracles were an invention of the priests who perpetrated a fraud upon an unsuspecting public.

The Bureau of Labor Statistics (BLS) well illustrates the superficiality and offhand manner of compiling statistics on the number of unemployed. One would think that knowing the number of unemployed, even in round percentages, would be treated as one of the more important economic indicators of how well or badly the economic expansions or contractions are doing. For one must take for granted that employment of the head of families serves a most important social purpose in building family cohesion as the bedrock of society. Similarly, but only to a slightly lesser degree, the importance of employment of all other members of society seeking a paying job should be the aim of every economic policy. To be able and want to work but not find any despite lengthy effort is the most demoralizing, dispiriting, and crushing blow to a person's self-esteem and self-reliance. To feel useless and unwanted by society is the equivalent of being condemned to a slow decay. The periodically published BLS figures on unemployment are eagerly awaited by the stock market, bond and financial markets, the central bank, labor unions, government policy planners, and various educational institutions, such as universities, colleges and trade schools. Given the great economic influence wielded by such statistics, one would think that extreme care would be exercised in their preparation since the results are never seriously questioned by those most interested in their accuracy and application.

The BLS obtains its unemployment statistics from a random survey of 60,000 households. Those who do not actively look for work, or are discouraged by lack of success, are not counted. Those who worked for at least one day in the month the survey is taken, or in the month prior, are counted as employed. Part-time workers are counted as employed regardless how minimal their hours. Those who looked for work in the month the survey is taken are counted as unemployed. Is such a survey reliable? Is such a survey sufficient for an unemployment report more closely watched than all other government reports because the results would represent the clearest indication of the direction of the economy? To survey at random a mere 60,000 households, surely a number that cannot be considered significant in light of over 50 million households in the U.S., by telephone and ask questions in a colloquial format? A total of 0.05% of the households in the U.S.? How many interviewees would take such calls from strangers and answer questions truthfully? How many persons would admit they are too discouraged to look for work? How about illegal aliens? What about those engaged in the substantial underground economy and not counted by the BLS? What kind of direction are statisticians getting when they count part-time workers as employed or those who worked only for one day in a month? If the unemployment rate hits the true mark it is by a fluke. Such porous, artless, and naïve compilations do not deserve serious treatment. It is a sad testimonial to the lack of discernment, or concern, on the part of users of these statistics that such easily manipulated and distorted figures, which do not merit credibility, should serve as a blueprint indicating the direction of the economy. If such untrustworthy figures are used, what do they tell us about the reliability of the economic planning? What does it tell us of the reliability of other government statistics compiled in a similar offhand manner related to growth rates, consumer spending, and the all-important consumer price index?

(7) Behavioral irregularity of humans, if the term has any use at all in view of the previous discussion about the fallacy of the single cause theory, applies equally to entrepreneurs, and most importantly to economists. It is the nature of capitalism and the free enterprise system to dodge regularity and order, which would imply stable prices and predictability. Instead, as every clever entrepreneur knows, it is the unexpected ups and downs of the economy, its instability and turmoil, its crises and upheavals that separate boys from men and create profitable opportunities for the crafty risk-taker and resourceful speculator. If the stock or commodities markets did not have high and low swings, they would be a boring place to do business and attract very few investors. It reminds one of the old bromide that businessmen like the level playing field, so that no one has the upper hand in the contest. But this is a benign subterfuge. The concept of a level playing field is a favored myth of free enterprisers—it just does not exist. No sooner do corporations compete but form alliances and combinations to stifle competition and gain the upper hand so that the advantage would be theirs. Similarly with the notion of equilibrium price. This is defined as the price when the supply of goods in a particular market matches demand and that price always seeks the equilibrium level. Also defined, speaking of graphs, as where the demand and supply curves cross. This is another example of pure imagery fit for economics students and their textbooks. In real life there is no equilibrium price which requires a mythical market to set a price at which all the goods are sold. As every businessman knows, if all the goods are sold at a given price, the price charged was too low. Similarly, if consumers purchased all the goods at a given price from willing sellers, the price they paid was too high. Businessmen set the price based upon full cost recovery plus the desired profit margin. The price at which all goods are sold to meet consumer demand is not part of the consideration, except perhaps in a post-holiday discount sale. A street vendor selling burritos who has no place to store the perishable food must dispose of his inventory by day's end at any price. But advertising this would give a wrong signal to his customers.

(8) Behavioral regularity of a human is predictable only if he seeks to satisfy self-preservation needs and how best to maximize life's comforts and

benefits. The more he is burdened with necessities, i.e., primary needs, the more his actions follow the basic pattern of survival, i.e., the natural order of things, and are predictable on that account because of their affinity with the vast majority of humans who share the common burdens of existence. Behavioral predictability becomes more complex and difficult the more independence from the basic burdens of existence a human achieves and who succeeds in advancing to the satisfaction of secondary needs. Behavioral predictability is most complex and difficult when humans achieve a status of complete freedom from the financial gravitational pull and escape from subservience to the natural order of things to enjoy the rewards and benefits such accomplishments have to offer. Since their conduct is freed from necessities, their activities and behavior are determined by a multiplicity of causes difficult to comprehend even by an astute observer because they do not conform to a set pattern. The more remote and distanced human actions are from the natural order of things, the more complex and unpredictable they become. Nature assigns but a brief span of existence to humans, for most long enough to become proficient in the struggle for existence. For the resourceful and perceptive, long enough to penetrate some of her secrets only to snuff out the candle of life just in time to protect what is concealed behind her veil.

CHAPTER 9, PART FOUR

RATIONAL ECONOMIC DECISIONS ARE THE EXCEPTIONS

(1) Behind the seeming order of Nature, the regularity of seasons, the regeneration of plant life after winter slumber, the rainfall or melting snow which starts with trickles of water and rivulets give way to majestic rivers, the heavy tropical rainfall breathing life into vegetation and animals which almost perished in the preceding drought—all these point to a well-planned grand rational design. But all these are superficial impressions of an observer influenced by appearances. For behind the seemingly orderly facade of Nature so pleasing to man reigns a brutal war of all against all, a savage struggle for survival, unchanging in its primitive ferocity and thirst for blood. Nature cares only about perpetuating the permanent struggle between unequals, the success of the strong and resourceful, however undeserving, and the defeat of the weak and inexperienced, however deserving, where pure chance encounter decides the outcome and promotes the evolutionary design in favor of the successful survivor. Man's idea of order contravenes Nature's design. A similar struggle takes place within human societies except, absent wars or violent conflict, there are some rules which limit the severity of the conflicts. But a degree of grimness is still present. When society can calmly countenance the anguish of masses of unemployed, the continued slavery and homelessness of children, the abuse of women in many areas of the world, neglect of the poor and aged, the starvation of so many while the rest enjoy the luxury of plenty, the lack of medical care or its total

195

absence, the ailing and physically suffering—they agonize in silence—
then the seeming rational order becomes the positive irrational disorder
as viewed and understood by man. The animal species is part of Nature
and thus embraces within its innermost being the irrationality and disorder inherited from Nature. It is the human race only, and then only a
favored segment of it, attempting to rise above the natural order of things
applicable to all living species, which achieved some success in mitigating
Nature's irrationality and instituted some order, a moral code to live by,
acting less aggressively and gave the human race some dignified standing
above other animal species. It gave the human race some assurance that
physical force would not resolve disputes, nor would superior cunning
drive the loser to the edge, but a legal system of criminal and civil laws
would level the playing field for most and provide equal opportunities to
all contestants, all for the advancement of social well-being. Moral codes,
however, cannot be enforced, only infractions of an ethical system can be
pursued by man's laws. Harsh experience teaches, however, that the concept of a level playing field and equality of opportunity for most contestants have no application in real life. On the contrary. In the field of economic endeavor, in particular, the clever and specially gifted see to it that
the playing field is never level, and those who have advanced somewhat
in the economic scale plot and manipulate events so that opportunities
are never equal even though such conduct violates morality. But in the
struggle for basic existence and in the effort to preserve some creature
comforts, morality always takes a back seat. Man's wavering between
aggressive self-seeking and morality has been the problem and measure
of civilization. The instinct of self-preservation is man's strongest motivation and takes precedence over rationality.

(2) Rational economic decisions imply not only a thorough review and
analysis of existing options but a foresight to discern and anticipate
future consequences of choices. It requires man to be capable of
divorcing his thinking process from prejudices, bias and prejudgment; it
further requires him to make judgments based upon a knowledge of the
subject and the guidance of intuition, a special innate faculty capable of
directly apprehending the choice of options. His thoughts would need to
be freed from the instinct of self-preservation, a quality possessed by
none pursuing primary needs, by some pursuing secondary and by most
satisfying tertiary needs. For the greatest obstacle to making rational
choices of options, even if it were possible to detach the mind from the
innermost instinct of self-preservation, is the fear of failure and panic

associated with possible privation and suffering. Economics deals with human activity most closely concerned with the effort to secure a living, i.e., satisfaction of wants related to the survival instinct and self-preservation. Its propositions, principles, and theories are all derived by application of rational analyses advanced by authors well beyond the concern with primary needs, are far from gaining unanimous acceptance by economists, lack universal relevance, contain too many variables, contradictions, and single-cause fallacies to replace man's natural intuition and self-preservation instinct as guides to practical everyday economic decisions. Based on the above, it can be stated that rational economic decisions, which by definition must be independent from intuition and instincts, do not meet realistic expectations and are for that reason rarely encountered, except in textbooks. Man striving to satisfy life's necessities, especially primary needs, will place far more reliance on his instincts and intuition, which he followed habitually since childhood, rather than on rational analyses, that cannot be considered in isolation. Rational economic decisions are not only the exception but have a most limited pragmatic application in practice.

(3)   An increase in the quantity of money raises prices and a reduction lowers them. An increase in the quantity of money and the consequent rise in prices could be offset by an increase in the supply of goods, which, if it rises faster than the quantity of money, would decrease prices. The same effect on prices would be achieved by the changing velocity rate turnover of money instead of altering the quantity of money. An increase in productivity does not mean an increase in the supply of goods offered on the market if the increase in goods is added to the inventory or removed from domestic consumption by export to foreign countries. An increase in the quantity of money does not affect prices if it results in increased savings or transfer to foreign countries. Production may be expanded, resulting in reduction of unit costs and the excess added to inventory, if the producer expects a rise in prices by withholding goods from the market. When more goods can be produced with less labor, prices tend to stabilize and the economy would expand without inflation. A tight labor market, i.e., a low rate of unemployment, would cause an inflationary wage-price spiral. Some level of unemployment would slow or stop inflation; a high rate of unemployment would reduce aggregate demand, lower prices and induce a recession. Raising the level of production and hiring more labor will increase wages and prices but not necessarily profits. Lowering the rate of growth of aggregate production would be

anti-inflationary if the population level were stabilized; if population is increasing, more consumers would compete for fewer goods and thus bid up prices and cause inflationary pressure. Increasing or decreasing government budget deficits increases or decreases inflationary pressures respectively. An increase of interest rates will slow economic activity, but increased savings will stimulate, in time, capital investments. Lower interest rates will reduce savings and stimulate the economy, but only if it increases aggregate demand.

It is evident that all the possible permutations of production, demand, supply of goods, quantity of money, employment, government budget surplus or deficits, population growth, interest rates and savings are almost too numerous for the human mind to grasp or control, even if well-versed in business affairs, in order to determine what effect the increase or decrease of each one will have on the others' increase or decrease. If one could take an X-ray of economics, the common denominator is the principle of more or less, of higher and lower, of increase or decrease, of bigger and smaller. Each constituent sector of the discipline affects the value of the other related sectors and their joint influence impacts the remainder of other component segments. One could draw various conclusions about the effect of an economic event, engage in disputations with others and still doubt whether the argued result would stand the test of time. If the personality factor is added to the equation, the psychology of the market, the optimism or pessimism of customers and producers, speculative anticipation, the influential role of speculators, the predilection or prejudices of the public, the total lack of objectivity, the influence of predictions and the herd behavior of the public, the impact of self-fulfilling prophecies—then one must inevitably conclude that the consequences of the interaction of components constituting typical and everyday economic activities cannot be rationally explained without inviting differing interpretations. The impossibility of single-cause explanations would frustrate the most qualified interpreter, resigned to abandon conventional definitions. One could justly conclude that rational decisions in economic matters are more the exceptions than the rule, decidedly more. This much can be said without hesitation: Reliance on the GDP, doubtful as compiled, as an indicator of progress is illusory. No matter with what glee the trumpeter announces annual growth, the principal weight should be given to adequate consumer demand at the right prices to make producers happy, tailoring production to expected customer needs; to unemployment at levels where it poses no danger to social stability; to inflation that has always been present since the time prices were catalogued, a fact pleasing to debtors and frowned upon by creditors; it rises incrementally and is assimilated as it contributes to a mood of optimism and stimulates the economy—all these constitute the most promising configurations of a politically acceptable economy and the best of all possible economic worlds achievable by a civilized society. However the ebb and flow of leading economic indicators forecast the ups and downs of business cycles, any activity in which human intrusion is the most important ingredient cannot avoid fluctuations. This is natural and unavoidable. When workers, consumers, producers, and financiers pursue their material self-interests, they do so without losing awareness of their contribution, and though some push harder than others, they prefer order and stability in the end. Workers press their demands, but wish producers no harm. Likewise, producers pursue their advantage, but desire consumers would understand and not harbor resentment. Financiers drive a hard bargain, but have a stake in the profitability of producers. Each one of them has an interest in the unbroken well-being of the other. Pure self-interest dictates that order and stability are preferable to disruption and disorder. For the sake of these mutual expectations there is a limit beyond which most dare not tread. But a special breed of economic predators emerged who maximize their profits by artificially destabilizing the markets, create chaos and distortion, always play the role of outsiders in pursuit of greed; unmindful of the disruptions, they are without remorse if rival competitors fall by the wayside and disappear from the scene. These are the speculators, who risk little to gain much even if such gain results in the collapse of businesses, wrecked fortunes, impaired well-being of society, or impoverishment of once prosperous countries. Their activities contribute nothing to the economy, serve no useful public function; they speculate against the trend, i.e., revel in the role as contrarian traders and are masters in spotting destabilizing weaknesses which they exploit to their advantage. They profit greatly from the futures markets, which seem to be tailored to satisfy their needs. It can be truly said of speculators that rational economic decisions are the exceptions.

(4) When Aztec and Inca maidens were slain by the Spanish conquistadors for refusing to part with their golden necklaces, a period in human history was born when man reached the lowest form of rapacity. They destroyed two great and well-ordered empires, slaughtered masses of their people, and subjugated the rest, all to satisfy their bewitched and

insatiable craving for the yellow metal. They risked their lives crossing the ocean in rickety caravels, waded through infested jungles and swamps, crossed high mountain peaks spurred on by the irresistible quest for gold. Accompanied by Dominican priests to give the Spanish brigands spiritual succor, whose religion of resplendent love failed to slow the murder of millions of innocent men, women and children. Instead, they devoted their energies to bring survivors into the fold of the Catholic faith by means of forcible, at times, bloody conversions. Gold (and silver) was shipped to Spain where it brought no peace but further bloody turmoil in financing aggressive imperial wars of the 16th century Spanish monarchs (Charles V, Philip II) and in the process, by flooding the country with gold coins, ruined commerce and impoverished the people of the empire as the influx of large quantities of gold fed a hyper-inflationary commodity price rise estimated at well over 500%. However, fate was just. All the ill-gotten wealth availed the Spanish nothing. After a few victories, the army's strength was spent, the power of Spain declined during the reign of subsequent monarchs, as did commerce and industry. Rational economic decisions were non-existent.

(5) From antiquity to the present, humans treated gold as if it were a divine substance, exercising an attraction as if charmed by a magic spell, always desired and trusted as a store of value, and in modern times treated by too many, though ill-advisedly, as the indisputable foundation of a sound monetary system. It certainly possessed unique qualities, such as durability, brightness, relatively high value per unit of weight, easy recognition, malleability, indestructibility, and convenient divisibility, qualities which were rated as ideal for use in commerce as a medium of exchange. But the attraction of gold for such use proved just as flawed, irrational, and full of unforeseen traps as the unbridled greed of hordes of conquistadors and their grasping and equally culpable monarchs, who squandered the plundered wealth on worthless adventures and in the process wreaked havoc upon the rest of Europe, by engaging in bloody conflicts and causing a ruinous price inflation. Gold blinded all who were seduced by its glitter, impaired their capacity for rational decisions, and brought out man's basest instincts. As a generally acceptable international, as opposed to national, medium of exchange, the influence of the gold standard has been relatively short-lived.

(6) A pure gold standard is one where all monetary stock is backed 100% by gold and the standard monetary unit consists of a fixed quantity of gold. Under the gold coin standard, all paper money and other metallic cur-

rency are redeemable in gold coins. Countries on the gold bullion standard provide for the purchase and sale of gold bullion by the government or central bank. Countries on the gold exchange standard provide for a fractional (i.e., not 100% backed) banking system tied to a fixed price of gold. The monetary unit in gold standard countries is the weight of a unit of gold which determines the number of dollars, pounds, etc., that may be made from an ounce of gold. It also determines the exchange rate with all other countries on the gold standard and thus keeps the value of money equal to a fixed amount of gold. In gold bullion standard countries, parity between gold and the circulating media is obtained by redeeming paper money in gold bullion at a fixed price. The quantity of gold held as reserves by a country will set a limit to all other forms of payment (paper money) that may be issued by that country. It is this limitation in the quantity of all other forms of payment which acts as a control and discipline and at the same time limits growth of the circulating media to the gold reserves held. Therefore, a pure gold standard would not support a stable price level of an expanding economy since prices will decline if gold held as reserves does not match economic growth, and the effect would be deflationary. Similarly, an excessive inflow of gold which exceeds economic growth would have an inflationary effect. These are fatal weaknesses which induced countries to abandon the gold standard. The world went off the gold standard in 1971 and also discontinued fixed exchange rates.

(7) The disadvantage of a gold standard is that it causes instability of the national currency but gives rise to foreign exchange stability. Payments for excess imports result in export of gold bullion, i.e., a decline in reserves and a resultant contraction of monetary stock. This depresses internal prices. To combat this trend, interest rates are raised (causing the attendant increase in financing costs) to discourage the physical outflow of gold. The reverse occurs when exports of goods exceed imports. The inflow of gold increases the reserves which allows an increase in the money supply; inflationary price increases are the result. If countries follow a deliberate policy of attracting the inflow of gold to increase the reserves, they would raise interest rates. Those countries, which successfully attract an inflow of gold, thereby increasing the reserves, experience economic expansion, price increases, and a short-term (about 10 years) inflationary climate, all of which have to be countermanded by lowering interest rates. The gold inflows and outflows, the constant interest rate and price movements, cause economic instability, unceasing turmoil,

opportunities for manipulation of the price mechanism and an ideal playground for speculators.

(8) The supply of money, prices, and economic growth of countries tied to an international gold standard depend on gold production, i.e., mining gold and adding to the world supply of gold. If gold production does not match economic growth, prices in terms of gold will decline. Expressed in another way, economic growth depends on the parallel production of gold, i.e., a shortage of gold would prevent needed expansion of money supplies to support economic growth and price stability. The value of gold cannot be a stable standard of value because it is subject to fluctuations in foreign and domestic markets caused by countries possessing either a surplus or shortage of gold in terms of the pricing structure and economic growth. Countries wishing to correct this imbalance have to resort to borrowing gold from, or lending gold to, each other in a sorry display of fidelity to an artificial and ill-designed system which may have had some application in the Middle Ages but is totally absurd when governments, or central banks, are quite competent to control the supply of fiat money, i.e., paper money, without any specie backing or ties to gold reserves. The international business community agreed to use the U.S. dollar for their reserves (instead of gold) and peg the exchange value of domestic currencies to the dollar.

(9) The gold bullion standard as an international arrangement for settlement of debts among countries lasted only from about 1875 till 1914, when the system was discarded after finally concluding that it was practically unworkable. The weaknesses were obvious and the benefits illusory; it created difficult problems for the monetary system and suffered from chronic instability. Economic growth was for too long bound up with an increase in the world's stock of gold, which had to be mined and paid for. The high cost of production of gold was considered a waste of resources. The owners of gold mines set their own policies by controlling production and pursued their own best interests. They treated the product as any other saleable commodity, deriving profitable price advantages by creating artificial shortages, causing instability and economic decline of countries in need of gold bullion. Abandoning the gold standard allowed countries to free themselves from dependence on gold production; from long periods of rising and falling prices; from uncontrollable economic upturns or downturns; from lending gold bullion to, or borrowing gold bullion from, other countries to temporarily and artificially increase the reserves to perpetuate a system that was flawed; in short, to be free from

the oppressive bondage which the gold standard imposed. To tie a country's well-being, employment, and productivity of its labor force; the inventive spirit of its scientists to improve the quality of products and method of production; the pricing system; interest rate fluctuations; the opportunities for a better life of its future generations; in short, to brighten the lives of its citizens, to the whims and circumstances of gold mining operators is the height of economic feeble-mindedness, more akin to the ignorance of the Spanish conquistadors and their monarchs than to the liberating spirit of the American and French revolutions, which freed man from bondage and subjection to artificial and oppressive conventions. Let the hard money proponents of the gold standard, intent on freeing the national currency from government manipulations, understand that abandoning the gold standard would not only free countries from much more sinister manipulators and speculators, but also from intrigue and collusion of gold mine operators.

(10) The gold standard was ill-conceived, the work of men who had a contrived interest in its existence. It proved to be much more damaging and unwielding than beneficial, and its proponents resorted before abandonment to disguise and deception (it was a deception from the start). The proponents failed to anticipate all the destabilizing consequences since rational thinking was not their strong suit. They placed greater reliance on faith than reason. These were mostly gullible men seeking a stronghold where there was none (nor could there be any), fearful of government manipulations when they themselves engaged in reprehensible intrigues and placed more faith in the resplendent metal than in the productive capacity and resourcefulness of a people, the real wealth of a country and store of value. Their ideas would have been more fitting centuries earlier, when settlement of international trade balances posed difficult problems and the introduction of the bill of exchange proved, for those early days, a much less trustworthy instrument of account settlements, although the bills circulated throughout Europe as a restricted kind of paper currency based upon the credit of the drawers and drawees. Rational economic decisions were indeed the rare exceptions since the pure gold standard had its beginnings when goldsmiths, of all people, issued warehouse receipts to their customers for stored gold and which were later circulated as paper money with 100% gold backing. They did this purely as a matter of convenience for themselves and their customers and had no conception on what course they embarked.

CHAPTER 9, PART FIVE

NATURAL AND MAN-CAUSED DISASTERS

(1) Nature's disasters, irreverently called "Acts of God", are major violent events which interrupt what humans perceive as the orderly working of Nature. Cataclysmic convulsions, akin to human apoplectic seizures, usually cause destruction of lives and property. Unlike the Victoria or Niagara Falls, the abrupt massive cascading of water in a steep fall of several hundred feet, noisy and powerful, called by man a sight of natural beauty revealing the hidden forces of Nature, the massive rush of water following heavy rainfall sweeping away a mountain village, causing loss of lives and property, is called a natural disaster. The absence of loss of lives and property damage excludes the former from the category of natural disaster. The distinction between the above two natural phenomena can be further exemplified:

    (a) The natural waterfalls—continuous, uninterrupted, a set course, anticipated effect, long duration. No disruption of any chain of events.

    (b) The massive inundation—sudden, of limited duration, no set course, unanticipated effect, disruption of the orderly chain of events.

Summarizing the description of natural disasters, it can be stated: Uncontrollable by man when they occur, powerful disrupters of human lifestyle, sudden and of limited duration, cause property damage and loss of human and animal lives.

(2) All natural disasters, such as floods, hurricanes, tornadoes, volcanic eruptions, mudslides and rockslides, forest and grass fires ignited by natural

phenomena, earthquakes, avalanches, sandstorms, all nowadays occur in inhabited areas because population density left no desirable regions uninhabited. Their effect can be partially mitigated by man taking the necessary precautions:

(a) Anticipating the occurrence by scientific forecasting and preparing for the impact.

(b) Making the necessary structural improvements to resist, withstand, and dilute the impact of destructive forces.

(c) Pulling up stakes and moving to a location determined not to be susceptible to natural forces beyond man's control.

It is pathetic to see, year after year, population centers suffer the onslaught and ravages of the same type of natural disasters; the victims dutifully burying their dead; the wounded recuperating, and the healthy survivors, thanking Providence for sparing them, restore the damaged property and normalcy to their lives. That is, until the next natural disaster strikes, and strike it will. It is only a question of "when" not "if".

(3) (As a form of literary license, the terms "Nature", "natural order", and "natural order of things" used throughout this Chapter were intentionally animated in order to make their attributes more meaningful without imputing at the same time anything spiritual or supernatural).

As is known to us up to the present, the planet Earth is the only one where living organisms, animal and human species evolved, developed, and reproduced. From inception, Nature placed impediments to their survival, frustrated their development and inhibited their choice of habitat by making their environment hostile to their reproduction. Hundreds died so one could survive Nature's grim design; most had to undergo painful adaptations to an inhospitable habitat or relocate to a more favorable environment. The unsuccessful suffered extinction. For the rules of survival permit no second best, no handicap or weakness, no blunder or failing but favored remorselessly and without pity the strong, cunning, adaptable and successful. Modern man, homo sapiens, was thrust into such a setting, forced to choose early on the most congenial climatic conditions, e.g., crowding areas adjacent to the Mediterranean, the fertile Mesopotamia, and the Nile delta, avoiding the hazards of the North and South poles. Elementary survival instincts dictated his choices. When a natural disaster disrupted his safety and/or ability to survive, he moved elsewhere to start all over again. Since population density was not a problem, there were many other places to choose from.

Nature and its natural order of things are guided by forces which promote the struggle for self-preservation and survival of the fittest, strongest and most cunning. No place is provided for the weak, timid, and unfit in Nature's scheme of things. They are ruthlessly and without pity cast aside as unworthy of existence. The natural order is not well adapted for human life even if it differs from the order governing the lives of other animal species. The planet Earth and all its natural outbursts, which to the human eye appear as violent upheavals, are the normal working of the natural process, a permanence of the natural order of things, adapted to its own evolution and rhythm of existence. There is no design for humans who are guided by rules opposed to the natural order, no place permanently adaptable as their habitat and no special forces are at work to provide a human-friendly environment. By populating the Earth, which only grudgingly accommodates human habitation, humans assumed the role of squatters and interlopers, forced to seek habitats whose environment is conducive to their survival. In the process, as they began to form social units, they established basic rules to facilitate communal living and mitigate the natural impediments to their existence by artificially changing and adapting the environment to suit their needs. But these were acts opposed to the natural order of things, for Nature's design does not accommodate human desires but opposes anything which would place the human species in a position of superiority to the natural order controlling other animal species. With the increase in their numbers and the formation of communities grew more numerous, humans had to design rules of conduct to govern the social interplay—these were the ethical rules. Such rules were enforceable and violators punished. Like the human neocortex, which was superimposed, in time, on the reptilian complex of the brain, so moral rules were established and, in time, superimposed on ethical rules to promote harmony and compatibility among members of more complex communities, which, unlike ethical rules, could not be legislated but held forth as paragons of civilized human conduct, the proudest achievement of man in his effort to oppose the natural order. The communities ultimately developed into modern nation-States and ethical and moral rules became the foundation which bound their members into a cohesive unit to impose their guidelines of order and regularity, of consistency and harmony, of tolerance and compassion upon the natural order whose design is antithetical to them.

(4) The conclusions of the foregoing can be summarized as follows:

    (a) What humans define as "natural disasters" are consequential evolutionary natural events of Nature's own regularity and evolution. The designation of events as natural disasters has no place in the natural design.

(b) Natural evolution is the foundation of natural design. The interminable struggle for existence and self-preservation favors the survival of the fittest, the strongest, the most efficient, the most cunning and adaptable.

(c) All species, except man, are completely subject to Nature's design.

(d) Man's rules of ethics and morality, compassion and consideration, fairness and rectitude have no place in the natural design and are opposed to it.

(e) The survival of the human species, unlike that of other animals, is founded on opposition to the natural order of things.

(f) The evolution of the human species from hunter-gatherers to specialized, industrial, technological, and organized nation-States, governed by laws and a system of justice was made possible by contravening, obstructing and opposing Nature's design.

(g) The maintenance and improvement of man's standard of living depends on his success in improving and adapting Nature's hostile environment to suit his needs.

When man aids the sick and ailing, the old and weak, the unfit and flawed, he is guided by ethical and moral convictions which are opposed to the natural design. When he creates financial institutions to assist his fellowman in starting or financing a business or the purchase of a residence, his conduct is in opposition to the natural order of things. When he assists his fellowman to recoup his losses whose property and family were devastated by a natural disaster, he contravenes the natural design. When man decides to relocate to a safer habitat after suffering catastrophic losses from a natural disaster, he is following the natural order of things. He is solely guided by his instinct of self-preservation in common with other animal species—the foundation of the natural design.

(5) As the world is becoming more densely inhabited and ever more population centers are established and expanded, many in new regions, natural disasters are happening more frequently than before, leaving behind ever greater havoc and destruction. More destructions take longer to restore, are costlier in terms of financial burdens imposed and more disruptive since more properties and people are affected. The financial compensation factor is only relevant in developed countries since in undeveloped regions the lack of government assistance, insurance coverage, the poverty of most people, and the absence of an adequate infrastructure,

such as hospital facilities, emergency food distribution, rebuilding of bridges and communication networks, convert most natural disasters into calamities of staggering proportions. The victims and their countries are forced to seek relief from international charitable organizations, which, due to the frequency of similar demands placed upon them, find it increasingly difficult to render adequate assistance. Not much can be done beyond basic relief barely sufficient for survival. There is little likelihood of permanent resettlement to safer areas. The situation is substantially different in well-to-do developed countries. When natural disasters inflict property destruction and loss of lives, those who had enough foresight and could afford sufficient casualty insurance had a first line of defense. The government would assist with grants and loans to cover any deficits and do the same for the uninsured lacking the financial means to rebuild or restore the damaged property and help rehabilitate their lives. But the experience would leave lasting scars and lost earnings might never be recouped. Only rarely does one hear about victims pulling up stakes and moving to safer areas to avoid the repetition of similar ordeals. For the majority, abandoning known neighborhoods and long-time neighbors is not an option and most are too proud to have their lives subverted by "Acts of God".

(6) Because increasingly more areas of the Earth are inhabited by more people due to unlimited procreation and the sheer number of natural disasters have admittedly not decreased, it follows that future natural disasters will devastate ever more populated regions, causing more havoc, greater financial losses, and more frequent disruption of civil order. There is bound to come a time when, notwithstanding the advance warning alerts, the most efficient structural improvements, the best adaptation of the environment to suit population needs, more people will come to the realization that they have exhausted, after having sustained repeated ordeals, all the reasonable means of opposing the inevitable, pay the price of submission to the harsh realities, and follow their instinct of self-preservation: abandon the disaster-prone regions and seek a safer habitat not known for exposure to natural disasters, regardless of the impact on the standard of living. Repeat natural disasters due to floods, volcanic eruptions, earthquakes, tornadoes, and hurricanes will, in time, induce many of the victims not to expose their well-being any longer to the terror of an uncertain future; to the high cost of rebuilding; to the injuries sustained and hazards of loss of family members; the adverse effect on their business, employment, and interrupted rhythm of their

lives. They will gradually abandon the disaster-prone habitat and resettle in safer regions which, though less desirable than those relinquished, nonetheless provide one blessing: relief from known natural disasters.

(7)   The presently inhabited areas were selected by choice and therefore rank among the superior or above average. When the inevitable global warming exacts its price, the sea level is expected to rise three to four feet in the 21st century. This is calculated to inundate, and render uninhabitable, all low coastal areas, swamp many large coastal cities, villages, populated islands, and even major parts of some countries (Bangladesh, with its present population of 127 million is projected to reach 211 million by the year 2050). A third of the world's coastal wetlands and 30% of the world's croplands will disappear. Global warming, however devastating its ramifications and effects may prove to be, cannot be considered a natural disaster but man-induced, the result of human mismanagement and excess self-gratification gone berserk. It requires mention because:

(a)   The resettlement and relocation of humans will be forced, not a matter of choice.

(b)   The land areas which will disappear or made uninhabitable are calculated to be between 10 to 15% of the total world habitable regions. The relocation would amount to the equivalent of a population explosion.

(c)   At present, the oceans cover three-fifths of the Earth.

(d)   Of the remaining two-fifths, counting rivers, lakes, high mountain ranges, rocky terrain, only about 60% are fit for habitation, inclusive land used for agricultural purposes. The higher sea level will salinize and contaminate rivers and further reduce a major part of potable and irrigation water supplies. With no human reproduction controls in place and global warming shrinking the habitable land of the world, recurrent natural disasters, such as earthquakes, floods and volcanic eruptions in particular, will have increasingly adverse impact on the viability of exposed population centers whose restoration and / or relocation of inhabitants will strain the financial resources of the affected countries to the limit. Everything points to higher costs and a lower standard of living. The second best arable land will be less productive even though utilizing more fertilizers; production facilities will be built on less land with smaller factories and require costly relocation to new population centers, competing for skilled labor. Producers will have to move where the labor is and not the other way, as was the past practice. Because of land use restrictions, office buildings, apartments, and homes will be smaller than before and accommodate more users. Construction codes will be revised to better withstand potentially destructive natural forces even though the intent was to relocate as far as possible to disaster-free regions. Similarly for bridges, roads and tunnels; everything will have to be better built, more costly, and smaller. "Smaller is better, less is best" will become the new maxim of mankind.

(8) Because of future crowding of living space, unrestrained population growth will be regarded as a man-made disaster. Enforcement controls may be the way of the future instituted to maintain at least zero-population growth, although the exigencies of the times are more than likely to cause the powers that be to establish planned population reductions, a reversion to the natural design applicable to other animal species. The urgency of the times may require recognition of a selection process, however distasteful to morality, based on the survival of the fittest, most cunning, adaptable and useful. The clock will be turned back, for the scarcity of habitable space would not permit the luxury of compassion and consideration to preserve among the living the aged, chronically ill, the crippled and useless, the mentally defective and incurable. Submission to Nature's design would cause the abandonment of the principle that human survival depended upon opposition to the natural order of things. The environment would be just as hostile as before because the relocation of "refugees" directed to regions already inhabited, mostly cities, would face new problems and difficulties, such as overcrowding, marginal housing facilities, diseases caused by substandard living conditions. National boundaries would be put to the test with hordes of "refugees" ignoring political borders in their search for safer havens. The moral rules of society would be severely tested: if there is just enough nourishment and medical care available for only 80% of the population, what happens to the 20% and who decides their fate? If accommodating the 20%, particularly the newcomers to the region, means inadequate diets for the 80%, untreated diseases, and a lower standard of living just adequate for survival, civil disturbances and widespread unrest are bound to be the result. Civil authorities, unable to cope with the turmoil by applying traditional rules of maintaining order, would be forced to resort to measures bearing little resemblance to civilized conduct.

All these dark prognostications of the hardships facing mankind in the not too distant future are the critical extrapolations from the conjunction of destabilizing events appearing on the horizon. The hazards of natural disasters and the companion perils of man's creation, namely, overpopulation and global warming, are the stumbling blocks of a future which will test the limits of human endurance and ingenuity.

(9)   What would be the impact of the newly created conditions on the national economy? What adjustments must be made, at a minimum, to economies as a result of the ongoing threat of natural disasters, overpopulation and global warming, all of them current phenomena increasingly making their mark felt? If the majority of people became deeply anguished and agitated just to persevere in their existence, suffer the impact on their lives of a polluted and hostile environment, exposed to dangerous and irreversible health-hazards of food and water containing highly toxic chemicals, all principally ascribable to the pre-eminence of a free-market economy—economists will have to stop ignoring non-traditional costs imposed by Nature's design. The changed conditions foreshadow civil turmoil, instability, unknown human and societal responses; expose mankind to new stresses and strains; require new approaches in handling problems by considering global and not solely national consequences. Further, it will require changes in the legal structure which would weaken property rights; strengthen the power of eminent domain; more stringent treatment of violators to control public disturbances that are bound to increase in intensity and frequency. The finances of most countries will be severely strained in caring for resettlements, human reproduction controls, and subsidies for scientific research seeking alternate sources of cleaner energy. Foremost, and this is a top priority regardless of the costs involved, governments must assume responsibility for removing the toxicity from water and unequivocally guarantee availability of adequate supplies of safe drinking water and unequivocally guarantee to consumers access to life-sustaining food free of carcinogens, bacteria and pathogens, or else accept the certainty of retribution for failure to discharge the duties of their office. Preventing ill-health and death of citizens because of ingesting contaminated nourishment takes priority over the prerogatives of a free-market economy. Business enterprises, their executives and directors, must be held accountable worldwide for the pollution their activities cause and forced to pay for the clean-up or be closed down. This should be a cost of doing business and economists take note. Countries ruled by responsible governments and responsive to their citizens' needs of unpolluted air, unpolluted water and unpolluted food, which should be added to their duties, must cease boasting about the wonders of achieving a budget surplus while bridges

are unsafe because of age and neglect; the highway infrastructure needs upgrading and the system expanded; airports are unable to handle passenger traffic efficiently and in need of increased facilities; the sewer and water pipes are crumbling; sewer treatment plants are overloaded; city and county water drainage is inadequate; hospitals cannot handle the patient load; the public school system is in need of repair and expansion; healthcare for the elderly and uninsured must be adequately funded; many prisons are outdated. Such facilities and services must be periodically expanded, retrofitted, renovated or rebuilt. Last but not least, the air is polluted, the drinking water fails mandated safety standards, and food is becoming progressively contaminated. The remedies will require substantial government investments and constant monitoring. Even though some of the obligations are those of cities or counties, shortage of funds prevents them from shouldering their responsibilities; a return of some of the national government's surplus, if any, would enable them to do so. Given these emergency conditions, no national government can claim a budget surplus; it can only have mishandled or inadequate appropriations. Just like a man who claims to have a large checking account but does not pay his debts.

(10) Solvent individuals and responsible private businesses customarily pay their debts; it is not only an obligation but a matter of pride. Such laudable qualities expected from private ownership cannot be equated with handling of debts by national governments. If the government expenditures exceed tax receipts and imports exceed exports, the deficit is usually covered by borrowing from private and institutional investors—as a stopgap measure and not a matter of habit. This is the price of living in a civilized society. In the U.S., such borrowings are owed in the form of interest bearing Treasury bills, notes and bonds, the totality of which constitutes the national debt. In short, most of the debt is long-term, owed to U.S. and foreign (38% of the total) investors and the general practice is to sell new government securities when the old ones fall due, rotating the debt and, in effect, paying interest only to the holders. The purpose of this digression is to discuss the wisdom of paying down and retiring the national debt with an occasional budget surplus.

In the U.S., the national debt is generally regarded with a sense of embarrassment, a blemish upon the national honor and placing an undue burden on future generations. Setting aside any reference to embarrassment, blemishes, or burdens, which can be summarily dismissed as puerile gibberish, U.S. government securities are the safest of all investments, abundant in the portfolios of life insurance companies, commercial banks, investments trusts, pension funds, private investors' holdings seeking absolute safety, U.S. government agencies and the Federal Reserve Banks. To want to retire the debt with funds derived from budget surpluses instead of funding the urgent needs outlined in the preceding paragraph is not only a sign of insensitivity bordering on cynicism but a display of ignorance of the function government securities perform. If the national debt were fully retired and budget surpluses could no longer be used to temporarily and partially pay down the debt, what investment policy would the government pursue? Invest in commercial bonds, stock market, commercial buildings or Peruvian railroads? How could monetary policy control sudden large increases in the money supply derived from debt retirement and avoid an inflationary spiral? The Federal Open-Market Committee, an adjunct of the Federal Reserve System, sets monetary policy by purchasing and selling government securities, thereby attempting to control the money supply; this activity is one of its main tools. How would life insurance companies and pension funds satisfy their need for safe investments? The answer is obvious: U.S. government securities are the safest, gilt-edged, and most sought-after investment of most financial and related institutions throughout the world which seek highest grade securities. As such, they are irreplaceable and nothing so far devised by financial experts could take their place. The talk about the efficacy of debt retirement is blind superpatriotism, a reversion to discredited mercantilism, totally ignoring investment requirements of major financial institutions.

(11) Throughout the world, major natural disasters happen so frequently that they seem to be always in the news. Disasters occur in developed and developing countries since Nature recognizes no political boundaries and losses of property and lives are equally unsparing. The disruption of lives of victims is equally devastating, except that aid, both financial and material, is more substantial and more speedily available in developed countries. It is also more costly. Frequently we read of casualty insurance companies sustaining huge losses and forced to cease operations due to the number of claims filed. Even though compensated by insurance, the economic impact is considerable and disruption of lives inestimable. Typically, production facilities, employment, supply of utilities, living quarters, food distribution, medical care, school facilities, and transportation infrastructure in the affected region are in disarray. A large inflow of funds from insurance companies, government aid and loans, and victims'

own resources are needed to restore normalcy. The flip side of the havoc created is the ensuing feverish restoration activity, bringing a period of prosperity, if one dare call it that, to the community. The sudden flurry of various building trades, the need for large supplies of building materials and building contractors, architects and engineers, restoration personnel all point to a period of intense profitable activity usually associated with prosperous times, albeit of short duration. One cannot help noticing a profound irony in all this, namely, some people profiting from the desolation of others as if natural disasters in which properties were leveled and lives lost were not all bad but had a compensating beneficial side. Perhaps Nature is sending man a taunting message: You have misused and squandered the Earth's gifts, polluted the ecosystem, opposed the natural order by disregarding population controls—vacate disaster-prone regions and confine your habitat to regions not vulnerable to natural disasters. Man has continued to ignore Nature's seeming admonition, a conclusion reached by any observer cataloguing natural disasters, and keeps profiting from his neighbor's suffering. The more destruction natural disasters cause, the more reconstruction industries and all the related trades profit from their neighbors' losses. Funds spent on rehabilitation stimulate enhanced economic activities in the same way as funds spent on new construction, or funds spent on replacing stolen property, an old machine, a sunken ship. Wealth is created for the fortunate few who owe their success to the caprice of fate. In developing countries, dependent on international support and individual donations, the end-result is the same. Goods and supplies are donated or paid for with donated funds; local labor paid with donated funds increases activities and stimulates the economy.

(12) Natural disasters are sudden manifestations of natural forces of limited duration which are injurious to man's well-being and destructive to property. Such natural forces are unaffected by man's activities, i.e., he plays no part in their occurrence. If man were absent from the scene, such phenomena would not be called disasters. If an earthquake were to occur in an uninhabited region, such as certain areas of the Arctic Circle, the event would not qualify as a disaster unless the repercussions affected humans. However, man by just living, breathing, and following his self-preservation instincts is the cause of certain disasters which, by reason of their magnitude and long duration, by far exceed any harm caused by natural forces. Whereas the elemental natural forces which manifest Nature's continuous revitalization and changing process are injurious to

man only (and certain animal species) if he happens to be in harm's way, man-caused disasters impair not only Nature's design but man wherever located. Global warming, degradation of the ecosystem, and population explosion are the most serious potential man-caused disasters, damaging not only the natural order but could bring about, if unimpeded, the extinction of homo sapiens. Man seems determined to follow a course that steers him to his inevitable doom, paying only feeble lip service to obvious signs of warning. He cannot comprehend that the planet Earth was not somehow designed for man exclusively, that it is not his oyster to exploit, abuse, and corrupt without suffering the consequences of his misdeeds. The cause of this mischief is his insatiable greed and drive for unlimited growth, believing in the maxim "more is better and most is best", which quest led him far beyond satisfying his needs and providing for his comforts in pursuit of self-preservation.

(13) Elected government leaders and legislators lack the competence to evaluate the gravity of man's vulnerability in the gathering storm. But even if competent to mitigate the increasing abuse of the Earth's resources, they would eventually incur the wrath and opposition of the business establishment, who, disposing of sufficient financial power, would rebuff imposition of restrictive tolerance levels and challenges to their self-promotion. The business community, which treats such warnings as the work of misguided agitators, would demand its government persevere in political correctness and be supportive of its strategy of free and expanding markets, greater profits, unfettered corporate colonialism, exploitation of global interests, and oppose the setting of acceptable limits of toxic chemicals in food and water. In case of natural disasters, the victims must retain the option to relocate since human nature argues against forced resettlement; such an approach would let politicians off the hook for not being forceful enough in deciding what is best for the people. Nothing will avail them, however, when confronting man-made disasters. Apart from failure to achieve an ecologically sustainable equilibrium and lack of success in initiating self-imposed procreation restraints, environmental toxicity, toxicity of drinking water, and the presence of highly toxic chemicals in food pose an ever growing peril to the physical and mental health of mankind. The responsible governments, their legislators and officials, who are also consumers, will pay a steep price for not devoting the required attention and for not being forceful enough in restraining commercial enterprises from polluting the nourishment, for failure to adequately inspect food processing plants, and lack of explicit

expert warnings to consumers about the hazards of ingesting polluted municipal water and polluted victuals purchased from approved establishments. Medical experts predict that consumers, and this also includes most of the producers and vendors who are also consumers, will inevitably suffer from various degrees of brain-damage, brain disorders, emotional afflictions, and toxic hepatitis due to ingesting food contaminated by toxic waste. It is hard to envisage the ordeal and opprobrium the complicit governments would have to endure if the majority of the populace suffered from brain-damage, incapable of understanding and following laws meant to keep civil order, electing their brain-damaged fellowmen to public office, and whose military commanders suffered from brain disorders. The same government authorities, whose negligence and dereliction of duty failed to maintain elementary health standards by showing explicit servile deference to business interests, would now have to assume the burden of governing and passing judgment on recalcitrant and belligerent brain defective people, for whose diminished capacity they must accept full responsibility and censure.

(14) Natural disasters are the embodiment of natural design. Man-caused disasters are the antithesis of natural design. Man's defiance of the natural order enabled him to advance far beyond the bleak conditions of generations ago, when there was little to differentiate his existence from that of animals. With the progressive betterment of his lifestyle, achieved in spite of many setbacks degrading his conduct below the level of wild beasts, culminating in the achievement of a standard of living far beyond the fanciest imagination of a mere few generations ago. Man truly believed he was at the point of subjugating Nature to serve his needs and comforts, self-assured the conquest was permanent. The decisive turning point was reached when the maintenance of his ever more lavish lifestyle adversely affected the ecosystem and biosphere to a degree that natural recuperative and restorative powers were unable to prevent permanent damage and degradation. Unmindful of the warning signals, man continued unperturbed on his course of abusing the natural process, until the onset of the inevitable backlash has begun to damage his physical health and sanity. From that moment on, man will have to devote a major part of his energies and ingenuity to discover remedies to battle newly generated diseases, including the toxic effect on his mind and body. Combating the newly man-created adverse environmental conditions of global warming will present man with only two choices:

(a) Change the lifestyle and discard ecosystem and biosphere pollutants, or discover clean replacements for the polluting substances. The former would diminish and reverse the benefits of many recent technological advances.

(b) Refuse to modify the lifestyle and procrastinate until the natural order forces the change upon him.

As far as major adjustments to economics are concerned, the foregoing discussion in this Chapter would lead, at a minimum, to these conclusions:

- Achievement of zero-population growth is a must and a further reduction to sustainable levels a top priority.
- Unlimited economic expansion will be a luxury of the past since aggregate demand will remain stable.
- There will be no overall GDP growth and the new era of limits will have arrived.
- Habitable land will be most sought after due to decreased availability. The cost of land and rents will command the highest price increases.
- Free-markets will be restricted and regulations mandated to control pollution as a result of production and to control contamination of products.
- Corporate globalization will have achieved its zenith and future production activities will target the home base.
- Because of constant population shifts, price competition would not be an effective tool of distribution.
- Emission trading, an obscene idea of incorrigible polluters, would not be acceptable.
- Medical research in genetic engineering and biotechnology will be the most financially rewarding enterprise.
- Business enterprises will be responsible for all pollution clean-up or be shut down. The clean-up cost would be part of production costs.
- Natural disasters will cause regional business interruptions. An accounting reserve should be maintained for such contingencies and treated as a cost of doing business.
- It will be more demanding for the average man just to satisfy primary needs.
- The limited availability of land and irrigation water for agricultural purposes will restrict the availability of food supplies; there are unlikely to be any food surpluses.

The future portends an era of limits. Natural and man-caused disasters will, of necessity, absorb more of man's attention and direct his energies toward alleviating their consequences. He would do poorly if he tried to mitigate the effects of natural disasters—there is only one option open. As far as man-caused disasters are concerned, he could succeed in damage control, but the indications point to no hopeful signs. We hear economists speak of pollution controls which must balance incremental benefits and costs to maximize value to consumers. In other words, we should look at costs and benefits in developing pollution regulations. There is no problem figuring the costs, but the benefits? How does one value the health benefits to society of less lung cancer, less emphysema, less brain disorder? Less pain and suffering? Mankind assuredly faces a desolate and gloomy future if we left it up to economists to recommend cost / benefit guidelines. At recently held conventions of most of the world's countries, assembled to agree on steps to counteract global warming and ecosystem degradation, the major developed countries displayed a mastery in obfuscating and procrastinating tactics—no doubt accommodating the wishes of their powerful industrial corporate interests. This left little hope for the success of the enterprise. There are no indications which would point to hopeful signs.

CHAPTER 9, PART SIX

THE DARK SIDE
OF COMPETITION

(1) Nature's design for organisms is the perpetual struggle for existence, the maintenance and prolongation of life, and the pursuit of activities conducive to that end. The struggle for existence involves differences in strength, skills, and the influence of shortages of nourishment and space. It is the existence of shortages that makes strength and skill meaningful in the effort to survive. The process which gives expression to that effort is called competition. Despite all the seeming abundance of resources that support life and space, shortages come about by the natural tendency of organisms to procreate in excess of available resources to sustain life and an abundance of space. Shortages are the principal means which restore some semblance of equilibrium between the number of organisms of a species and available resources and space. But the process never restores a perfect balance since that would make shortages and competition meaningless; without them, Nature's design for the perpetual struggle for existence of the species would be nullified. The struggle for existence among organisms of the same species, or between different species, inevitably improves the faculties of survivors and enfeebles those of losers who, cut off from ample resources, face a slow death or endure debilitating hardships inhabiting marginal areas. All species, including human, respond naturally to circumstances that create shortages; humans not only respond robustly, but driven by the quest for economic gain create conditions of artificial shortages, thereby intensifying competition.

221

They are the only species which would contrive make-believe shortages to intensify competition and also artificially prolong it by forming associations to further their continuity.

(2) As an artificial prop to sharpen strength and skills in order to improve the ability to compete without incurring finality for the losers, man invented the art of sport, a contest subject to rules and limited duration to test the proficiency of contestants and provide for a winner and loser to be declared at the end of the contest, unless the result is a draw. The contest of sports has the advantage in that it can be repeated as often as desired with the same contestants alternating as winners or losers and no finality attaches to the outcome. It can be said that sports are man's attempt to camouflage Nature's oppressive struggle for existence, which offends his sense of fairness and morality. It is a test and competition in which the concept of shortages is reflected in the differences in strength and skills, often subject to extensive rules to add complexity to man's simulation of his version of the natural design. But man cannot improve upon Nature's design and must accept the struggle for existence and the competition involved in that contest as applicable to all species.

(3) As a member of a community, man competes to persevere in existence; the competition is the more intense the more primary needs absorb such effort. A hermit, for example, who lives alone in the wilderness, competes with natural forces; he must maintain an upper hand or else natural forces would overwhelm him. When there are no shortages (real or artificial), i.e., resources and space are abundant, there can be no competition. For competition to take place there must be more demand than availability so that some demand would not be satisfied. This enables the producer, seller or supplier, to increase prices sufficiently to reduce demand just enough to exceed supplies in order to retain the economic advantage of competition among consumers. If there are two or more sellers and the aggregate supplies exceed demand, competition among sellers would reduce prices to levels just sufficient for supplies to exceed demand and shift the competition to suppliers. For competition to exist, there must either be more demand than supplies, or more supplies than demand, a shortage of supplies in the former and a shortage of demand in the latter. These conditions do not apply to fire sales, or where spoilage is a factor, or the desire of sellers to dispose of all the inventory to make room for new merchandise. Prices would have to be lowered sufficiently to dispose of all goods.

Profit maximization is the avowed aim of every business. The results of such efforts are the gaining of a competitive advantage and secure a larger share of the market. To be a successful competitor, prices being equal, a business must offer more attractive benefits than rivals, such as place utility (as in neighborhood stores), credit terms, courtesy to customers, free delivery, convenient parking, and, if possible, noticeable product differentiation which would make its product more desirable. The more profitable the business operation, the more benefits can be offered to customers above those put forward by less successful competitors and point with pride to have provided a better service to customers. These are the criteria of a well-ordered business. The larger enterprises can also take advantage of economies of scale, providing a larger output at lower unit costs; greater division of labor; more specialized equipment and less disruption to production caused by the breakdown of any piece of equipment. All these point to a more favorable competitive advantage and larger profits.

(4) Profit maximization often has a dark side. Businesses falling behind in the contest and lacking scruples will resort to underhanded means, if necessary, to keep their head above water. They engage in unfair competition, employing practices their rivals are unwilling to utilize—the criteria of losers. The quality of the product may be cheapened, the size made ever so slightly smaller to escape notice, employees are required to work long hours and short changed on overtime pay, health and safety standards are violated. In short, socially undesirable practices are followed to gain an unfair competitive edge. They take the final step and go global, moving production facilities to an undeveloped country lacking pollution and labor regulations, employing local workers and child labor at a fraction of the home base pay, assured from experience that consumers, as a rule, care little about the reasons behind lower prices. If these measures do not pay off, they might opt for cutthroat competition by successively reducing prices and engaging in a form of price-war. If it continues long enough, they and many other reluctant participants would be forced out of business. There is less cutthroat competition during prosperous times than during periods of economic downturn.

Profit maximization can take other forms. The financially stronger enterprise could gain a larger share of the market by acquiring competing businesses or merge with them, employ vertical integration with enterprises in various stages of production, engage in hostile takeovers or leveraged buyouts, agree with competitors on production quotas and minimum prices, induce the government to grant subsidies or impose tariffs on imports. Ownership of patent rights, trade-names, or franchises give owners a singular competitive advantage. They could participate in consensual sharing of the market, form trade associations to minimize competition, or take part in gentlemen's agreements to stifle competition. It is an old aphorism that businesses which are in the forefront of promoting the efficacy of competition seek protection when the contest begins to hurt. Competition on a "level playing field" is a daydream of free-traders—it is seldom a contest of equals facing similar obstacles and objectives. The larger enterprises enjoy a decided advantage.

(5) Competition often involves foreign markets. Export-oriented business firms, if they are large enough to command the required attention, receive export-subsidies from their government if it has a stake in encouraging exports, either in promoting trade and employment or needing to increase its foreign currency reserves to pay for imports. Another method, underhanded but effective, utilized by a government of an export-oriented economy or a government desirous of giving exporters an artificial competitive edge, is to devalue its currency vis-à-vis foreign competitors. The exporter can maintain its profit margin and effectively undersell exports in foreign countries, or increase the price and improve the products sufficiently to disrupt the "level playing field". This method also protects domestic producers or traders against competing foreign imports by making the latter more expensive and forces importers to reduce the profit margin to stay competitive. A country dependent on imports of raw materials for its production plants and exports finished goods would want to raise the value of its currency artificially in the foreign exchange markets and derive a price advantage of cheaper imports and rely on the efficiency of domestic producers to offset the price handicap of exports. But most other countries could effectively countermand the currency manipulations by engaging in their own offsetting maneuvers. The result would be instability in foreign exchange markets, made to order for international currency speculators, for such currencies would necessarily fluctuate due to the export-import variations. Rates of exchange of foreign currencies are never stable but freely fluctuate with supplies and demand like any other commodity even without manipulative interference, based upon surpluses or deficits in current-account balances among countries. In the final analysis, the exchange rate of all currencies should be based upon their respective constant purchasing power of a fixed basket of commodities; this is the only true comparative measure of a currency value.

(6)   The drive of the typical business enterprise for constant growth and a greater share of the market, improved production efficiencies, increased labor productivity, and larger annual returns to stockholders, i.e., the quest for unceasing profit maximization as the only barometer of success in a world of hostile takeovers, failed competitors, automation of production, employee layoffs, and globalization to achieve further cost-savings—if carried to its logical conclusion—could well doom the free-market capitalist system. Inventory build-ups, regardless of purpose, add nothing to economic stability; the structurally unemployed and the underemployed do not make desirable customers; the gnawing poverty stalking over 50% of the world's population (3 billion people live on $2.00 per day, or less) without hope of change for the better cannot be conducive to demand stimulation. Faced with such scaled down world-wide consumer spending, business enterprises would do well just to hold their own, be profitable enough to return satisfactory and steady returns to investors without encouraging the expectations of constant annual revenue growth, and paying their employees a fair living wage. It is not the business of business to stimulate repeat exuberant expectations of stock market traders and hucksters (If they are so smart, why aren't they rich?) and be judged primarily by the steadily escalating profits, no matter how achieved and no matter how many of their lesser equals were trampled in the process. The real economy, the aggregate result of the down-to-earth hustle of small and medium-size hard working and knowledge-able entrepreneurs, who are in it for the long haul and not just for the stock options as a reward for short-term results—is not the deceptive stock market economy driven by slick and captious casino gamblers encouraged by hired perennial optimists who, with their benighted intuition, judge the soundness of an economy by the profit targets of listed companies. The criterion being whether they would meet the predicted earning targets or just routinely repeat prior year's results. Stock market traders, who brandish their self-serving limited outlook as central to the economy, are responsible for the creation of bubble economies in which manipulated rising stock prices and the paper profits they generate—totally divorced from the merits attributable to long-term stability and adequate capitalization of a company—give investors the feeling of wealth. Gloom and despair drift through the stock market if too many listed companies fail to meet the projected earning target (by reason of faulty forecasts or management intrigue) and the preferred explanation of the gurus for their characteristic misjudgment is the "general weakness

of the economy". The domino effect of such sophistry could even bring about a recession. But there is no correlation between some missed earning targets and the health of an economy. The stock market traders are the ones who profit from exaggerated expectations of projected earnings; they manage to boost sales of such touted shares and earn huge commissions in recommending them to investors. But the stock market's ups and downs are not a reflection of the economy. The decision of large investors (financial institutions and mutual funds) to liquidate their position or take advantage of bargain purchases, causing dramatic swings in the market averages, have a lot to with the whims of institutional traders but nothing with the health of the economy. The listed companies' managers are not alarmed if the earnings are less than predicted or less than the year before; they could bring to mind any number of reasons that make sense—the operations could undergo a number of adjustments, some of them with predictable results, others just failed to meet expectations. The exaggerated influence of large traders is reason enough by itself to destabilize stock markets, aggravate the trend and abet the herd instinct, placing markets in an unreal world of fairy tale totally disconnected from main street, the real productive and industrious work performed daily by other segments of the economy. Since the market value of a company's listed shares depends on existing and future expectation of higher earnings, which is also the confidence index of stockholders, it follows that financially sound companies following a steady course and conservative practices are of no interest to traders and speculators. Financial discipline is frowned upon as not forward-moving; accommodating management is expected to diversify (buying businesses they know nothing about) by seeking acquisitions, mergers and the inevitable leveraged buyouts, all exciting but perilous steps seldom conducive to efficiency or profit maximization, but always requiring burdensome debts and possibly costly divestitures.

The economic malaise caused by overzealous pursuits of ever greater earnings, growth without limits, the superficial monetary worth which pervades the thinking of stock market pundits cannot be localized but spreads to economies worldwide due to globalization, rapid unmolested movement of capital, and most importantly, due to the almost instantaneous dissemination of information. There are great cultural differences among the various countries traceable to historical and religious dissimilar backgrounds, but there is total unanimity, for the present, on the subject of free-market and free enterprise. What took most developed coun-

tries over 200 years to fine-tune and experience was adopted by the interacting developing countries in a matter of a few years—a time far too
short to establish a strong middle class, a vital stabilizer to help navigate
the economy in troubled waters. As long as business is profitable,
investors and producing countries benefit from the inflow of capital.
Absent a middle class, most of the local income flows to the minority
ruling elite and the nouveau riche; factory workers just earn base subsistence wages. But should problems develop, the fall could be painful and
rapid. The global economy is, by its nature, at great risk because of the
domino effect among interlinked financial markets, aggravating economic conditions worldwide owing to the free and swift movement of
investment capital that would cause a global slowdown by exporting economic crises. Liquidation of foreign holdings, rising unemployment, and
falling output result from overreacting and nervous investors, duped by
the bubble economies created by pivotal stock markets (New York,
London, Tokyo, Frankfurt) in search of unlimited growth and ever
greater earning targets.

(7) Economists invented the concept "perfect competition", which has three
stated characteristics:

(a) there are many sellers

(b) they sell the same product

(c) there is free entry into the industry

It is generally admitted that perfect competition does not exist in the
business world but serves well as a model against which actual competition can be measured. It requires many sellers so that no one seller's
increase in supply, or pulling out of the market, would affect prices. It is
assumed they sell the same product, although in a competitive industry it
is unlikely that the product would be identical in all respects. Sellers are
free to enter or leave the industry and their action would not affect prices.
One cannot critique the model since the assumptions are hypothetical
and admitted as such. It is necessary to mention three other characteristics essential to the concept but not included above:

(a) *Shortages*

For competition to exist there must be an imbalance between
demand and supplies. Either there are too few consumers and too
many suppliers or too few suppliers and too many consumers. Competition does not have a limited duration unless a theoretical price
equilibrium is achieved. If that state is attained and at that price
quantity demanded equals quantity supplied, competition ceases.

But prior to the state of equilibrium, competition due to shortages existed. If there is an increase in supply, the equilibrium price will decline due to a shortage of demand. If there is a decrease in supply, the equilibrium price will rise due to a surplus of demand. The supplier of goods or services for which there is no substitute is said to have a monopoly—there is competition and a shortage if demand exceeds supplies, but supplies would never exceed demand since the monopoly-supplier would reduce the quantity offered and maintain an artificial shortage to achieve the desired price level. Product differentiation, where a consumer prefers the product of one supplier over that of another even though prices are the same, creates a condition which nullifies competition.

(b) *Informed consumers*

For competition to be effective, consumers must have information about the product and supplier to form an intelligent judgment. They must recognize product differentiation, if it exists, and know the reputation of the supplier—whether the supplier can deliver the quantity desired and is willing to warrant the product for an acceptable period, whether the price of the product is expected to rise or fall, whether an improved product would make the present one obsolete in the near future, whether there is price competition among suppliers and which one is willing to offer discounts. The consumer should be informed about the various locations of suppliers and whether transportation or freight charges would be cost-effective. But it is difficult to find a market in which complete consumer information exists. More often than not, consumers possess a patchwork of information gathered from advertising media or word-of-mouth and, as a rule, cannot be bothered with too many details.

(c) *Category of consumers*

Besides product differentiation there is also consumer differentiation, i.e., consumers with different cultural, financial, educational, marital and age backgrounds. A particular product and supplier will have a different appeal and attraction to a varied category of consumers. Customer habits and loyalty, regardless of price differences, play an important part in consumer demand. Some advertisers and suppliers appeal strongly to consumer pride, arrogance, even snobbishness, fully aware that price is of no particular importance to them. On the contrary, higher prices for the same product stimulate more demand as validating expensive tastes and selective consumerism, and such customers use this means to exhibit contempt for price-competition as an activity beneath their dignity. Suppliers selling necessities and luxury items will maintain a price-flexibility for each category. Consumer demand to satisfy primary needs will seek sources where competition is the most intense and the pricing most flexible. The concept of perfect competition, therefore, does not depend only on many sellers who sell the same product and have unobstructed entry into the industry, but also on the category of consumers who are in the market for a specific product and possibly seek a particular supplier, regardless of price, known to them and with whom they developed a satisfactory business relationship in the past.

(8) Conceived in the totality of its components which make business activities, in general, a world of ups and downs, of successful enterprises and failures, allowing reasonable time for each ascent and descent to develop its own course by giving due regard to the human element which permeates the scene, it can be stated that economic stability is an oxymoron. Granted that material self-interest is the spark that drives humanity, economic conditions are inherently unstable due to the effect of unceasing competition of conflicting human interests. Man guided by material self-interest makes factionalism possible, which enables the contending segments of the economy to place no limits on the effort to gain the upper hand in realizing the desired ends. All competition in the commercial world is based upon such conflict and promotes a morality that no attention need be paid to the discomfort or misfortune inflicted on the loser, who is expected to play by the rules and accept the loss or disadvantage gracefully. Humans adept in such hard-nosed conduct are destined to gain success over their rivals. They should be well aware that for each success gained, they may themselves fall victim to one who is more adept in not playing by the rules, someone more skilled in using underhanded means, who in turn can ultimately expect the same fate.

Fair competition means playing by the rules. Unfair competition involves taking advantage of a rival's trust; a form of cheating as in head-start, i.e., gaining an advantage by some underhanded means, plain lying or misinformation, cynical contempt for the truth, duplicity, or hoax. Competition is not unfair if one party outsmarts the other by cunning, better information or preparation, harder effort, better strategy and timing.

(9) The classical economists, who preached the efficacy of a total and unhindered free-market without regulatory interference, had no idea what harm could be inflicted on unsuspecting consumers by selling unsafe

food products; the irreparable damage caused to children's brains by exposing them to consumption of food containing traces of PCB and mercury. The blame can be laid squarely at the doorstep of intense competition and the reluctance of competitors to expend sufficient funds and time on research and supervision of quality control for fear of falling behind in the contest for an ever bigger share of the market. Producers who are guilty of such corruption cannot claim ignorance but an execrable quality of turning a blind eye to the interest of consumers and pursuing insatiable financial self-seeking—they hope and pray their misdeeds will go undetected. Pesticides used in farming are implicated in the increased incidence of leukemia and lymphoma, as well as cancers of the brain, breast, testes and ovaries. 71 different ingredients in pesticide cause cancer in humans and animals. Such pesticides are used in the production of major crops, including apples, tomatoes, potatoes, grapes, peaches, pears and spinach, to name some of the best known fruits and vegetables. If one eats chickens containing antibiotic resistant E. coli, the resultant sickness may not be helped with antibiotics. Nuclear irradiation stations are used ever more frequently to kill the bugs in ground meat—a pound of hamburger may receive the equivalent of millions of chest X-rays. Suppliers who sell these products and in the process engage in intensive competition resist any form of regulation as intrusive interference. As stated before, it is known to some suppliers that their food is contaminated and harmful to consumers. Who are these people? They lead normal lives, have families and children, live in well-kept homes, are educated, most of them attend religious services. But the intense competition, the pursuit of material self-interest without limits blinds them to their actions and immunizes their feelings to the terrible wrongs, nay crimes, which are committed in the name of maintaining profitable operations. What about tobacco growers and cigarette manufacturers? Do they need more information and studies to prove that the use of their product causes premature death to millions of users? Their products have never been anything but harmful to humans despite many efforts to modify the contents and cynically mislead the public, causing three million people to die yearly worldwide from tobacco-induced illnesses. They too have families and are well educated, yet their conduct is criminal. They too are engaged in intense competition without limits, plain lying and misinformation, contempt for the truth, participants in the most perverse hoax. All their misdeeds are committed in pursuit to further their material self-interest in the name of profitable operations. This is the sort of mind set these men share with common criminals, a disgrace to the free enterprise system, which was brought about to deliver the best-priced and most wholesome product to the consumer as a result of intense competition among producers. If the punishment meant certain long-term imprisonment for the culprits instead of a mere fine, these outrages against humanity would cease. The airline transportation system, where safety is the pride and chief aim of the various carriers, provides service to millions of trusting customers who board the planes in the belief that the best pilots, the most competent mechanics and maintenance personnel money can buy assure their safe passage. But the profit margin is squeezed to its narrowest by cutthroat competition, which forces airline companies to cut corners on passenger safety and service, require long pilot flying-time, which is in itself a hazard, and tolerate slack supervision of ground mechanics. Once again, guided by material self-interest and experiencing intense competition, the self-preservation instinct pushes all knowledge of risks, acts of outright negligence and deceitful attitudes into the background so that the enterprise can stay afloat. What kind of men manage steel, chemical, electrical, and other manufactures who avert their eyes to the toxic waste they dump into rivers, lakes or oceans, rather than spend the necessary funds on clean-up, a cost which would reduce their profit margin and make them less competitive? They and their ilk are the product of a tenacious breed of scheming corporate executives, whose strength lies in fooling the public and taking advantage of the public's ignorance. These are the costs their more efficient and principled competitors manage to absorb. Some of the unsafe automobile and accessories producers, operators of pollution-causing oil refineries, and many other fabricators of contaminated products consistently denounce any regulatory intervention as unwarranted interference with the private sector. They are, however, guilty of illegal conduct and should be treated as outcasts by the business community, for they give free enterprise a bad name and expose the dark side of competition.

(10) In a free economy, production and consumption are controlled through the price mechanism. Companies which produce in excess of requirements will cut back on production to reduce surplus inventories so as to maintain price stability. Those that find that inventories are below requirements will increase production to restore some balance between supplies and demand. All this is performed routinely and in the ordinary course of business. There is a correlation between unit costs and desired

profit margins as limited by industry practices and competition. Some-times competition is so intense that drastic reduction in price is called for with the producer seeking to recover variable costs only. These are mostly producers of brand name products who invested sizeable capital in development and advertising and who built a reputation for honorable business dealings. Similarly, most wholesalers and retailers value the relationship and trust built with their clientele as an irreplaceable com-modity to be maintained at all costs. To illustrate, during heat waves and floods, window air-conditioning units, electrical fans, and bottled water are soon sold out due to sudden heavy demand. No well-established pro-ducer or dealer would raise prices because of potential demand-pull inflationary price pressures. The last unit would sell at the same price as the first. No customer price gouging will occur even though abnormal conditions present an abundance of opportunities. The producers and sellers incurred no increased costs of their product, did not require price increases to maintain their profit margin and could not, in good con-science, take advantage of the temporary predicament of others by increasing prices of products in short supply because of an emergency. The existence of competition as a requisite for the effective operation of the law of supply and demand is not applicable in the above cited case. If just prior to the above emergency one-half of the supplies were destroyed by fire and the excess demand consequently greater (disre-garding losses covered by insurance), wholesalers and retailers did not incur any cost increases and therefore will not be forced to raise prices—as to them the situation is the same as if they sold only one-half of the inventory. But the producer does not fare as well. By disposing of only one-half of the budgeted production, the failure to recover all of the fixed and variable costs would force him to raise prices, provided they are still competitive and the share of the market is not significant.

The zeal for profit maximization and opportunity to take advantage of the above producer's predicament would permit competitors to raise prices and thus reap windfall profits. Such an exploitation of an unearned advantage may seem clever for the short run, but the benefits are soon dissipated by absorption into the eventual pricing system. Greater than customary profit margins would cause labor to demand higher wages, attract new competition (both competent and incompetent) adversely affecting prices, incur customer ill will for engaging in unwarranted prof-iteering, and finally, destabilize the market for the product. Public oppro-brium can be justly resisted if price increases are caused by higher costs.

But the public and business community will view price gouging and crass profiteering as a blemish on the free enterprise system, as unrestrained self-seeking, immodest greed, woebegone regression to the dark past of rapacious feuds when public interest was damned. How is one to explain, let alone justify, the general price increase of grapefruits or oranges because a regional frost destroyed the crops without affecting other growers? Pure opportunism and greed. Why do gasoline refineries routinely raise the price of existing inventories the moment an increase in the price of oil is announced by oil producers? Future purchases of oil are affected, but not existing contracts, which are completed under the old price. Yet prices are increased for all existing inventories for oil supplied by previously negotiated contracts. Pure opportunism and greed. Inventories which have to be replaced at higher costs in the future would justify future price increases. When there are no increases in oil prices, why do gasoline prices increase in summer and heating oil in winter, both blamed on tight supplies and distribution problems? These are mostly artificial contrivances and pure deceptions. The raw material and production costs have not changed unless regulations mandate some expensive seasonal additives to gasoline products, in which case the problem is regional and seasonal—an event a smart producer should be able to anticipate and average his costs. Sales are usually brisk, do not require more effort and turnover is faster. Is it credible that experienced operators are unable to forecast increased seasonal consumption occurring with routine regularity each year, and provide for such eventualities? A more likely explanation is that supplies are deliberately kept off the market and all producers, despite competition, share in the windfall with prices set at the level charged by the least efficient and most expensive producer. For if the situation were reversed and oil prices fall, the refineries seldom lower their prices until all the higher-priced oil is sold. No one on the outside is sufficiently well-informed to see through these sharp practices. There are shortages but no competition to affect prices. Who are these sharpies who catch the consumers off guard, cause market turmoil and financial hardship to gasoline users and homeowners dependent on heating oil to make it through the winter? They and their fellow price gougers ill-use the economic freedom appropriate for principled entrepreneurs and who, for the sake of an extra income gained by duplicitous practices, show an insensitivity for the public bordering on contempt. Many other similar disreputable practices could be cited, but the above examples suffice to make the point: The world is getting smaller and such abuses more notorious. Sooner or later, they will generate a hostile reaction by the deceived. The principled entrepreneurs who care enough to preserve the free enterprise system had better start policing their own before the reprobates impair public tolerance beyond repair.

CHAPTER 10

THE PROBLEMS OF
A GLOBAL ECONOMY

(1) Imperialism is the acquisition by forceful means of regions belonging to other political entities by States which have the wherewithal to accomplish such objectives, imposing their rule by force and engaging in economic exploitation. Most justified such acquisitions by declaring that the conquered profited by sharing in the advantages civilization had to offer. But the conquest itself controverted the spurious benefits of civilization, for to the conquered the meaning was not the same. To them it signified a condition of political and economic suppression, privation and hardship, poverty, of feeling exploited—they suffered the abuse by their more developed conquerors. Such brazen military conquests are no longer politically correct, no longer acceptable by the community of nations. Its crude form has been replaced by a more polished process accomplishing the same purpose without flagrantly offending the sensibilities of other developed nations. Imperialism has been driven by the quest for economic exploitation, modified by the new industrialism of the 19th century focusing on ample sources of raw materials for their factories and augment the food supply for their growing population. The leading industrial nations manufactured products for which the market was highly profitable, resulting in great accumulation of surplus capital. This capital in the hands of manufacturing corporations (replaced later by major international banks and investment enterprises) exerted great pressure to locate new investment opportunities in foreign countries, as there

were only limited opportunities for expansion in the domestic economy. The wealthy corporations became, in time, powerful enough to influence the foreign policy of their governments in the direction of not only securing foreign markets but also enabling the transfer of production facilities to foreign countries and pass legislation to accommodate such investments.

(2)   All policies of imperialism have been conducted for economic gain from the beginning of recorded history. At first, it was for outright plunder, tribute and slaves. When technological means began to improve, it was the coordinated search of foreign markets for excess domestic products which led to the growing and systematic development of international trade. As Europe grew in wealth, the First Crusade (1096–1099) opened new commercial communications with Muslims in the Near East, although the stated intention of the Crusades was a murderous religious military conquest. The ruling and rich classes began to manifest the newly gained elevated status by eating and dressing in a different way from the rest of the poorer population. Spices, exotic fruits, ivory, and silk were the products increasingly in demand and initially responsible for the opening of the lucrative trade in the Mediterranean. The desire for conspicuous consumption opened new markets for trading and exchange of products, exploited initially in an organized manner by the clever Venetians, the most capable and resourceful merchants of their day. Not being exceptions to the rule, their original peaceful trading was supplemented by rapacious conquests and exploitation of conquered territories in search of more riches and markets, until they too fell victims (1797) to a more resourceful military imperialist, Napoleon Bonaparte. Modern European colonialism began about the early 16th century following the discovery of a sea route around the southern tip of Africa (1488) and the discovery of America (1492). European countries which possessed the requisite sea power (England, Spain, Portugal and the Netherlands) established colonies throughout the world by military conquest and population settlements; these colonies were politically oppressed and economically exploited—the trade in commodities was mostly one-way. As the colonial settlements became more populous, it became counterproductive to continue their subjugation; the reins had to be loosened and enough freedom granted to retain the economic and political ties to the home country. By the 20th century, most of the former colonies gained complete political independence and began to participate, on their own, in the free enterprise and competitive capitalist system, searching for the

most lucrative markets and making their own economic alliances and trade pacts. The economic environment changed completely, however, when capital migration arose from the desire to maximize profits, resulting in a new form of imperialism, a seemingly benign and restrained variety. The pressure of capital needing investment outlets abroad evolved in the rebirth of an economic, financial, and industrial exploitation in the guise of a new genre: commercial globalization and economic colonialism.

(3)   The accepted connotation of the term "slave" is one of bondage, of someone completely owned as property, forced to work for and subject to the absolute control of his master. This term, for lack of a better one, also imparts more than any other the non-literal, figurative, and, by transference, a more suitable meaning the condition of man as he shares the burdens of existence with the majority of mankind and whose energies are wholly consumed with the effort of self-preservation, the effort to persevere in maintaining his basic existence. Such humans are limited by these confining circumstances from which few manage to free themselves, entangled with necessities to satisfy needs and whose freedom of choice and actions are limited by these endeavors. Although forcible slavery, in the literal sense, has been abolished by the early 21st century, pockets of this condition still exist in Pakistan, India and Brazil (and a few other countries in Asia) of indentured unfortunates working off their debt to creditors. But a man also can be said to fit the description of a slave, although lacking freedom of action, who is nevertheless in possession of freedom of speech, choice of occupation, in possession of his constitutional rights and liberty protected by an existing legal system, a slave notwithstanding because forced by circumstances of his needs to apply all his energies in earning a livelihood, barely satisfying his wants and financial obligations. It is an ongoing effort and without respite. He could regain his freedom of choice and action by disposing of a sufficient discretionary surplus—but then he would no longer be referred to as slave. All subsequent references to slaves or slavery, unless otherwise stated, are embraced by the above definition and as related in prior Chapters.

(4)   All civilizations were depended on, and made possible, by slavery, which created a sufficient discretionary surplus for the minority to enable that segment of society to enjoy the freedom of choice and action in pursuit of interests other than satisfying primary needs. There always existed a gap between the wealthy and poor, between the haves and have-nots, but the chasm has never been as wide as at present; it is widening with the

passing of every year. The well-being of some depends on the privation of the many. And so it is with nation-States which participate unequally in the benefits civilization has to offer. The gap in the possession of a discretionary surplus applies equally to nation-States, between the wealthy and struggling, between the developed and undeveloped countries. There too the gap is progressively widening with each year in favor of the former. If enough inducements are offered to help their weaker economy, the undeveloped countries have little choice but to consent to the business advantages demanded unilaterally by their economically superior foreign counterparts, who negotiate from a position of strength and with the funding, if necessary, from powerful international banking consortiums. The playing field is never level. The transnational corporations command not only superior wealth, but are more business-experienced and possess far better know-how of commerce than their foreign opposite numbers to tilt the arrangements in their favor. But this impediment is temporary since, in due time, the latter are bound to gain in experience and acquire the technical knowledge to deal with the transnationals on more equal terms.

(5)   Transnational corporations invest in offshore enterprises for the following business reasons:

(a)   To move production facilities closer to markets and save in freight charges, custom duties and tariffs, if applicable. Also, the avoidance of the risk of currency fluctuations is a consideration. The products are sold locally and labor cost saving is not a prime consideration.

(b)   To save in labor costs and/or avoid restrictive and costly environmental regulations applicable in domestic production. The goods produced would be mostly offered for export, mainly for the home country market.

The rest of this Chapter will analyze the second alternative.

The Random House Dictionary of English language defines the term "exploit", in part, "to use selfishly for one's own ends". The Webster New World Dictionary defines it, in part, "to make unethical use of one's own advantage or profit; to make profit from the labor of others". If one were to accept these definitions, one would have to conclude that there is nothing odious in stating, for example, that A exploits B, because that is the way business is typically conducted and no businessman could be faulted. The "unethical" part of the definition is out of place as it would be against the laws in most States to be charged with unethical conduct; "immoral" would make more sense. But the above definitions miss their mark. A more appropriate definition should refer to some inherent abuse, such as "knowingly maximizing profit or some other advantage at the expense of another, by one who is sufficiently knowledgeable and financially secure, and who is negotiating with someone experiencing a position of temporary weakness and unable to conclude a more desirable agreement." Such a definition would fit the negation of the "level playing field". The incentive for corporate globalization is to maximize profits by reducing labor costs and avoid the cost of clean-up of any pollution production may cause; to be exempt from regulatory discipline, such as safe working conditions, overtime pay, health benefits, workers' compensation insurance, retirement benefits and termination pay; to obtain the benefits of a tax haven for an extended period and to be free from any government control, supervision or interference. The global capitalist system created a reprise of the former economic imperialism, to pursue the customs of freebooters in practicing economic exploitation, deriving an economic advantage in a skewed playing field favoring their interests. Lastly, they repudiated the longstanding economic principle that the inefficient and noncompetitive should seek every means to reform, change products, or sell the enterprise to a more efficient operator rather than abandon the community and employees and shift operations ("escape" would be a more appropriate description) to an undeveloped country to practice corporate globalism. What example are they setting for the business community? And what lesson for the home government? If labor becomes too demanding (they are the predominant consumers) and government regulations too confining by legislating essential health and safety standards (it is the ultimate protector of the free enterprise system), producers simply thwart such demands by threatening to shut down business, abandon employees, and leave the country for greener pastures, assured that their foreign production can be freely imported to the home country, without the imposition of custom duties and tariffs. The jury is still out on whether this kind of abuse of the free enterprise system benefits the country and community or causes irreparable harm. For countries do not exist to sustain economies, but economies exist to sustain countries.

(6) It is the nature of production enterprises to seek continuous expansion of markets for their products. They will be hampered, in due time, by the limitations of market potential within their political borders. They spare no attempt to expand markets beyond the borders—this is the essence of the capitalist free enterprise system. Effective demand is the driving force of any economy and is dependent upon the purchasing power of con-

sumers. Demand of the unemployed and underemployed (which includes the part-time employed) is necessarily limited to bare necessities needed for survival and affects the overall percentage of production capacity utilization of producers. If a production enterprise moves its factory to a foreign country, the resultant unemployed will, of necessity, reduce their demands which would not be fully restored by the price reduction of cheaper global imports nor the compensating reemployment at reduced wages. In a mass-consumer society, unemployment will always cause a reduction in effective demand, which, in turn, would lead to further reduced employment due to downsizing of the production capacity. The world economy cannot continue to prosper at a projected increasing pace if globalization is carried to excess; the resultant decrease in spending ability of the marginally employed (many would find reemployment only at reduced wage levels), the increased availability of goods would flood the markets and exceed the ability of consumers to absorb domestic production and global imports. Globalization and global free-trade are a temporary economic benefit only because, like all capitalist expansions, a point of market-saturation is reached and there are no other horizons to exploit. Economic slowdowns and recessions are the result of the inevitable failure of effective demand and oversupply. The concept of a global economy is faulted and carries within it the seeds of its own demise (in the long run), because the benefits of lower costs are not the panacea when insufficient demand is a permanent risk.

If a vigilant producer discovers that he would have to pay only $1.00 per hour for labor if he moved his plant offshore and still achieve the same production, as opposed to his current payment of $25.00 per hour, his decision would be a foregone conclusion. But how long would this advantage last? The $1.00 per hour employee cannot be counted as an effective consumer, and his former employee, making now substantially less than before (if he is reemployed), can barely satisfy primary needs. Would not a competitor eagerly want to participate in such a profitable business and would not competition cause overproduction and reduce the profit margin? Steel production became so highly profitable that global steelmaking capacity is now 1 billion tons per year (2002) and annual demand is only 700 million tons. Thailand, India, and Indonesia are counted among the recently established producers. Not only did it help drive prices down (35%), but there are too many unprofitable steelmakers and some of them were forced to shut down. Reduced purchasing power means reduced demand; global business requires uninterrupted expansion and growth, which demands more consumers, i.e., unlimited population growth. A sustainable population growth, or zero-population growth, is anathema to global free-trade and to the capitalist system, which is based on steady growth. Population growth must come to an end when Nature forces the limit and compels a population reduction back to sustainable levels. A profitable global free-trade system cannot be sustained for too long because its foundation is flawed: It is dependent on steady population growth, steady increase in demand, and steady increase in spendable income—its protagonists are blinded by the initial success and are guilty of reckless optimism. It is purely a temporary arrangement of limited duration.

It is a grim symptom of the impaired income distribution system if so many countries can prosper with so many hundreds of million out of work, 3 billion earning $2.00 per day or less, and 250 million children—ages 5 to 15—working full-time or part-time, somewhere in the world every day producing goods many of which are marketed in developed countries. Most of these children are working under exploitative and hazardous conditions of little interest to consumers. The growing discrepancy between the haves and have-nots is staggering. The benefits of globalization mean nothing to them; it will not reduce their plight or poverty, but will suffer equally the hazards of unlimited economic growth, such as foul air, pollution and environmental degradation without medical relief for the added exposure. There is nothing in the capitalist system to warn protagonists that they may be pushing the envelope too far; that sustaining unlimited growth is not feasible; that sooner or later global warming, that inevitable consequence of unrestrained population growth and excessive global mass-consumerism, would adversely impact the well-being of man regardless of economic achievements or dispersal of global productive capacity; that perhaps the single-minded compulsion for ever greater profits may turn out to be counter-productive and undermine the capitalist system itself. It is inconceivable, contrary to the claim of confirmed defenders, for the global economy to grow its way out of poverty and environmental problems.

(7) Profit-seeking capital opened the world to international investors—capital has become borderless. It is the logical culmination of a system inherently expansionary, intolerant of political borders and regulatory confinements. It has shown this proclivity especially in the 19th and 20th centuries by initiating many aggressive wars of conquest to gain new markets and economic advantage, although appropriately camouflaged by patriotic fervor or other nationalist causes. Few soldiers died on the

battlefield aware of the real causes of aggressive wars for which they paid the ultimate price. Superior technology has made major wars impractical and unnecessary to achieve the desired ends—massive accumulation of capital has found the means in global free-trade and practically achieved the same ends. In unholy secretive alliances of the leading elites in the world of business, politics and finance, members of the Business Round-table, the Bildeberg Conference, the Trilateral Commission and the Council on Foreign Relations—all in biased interlocking relationships—meet regularly and privately to provide a forum for the exchange of ideas, culminating in the concept of controlling the economies of the world's countries. These members, who have no intention of firing a shot in anger, set out from the beginning to plan, with remarkable patience, efficiency and secrecy, nothing short of globalization of the world economy. The aura of secrecy cannot but help raise the public charge of conspiracy, but this view is highly overrated and gives them too much credit. They managed, however, to prepare the way for national governments to pass the necessary legislation to approve international treaty organizations, such as the General Agreement on Tariffs and Trade (GATT), the World Trade Organization (WTO), the International Monetary Fund (IMF), the International Bank for Reconstruction and Development (the World Bank), and the North American Free Trade Agreement (NAFTA)—all these are principal tools to maintain control over global management and supervision of international investments, loans, transnational corporate operations, and debt renegotiations with developed and undeveloped countries. These organizations collectively exercise vast powers to remove any and all obstacles to international commerce, any restrictive trade regulations of countries and guarantee that foreign investors have the same rights and freedom of action as their domestic counterparts. Their authority supersedes existing legislation of participating countries when matters of conflict arise. The organization wielding the most pervasive authority is the World Trade Organization (WTO), which has both legislative and judicial powers to eliminate all imposed barriers to international trade and competition, powers that are unilateral and wholly undemocratic, administered by unelected officials headquartered in Geneva, Switzerland. The general public is not aware of the extent of its reach; for that matter, most of the legislators who voted for its establishment never read or understood the full text of the agreement. There was a purpose why its sponsors moved furtively—they did not want to provoke a public debate or any debate.

(8) Global corporations, most of them transnational conglomerates, exercise great political influence at home and abroad due to their financial strength. Their main objective in going global, apart from the internal urges to expand, is to maximize profits, minimize labor costs, be exempt from any restrictive rules or regulations affecting labor or environment, and have the same rights in foreign countries as domestic corporations. In short, rules of the market must be reshaped in their favor so that Third World countries, the prime targets of global corporations, would become increasingly dependent upon global trading to sustain their economies. To add to the dependence, institutions such as the World Bank are requested to loan funds for various infrastructure improvements, such as roads, bridges or dams—most of them not cost effective—but adding to the dependence and need for ever larger exports of natural resources, such as timber and other minerals, to service interest on loans and pay back the principal. If an undeveloped country had an economy that was out of balance in the first place or later encounters difficulties servicing the loan, the IMF stands ready to get involved with its structural adjustment program, to make sure that the economy of the debtor is more compliant with global development. How is this metamorphosis achieved? What changes are demanded? Government participation in the economy must be curtailed; all restrictions on foreign investments have to be removed; aggressive privatization of State-controlled businesses is encouraged; social spending costs are to be curtailed; corporate taxes should be lowered; export of natural resources, such as minerals and agricultural products, are encouraged; the conversion of small scale agriculture to corporate export-oriented mono-culture is urged; currency devaluation is recommended so that the debtor derives an export advantage and its products are more competitive in foreign markets. All these provisions, however, really benefit international bankers and transnational corporations in that the principles of free-trade are exploited, the rules of free-market capitalism thrust upon the host country, which, in turn, inevitably becomes more dependent on imports of goods and services, though at higher prices due to currency devaluation. The debtor has little choice but to accept the recommendations, which are really demands, and comply fully—shades of exploitative colonialism.

(9) Even if a debtor has a democratic form of government, the demands as outlined in the preceding paragraph to restructure the economy are not submitted for approval by the majority of legislative bodies but, of necessity, decided behind closed doors by few of the leading politicians and

businessmen, who are the main beneficiaries of the new economic arrangement. But then democratic principles do not guide transnational corporations or the World Trade Organization, whose chief function is to foster suitable trade relations among its members, resolve disputes, and serve as a forum for multilateral trade negotiations. The WTO is already among the most powerful, secretive and unelected bodies; it follows rules which are uniquely undemocratic. Carrying out its mandate in secrecy by a tribunal of mostly appointed corporate lawyers located in Geneva it will, upon a complaint filed by a member against another member, unilaterally approve punitive sanctions against deemed offenders charged with interfering or restricting the free flow of commerce, or impeding the ability of members to compete unhindered in a member-country. It represents the culmination of clandestine efforts to create a global market safe for multinational corporations and international financial institutions. In the process, human rights, benefits and necessities, are completely subordinated to the right of making a profit. The expansion of international trade and investments which promote economic growth are considered foundational to the enhancement of the general welfare. It will be shown that this assumption is flawed.

The list of possible violations which would trigger WTO sanctions is formidable. It challenges local and national environmental regulations as illegal restraints of trade; it proscribes any legislation which interdicts contracts with slave-labor countries as interference with the free flow of business; it mandates removal of investment restrictions and lower corporate taxes; foreign companies are to be given "national treatment", i.e., treated exactly as if they were host country companies; it considers as illegal trade barriers any laws which prohibit carcinogenic food additives, asbestos insulation, raw log exports causing harmful deforestation, import of beef tainted with growth hormones. The WTO is not designed to protect democratic principles. It has the power to challenge the right of nations to pass laws favored by the majority to safeguard the health and well-being of citizens, if they restrict or interfere with international trade. All these measures are intended to overrule the democratic decision-making process of developed and developing countries (the latter more forcefully) and support the elimination of restrictions which inhibit the unhindered activities of international business enterprises.

(10) What are the business principles which guide transnational corporations? These can be reduced to a few basics:

• They must show a profit.

- Concerted effort must be made to increase the per share profit in each succeeding year.
- Volume of business must grow each year.
- Increased profits and growth should be pursued because they are favorably rated by the stock markets and enhance the values of executive stock-options.
- Predatory and aggressive pursuit of interests should guide management, and morality must never be a consideration.
- Management must constantly seek to improve advantages in the competitive edge.
- Expansionary interests are viewed as global and political borders should be ignored.
- Their first duty is to stockholders and not to national or community interests.
- The duty of managing executives is to prefer profits over morality.
- The Board of Directors should favor a policy that all employees are expendable, be they executives or production labor.

Critics observing these corporations guided by such principles, devoid of any long-term loyalties to alliances or employees, lacking any duty or responsibility to their community or country which created these "artificial persons" and passed laws that made their success possible, can well understand their motivation although puzzled by their ruthless Machiavellian principles of expediency. They form self-serving global strategic alliances when it suits their purpose and terminate them for the same reasons; move their operations overseas and ignore the interests of employees or the damage sustained by their community which provided an economic climate for business to thrive. In short, their culture can be said to conform to the typical patterns exhibited by amoral, cutthroat and exploitative business enterprises.

(11) Globalization, i.e., the unobstructed movement of capital, production facilities and trade to any country of choice, is the culmination of the concept of free enterprise, i.e., that any business can produce anything anyplace and sell it anywhere else. Surplus capital had to find outlets where it could be more profitably invested. Utilization of these means to maximize profits will further augment the capital surplus, which, in time, will become less productive, even unproductive, for lack of available profitable investment opportunities. Just like excess capital had to move beyond the confines of the original borders and seek productive investments globally, continuous profitable expansion cannot be sustained

interminably since capital accumulation will exceed its utilization and global demand. The capacity to produce consumer goods will, in time, by far exceed demand in the global markets for such goods. The geographic limits of nation-States will become the limits of the global geography. The interminable accumulation of wealth will cease to have its former significance due to the diminished investment potential; no longer will the persistent demand for more free trade, more free enterprise, and unhindered competition have the former significance because their very application brought about a surfeit of redundant capital accumulation. Banks would no longer seek major deposits to invest. They would no longer pay interest on such deposits but charge a fee for safeguarding such funds. The scale of advantages will tilt against the lure of moving offshore, or meet the emerging markets, because the gospel of steadily rising profits associated with the drive for growth as preached by free-market capitalism will have lost the attraction enjoyed in its early halcyon days. The policy of recklessly pursuing downsizing of the domestic labor force and totally abandoning employees by moving production offshore, the drive for a large-scale technological revolution resulting in a new generation of robotic workers, and the escalating automation of the manufacturing industry have all made millions upon millions of willing workers in the industrialized countries superfluous and unwanted. No system of government, democratic in particular, can for long passively countenance the plight of these potential customers without taking corrective steps; these human beings made irrelevant by a flawed economic system tilted to briefly benefit the few in search for ever greater profit margins and ever more extravagant returns to stockholders. The answer is not the availability of low paying jobs, particularly in the service industry, where the worker has to labor long hours or hold several jobs to meet the responsibility to his family, or both husband and wife must have gainful employment to make ends meet. The latter condition cannot but adversely affect family life and the upbringing of children—the community and State will suffer if dysfunctional families are the result. The elitist establishments that favor global free-trade and the importance of continual growth must, in time, abandon the permanence of these benefits as a self-deception. The prosperity created for a mere minority would generate an inevitable permanent contraction of the economy, with the consequences adversely affecting all segments of society. The silent majority has the natural law on its side. For if the gap between the super-haves and the haves on one side, and the have-nots on the other side, reaches reproachful disparity, the former must be mindful that Nature recognizes no property rights nor the right to practice global free-trade capitalism, which are artificial creations calculated to benefit the ideology of special interests. Such rights flow from the institutionalized explicit consent of the majority of citizens or from their silent acquiescence. The drive for economic security is fundamental to man. He has the duty, and therefore the right, granted by his State to do everything within his power and within the law to persevere in his existence and do likewise for his family. There is nothing sacrosanct about the global free-trade capitalist system; it is the logical result of the historical dialectic of free capital finding full expression in a suitable permissive economic system with minimum regulations and maximum of freedom. There were other systems once flourishing, but later forcibly discarded due to the rise of inevitable internal contradictions and defects all systems develop in time: the divine right of kings, the feudal system, forcible slavery, the glorification of the State—just to name a few. All supporters of such systems hid behind the mistaken claim of their inevitability and historical destiny. Should a system fail because of chronic defects and extreme exploitation, which would be consistent with the fatuous human custom of carrying most original beneficial designs to excess by immoderation until the harm exceeds the benefits, then it behooves that the failed system be repudiated. This is the harsh lesson of history. Corporate globalism rests on a flawed premise that transitory success offshore would compensate for deficiencies caused at home; that more affordable goods, the result chiefly of cheaper labor, can induce ongoing global mass-consumerism when the very act of going global has impaired the purchasing power of average consumers to the point where effective demand cannot match the abundant supplies; that a majority of mankind lacks sufficient means and has become irrelevant as consumers; that very little of the prosperity enjoyed by the successful minority has benefited the majority; that the GDP, in that it equates total increase in output with improved national well-being and progress, is a fraud perpetrated upon the public; that permanent growth, the basis of globalization, is not sustainable since the bounties of Nature are not inexhaustible because man is unable and unwilling to control population increases. The WTO, NAFTA, the World Bank, the IMF, the major international banks and leading transnational corporations, are all linked together in a netlike world of inscrutable alliances and self-serving ideologies, flouting conventional business and banking practices, and exploit to the limit the preferments they claim as their special domain.

Colonial rules of old were subverted by national liberation movements which hungered for freedom possessed by their subjugators. The
present-day host countries offering investment opportunities to multinational corporations and international banks may do likewise if they feel
their sovereignty compromised, particularly if a persistent global recession were to intensify. Persisting financial pressures could create a reaction against global economic policies and result in protectionism.

(12) It is premature to judge what lasting impact television, cellular phones
and computers have made on the institutions and cultures of developing
nations. The WTO, IMF and World Bank have certainly adversely
affected the lives of their population by subverting the political institutions and depriving their citizens of certain fundamental rights they
enjoyed for uncounted generations, e.g., farming the family plot, state
administered enterprises, government spending on health and education.
Cortez and Pizarro had little effect on the culture of the Aztec and Inca
nations except the forcible adoption of the Catholic religion. Early English colonists settling in North America had minimal cultural effect upon
the native Indians except they managed to exterminate almost all of
them. The Spanish invaders sought to extend the power of the monarchy
and subjugate the native population as slaves to work in the mines and
fields; the English settlers needed land to make room for the increasing
immigration of newcomers. But then the culture of the Aztec, Inca, and
native Indian nations was superior to that of their usurpers. Apart from
cooperating in the opening of production facilities oriented mainly
toward export, the developing countries will be hard put to assimilate any
significant part of the Western-style culture of mass-consumerism. What
have global purveyors of the new world order brought them? They
enriched a few of their elites, to be sure, and further increased the gap
between the rich and poor. But the new market-driven world, culminating in economic globalization, brought them increasing financial
instability due to possible overcapacity and dependence on the continuing prosperity of developed countries, the chief buyers of their exports;
they successfully propagated the ideology that there is no alternative to
globalization; they are the bearers of a culture which countenances with
equanimity the plight of the unemployed, underemployed, the unhealthy
working conditions in some of the plants (textiles, in particular) and the
reduction of basic social services. The developed countries' economic
system, which pride themselves on promoting a consumer-oriented
economy at home, will be hard put to convince the developing countries

that an export-oriented economy would bring them equal prosperity. But what are developing countries to think of the United States, the chief protagonist of the new global ideology and the chief exponent of its efficacy and benefits, where 40 million of its citizens live below poverty level; 45 million are without health insurance; 15 million children go to bed hungry; business profitability is sought by employee layoffs and plant downsizings occur almost daily; millions of workers are forced to derive earnings from more than one job to keep head above water; the gap between the rich and poor is the widest ever and increasing yearly despite borderless competition; greed is acceptable and not considered immoral; agribusiness lobbies for the elimination of farm subsidies to small family farmers, which causes the bankruptcy of many; major lender-banks find it more profitable to invest overseas than finance local enterprises, relieve unemployment, and foster an expansion of the economy. It is apparent that the borderless free trade has not helped all segments of society in the U.S.; it has helped the powerful and financially dominant components to register record gains with miniscule benefits trickling down to the rest, except that imports are priced more favorably (with the help of a strong dollar), benefiting the average consumer and minimizing inflationary pressures. These details cannot but be noticed by offshore exporters with some sense of disquiet since it is apparent who chiefly benefits from their export-oriented economy. What will happen to their well-being if world export deceleration should cause falling profits to global corporations? Will they be financially strong enough to withstand an economic downturn or a prolonged recession? It is only a question of time. The economy of free-trade was first confined within national borders. Expansion made it global and borderless; the whole world became the new markets, but new borders nevertheless, with no new untapped markets to conquer. Hence growth and expansion have their limits and market distortions due to overcapacity will bring on cutthroat competition, unemployment and destabilized economies. A reversion to protectionist policies by developed countries, even if temporary, would doom many a global dream. Too much blind faith has been placed in the efficacy of global markets.

CHAPTER 11

THE FLAWS OF A FREE-MARKET GLOBAL ECONOMY

(1) The time will surely come, rather sooner than later, when mainstream economists will concede that the global economy which they so eagerly preached is not the solution of the world's economic problems. On the contrary, globalization has been responsible for preaching the merits of sustainable economic growth, which is not only responsible for exacerbating harmful inequalities within countries and damaging to social harmony, but carries the seeds of its own demise and possibly that of free-market capitalism. For globalization stands for uninterrupted growing markets and more competition mainly by lowering labor costs, or downsizing the work force as a cost-cutting measure to attract new price-conscious consumers, while at the same time reducing the purchasing power of a large segment of the buying public. Corporate executives of transnational corporations, driven by the frenzy of accumulation of profits, in complete disregard of the long-term consequences of such a policy if applied globally, forgot Henry Ford's wise statement, "If you cut wages, you just cut the number of your customers." It could not be otherwise. For the impetus for going global is that the production capacity exceeds demand—either the product is beyond the reach of too many consumers, or there just are not enough customers and producers seeking consumers with adequate purchasing power in other countries. When corporations and/or capital move abroad, the market for domestic jobs is reduced and so are wages. Lower wages and fewer jobs cannot help but reduce con-

sumer demand. Cost-cutting results in lower wages or reduced labor force, and moving production offshore may hamper a company's effort to increase its overall market-share, particularly if such labor-saving policy is widespread in the corporate world. The unemployed and those otherwise employable but forced to take lower paying jobs would not qualify as members of a mass-consumer society; the much touted cheaper imports and lower priced goods made available by competition would not likely restore demand; the available spending is restricted to the purchase of necessities to sustain life.

(2) As a result of intense competition and technologically improved production processes, some of the more efficient labor force can expect higher remuneration, but there will also be reduced compensation and layoffs of those considered dispensable by employers and unable to keep up with the new standards demanded. This situation can be expected to apply to developed countries. The more production processes are technologically simplified, the less the training and skill required of workers—producers can move their facilities offshore, where an abundant local supply of unskilled labor can be easily trained and put to work for substantially lower compensation than earned by their counterparts in developed countries. Globalization has the effect of depressing wages in developed and developing countries. In the former, by creating surplus labor due to technological improvements and production facilities moving overseas; in the latter, by taking advantage of surplus labor caused by overpopulation— these countries are responsible for 90% of the world's annual population growth. All this cannot help but have an adverse effect on the standard of living and unfavorably impact the whole economy, causing contraction due to decrease in general spending capacity. Overcapacity is the curse of a free-market economy and causes fluctuating business cycles attributable to reduced spending, which negatively affects output thus adding to the redundant labor pool. Reduced spending is caused by depressed wages, unemployment and underemployment. Effective demand is the lubricant of trade and the driving force of an economy; the segment of population that lacks the means to purchase the products offered even by the most efficient producers does not participate in the blessings a progressive economy is capable of providing. This failure provokes additional cost-cutting measures which primarily depress the remuneration of labor and lead to additional unemployment and underemployment.

(3) Competition among producers results in the most efficient gaining a larger share of the market and capable of initiating cost-cutting measures

by reducing, among others, the compensation of labor. Competition between employed and unemployed labor will, of necessity, result in reduced compensation since those willing to work for less are more likely to gain and retain employment. Working for less will lower discretionary surplus and consumer demand, cut back production and, in turn, further reduce compensation and employment. The dynamics of such shifting economic forces and the certain changes they produce in relation to one another appear to be inevitable and point not only to an impaired order but mark a state of permanence. The ebb and flow affecting a producer's efficiency, compensation of labor, and effective demand, cannot be micro-managed by the human hand, or the celebrated invisible hand—it does not exist. It is apparent that human intelligence is not capable of improving upon the natural order of things to minimize the effects of these economic forces and make their interrelationship more harmonious. If these economic forces are projected on a global scale, the human hand is that much further removed from affecting their determined interrelationship.

The global economy is subject to spasms of ever greater and prolonged economic contractions, followed by temporary periods of economic recovery due to the growing gap between the affluent and the poor, both in wealth and numbers. While global production stimulated by international capital embraces few limits, the constrains of real disposable income and widening demand gap caused by the growing maldistribution of income make a mockery of what is so glowingly referred to as the magic of the marketplace. Before globalization, the economies of countries were affected variously by economic growth, prosperity or stagnation; after globalization, countries marched in lock step pursuing a global free-market economy influenced to a varying degree by the prevailing worldwide economic well-being, malaise or knowledge of the market.

(4) To mainstream economists limits of natural resources, limits of waste absorption, limits to the pollution of the atmosphere are not topics which would deflect their thinking from advocating market fundamentalism. According to them, such subjects are best left to the dilettantes; they are beyond the bounds of their thinking and that is why their obsession with constant growth is based on faulty fundamentals, completely oblivious to the frictions and instability caused by continuous growth. Following the logic of free-market capitalism, they spread the view that globalization is inevitable, the culmination of a free economy from which there is no retreat. It does not require a word from the philosophers to spell-out the

obvious, namely, that no human action is an end in itself and that, by the warrant of history, anything contrived by humans is but transitory, to be reshaped or discarded by future generations, or collapse from its own defects and contradictions. Specifically, any system designed by man to guide, control, or regulate any form of human association is bound to contain flaws and contradictions, which are destined to spell modifications the higher its aim or reach. Free-market capitalism, whose growth was formerly restrained by political boundaries and cautious business judgment, overcame such obstacles. Fully captivated by the mind-set which preached the efficacy of sustained growth, the CEOs of major corporations maximized growth by expanding their profitable activities into the untapped global markets. But, in time, due to the inbred tendency to overproduce and gain an advantage over competitors, global markets will become saturated; overcapacity will cause an outright termination of growth of the global economy with no additional expansion possible. Apart from limits to population growth, limits to the degradation of the environment, limits to effective consumer spending, globalization is bound to reach, in time, its own limits since expansion of corporate productivity will have penetrated and straddled all available global markets. Economic growth will have to give way to economic development: for the former there are no more horizons to conquer; the latter is only limited by man's ingeniousness. Corporations could achieve growth by absorbing each other—merger or acquisition—but such moves would not represent overall growth of the economy.

(5) As with any genre of human endeavor, successful participants always seek ways not to be unseated by their rivals. Corporations are opposed to free-trade once they become global. They spare no efforts to stifle competition in order to maintain an upper hand in a playing field tilted in their favor; they do not champion democratic regimes but prefer authoritarian rule of military dictatorships, for otherwise Standard Adjustment Programs, so enthusiastically embraced by them for granting exclusive prerogatives and so favored by the IMF, would not likely be voted favorably by the host country's legislature because its measures are punishing to local popular interests. They will do anything within their power, legal or illegal, to protect the advantages gained; promise the host countries that their corporate activities would raise the standard of living. At the request of the IMF and in furtherance of their special interests, local currencies are devalued to encourage exports, discourage imports, contribute to inflation and shortages of consumer goods, competition among

employees, lower wages and higher unemployment—all these tend to lower the standard of living. Global businesses vehemently resist governmental regulatory authority for fear of interfering with unfettered exploitation of trade or economic advantages, in particular, punitive fines assessed for acts damaging to public health and safety, yet they are most gratified to be under the autocratic regulatory regime of the WTO (although business-friendly, it hands down peremptory orders in deciding trade disputes), which, on the one hand, encourages free-trade globalism and increased protection for corporate interests against governmental interference, and on the other hand, submits transnational corporate interests to imperious rules and oversight, such as ruling in patent disputes or infringements between business establishments, corporate activities that interfere with competition, or established international corporate compacts deemed to be damaging to trade.

(6)   Nature is finite as a source of nourishment and energy; there are limits to the exploitation of the ecosystem which will interdict in a demonstrative and unmistakable manner unlimited population increases and unrestrained economic growth. Globalism stands for ever expanding markets and an ever expanding customer-base, i.e., global mass consumerism, to support global output. Economic growth involves increased production and increased sales for an expanding market. In the process, more raw materials, energy and technology are utilized. Increased depletion of raw materials and most of the present sources of energy are not only nonrenewable resources whose availability is limited but diminish the biodiversity and poison the biosphere beyond its regenerative capacity, making any progress achieved lose its relevance. A correspondingly necessary expansion of a consumer base not only means reaching potential purchasers who currently are not counted as customers but an enlarged population base, i.e., population growth. The assimilative capacity of the ecosystem cannot indefinitely absorb a population growth. Cultivated land used for food production, living space, potable water supply so essential for human survival, landfill sites to accommodate the increased wastes generated are all becoming insufficient to provide for unlimited population increases—without even considering the worsening air pollution, harmful climate changes and degradation of the ecosystem—with the inevitable result that future population growth will be coerced to moderate and eventually come to an end by the force of adverse circumstances of its own making until some stability is reached, a zero-population growth. It is said that production costs will increase faster than ben-

efits, in which case it would become unprofitable to continue the level of output, but this would not by itself constitute a limitation of economic growth. This will come to pass when the fragility of natural forces is not capable of supporting the assimilation of a population sprawl. Zero-population growth would retard, and ultimately terminate, economic growth because entrepreneurs will not increase production unless they can profitably dispose of the output; the dawn of a steady-state economy will have arrived. No more business expectations of ever greater annual profits and no more improvident short-term planning by anxious corporate executives driven by unrestrained greed, ever eager to line their pockets rather than plan what benefits the real long-term corporate interests. Sustainable growth, in general, will have to give way to sustainable development, i.e., more technologically improved production and distribution, less urgency for continuously increased profits and minimized costs, but rather more attention paid to greater product utility, advances in improving product quality and desirability, and greater concern for the enduring viability of the environment so essential for the well-being of the human race. Unhealthy people make good patients but bad customers.

Zero-population growth would soon cause output reductions; without economic growth, the vaunted inevitability of globalism's success would evaporate; capital and production would have to concentrate on domestic markets and gradually disengage from foreign involvements in order to increase the purchasing power of consumers. There may not be any limits to wealth accumulation, but a sustainable economy based on intensive development rather than growth would require a more equitable income distribution; people with limited means do not make desirable customers. If a country's economy was historically directed toward growth in order to raise the standard of living of the less favored in the hope that an expanded economy would reduce the gap between the rich and poor, a simpler and surer method would be to seek ways to achieve a more equitable distribution of income. Producers and merchants could finally reach the conclusion that the foundation of a healthy economy is an effective demand and consumer confidence. Subsidy is not an ugly word for conglomerates and multinational corporations; those inveterate advocates of free-market capitalism, for most governments are always generous in awarding grants, such as support for research, tax concessions, rescue of failing major businesses or other financial incentives, procured not only by busy lobbyists and the expected paybacks for substantial political party support during elections, but also because of the "good for business" mantra. It is in the interest of business (and governments) to maintain a moderate sustainable prosperity without extreme economic swings of ups and downs, from contraction to recovery and back to contraction, as if ordained and predetermined by the "mystique" of the market. The "mystique"—and there is none—is the lack of foresight and incompetence of entrepreneurs in failing to match output with consumer demand and therefore blunder in giving rise to persistent business cycles. A more equitable income distribution would not only be "good for business" by encouraging corporate-friendly consumerism, but increase the consumer-base by raising the standard of living of those presently barely able to satisfy primary needs.

(7)   The rising unemployment in most developed countries which are deeply involved in globalization is attributable to a weakening of the global economy. Multinational corporations are experiencing lower profits because of a drop in demand for their goods and are resorting to cost-cutting measures, foremost among which are employee layoffs, outright reduction in compensation of retained employees and cutbacks in average weekly hours worked. Globalization has been a boon to world trade in that it achieved generally lower consumer prices for goods due to more intense competition, lower labor costs, and a greater selection of goods for consumers; on the flip side, it accounted for excessive capacity utilization and unsold inventories for which corporate management policies are responsible. The fallout is overproduction of goods beyond the capacity of global markets to absorb. Prices are of no consequence if demand is insufficient when consumers do not need the product, or the global market is oversold and oversupplied. The blame for these market distortions can be credited to the reckless self-seeking of overzealous corporate managers pursuing a policy of aggressively driven growth and maximization of profits—made respectable by advocates of the global economy—without paying heed to the consequences. The resulting decline in corporate earnings causes a contraction in capital investments for plant and machinery modernization, technological research for the improvement of products or product substitution, and the inevitable employment cutbacks. Corporate executives seek economic predictability, but the nature of their duties and self-preservation instinct find them inclined to misread the markets, an endemic occupational frailty from which there is no escape. There is no "invisible hand" which keeps business executives straying from the intended course, for the accurate predictability of a complex market, especially one extended

over the global basis, is beyond the capacity of even the most knowledgeable humans. It is said that markets do not err, humans do. This is a
false aphorism of economists. Every market is the conjunction of human
calculations and miscalculations, with a touch of human frailties, greed
and cunning combined in varied proportions. As far as business in general is concerned, it must be more than a coincidence that the larger the
corporate operation the less capable and more mistake-prone its top
executives, for in the hierarchy of corporate management the working of
Peter's Principle applies, i.e., executives tend to rise to their level of
incompetence and work is accomplished by those executives of lower
rank who have not been promoted to their level of incompetence. As for
forecasting the working of global markets, and that applies to any market
unless rigged by scoundrels, the imponderable variables of the multiplicity of human actions make any calculation unreliable and unfit to
serve as trustworthy guidelines. This can be said of the whole subject of
economics, which relies on interesting theoretical models but falls short
of the reality test because it attempts to institutionalize human greed,
frailty, and erratic behavior. Therefore, management which expanded
domestic companies into global enterprises advocating globalization of
the free-market economy, causing local unpredictable markets prone to
somewhat manageable misjudgments to become totally incomprehensible and uncontrollable global trading networks, subject not only to
manipulation by grasping speculators and the unpredictable whims of
international financial institutions, but also the victim of misguided and
incompetent business leaders engaged in market-distortion practices,
incapable of focusing because of their myopic vision. For had they
viewed globalization in the proper perspective and fully understood the
consequences of too many businesses wishing to globalize, they would
have realized that moving plants offshore to maximize profits by dis-
placing domestic employees with cheaper labor of the host country
would not only depress the domestic labor market but, in the long run,
dampen consumer demand, weaken consumer confidence, depress consumer prices, decrease corporate profits resulting in more employee layoffs, and cause a worldwide prolonged economic downturn. The downward spiral could be of long duration since globalization, by supporting
the frenzy of accumulation, widens the gap between the rich and poor,
with the latter experiencing a regressive shift in income and contribute to
the imbalance between supply and demand.

If management of global corporations paid attention to their real long-term interests, namely, maintaining a growing economy that is based on a solid foundation, they would shudder at the thought of a decline in employee compensation, full-time jobs converted to part-time, unemployment, and consider the resulting lower disposable income of most consumers a curse to be avoided at all costs. But this would be too much to expect. Global corporate leaders look on with equanimity as year by year a greater percentage of willing and able employees become redundant, with no role to play in the global economy. This bodes ill for corporate growth since demand for goods will certainly decline.

(8)   Third World countries consented to globalization in the hope, as outlined by industrial countries, that it would stimulate their economy, reduce unemployment and raise the standard of living. It was more than blind faith in the efficacy of the free-market since arguments for adoption were persuasive, on paper. It was taken for granted that the parties would deal fairly with each other, that agreements negotiated benefited all signatories as evenly as practicable, and that the advantages of joining with the most successful of the world's free enterprise entrepreneurs would grow with the passing of time. They were assured that economic growth would reduce the level of poverty. Such forecasts seemed a salvation to countries whose economy was stagnant and floundering in the morass of hopelessness. But there was a steep price to pay. Globalization, which required submission to stringent new regulations, gradually became to be perceived as a new form of colonialism. There was no alternative, and greed of the stronger eventually intruded upon the interests of the weaker. The initial enthusiasm turned into resentment as the high expectations proved to be misplaced. The whole apparatus of power, whose involvement was essential in the implementation of globalization, was tilted in favor of industrial countries. It simply was overlooked by all sides that the success of globalization depended on the continued prosperity of industrial nations—a critical condition which never occurred in the annals of history and, in turn, depended upon a high degree of continued consumer spending. The IMF and World Bank, with their Structural Adjustment Programs, imposed humiliating invasive requirements as a condition of funding, most of which would have been rejected out-of-hand by rich countries. Even though initially accepted, they were resented as unworkable, burdensome and unacceptable violations of traditional customs of Third World countries. The IMF and World Bank not only violated the rule of impartiality but acted as quasi-agents for international banks, other creditors, and global corporations to help them

achieve economic domination by offering attractive infrastructure development aid ostensibly to eradicate poverty, but in effect, through repeated lending, turn debtor countries into economic dependencies. The IMF, almost invariably, required the raising of interest rates and devaluation of borrower's currency to increase exports and decrease imports, in order to improve the balance of payments and, in this manner, enable borrowers to service their debts. Most of the debtors, through inexperience, graft or mismanagement, will never be able to repay their loans; they will have to borrow more money to repay principal and interest installments as they become due. The humiliation and constant pressure on debtor countries to avoid default, in time, will give rise to discontent with the strictures globalization imposed, which, in their view, subjected them to conditions of economic slavery. Third World nations were encouraged to increase their exports by concentrating on what they could produce best and most efficiently, but in doing so, they became too dependent on import of necessities, mostly agricultural products, which they ceased producing (the weakness of David Ricardo's theory). They viewed this as an artificial arrangement imposed by scheming Western leaders who mistakenly believed in the merits of such programs. These, in fact, accelerated the impoverization of borrowers and eventual default on their debt. The financial bankruptcy of many of the poorest and not so poor Third World countries, which are indebted to the IMF, World Bank, and other international banks in amounts that cannot possibly be repaid, has been well known to the lenders. These creditors, however, instead of recognizing the flawed and, at times, irresponsible lending practices and easing some of the imposed stringent conditions, proceeded to grant additional loans to assist debtors to repay some of their obligations to the very same creditors. In this way, lenders could cynically claim that their loans were sound and repayable.

The needlessly harsh conditions imposed by the IMF and World Bank could trigger, in due time, hostile repercussions from the populace of impoverished nations, whose governments squandered what little resources they had to sustain them. Beguiled by blandishments of global business activists, Third World governments (and some emerging nations) adopted the requested austerity measures to qualify for the promised lending programs. Such loans, however, tended to entrap them into successively greater dependence upon future borrowing, and only the pressure on major industrial nations to avoid possible financial collapse, and the attendant negative publicity, induced lenders to renegotiate the terms of loans, including forgiving part of the debt to ease the financial burden on unstable poorer countries. Industrial nations have to maintain the myth of the inevitability of globalization and the beneficial effects flowing to all participants. Lackluster performance could call into question the soundness of the undertaking and the motives of its sponsors. Only in this artificial and contrived manner could a plan of borderless business expansion, conceived in ignorance of human nature by originators of limited intelligence who lacked the necessary foresight to design a sustainable world-wide plan, preserve the semblance of order. Such a plan would be beyond the capacity of even the most intelligent designers, who could not have noticed the inherent flaws leading to its impermanence and ultimate failure. So much for the new world order.

(9) A free-market (free-trade) economy can be said to exist if prices are determined by the unregulated interchange of supply and demand; the same applies to allocation of resources. In other words, there are no traces of a centrally planned economy. The effect of competition is central in setting prices, raising or lowering production, and achieving technological product efficiency so essential in maintaining a free-market economy. Restrictions imposed by government regulations in the interest of public policy, such as minimum wage, overtime pay, or compensation insurance for job-related injuries, would not interfere with free-trade if observed equally by all competitors. The same applies to government imposed tariffs and subsidies, but these are prone to misuse resulting in the subversion of reciprocity. It is theoretically conceivable that government regulations with respect to wages could apply equally to all competitors, domestic and foreign, so as to preserve a balanced access to markets; the same could apply, in theory, to tariffs on imports as long as there is mutuality. With regard to government subsidies on exports, the requisite transparency is, more often than not, lacking to put competitors on notice. In the case of cross-subsidization occasioned by businesses producing multiple products, a particular product is sold at cost, or below cost, and profits recouped from income derived from other products, the intent being to achieve a calculated market advantage and confound competitors.

There is a window of opportunity enabling business enterprises to enjoy the benefits of a free-market economy limited only, at the lower end, by the requirements of a government sponsored social safety net, and at the upper limit, restricted by various legislated product-safety regulations, inspections of targeted production, and product handling facilities to ensure public health and monitor other business activities to bring about compliance with laws prohibiting activities in restraint of trade. It is in the interest of the business community to observe these limits imposed on a free-market economy and preserve the benefits of the vast advantages it offers. The benefits and advantages are the greater the more universally, i.e., globally, these limitations are equally observed and voluntary compliance is achieved in good faith. But such expectations are illusory. No sooner do leaders of business enterprises convene to negotiate than one tries to get the better of the other and morality is almost never a consideration—the law of self-preservation is paramount. Globalization has opened the door for business to engage in activities which are in complete contempt of the concept of reciprocity of advantages and exploit the weakness of trading partners in order to maximize profits. There can be no talk of an even playing field. Under competitive pressures to create and make the most of profitable opportunities, business enterprises constantly seek to enlarge the window of a free-market economy by attempts to evade, covertly or overtly, the confines of the upper and lower limits set by regulatory authorities. Agreements on reciprocity of benefits are violated, the gaining of unilateral advantages are disguised as essential changes to established limits, the narrowest views are proclaimed that such conduct will improve the business climate. But such conduct benefits the more powerful only and damages the business interests of the weaker. In the end, it will prove to be destructive to the free-market economy. Such self-serving and opportunistic conduct is bound to damage the confidence placed in business arrangements negotiated between industrial nations, their corporations and Third World countries. A global economy is not sustainable unless industrial nations, these arch-protagonists of the merits of a free-market economy, conduct their business activities in accordance with the principles they espouse— no politically or business motivated protectionism, no absence of reciprocity, no hidden subsidies, no unilaterally imposed tariffs on imports, and no imposed Structural Adjustment Programs—these anti-democratic and colonial inventions of international bankers.

(10) The burden is on industrial nations to observe the rules of reciprocity. Even though all WTO member countries are committed to observe the rules against interference with international trade competition, it is politically difficult for developed countries not to heed the requests for financial assistance by certain domestic segments of the commercial establishment unable to meet foreign competition. Such establishments either seek imposition of tariffs as protection against imports, or export subsi-

dies to make them more competitive on the international scene. Tariffs and subsidies are artificial contrivances assisting enterprises unable to compete effectively, frustrate the benefits derived from competition, and undermine the advantages of a free-market economy. These measures can be challenged by any WTO member and seek intervention upon filing of a complaint. If deemed justified and the dispute cannot be resolved, the WTO would order the offending country to cease the infraction. If ordered to comply and the offending country ignores the directive, the WTO can impose sanctions to enforce compliance. Very few, if any, developing countries would consider seeking the help of the WTO in resolving disputes with developed countries for fear of retribution by the latter and the impediments their weaker position poses with the arbiter. Industrialized countries consider the organizational structure of the WTO as imposing permanent restraints upon developing countries, which, if brazen enough, could challenge their stronger counterparts to observe the reciprocity rules of global economic integration and compel balanced trade conventions among all the members. In Third World countries, there is a sense of injustice and a feeling that there must be something wrong with a system which, despite glowing reports to raise their level of well-being, failed to achieve noticeable improvements. On the contrary, they maintain that the global economic system is not only rigged to foreclose any improvements in their standard of living but lowers their status to that of colonial dependencies. It is difficult to understand why international monetary institutions established by the most powerful industrial countries and literally controlled by them can exact painful structural adjustments from Third World countries, and in the process undermine their ability to encourage exports by imposing selective import tariffs to thwart such exports in order to satisfy appeals from domestic interests. No wonder such cynical conduct breeds defiance and hostility. And when one adds to the mix irresponsible lenders who condition their loans upon the borrowers' capacity to increase exports, one is forced to reach the inescapable conclusion: the principles of global trade are flawed and must be corrected.

The WTO, IMF and World Bank are designed to serve the interests of global corporations. Despite their standard advocacy of global free-market economic policies, they consistently demand invasive and stringent structural changes from developing countries to minimize investment and lending risks of international financial institutions. Such policies, however, require rethinking since their usefulness is of questionable permanent effectiveness; the requested changes invariably involve draconian cuts in social services, a balanced budget, privatization of government owned enterprises, currency devaluation, deregulation of international commerce and banking, changes which would be strongly resisted as unworkable by most developed countries. Since such requests are made to impoverished nations whose economy is on the verge of instability and fiscal difficulties, they cause popular discord bordering on defiance; most Third World governments have to resort to undemocratic measures to restore and maintain order; such operations require substantial loans to mobilize armies and support competent police forces. As if guided by some invisible hand, burdensome debts are almost always a consequence of restructuring.

Neoclassical economic policies are favored by most champions of capitalism. All government interference is considered a hindrance—or so the preaching goes. The free interplay of market forces is the best solution to all economic problems and although there will be winners or losers, compliance with that philosophy will render the right results: reward for the most efficient and most enterprising. The global economy and mobile international capital in search of the most lucrative global investments are considered the apogee of neoclassical economics, preaching that doctrine to the rest of the world. Developing countries are urged to adopt its principles as the surest permanent release from the shackles of poverty.

Industrial nations proclaim the redeeming value of a free-market economy but are its chief corrupters. It could not be otherwise, for the economically strongest and industrially wealthiest nations do not practice fair and open competition unless it serves their interests. To answer the pleas of its powerful constituent major corporations, trade associations, and multinationals to thwart the inroads of the more vexatious foreign competitors, accommodating governments grant subsidies, impose tariffs and quotas, manipulate currencies, pass selective anti-dumping laws, exempt part of export income from taxation, partially waive regulations against degradation of the environment, expand or restrict specific international credits, and threaten to withdraw participation, if necessary, from previously approved international conventions. All such measures are embraced to give exporters an artificial edge against foreign competitors and assist them to compete more effectively in foreign markets. Opposition to globalization will grow when disadvantaged countries realize that their share of the pie is not likely to increase. And when hapless countries and their citizens comprehend that the system was rigged against their interests from the start, the inevitable reaction could lead to a dramatic surge in nationalistic and anti-globalization sentiments.

(11) Most Third World nations consider the foremost industrialized countries, the United States in particular, to be the biggest obstacles to their economic advancement. These countries set up trade barriers, such as tariffs, subsidies, quotas, and anti-dumping policies mainly to protect agriculture, textile, and clothing industries, steelmakers—to name the most prominent—from more efficient competitors located in developing countries. Such artificial impediments shelter politically influential but inefficient industries from competition and result in overproduction. Subsidies invariably insulate aided industries from the effects of economic downturns and export losses to more qualified competitors. All these man-made measures not only adversely interfere with the export growth of Third World economies but contravene the high-minded sermonizing by advocates of free-market economics, whose constant reassurances about the wonders and inevitability of a global economy induced developing poorer countries to join the club. These artificial impediments interfere with essential income from exports and not only make it more difficult, at times impossible, to service the debt incurred just to become more export-oriented, but the culprits are the very countries with the largest shareholder stake in the lender institutions—the IMF and World Bank. It is even said derisively that the IMF is a branch of the U.S. Treasury Department.

One of the functions of the WTO is to serve as a forum for future multilateral trade negotiations among its member countries. These are practically ongoing from year to year and proposed changes require unanimous approval of member delegations. The opportunity will surely present itself at some future date for developing countries to have their grievances heard, paramount among which are hindrances to selective exports. The time will come when some of the Third World countries will remind their wealthier counterparts that flaws beset the practice of free-market global economies as presently constituted. The wealthy countries would be well advised to review their economic policies, eliminate artificial hindrances to international trade, and make substantial adjustments in response to reasonable criticism. Each nation must have a stake in the global economic system. The design of the new economic experiment is defective and unworkable with the best of intentions. It is therefore understandable that of the world's poorest countries most of them have lost ground after years of trading with multinationals. The wealthy international money managers and global corporations have reaped great benefits from their contrived economic experiment and grown richer.

(12) There are no absolute winners in Nature's scheme of things. The weak are compensated with certain uplifting qualities which the strong have to do without. There are compensating balances and unintended consequences. Developed countries saw the removal of some of their major industries overseas to maximize profits from the use of cheaper labor, left a vacuum behind of unemployed, unemployable and underemployed labor; caused an interrupted income stream which cannot help but affect aggregate demand and result in a retreating economy; left the affected segment of population and support industries impoverished and destitute. What justification was offered? Commerce and capital must not be hemmed in by man-made national boundaries but free to locate anywhere to exploit more profitable opportunities. The result is a steadily rising unemployment waiting for technological changes to create new employment opportunities. But the economic climate has changed radically; the temptation of new inventor-enterprises to follow the known blueprint of labor-saving incentives abroad would override any domestic considerations. The exodus of many commercial enterprises from developed countries has, to all intents and purposes, permanently reduced the industrial and employment base in those countries; left a discernible void which no amount of global integration could rectify—only uninterrupted prosperity could make a noticeable dent. Permanent global prosperity, however, is a pipe dream of deluded optimists, a condition which is not only without precedent but a theoretical and practical impossibility. No economy can be made recession-proof. Anything less than uninterrupted prosperity would peg the rate of unemployment at levels considered unacceptable by civilized societies. A reduced industrial base, which is likely to assume features of semi-permanence, may yet prove to be the bane of developed countries favoring globalization at any price, a collection of highhanded practices.

Most Third World countries have for decades, nay centuries, enjoyed a modest standard of living, based around the basic family plot of agricultural land from which they managed to eke out a bare subsistence. Whatever small surplus an occasional good crop produced was brought to the village or town market to be sold or exchanged for other necessities. Such economic conditions embraced the major part of the population; satisfying such primary needs, i.e., basic necessities for survival, was the chief preoccupation. Then came multinational global corporations and international lending institutions, ostensibly to raise the standard of living (especially for the mostly autocratic ruling elites) and help bring about the hoped for sustained economic growth. They offered what were locally considered immense loans for expensive infrastructure improvements and helped create an export-oriented and free-market economy to lessen the extensive poverty. This required the inevitable Structural Adjustment Program to make the economic potential creditworthy, market-oriented and therefore acceptable to international lenders, who were not only most anxious to make lucrative investments but assure timely loan repayments. Adjustment programs disrupted the culture and social fabric of developing countries by requiring privatization of government owned facilities, reduction of social programs, transfer of small family owned farms to giant foreign corporate agribusiness manufacturers, and as a result became dependent on foreign food imports. Most developing countries' agricultural products are exported by foreign multinational corporations; formerly self-sufficient, this makes them dependent on foreign food imports customarily handled by international trading companies. The displaced farmers augment the pool of surplus labor and compete for work in the new export-oriented factories. An uninterrupted global prosperity (an impossibility, as mentioned above) could have brought about some economic growth and raised their standard of living. It did not happen, not only because the global economy did not enjoy the benefits of a prolonged prosperity, but mainly because the global system is flawed and favors the rich developed countries. It must be made more evenhanded and balanced to ensure the continued and willing participation of poor countries. An economic contraction, or broadbased recession, would adversely affect the economies of industrialized nations, but the effect on Third World countries would be moderate—the industrial base is generally a minor segment of the economy. Under such circumstances, a return to the family owned plot is inevitable for the unemployed and destitute. In an economic downturn, the advantage of poor nations is the small acceptable adjustment necessary to compensate for the changed conditions and satisfy solely basic primary needs, a part of their age-old culture. In most industrialized countries, failure on the part of its citizenry to satisfy the accustomed secondary needs, reduced by the debilitating circumstances of grappling with unaccustomed onerous primary needs, would lead to unrest, class conflict, even upheaval. Barring conditions of war, middle class citizens, in particular, take for granted a graduated level of affluence and steadily improving standard of living, evidence of prosperity and economic growth. Even for winners in the global shakedown of poor countries, the initial years of surging prosperity will, slowly but steadily, give way to a lackluster contraction because of globalization. The unceasing economic growth contains the seeds of its own demise.

CHAPTER 12

CAPITALISM AND THE GROWING PROBLEM OF UNEMPLOYMENT AND POVERTY

(1)   Before major corporations appeared on the scene, business enterprises were managed and owned by the same individual, his family, or other related individuals, who were also actively engaged in the production and trading process, i.e., the producers, traders, and managers were also the owners. Such enterprises were necessarily of small capacity because expansion capital could only be provided from profits earned. But there were a few striking exceptions, particularly in the banking business, remarkable because of the genius of the patriarch-founders, who were blessed with sons of exceptional ability. The Fugger and Rothschild families founded major European merchant banking dynasties and were variously dominant between the 15th and 19th centuries. In areas other than banking, particularly as a result of the Industrial Revolution, there was a gradual separation of those who provided labor and those who owned equipment, furnished raw materials and provided management. This marked the beginning of the capitalistic system. Due to competition, enterprises sought an ever greater share of the market, and this required larger capital investments to accommodate expanded production facilities. Owner-managers maintained a decreasing control of companies as the number of stockholders increased and, in time because of growth, ownership and management were separated; they became publicly owned and traded companies. When the stock of companies became publicly traded, ownership became increasingly diversified, with control of major

companies placed in the hands of professional managers. The latter, most of whom merely owned an insignificant percentage of the shareholdings, assumed the functions previously exercised by owners and, in the process, acquired a vested interest in preserving their control as managers. But this is not capitalism. These managers are salaried employees, participating in perquisites, such as use of company cars and aircraft, various insurance benefits including life insurance and pension plans, use of company dining rooms, opportunities to engage in insider trading, earning substantial bonuses, company stock options, and generous termination payments. Ensconced in their corporate ivory towers, they enjoy most of the privileges of owners but suffer none of the financial perils, such as exposing their personal net worth to the risk of business failure. When their companies obtain credit lines from financial institutions, they are not asked for personal guarantees, and if asked, would most assuredly decline. They only risk termination of employment which happens principally in cases of gross incompetence or retirement. The baker, plumber or carpenter, to name just a few, as sole owners of their respective companies, are the true capitalists, the genuine risk-takers, the venture capitalists, enjoying none of the protection accorded corporate managers. The latter are not the owners of the means of production and distribution but represent absentee stockholder-owners, a type of economic system more akin to quasi-socialism, a system based on common ownership of the means of production and distribution. Yet to hear these corporate executive managers, especially of major corporations, sheltered under a corporate umbrella, these salaried employees who managed to advance to the top ranks, appointed by and serving at the pleasure of corporate directors (elected by absentee stockholder-owners), spout the efficacy of risk-taking and free-market capitalism, represent their kind as the paragon of the capitalistic system, when in reality they only vigorously defend their vested employee interests and the enjoyment of free corporate perquisites. The primary function of these managers is to expand corporate profits and procure a progressively larger percentage of the market, so that corporate shares would appreciate in value and the majority of stockholders (millions in many cases) approve their performance. Therein lies the problem. The relationship between executive managers and directors (the latter are required to monitor the former and are their bosses) can, in time, become one of coziness; the existence of interlocking directorates are conducive to corporate intrigues and the lack of separation between them is detrimental to the interests of stockholders. Management actions tend to become secretive by design; the proverbial executive suite becomes one of privilege and distinct power within; insider corporate loans and stock trading are common; executive compensations and benefits are routinely reviewed to better than match the scale paid by other successful corporations to attract and retain skilled personnel; greed and self-seeking are rampant. But as long as corporate shares increase in value, the concerns of stockholders are not aroused. For greed is just as common among stockholders (some of the largest are impersonal mutual funds, constantly in search of more profitable investments) as among corporate managers; activities detrimental to community or national interests are condoned, or winked at, as long as the aim is to maximize corporate profits.

(2)   This distinct class of corporate executive managers guiding the largest corporations and financial institutions share related interests; generously support political institutions favorable to their undertaking; collectively exercise the necessary political influence to bring about a favorable business climate. Formerly the priests, then the kings, followed by the papacy, emperors, capitalists, and finally corporate managers, these present-day wielders of power and influence, relatively few in number considering their impact on world events, act in concert globally to maintain a favorable political climate, a social and economic order conducive to global economic integration, interlinked financial markets, and total freedom for capital seeking global investment opportunities, in short, a new world order. They comprise the new elite and select, the most influential and well compensated segment of society, directing their energies solely toward accumulation of wealth as the main focus of life's purpose to the exclusion of all other considerations, such as the well-being of outsiders; possess the ability to manipulate information and events to camouflage their true intentions for fear of being discredited; follow an agenda undemocratic in practice and anti-democratic in principle. These seekers of unlimited wealth and power constitute a new form of oligarchy, the preeminent influence of the wealthy, limited in number, who believe that inequality in wealth justifies inequality of rights of the lesser endowed. These are the managers of supranational corporations, who plot to reshape national economies in complete disregard of national interests, in order that their successful entry into global markets would reach the zenith of aggrandizement.

(3)   The new globalism created by multinational corporate managers (this would include most of the major corporations) has been successful, for

now; the regimen they dispense has enriched their coffers; they brought good news to stockholders who not only received larger dividends but their holdings were enhanced in value. But this new order is flawed and has many dark sides. It created conditions of unemployment and under-employment in advanced industrial as well as undeveloped countries, which have the features of semi-permanence (there are just too many people and the production technology is too efficient), greater poverty and disorder in the latter. The new globalism has created massive debts which are not likely to be fully repaid, not only creating hardships for debtor developing countries but possible conditions of instability for lender institutions. The darkest side, however, has been the propagation and acceptance of a new philosophy of wealth, a culture of insatiable acquisitiveness and overemphasis on moneymaking as the foremost aim of existence. Wealth and enrichment equal success, dispassionate and amoral, as the new symbol of man's proud achievements. Man's efforts to persevere underlie activities of his very existence, the satisfaction of pri-mary needs, and the creation of some discretionary surplus to avoid bondage. An average education, reasonably good health, freedom to choose gainful activities one is best suited for can achieve, if pursued dili-gently, a level of income more than sufficient to satisfy primary needs. For the average man, the pressing pursuit of moneymaking tapers off progressively the more he reaches a level of income in excess of his needs. It would surely represent a sorry existence for man if his pursuits were confined solely to the creation of wealth, to the exclusion of other activities regardless of the level of comfort achieved. Yet this is exactly what the oligarchic order of global corporate managers represents. Under the guise of professing the efficacy of the capitalistic system, which, at a minimum, encompasses private ownership of the means of production and distribution, the taking of financial risks, unlimited competition, a free-market, opposition to governmental interference and intervention— these corporate executive managers, these employees of the real owners, do not own the means of production and distribution; are not risk takers but hide behind the corporate shield; once successful, conspire to limit competition; corrupt the free-market process by seeking governmental intervention when the need for subsidies, tariffs, or tax concessions arises. They do not represent the capitalistic system but its dismal accretions: unlimited acquisitiveness and overemphasis on moneymaking. Yet they symbolize the culture of the new global economic order and are most disingenuous in their claims. It is natural for man to follow his instinct of self-preservation and to leave no stone unturned, regardless of moral considerations, to satisfy his primary needs. This is his duty and right co-extensive with his capacity to perform. If he has the wherewithal, he will manage to satisfy secondary needs; the apex of success is reached when man's discretionary surplus is capable of satisfying tertiary needs, a condition which places him far beyond the gravitational pull of necessities, circumstances limited to but a few of the financially most successful and privileged, the financial elite of the world. The corporate executive managers of the larger corporations belong to this select group.

(4)   The fundamental flaws of the economics of globalization were described in prior Chapters. In this Chapter some of its other defects will be adduced.

How can the corporate management elite preach the efficacy and beneficial attributes of global capitalism when they are its shadowy interlopers and corrupters? How can a sovereign Third World nation govern itself when confronted by global speculation, disruption of its culture by multinational corporations, and exposed to the hegemony of the IMF? How can the corporate management elite of multinationals, the privileged few who live in undisguised luxury, have anything in common with the world's poor and have any understanding of their plight? They have shown no concern for the unemployed and poor in their own country. They must surely know, or at least consider the possibility, that developing nations would view their promises of improved conditions with suspicion and react with understandable hostility if they fail to develop. Of the global population, 65% live in poverty and are beginning to show anger for suffering unyielding misery. This number keeps growing year by year, and no economic system presently known to man can provide a key to tackling the problem. Is it possible that the free enterprise and competitive capitalistic system are so efficient that they provided a production and service technology which progressively manages to produce more goods with less labor? Is the system that defective to cause a constantly worsening maldistribution of wealth as to preclude an ever greater majority of mankind from participating in the economic process and share the benefits of effective consumers? One thing can be stated unequivocally: unlimited acquisitiveness and overemphasis on money-making, that obdurate mantra of corporate executive managers, will not provide the solution. Adam Smith (1723–1790) was on target when he warned that a separation between business ownership and management could lead to possible abuse. But he could not foresee that such a separation could bring forth a management elite aggressively pursuing its own interests and in the process manage unwittingly to pervert and impair the capitalistic system.

The corporate management elite of multinationals is intellectually unprepared and culturally ill-equipped to confront Third World countries as coequals. On the contrary and by the nature of things, the background of individual executives and their financial standing incline them to a position of superiority vis-a-vis their poorer counterparts, which they consider as sufficient reason in not negotiating agreements based on reciprocity. Additionally, accurate prognostications of the direction of global markets are beyond the vision of multinational executives; frequent miscalculations are viewed as efforts to engage in sinister entrapment and prompt understandable mistrust and apprehension on the part of their poorer trading partners, circumstances not conducive to lasting cooperation. Multinational agreements without transparent reciprocity and acceptable compensatory measures are bound to arouse lack of confidence; the injured party has every moral, if not legal, right not to be bound by its detrimental provisions, if they are based on inequality: getting the short end of the bargain involving underhanded procedures; clever maneuvers by taking advantage of the weaker's shortcomings; misplaced reliance on continued global prosperity; no noticeable relief of poverty and unemployment; growing dependence on burdensome loans; the threat of capital flight if future demands are disputed. The global managerial elite, unable to disguise its arrogance and pride, is not capable, on that account, of concluding lasting agreements with Third World nations in furtherance of global trade which would withstand the test of changed circumstances.

(5) Unless seriously incapacitated or suffering from a disabling illness, it is the natural instinct of humans to be gainfully employed in some field of activity promoting self-preservation and contribute to the overall well-being of society. It can be taken as axiomatic that the gainfully employed benefit more from society's well-being than they contribute to it, regardless of their participation. Prosperous countries provide financial benefits to the unemployed for some defined period of time, even though, as unemployed, they contribute nothing to the well-being of society except use the support payments to purchase necessities and satisfy other obligations. Unless employment is terminated for willful misconduct or the termination is voluntary, it is incumbent upon a well-managed modern State to:

(a) Provide unemployment benefits for a specific period.

(b) Maintain facilities aiding the unemployed to find employment.

(c) Offer job training programs in occupations more in demand.

(d) If the number of unemployed exceeds a targeted percentage of the labor force, it must sponsor public works programs for the unemployed.

Be it structural, technological, frictional, or cyclical unemployment, the State must make available to the unemployed, at a minimum, the assistance outlined above as a matter of right and not charity. For it behooves its interest not to make the period of unemployment a humiliating and financially embarrassing experience and avoid bringing about a feeling of resentment toward the political authorities and business establishment. It is the duty of the State to keep the economy at levels providing maximum employment at compensation sufficient, at a minimum, to keep body and soul together.

(6) Unemployment must be treated as a social evil, a disruption of the economic and civil order, particularly if those affected are the sole support of families with children. It causes loss of confidence and self-esteem, the hardship of financial stress and doing without, crimes, suicides, juvenile delinquency, mental and physical disorders. It is a blight on the body politic and a contemptible, ill-considered economic theory which holds that a certain percentage of unemployment is desirable to keep inflationary pressures under control. It is reasoned, evidently by those whose jobs are not in jeopardy, that full employment by itself would bring on upward pressures on wages, reduce profits, force businesses to raise prices and thus cause an inflationary spiral, a condition not desirable to maintain a stable economy. It is, however, the result of simplistic theories based upon unreliable economic models to arbitrarily select one particular out of many antecedents and assign to it the attribute of cause. This is one of the major fallacies of economics, not an experimental science but an observational discipline, and as such, susceptible to misleading conclusions influenced by the observer's preconceived agenda. Inflationary pressures are due to a multiplicity of causes besides the labor issue:

(a) Increase in velocity of money in circulation.

(b) Excessive demand for goods and services.

(c) Increase of the quantity of money in circulation.

(d) Devaluation of currency to benefit exports at the expense of imports.

(e) Easing of credit policies.

(f) Monopolistic price increases.

(g) Conspiracy among suppliers to raise prices.

(h) Lack of competition among suppliers.

(i) Price increases in anticipation of shortages caused by strikes, influence of inclement weather upon crops, natural disasters, political instability.

(j) Foreign price increases of essential raw material imports.

(k) Economic panics due to psychological causes.

(l) Speculation in the commodities markets.

(m) Foreign influences and international cartels.

(n) Producers' and suppliers' greed.

Any one of the above listed causes, in conjunction with some others, could disrupt price stability and shake producers' and consumers' confidence. A theoretical full employment would put pressure on wages; an increase in worker productivity or technological improvements in the production and distribution process could maintain, or even increase, the desired profit-margin. It is the height of obtuseness to protect price stability by attempts to maintain a rate of unemployment at artificial levels.

(7) A low rate of unemployment, a condition to be desired by any civilized society not only as a matter of social equity but beneficial to social order, increases aggregate spending because there are more consumers with real disposable income. It is, however, the favored propaganda repertoire of stock market traders and speculators to convince the public and fiscal authorities that almost full employment is unmitigated bad economic news, signaling the onset of positive inflationary pressures, anticipating a stock sell-off and a decline in stock values due to loss of investor confidence. Are they concerned that a profit squeeze would result in lower stock prices? One gets the impression, based upon the stock market performance over the last few decades, that market fundamentals have been replaced by investor exuberance or gloominess and that any connection between market value of traded shares, price/earning ratio and price/sales ratio, are purely academic and only formerly of reliable consequence. Do they really believe their own statements or attempt to sway the investing public with specious theatrics based on non-news? One is reminded on hearing stock analysts forecast market trends, expectations and explanations of incessant price volatility of the ancient priestly oracles shrouded in mystery and communicated to trusting but unsuspecting congregants. Expressed in another way, speechifying by stock market traders does not require a grasp of economics but a course in Psychology 101. How else is one to judge the substance underlying price volatility on

any particular day if based on flimsy trivialities, such as: the stock market soared as investors searched for bargains; the market declined sharply on profit-taking; the market rose sharply in expectation that mutual funds would unload their surplus cash; the market declined as investors reduced their holdings before the holidays; investors were selling because of pessimism about the economy; the next day, investors were buying because of optimism about the economy; the decline in consumer confidence was larger than expected and this had a negative effect on market performance. And so on. There is no connection between such flightiness, such non-news, and the real value of shares. This is casino speculation, day trading pure and simple.

Major corporations find it profitable, at times, to stimulate inflation and, at other times, to depress prices (to reduce excess inventories), a plain indication that economic realities can be manipulated and that economic fundamentals are mostly contrived if there is enough motivation to engage in such intrigues.

Stock market traders prosper on price instability, market volatility and unexpected market movements, which are conducive to short-term profit expectations and therefore generate a high volume of market activity—the bread and butter of traders. A high employment rate and the consequent possible upward pressure on wages are viewed by stock traders as price-destabilizing, whereas excessive corporate executive compensations, which have soared over the course of only a decade to extremes previously considered unthinkable, are viewed with admiring applause as the legitimate rewards of successful business leaders in a free enterprise economy. Such excessive executive compensation is nowadays the standard with major corporations, seemingly disconnected from measurable achievements. Viewing the results of most corporate performances, high compensation of management executives appears to be the expected norm rather than the exception, regardless of above or below projected corporate earnings. Unlike wage-hikes of labor, which are expected to be tied to increased productivity or else treated as inflationary, executive managers encounter little opposition from corporate directors to their ever escalating exorbitant demands for higher compensation, as if it were a matter of prestige rather than reward to see which one of the corporations could afford to pay the most—not a word is ever said about inflationary pressures. Just two decades ago, the average compensation of CEOs of major corporations in the United States used to be about $300,000 per year. At present (2002), compensation—salary, bonuses, stock-options—is above $15 million per annum; this would amount to 500 times the annual pay of average workers. This corresponds to an astounding ratio. Annual executive compensations of $40 million (and above) are on record, a stratospheric ratio of 1,300 to 1. The compensation of the lower corporate executive echelon is not far behind. Is such excessive enrichment good for the economy? A critical observer of such financial self-seeking should not be regarded as cynical or envious, but how much more than an average hourly paid worker could such a highly-paid executive spend on consumer goods and contribute to economic growth? He can only eat enough to keep fit, drive a few expensive cars, own some vacation homes, wear a number of expensive clothes, take a vacation only so often. However one chooses the range, it would not amount to more than thirty times the consumption of an average worker. These executives, and others similarly positioned, driven by the frenzy of accumulation, engage in hollow sophistries when they treat high employment and labor demands for wage adjustments as contributing to an inflationary wage-price spiral, when, in fact, the demands for wage adjustment are mostly efforts to correct regressive shifts in income due to general price increases and thus narrow the gap between nominal and real wages. The different characterization of the two kinds of compensations is only a matter of power and influence.

(8)   A few comments about inflation. The simplest explanation is when too much money (demand) chases too few goods (supplies), the price of goods will tend to rise, i.e., when the demand for raw materials and labor exceeds the supply (cost-push inflation), prices go up. Manufacturers raise the price they charge merchants for the finished product, who, in turn, raise the price they charge consumers. However, a moderate 2% to 4% per annum inflation is an acceptable criterion accompanying economic growth. Inflation has been a fact of economic life since recorded history. No matter how successful anti-inflationary measures may be, the phenomenon of an ongoing moderate inflation seems unstoppable. How do price increases affect investors? It is realistic to expect the average investor to want to hedge against inflation, i.e., make investments which would at least increase in value relative to general prices. The most desired investment hedges are common stocks (equity securities) and real estate, with the latter requiring a degree of sophistication not common with the general public. This leaves equity securities as the most popular hedge against inflation, handled by special institutions well-staffed with professional market analysts and technical advisors to guide the uniniti-

ated as well as the experienced investors. It would certainly seem most disingenuous for stock market professionals to characterize increased employment as a blight on the economy, when the very existence of potential price instability causes most investors to divert their capital into equity securities and keep the stock market professionals busier than ever—one would think the latter would welcome such economic indicators. Yet these are the same professionals who regard a rise in joblessness with approval—a condition detached from price instability.

(9) The condition of unemployment thus far commented upon has been that of industrialized countries traditionally with a stable economy which can afford to maintain a safety net, i.e., transfer payments, such as unemployment compensation, to keep those out of work from sinking into dire poverty. The unemployed fare incomparably worse in Third World countries, where unemployment is an unmanageable calamity, not only leading to stark poverty but also to starvation. The economy is marginal, safety nets mostly non-existent, the unemployed and underemployed constitute a large percentage of the population, and the supply of potential workers is inexhaustible. Unlimited population increases keep the countries poor, life is cheap, education limited, health services inadequate and the employment potential discouraging. The over 3 billion workers, more than one half the world's population, living mostly in developing and emerging countries, who earn $2.00 per day or less, cannot be realistically counted as employed. Most of these suffer from hunger, live in poverty and without hope for an improvement in the future. The United Nations Population Fund reported (12/7/01) that the world's population is projected to reach 9.3 billion by 2050, and that 4.2 billion will live in countries where their basic needs cannot be met, i.e., live in poverty. The International Labor Organization (a U.N. affiliate) warns that at least 500 million new jobs will be needed over the next 10 years to accommodate new arrivals in the job market.

Advanced manufacturing technology makes it more than likely that fewer and fewer workers will be needed in the future to produce all the goods required. What is the answer? More than one-half of the world's population does not participate in the economic process and is not needed to satisfy the demands of consumers? Without mincing any words, it is apparent that these people are of no use to society, they are redundant, continue to reproduce without limits, and most require food subventions to keep them from starving. Global poverty and the lack of global employment opportunities are not the result of some natural law.

Without suggesting there is necessarily an equitable solution to these problems consistent with the cutthroat culture nurtured in industrialized countries, it can be stated that they are caused by the free-market oriented economy; flawed income distribution; defective allocation of resources; the inordinate frenzy and drive for income accumulation; immoderate consumer lifestyle; encouragement of greed and self-seeking; and most importantly, by the incompetence, ignorance, and lack of foresight of Western business and political leaders, who exercise a major influence on world economic affairs and whose control of large financial resources could give them the power to play a great role in determining the material well-being of mankind unmatched in the history of civilization but for their lack of resolve and refusal to countenance the dangers of inaction. These well-fed men of influence, well positioned and prosperous, whose intellectual horizon excludes those not sharing their common circumstances, consider their privileged standing unassailable and see no gain or urgency to get involved with the problems of the permanently unemployed and the plight of the poor. Perhaps they consider their approach backed by historical precedent—they don't feel threatened. But history has sometimes fooled the self-assured and self-righteous. The flawed conditions which brought about the economically underprivileged could be perceptibly lessened by Western business and political leaders, if they were minded to make increased employment one of the goals of economic policy. But they avoided such efforts for lack of purpose and incentive. As a consequence, the day could come when the world's disadvantaged would explode out of their misery and provoke a turmoil menacing the far-flung interests of the privileged. The worldwide capital investments of global corporations, dependent for their security upon the notoriously unstable police powers of developing countries, are particularly vulnerable to the moods of the mob. The maintenance of worldwide political and social tranquility are the cornerstone of globalization. Technology is too far advanced to ignore the lessons of history.

(10) Is it theoretically possible to have full employment? Some countries may succeed in keeping levels of employment at a maximum by maintaining production capacity at close to 100% and export the excess goods. But such a plan could not be available to all countries simultaneously, since, under the described conditions, some of them would have to be net importers. On a global basis, given the present steadily increasing population, no matter how well-educated and technically qualified, a signifi-

cant unemployment reduction is not attainable. There was a historical precedent in 14th century Europe, which brought about a shortage of labor and hastened radical changes in the social stratification, unthinkable before the calamity. What became known as the Black Death (1347–1351), a plague which eliminated about one-half of the population, a disaster that affected all aspects of life. After the plague subsided, there was no unemployment; laborers demanded, and received, a living wage. But with population increases exploding in the 19th century and thereafter, unemployment and poverty rose to levels not experienced before—the leverage labor gained centuries earlier was dissipated. It follows, therefore, that the primary cause of unacceptable levels of unemployment is overpopulation. The secondary cause of unemployment is the lack of effective demand which inhibits capital investments in manufacturing plants. The depressing standard of living of more than 50% of mankind makes a mitigation of the unemployment problem unfeasible. The distinction between cause and effect is blurred—it is a vicious circle. Technological production improvements are an ongoing process, requiring less labor by increasing worker productivity. The surplus labor joins the ranks of the unemployed and poor whose lowered standard of living can afford only the barest of necessities. This lowers consumer demand, decreases factory production and service industries, and lessens the need for labor. The unemployment and poverty problems just defy resolution in a capitalistic free-market economy. Barring another calamity of the order of the 14th century when Nature helped solve the problem for a few centuries, the ever increasing unneeded surplus humanity is the result of a linkage of conflicting man-made and flawed economic forces, the result of man's neglect, lack of motivation and absence of inspiration. Even if man's conscience were sufficiently provoked to undertake an improvement in the plight of the disadvantaged, such efforts are bound to fail because:

(a) There just is not enough discretionary wealth at the disposal of the rich nations to rehabilitate the disadvantaged, reform the flawed global economic system to create new vehicles of employment, and raise the standard of living to levels of minimum human dignity without substantially lowering the standard of living of their own citizenry. This they could only do with the consent of those affected, whose consent would be contrary to anything known about human nature, or else risk violent resistance and turbulence of major proportions.

(b) The human intellect and ingenuity are inadequate to comprehend and resolve the complexities such a grand scheme would entail; contemporary science and other disciplines provide no keys to a solution.

(c) The business and political leaders of rich nations lack the necessary courage to confront the risks involved in such an undertaking of remedial action.

(d) The business leaders of wealthy nations consider their global influence unassailable and would, on that account, hesitate to place their capital at risk for seemingly insoluble social failings and consider the financial benefits, at best, problematic. They see no reason to view the permanence of the status quo, however defective and reprehensible, as a threat to their financial standing.

(e) Society has been overly indifferent for too long in permitting unemployment, underemployment and poverty to reach unmanageable levels. It may be too late to find an economic solution even with the best of intentions, which is not the case.

(f) Those of the general public who managed to make ends meet and feel secure in their circumstances, or do much better than that, are too terrified of possibly losing some of the comforts of financial security to risk participating in any political movement to improve the lot of the less fortunate.

(11) The sound functioning of society has a constant need for services which can be adequately performed by untrained labor with a minimal education. There is always an abundant availability of those marginally qualified, whose jobs, despite their low skills, have always been in demand as fulfilling an essential and indispensable service to society despite the low pay and marginal benefits affordable with the wages offered; they manage to keep just at the poverty level. It is difficult to imagine how a Western-style society could function without the services of cleaners, security guards, watchmen, housemaids, messengers, parking attendants, hamburger flippers, etc. These are the level four wage earners. Next up are the semi-skilled with at least a high school education; their earnings keep them above the poverty level. Society could not function without their services; they are the hospital nurses, nursing home caretakers, supermarket employees, city garbage collectors, low-level clerical workers, office receptionists, etc. These are the level three wage earners. Next up are the skilled with a college education or other trade proficiency. They belong to the middle class; their earnings enable them to satisfy secondary needs and dispose of a discretionary surplus; they belong to the

professional and skilled-trade class—engineers, plumbers, electricians, carpenters, accountants, stock market traders, physicians, architects, small and medium size business entrepreneurs, etc. These are the level two income earners. Next up are the level two earners who demonstrated exceptional skills and aptitude to join the ranks of the select in the business world—the corporate executive managers and successful business entrepreneurs. Those reaching the top management of major corporations belong to this elite, the leaders who help shape policies of the business world (to this group also belong large private investors). These are the level one income earners, whose pay and discretionary surplus are large enough to escape from the gravitational pull of any conceivable necessities encountered by humans; however, society could function without their services. They manage multi-plant major corporations with far-flung subsidiaries all over the world; owe no loyalty to society or country that created a climate for their success; ready and willing to pull up stakes and move one or more of their managed plants offshore to profit from cheap labor, or downsize their operations at a moment's notice; abandon their employees, many with long service records, who join the ranks of the unemployed, or unemployable if above a certain age, and conveniently thrust the financial burden upon society to take care of them. Future experience may yet demonstrate that society could be better off without the non-ownership executive elite and instead patronize medium and small size business enterprises operated by hands-on owner-managers, who understand the value of good community relationship and the loyalty of seasoned employees. More jobs are created by small business enterprises than by any other employers. Nor do they constantly search, unlike major corporations, for offshore shelters, in order to take advantage of tax loopholes and legally avoid paying their fair share of income taxes. Most of these shelters are sham transactions, no more than fictional headquarters and folders in a filing cabinet, which violate the spirit, if not the letter, of tax laws; set a flawed example to the general public of tax compliance; deprive the State and local communities of their fair share of tax collections; but worst of all, set a sordid example to the investing public that a clever search for tax loopholes is just as important, if not more so, for the bottom line profits as implementing production savings or capturing a major share of global markets.

(12) Excluding the small and medium size business entrepreneurs, independent contractors, and large private investors who do not rate the status as employees, the four levels of income earners have one thing in common:

each could be terminated arbitrarily at a moment's notice, with or without cause, contract or no contract. Level three and four unemployed would face great insecurity until re-employed. Level two unemployed would find, because of their discretionary surplus, some safety in their savings until re-employed, although they too would experience insecurity for fear of diminishing their surplus. The security of the level one unemployed is not affected because their discretionary surplus is sufficient to provide for a lifestyle of their choice and their level of creature comforts are never in jeopardy. Pride and boredom would induce them to seek re-employment.

It seems as if some invisible hand has compartmentalized the levels of earners of income in a society, in any form of society functionally sustainable as a cohesive whole, each level complementing the other, each level structurally delineated, more indispensable in a descending scale, but wielding power and influence in an ascending scale proportional to the income earned. The highest income earners protect their station by safeguarding the societal configuration of income levels. Levels four and three are the poor; level two represents the middle class with the upper segment composed of the well-to-do; the rich comprise level one income earners. Basically, the strata of society can be divided according to the degree of financial security achieved: the poor, low income, well-to-do, and the rich, or simply, the well-to-do and the poor.

The study of the interacting forces in organized societies should be founded on things as they are rather than on things as they ought to be. It cannot be based on man's virtues (as the ancient Greeks understood them), where there are none; nor on man's morality, which is not a reliable basis for man's conduct. It must be framed by the dictates of natural laws, the most reliable basis of understanding the unchangeable man's motives and actions: the instinct of self-preservation, avoidance of suffering and the pursuit of creature comforts.

When the laws of Nature prevailed, the weak succumbed to the strong in the struggle for self-preservation. As population increased, the need arose to safeguard life and property and prevent the strong from dispossessing the weak by forcible means. Political society was formed, rulers and instrumentalities of government selected or self-appointed to institute laws to protect life against assault and establish rights of property ownership. Predictably, the well-to-do property owners (the minority) and the political leadership developed a close community of interest because the former paid most of the assessments (taxes) for the support of the latter. The non-propertied (the majority) exercised little or no influence on the political leadership. The institution of government followed its own rules of self-preservation by providing just enough security for the governed to justify its existence, but vigilant not to grant too much security for fear that the need for its own existence would diminish. The political leadership developed its own power to influence the course of events; to preclude members of society from violating the rights of each other and consequently prevent a challenge to its own authority. In the context of shifting balances of power, the political leadership would join forces with the property owners, or vice versa, against the non-propertied because their interests are correlated; it would therefore, on that account, never join forces with the non-propertied against the property owners. Such interaction of friendly and opposed segments of society and the linking of the one against the other constitute the drama played out by political societies since recorded history. The preceding simplified version of the dynamics of constantly shifting balances, each striving to acquire more power to ensure its security, exemplifies the struggle for a greater share of the pie, commencing with the ancient conflict between master and slave, continuing between the haves and the have-nots, the wealthy and the wage-slave, the rich and the poor. The rich feel more secure if the poor are insecure; the poor feel more secure if the rich are in retreat; the political leaders feel more secure if they possess the power to diminish the security of the rich and poor.

(13) The economic system best suited to accommodate the conflicting interests and the varying aptitudes of man is, for a lack of anything more expedient, a partly regulated democratic capitalism. Some regulations are necessary to ensure unimpeded business competition; protect consumers against product mislabeling and contamination; protect investors against false financial reports and fraud, to name just a few. For man's struggle for self-preservation requires unhindered exercise of efforts to gain security (freedom) and protection of his gains (property rights). Any political system which denies man freedom to follow profitable activities and enjoyment of his gains, inhibits his basic natural instincts which would, barring any incapacity, motivate him to overcome this handicap by any means, peaceful or violent. This is the stuff political uprisings and revolutions are made of. In a democratic society in which redress can be achieved by non-violent means (that is, in most situations), man's quest to assert his basic natural instincts finds expression in the contest for greater financial security.

As noted above, a partly regulated democratic capitalistic system is best suited to give expression to man's basic natural instincts. How ironic, therefore, that the most vociferous protagonists of the capitalistic system are the executives of major corporations who manage the property belonging to investors, the true owners, and who are accountable to the corporate directors for their managerial competence; these employees convincingly camouflage what they know to be fiction to protect their lucrative fiefdom. But then simulation and dissimulation are the ways of Nature, for wherever the minority is dominant, deception, bluff, and guile are more effective in preserving control then crude force. For many centuries, society was dominated by a small circle of a priestly hierarchy whose chief weapon was the spurious claim of divine intervention and absolution of sins, forces which retained their sway as long as the laity remained credulous. It is even more ironic that once these executive managers of major corporations attain pre-eminence in their field of endeavor—these corruptors and interlopers of capitalism—connive to seek government subsidies, interfere with competition, solicit guarantees against expropriations and underwriting of loans, criteria which are wholly inconsistent with risk capitalism; intrigue with their respective governments and their agencies to establish spheres of political and eco-nomic hegemony by a process they call globalization. They seek world-wide expansion of their particular interests by entering into unenforce-able bilateral agreements with less developed Third World and emerging countries and take advantage of their weaker economic circumstances. But in doing so they have crossed the Rubicon—there is no cost-free return to the status quo ante. For these corporate executive managers, limited by training and experience to view corporate profits as para-mount to the exclusion of all other mundane considerations, are unqual-ified to contemplate the permanently damaging economic consequences their relocation inflicted upon employment, growth, and general well-being of their home country, and the risks to which their far flung oper-ations could be exposed. Their international investments depend on the enduring political and economic stability of host countries where ruling parties are often replaced by an unexpected coup, raising the specter that agreements solemnly concluded could be modified or even abrogated; where repatriation of profits, repayment of loans, and massive exports would most assuredly contribute to a damaging inflation and impoverish the great majority of the population, causing unrest, possible violent dis-turbances, and demands for restoration of income parity, which the host country could not meet for fear of violating bilateral agreements with the IMF and the destabilizing consequences such a breach would incur. Disagreements dealing with the establishment of plant facilities could lead to expropriation; popular disturbances by malcontents as a result of deprivations would target production output or interfere with exports and endanger the safety of foreign personnel. All these potential risks should have been weighed by global corporate executives but for the implicit reliance on their respective governments to implement expedient bail outs of the total capital investments or, if necessary, initiate military actions to restore order. Citizens of the home country would never be told that their sons and daughters could be dying in far-off places to protect global financial investments. If all the potential costs of protecting foreign investments were internalized, offshore operations could not compete with domestic producers. Multinational corporations, with their extensive global investments, may ultimately leave no option to their home countries but to be drawn into the role of global policemen.

(14) Worldwide unemployment, underemployment, and the resultant poverty have become unmanageable because their numbers are staggering (over 50% of the world population) and because their concentration is largely in developing countries, which additionally have to absorb most of the annual population increases (100 million). Globalization has made, at best, a miniscule dent in the unemployment facing developing countries, but these were more than offset by the difficulties created in the home countries. Even leaders of Western countries admit that the hopes generated by their economic advisors, including corporate executive managers, that globalization was the panacea and the means to raise the income of the world's poorest people were misplaced. Fast-paced growth and cross-border investments promising riches but not delivering proved to be empty promises. A World Bank survey (March 2001) stated that private annual capital flows to developing countries fell from $300 billion in 1997 to just over $150 billion in 2001. Industrialized countries cannot passively countenance the plight of the major part of humanity sinking into the morass of poverty, leading to starvation and fatal contagious diseases, if for no other reason but self-interest; fatal contagions could not be confined to areas of their origin. But industrialized countries can even less passively countenance the poverty related evils of child labor, estimated at several hundred million, mainly in Brazil, Haiti, India, and even in the United States, working chiefly on plantations, farms, and in garment factories; to these evils must be added the bonded slavery of child-prostitu-

tion, especially in Thailand, known to well-to-do Europeans as the sexual playground of choice. Western countries must be further dismayed that African slave-trade is still well and alive, mainly in Sudan, where slaves are bought and sold as if nothing changed since several centuries ago. In the wealthiest country, the United States, garment industry sweatshops are still doing well, exploiting mostly non-English speaking immigrant employees by working them double the hours at well below minimum pay despite strict laws against such abuses, selling their merchandise to eager brokers, and justifying such outrages as necessary to meet foreign competition. Greed finds all manner of justification.

In light of such tolerated abuses driven by the profit-motive, do any political and business leaders of Western countries really care to mitigate the plight of the unemployed, underemployed and the poor? Those who are financially well-off and dispose of a large enough discretionary surplus to assure them stability in the face of any foreseeable exigency, have they not gained enough security to defy the natural order of things? Does the instinctive compulsion to pursue the dictates of self-preservation to the reckless exclusion of moral imperatives obscure and confound the perception of their long-term interests, even though self-preservation is no longer an overriding financial motive? Defiance of the natural order of things, i.e., Nature, elevates man from the pursuit of instincts in common with the animal species to want to mitigate the plight of the less fortunate—a sign of moral purpose, a manifestation of morality. Society cannot demand of man that he set aside, or impede, his instinct of self-preservation and engage in activities from which that instinct is absent, unless he attained a degree of financial security to guard him against all unanticipated contingencies. For a society is called civilized not because it produced great painters, architects, poets, sculptors, etc.—most of whom were well paid for their efforts and received ample acclaim during their lifetime—but because a large number of selfless and motivated citizenry possessed enough strength of character and dedication to set aside Nature's imperatives and for whatever reason, be it adequate financial security, internal fortitude or religious conviction, refused to overlook the torment of others and banded together with those similarly minded to mitigate not only the plight of their suffering neighbors but of humanity at large, working silently, without acclaim, fanfare or publicity—noblesse oblige. To follow the dictates of Nature is to promote the strong, cunning and tenacious, i.e., the useful, and abandon the weak, helpless and ailing, i.e., the useless and unwanted. To do otherwise is to frustrate the natural order of things and, by opposing it, free man from the burden of animal instincts and reach the highest plateau where moral conduct carries the day; to have reached that stage is to join the true forces of civilization.

One would have expected that major corporate executive managers, that wealthy business leadership elite, who bear the major responsibility of planning the new economic global order and for whom the mundane struggle for self-preservation should have been relegated to secondary importance, would be eminently positioned to ponder the dismal state of societies burdened by the calamity of the world's unemployed, under-employed, and poor, a state of affairs in which they were not the silent bystanders. Instead of engaging in an uninterrupted frenzy of accumula-tion, piling earnings upon earnings, so that the possession of wealth became an end game instead of a means to an end, well assured of the proverbial secure nest egg, one would have expected that they would set aside a part of their busy schedule to reflect upon the grievances of the disadvantaged and not permit their unhappy circumstances to slide into permanence without raising their collective hand. Even if sufficiently aroused, however, it is beyond the competence of any group of men to find a total solution to the problem—it has gone beyond the point of no return, but a partial mitigation in isolated instances is certainly within reach. These well-positioned executive managers, who contrived to exploit the loopholes of the capitalistic system, these prosperous leaders of the business world, should be expected to want to deflect some of their tarnished reputation by betraying a tinge of remorse for wittingly con-tributing to the problem, and join together to lessen the anguish of the unemployed, which, to say the least, represents the dark side of capi-talism. Unemployment and poverty give civilization a black eye, espe-cially when juxtaposed with unrestrained consumption and conspicuous wealth, a mark of a dysfunctional economic system and of humanity in distress. But no voice is heard, no hand lifted, no remorse shown, no time set aside—the elite kept silent, totally distanced and unconcerned. Sepa-rate and apart from the prosperous business leaders, Western govern-ments, their collective conscience aroused, have come to the somber con-clusion, even though belatedly, that financial aid to the poor countries is in their own interest since poverty is linked to terrorism and the security of rich countries could well depend on helping the poor. But such aid, though alleviating some misery, is not the answer since it is charity without addressing the core problem: jobs.

But there was one remarkable exception. Fate was unkind to this uncommon humanist (he was 56 years old when killed in a plane crash), but fortunate to have a son, Jan, to take his place and guide the giant enterprise. The father's and founder's name was Tomás Bata (pronounced Batia), 1876–1932, the most prominent industrialist of Czechoslovakia, the founder of the largest shoe manufactory and shoe retail business in the world, with 4,700 company-owned retail stores in every populated center of Czechoslovakia and in well over several hundred cities all over the world, including 100,000 franchise retail stores. A truly global enterprise, reaching a production capacity of 170 million pairs of shoes per year (1994), offering quality products at reasonable prices. Headquartered in Zlin, a company town modeled after modern American cities, the Bata companies (they were family owned) expanded into non-footwear products, such as automobile tires, using their Asian rubber plantation as a source of raw materials. They provided local company employees with many benefits, such as housing, health insurance and pensions, free treatment in company-owned hospitals, and free education in company owned schools. Bata companies later expanded into rail services, construction, insurance, publishing and a tannery in Zlin. Tomás believed that a focus on people and public service was critical for business success; revolutionized the treatment of employees and labor conditions; created opportunities for development and advancement, and added compensation for employees based on achievement; organized operations into autonomous workshops and departments (profit-centers) allowing employees to contribute ideas, stimulate production and share in the increased profits; made it a priority to contribute to the economy of any new market his companies entered. He clearly thought of his business enterprise as an instrument for social good for everyone and his company the means of lifting the living standards of people. His views were intended to affect the outlook for all business enterprises, a clarion call for better relationship with customers and employees, to quote: "Do not pursue money, he who pursues money will never achieve it. Serve! If you serve as best as you can, you will not be able to escape money ... use your enterprise to make the world a better place. Make it your aim ... It is remarkable that we can find the greatest number of wealthy tradesmen and a population on a high standard of living in countries with a high level of business morality." What a message! If heeded, corporate globalism as presently constituted would not have been possible. He would have condemned the IMF and WTO as destructive of man's dignity, immoral, and the creation of intellectually unenlightened bureaucrats. Not content with his accomplishments, Jan Bata set out in 1938 to effect major improvements in the outlook, education, and attitude of future leaders in the world of business, in particular, the up-and-coming entrepreneurs and executive managers. He proposed to establish and finance an exclusive Superior Academy of Business Management, with admission restricted to sons of business-millionaires as the most likely prospects to become business leaders. The avowed aim was to prepare leaders for the necessary changes in national and international commerce considered necessary to maintain a democratic capitalistic economy, stressing the importance of maintaining good labor relations by extending essential benefits so as to cultivate incentives, loyalty, and reduce unemployment by providing on-job training for unskilled applicants as part of a constructive national policy; not to let the zeal for profits gain the upper hand to the exclusion of other considerations. These were part of a curriculum worthy of a new kind of business leadership. The project was aborted by the Nazi invasion of Czechoslovakia in March 1939.

(15) There will always be poor people as a result of poverty-level wages, a condition where needs are barely satisfied; a quality of life which is harsh and difficult to bear; a situation from which the dignity of man is absent. In most countries it does not imply starvation but lack of adequate healthcare, a deficient diet, degrading and painful circumstances for the aged. The poor suffer. Not all people can qualify for a university education, or even graduate from high school. Lack of education disqualifies most young people from obtaining employment paying more than poverty-level wages. But then the present economic system has a constant need for such employees of limited education and short on qualifications to fill level four jobs—there will always be a market for such work. Who would want to perform such menial work if all applicants had a university education? Without them society could not function. Nature will come to the rescue. Not only do some youngsters lack the opportunity, stamina, ambition, or parental encouragement to get an adequate education, but many lack the right combination of genes which inhibit their comprehension and judgment—most of them are destined for low-paying jobs. There were some men and women of poor background and limited education who made a name for themselves and were counted among the most successful—but these were the exceptions. Certain pedagogues would argue that any group of children from a poor neighborhood, selected at random, could be taught any discipline regardless of

predisposed genetic make-up. Perhaps. But how many students would excel driven by ambition to continue their learning unaffected by a life of poverty? Would they not be forced to seek employment as soon as partially qualified and abandon further education, to escape from the clutches of poverty? What about those students who experience dramatic increases in learning disabilities because of diets deficient in nutrients and proteins, suffer from ongoing conditions of hunger, all attributable to poverty? And those who live in poor neighborhoods exposed to PCBs, which are tied to learning disabilities such as lack of coordination, poor memory, low reading comprehension and diminished IQ? It must be taken for granted that the poor are more susceptible to these disabilities than the well-to-do, which handicap haunts them for the rest of their lives and perpetuates their poverty. It is true that there are students in every class who reach the top of the ladder; competition demands excellence and some reach it effortlessly, given fewer handicaps and the right combination of genes. How else could one explain a Kasparov, Menuhin or Toscanini? How else could one explain a Churchill or Einstein who, despite a poor showing in school, achieved world-class? But these were the notable exceptions. The working poor and unemployed do not partake in the benefits a prosperous society has to offer. Economists of all stripes make no reference to them, as if they did not exist, even though they constitute more than one-half of the world's population and are becoming more numerous. Access to television and print media makes them aware of their shortcomings, for they learn how the other half profits from the good life. But those who are able to satisfy secondary and tertiary needs, namely the well-to-do and wealthy, cannot permit with impunity the indignities to which the poor are exposed without concrete efforts to lighten their burden, even if not wholly effective. Large enough financial grants, governmental and private, employed in the right places could have an impact, albeit limited. The poor are not organized as a cohesive force, do not have the wherewithal to change the system by force of arms or any other violent means to improve their lot because intelligence, organization and power are with their would-be adversaries. They could cause enough turmoil and disorder to make the life of haves less enjoyable, more stressful in coping with daily inconveniences. As mentioned above, there is nothing within the power of business and political leaders, however intellectually endowed, to better the lot of the poor beyond minor improvements of their circumstances. The collective selfishness and indifference of the wealthy have contributed, over time, to the despair of the dispossessed. Not only does poverty conspire against democracy, but no one can feel safe while so many are suffering. No less than a director of the WTO called global poverty "a time bomb lodged against the heart of liberty" (March 2002).

There are only two options available:

(a) Narrow the gap between the rich and poor by effecting a comprehensive and sweeping redistribution of income, which would make the poor richer and the rich poorer. The probabilities of a voluntary relinquishment or disgorgement are non-existent. It would violate man's instinct of self-preservation. This is not an option.

(b) Nature may reduce the excess population gradually but irresistibly over a century or two, if there is that much time left, which would result in better lives for the remainder, the former disadvantaged especially. The process would be harsh and affect with greater impact the most vulnerable sector of the population, namely the poor. Even the present (2001) world population of 6 billion is too large to sustain a viable environment and ecosystem by just existing, i.e., breathing, consuming, commuting, polluting, procreating, and causing garbage to accumulate. Man is not going to reform and cease the abuse of Nature's life-giving forces, since the profit motive is too strong and life too enjoyable for the haves to adjust and downgrade their lifestyle out of concern for the putative survival of some segments of humanity. But Nature will do it for them with their unwitting assistance. Pesticides cause leukemia and lymphoma cancers of the brain, breast, testes and ovaries; agricultural chemicals leak into hundreds of rivers, making fish unsafe to eat, water unsafe to drink; food-borne pathogens infect millions of people a year, the bugs pass to humans through beef, chicken and pork; antibiotics fed to animals eventually cause disease-organisms to mutate stronger; hundreds of nuclear irradiation stations are built to help kill the bugs, and the average pound of hamburger may receive the equivalent of millions of chest X-rays; more food resources are progressively grown on less productive land requiring more intensive methods of cultivation, fortified artificially by pesticides and fertilizers damaging to the ecosystem and humans; excessive application of synthetic compounds used as refrigerants, solvents, and aerosol propellants will damage the Earth's protective ozone layer, causing skin cancer, cataracts, and damage to the immune system; too many automobiles and smokestacks spew exhausts and fumes into the atmosphere causing acid rains due to excessive concentration of sulfur and nitrogen oxides, resulting in polluted and lifeless lakes, ruined fisheries and dying forests; extensive commercial clearing of tropical rain forests, which absorb carbon dioxide, Nature's own filtering process, will contribute to global warming and climate changes affecting agricultural productivity and therefore the food supply; chemical air pollutants due to overloading of oceans with industrial wastes, sewage and garbage will help lower man's immune system and his resistance to deadly viruses and bacteria; the most damaging poisons—PCB, DDT and dioxin—cannot be excreted but accumulate in human bodies with each additional exposure; countless millions of humans are born deformed, mentally impaired, psychologically and neurologically damaged because of the havoc inflicted on male and female fertility by synthetic chemicals.

It is clear that the ravages caused by man's devastation of the environment and ecosystem directly endanger the health and sanity of humans; they will require massive doses of medical care, which is at present already in short supply and expensive. It will be available, first and foremost, to those who can afford to pay for the needed medical services, i.e., the haves. There are just not enough physicians, hospitals, or clinics to treat the masses of low-income patients who would require more intensive medical care because of their greater propensity and predisposition to illnesses and other debilitating disorders. Survival of the fittest, Nature's inexorable and uncompromising selection process, will doom the frail and sickly, those unable to afford proper medical care and an adequate diet. Deaths will exceed births—excess population, i.e., the poor, will slowly diminish—until the environmental and ecological balances are restored to sustainable levels. Morality or other civilizing influences will not be effective enough to hinder or derail this forced natural correction; the overly aggressive, profit-oriented, and insatiable desires of man are the cause and bear the burden of guilt. This is a more realistic option, but degrading humankind to the level of animal species.

(16) The aims of morality and Nature are antithetical. Anyone who grasps this concept would denounce the practice of medicine as a black art for saving and prolonging the life of the otherwise unfit and consigned by Nature to the dustheap. Even though the science of medicine, its research and accomplishments, have become the wondrous glory of man, making the pain of existence bearable for most humans, the fair distribution of its benefits lags far behind. Likewise, food production has

reached a level of accomplishments which could provide enough nourishment for everyone—a credit to man's inventive genius—but for the faulty distribution. It only adds insult to injury for the undernourished to learn that surplus food is rotting in warehouses, or fed to pigs, or destroyed to avoid spoilage, because adequate means of distribution are lacking for shipments to impoverished countries, particularly if the intent is charitable. Nor is it encouraging for the undernourished to learn that life-saving food is intentionally destroyed by man to maintain price stability or to raise prices by creating artificial shortages. Though the failure of adequate distribution of medical care and nourishment may serve Nature's purpose in dispensing with the poor, it offends the moral dignity of man because these problems are preventable and cause unnecessary suffering; it is especially vexing when children are victimized. According to the head of the U.N. Food and Agriculture Organization (2002), around 815 million people—13% of the world's population—suffer from hunger and malnutrition, mostly in developing countries. Almost 11 million children, most of them babies, die each year from preventable causes; 600 million children around the world live in impoverished conditions; of this number, 150 million suffer from malnutrition. Poor diet and sanitation in early childhood make them more susceptible to diseases. If all children were immunized against measles in their first year, most of the 600,000 deaths caused by the disease annually could be prevented; and all this misery and pain inflicted despite Western countries providing considerable, though inadequate, funding to U.N. health organizations. The contest between charity and Nature's way simply favors the latter; the harsh reality is that even if the pain of adults and suffering children were eliminated, the economic system, as presently constituted, has no need for them: they are destined to remain a drain upon the resources of industrialized societies. There is a lot of unavoidable hypocrisy going on here. One-half of the world's population is not needed for the other half to function effectively? It would be unthinkable to float such an observation. Instead, the self-assured well-to-do are too preoccupied preaching that economic expansion and growth would, in time, improve the overall financial conditions, lifting all the boats when in reality lifting the yachts only; the other self-assured of either moral or religious persuasion relieve their deep-rooted feeling of guilt for the blatant injustice of it all by contributing to charitable relief organizations; the rest of the working half, forced to keep their nose to the grindstone by financial circumstances and eking out a decent living, don't have the

time, money, inclination, or understanding to get too exercised by the
economic torment or physical affliction of others. Everyone wishes for
the problem to somehow go away because they are paralyzed by the
prospect of forced personal entanglements or any interference with their
lifestyle—not much concern for sacrificing for the common good, be it
national or international. This is the way of man, that fragile, hedging and
inconstant species, when put to the test of going against the natural order.
The occasional caring individual who agonizes over the suffering of his
fellowmen, his efforts almost always thwarted by the uncaring attitude of
others, finds the obstacles placed in his path would slow his pace to an
ineffectual crawl—the general apathy is too daunting.

(17) Nature works in its own unpredictable ways; it is purely coincidental if,
on occasion, it accords with man's purpose. Nature luxuriated before man
came on the scene and will do so after he departs. His momentary sojourn
is just a blip on the screen of time, the victim of a faulty design in that he
went beyond, and disregarded, Nature's firm limitations imposed on him.
This misstep, this vanity, can be attributed to the influence of theology
upon man's views of Nature as existing solely for his benefit to use as he
pleases. Based on this ill-founded belief, man proceeded to exploit
Nature's gifts with reckless abandon—nothing will shield him from the
consequences of this trespass. He exceeded the narrow perimeter of his
existence by degrading the environment and ecosystem, polluting the
atmosphere, and progressively poisoning the food which nourishes his
fragile body. But he could not do otherwise. Like the tragic Hamlet who
suffered from one particular fault, so man, who shares the effort to persevere in existence with all other animal species as limited by the natural
order, managed to exceed that limit driven by an insatiable greed (his
particular fault) to surpass by far his basic needs for security. This incessant drive for ever greater security beyond all reasonable needs takes on
the mantle of an increasing drive to accumulate ever more wealth, will-
fully unmindful of the damage caused to his life-sustaining habitat and
the injury inflicted upon his fellowmen. To this end, the discipline of
classical economics was designed to place this crude pursuit of wealth
within a framework of probity. Economics ignores the negative consequences of that pursuit upon man's moral fiber; its protagonists declaim
that to be credible economics has to be amoral. But if morality were
injected into its design it would self-destruct. Therein lies its shortcoming as a reliable guide to man's pursuit of a living; based upon
anaemic econometrics, it treats man as a cool and calculating machine

when, in fact, he is mostly guided by passion and impulse. Generally speaking, the pursuit of wealth is necessarily amoral until it equals man's need for a level of security commensurate with his resourcefulness and station. Beyond that, the pursuit of wealth becomes immoral, overreaching and destabilizes the psyche of man and the viable equilibrium of society.

When it comes to efficiency and competition, economics preaches the mantra "bigger is better and biggest is best." But this exemplifies another case of solely concentrating upon an isolated aspect of the economic whole, ignoring the necessary contribution of non-monetary elements to the well-being of society, in particular, the benefits of lower unemployment. It is true, for example, that an owner of a chain of retail stores can offer the public products cheaper than individually owned retail stores due to achievable cost-cutting measures. That is what Economics 101 teaches. But what it does not teach is that the benefits of greater per store employment resulting in better customer service would likely more than offset the price disadvantage. The individual store owner will, of necessity:

(a) Employ more people per volume of sales.

(b) Partake in hands-on management.

(c) Employ no more than a necessary nucleus of employees, less susceptible to downsizing if sales falter.

(d) More likely pay a higher living wage to reduce turnover and the cost of training new employees.

(e) Increase employee loyalty because of owner supervision; loyal employees are more motivated to provide better service to customers.

The single store would not only benefit more from customer loyalty but also contribute to the overall reduction of unemployment and therefore to the increase of aggregate demand, if such a trend were to be extended nationwide and globally; it is more suitable for the service sector than manufacturing.

The financial burden for support of the unemployed falls on the State; funds for this support are collected from employers as unemployment taxes, a cost which is passed on to consumers in higher prices for the products sold. The indirect non-monetary cost of unemployment, such as its degrading and destabilizing effects, is a load imposed upon the community to deal with. There are assuredly costs associated in alleviating the trauma affecting those exposed to prolonged unemployment.

The business community must be required to share such costs as a matter of equity; without fail, however, those enterprises which chose to dump their employees and move offshore to profit from cheap labor should be especially targeted for such levies. As homeowners, the unemployed may lose their home; fall behind on car and furniture payments (causing losses to lenders who are forced to recoup their losses by raising the cost to new borrowers); forced to neglect their general healthcare and that of their family (which could later lead to increased need for medical services); their children may have to abandon costly higher education, seek low-paying entry-level jobs and depress wages; financial hardships may cause the breakup of the family unit, lead to crime or participation in the underground economy and tax-evasion; their plight could cause mental problems, higher consumption of alcohol and lead to crime. But the classical and conventional economists not only ignore these problems but externalize the costs involved, unmindful of the basic principle that all costs passed on to outsiders to deal with must ultimately be recovered from some earners of income, the burden borne by either commerce or individuals (whose purchasing power would be reduced) and the assessments passed on in higher prices to consumers. A new philosophy of responsible conduct should mandate that all business entities, which externalize costs as a matter of convenience or expense saving, should be charged pro-rata for the consequential expenses passed on to State authorities as a result of such conduct and not permit them to perpetuate the overdone myth of acting in the name of efficiency. Enterprises which take great pride in becoming more efficient by achieving labor savings and becoming "leaner and meaner" may, in the long run, face customers and a public who will have likewise become "leaner and meaner".

(18) The political and business potentates, assisted by the free enterprise theories of tenured economists, have managed to make over one-half of the Earth's population irrelevant, superfluous and unwanted; the majority of people live below the poverty line and the numbers are steadily increasing. The national economies of Western countries have become global in full expectation that the resulting increased trade and growth would not only make their own economies more prosperous but also help developing countries reduce the general level of poverty. Such an endeavor would take time and require a condition of worldwide political stability to reassure potential institutional and private investors that the needed international capital investments would not only be profitable but also repayable. There is little time and there has never been worldwide

political stability. One cannot fail but get the impression that the rich countries treat unemployment and poverty as if they were a 19th century problem, the objects of occasional charity and token condescension. The present numbers, however, are too large and too visible. The seeming collective permanence signals a hopelessness never experienced before; there are no new ideas or solutions on the horizon. The world has come to accept their plight as the unavoidable and inevitable result of a profit and efficiency-oriented economic and social order—the price paid by losers in a competitive capitalistic economy. But the price does not have to be that steep for capitalism to bloom. Bonded with political freedom, capitalism involves the equal right of all individuals to freely choose the means of securing a living (within legally prescribed limits equally applicable to all), assume the risks involved, own the means of production and distribution, and seek the most profitable allocation of resources. Political stability is essential for capitalism to function. Although it is flawed, as is the case with any system designed by man dealing with the interaction of people, it is, nevertheless, the only known system viable in the long-run. But for the present, capitalism is not blooming; it has developed defects by unwitting corruptors. Massive unemployment and poverty are more the result of ineptitude and overreaching by the political and business leadership than any intrinsic deficiencies. Who are the chief culprits? None other than the executive managers of major corporations and the corrupt political leadership whose transgression against, and abuse of, the capitalistic system were catalogued in this Chapter. Additionally, major corporate interests wield too much power for the proper functioning of the national and global economy; corporate interests exercise too much influence on domestic and foreign policy; they are by far too large in relation to small and middle-sized businesses; most of their executives are scandalously overpaid and do not represent the champions of capitalism; own too many subsidiaries of questionable integration; the conduct of their top management is too secretive and conspiratorial; violate and ignore tepid efforts by administrative authorities to keep them in line, and when accused of wrongdoing, government lawyers are generally no match for their high-priced legal experts. The most effective reforms should prohibit horizontal mergers, acquisitions and subsidiaries (which invariably result in termination of "excess" employees), making corporate officers and directors personally liable for breach of their fiduciary duties and other law violations, and not excluding imprisonment and fines as punishment for their misdeeds.

Classical economics deals with people making informed decisions, intelligent choices and following the most profitable incentives, but the world of business is not guided by such thoughtful players. It favors large corporations; the promotion of small and medium-size businesses—which are critical to job creation—would be contrary to its logic. Political leaders should favor employment-oriented economies as the only key to a lasting and calibrated prosperity for all, leading to a tenuous balance of conflicting social forces. The present efficient economies are not conducive to social tranquility and would lose their luster if forced to internalize all costs. Camouflaging and evading the payment of all true costs and creating fictions to cut corners on their fair share of income taxes—all these to maximize profits—is more akin to the way of free-booters than behooves the rights and privileges of artificial persons.

(19) Do the well-to-do really think that life can go on with the accustomed aplomb even though one-half of the world's population looks on resentfully? Don't they suspect that their efforts to find a solution are seen as more akin to benign neglect and looked upon with suspicion as not really seeking to mitigate conditions of distress, but rather engage in perfidious waiting games to let Nature seal the inevitable? Even if so, none of the potentates would ever think of admitting complicity in such a Machiavellian scheme. It is, however, incontrovertible that political and business establishments are not only aware of the corrosive effect extended unemployment and poverty have on the mind of the distressed in that the resulting fatigue might vitiate their future ability to responsibly rejoin the economic scene, but are also very mindful that the political activism of the distressed could be impaired, quietly hoping for the unthinkable to happen. But lacking any practical and workable solutions to the problems of massive poverty (extended unemployment equals poverty); fearful their lethargy could result in unintended consequences, such as placing their security at risk; apprehensive that the ever increasing demands for financial aid would, in time, overwhelm their resources without raising any hope of lasting solutions—the political and business elite could be expected to rely on natural forces to free them and their preferred social order from the threat of upsetting the status quo. If they guessed right, Nature would provide the desired, albeit only a temporary, solution. But what if they guessed wrong? The ravages of new untreatable diseases, toxins suppressing the immune system making the body unable to conquer all the diseases; cancer-causing pesticides; food borne pathogens—all these man-caused disasters could spell doom in a devastating demon-

stration of Nature's awesome power to restore the natural equilibrium by bringing all humans to an ungraceful downsizing, without distinction between the haves and the have-nots. The impact of diseases could be the great equalizer.

An economic climate which permits the reckless failure to impose limits upon man's insatiable greed to accumulate wealth beyond all reasonable needs and permits the calculated abandonment of the disadvantaged to their fate culminates in a society which is dysfunctional; the inevitable Nature's intervention could only provide temporary respite from man's abuse of the capitalistic system. For human greed and recklessness are beyond redemption; given a temporary respite as a result of natural forces and the ensuing social tranquility based on an overall level of an emerging prosperity, humans will resume to procreate beyond the capacity for any future economy to accommodate the population increase. Unless the economic infrastructure is redesigned to eradicate most of its glaring defects—a course that would require selective limitations imposed upon democratic capitalism and human procreation—a resurgence of large-scale and prolonged unemployment and poverty are certain to reappear to plague the more fortunate and again endanger social tranquility. Man will have learned nothing from past experience: that one-half cannot prosper while the other half endures exclusion; that economic growth has limits and must embrace all; that prosperity is based on maximum effective customer demand by all, the only incontrovertible principle of economics.

The goal posts must be moved and the rules of the game changed.

CHAPTER 13

MAN'S SLAVERY
The Literal and Virtual

(1)   The generally accepted meaning of slavery is when humans are completely owned as chattels by a master, forced to work for him and do his bidding under his absolute control, for little or no pay, their wages being the nourishment, clothing, and shelter the master deemed fit to provide, laboring until sold to another slaveholder, too ill to be useful or released from the misery by death, serving under demeaning conditions and destructive to dignity and health. Slave-trade has been a most profitable occupation since recorded history, increasing or decreasing with the changing demand for slaves. But the demand for slaves always exceeded supply even up to the present, and although slave-trade was outlawed in the 19th century, there still exists a brisk market for chattel-slaves, indentured servants and prostitutes, with the latter much in demand by Western societies. Chattel-slavery, forced labor, debt bondage labor, sexual slavery and serfdom, all meaning involuntary servitude of one kind or another, historically fulfilled a social and economic need indispensable to the well-being and proper functioning of all societies; chattel-slavery and serfdom were abolished in the 19th century; slavery of children, debt bondage and sexual slavery are still practiced up to the present. Chattel-slavery was responsible for providing Europe (15th–18th centuries) with prosperity based upon an abundance of products, such as sugar, coffee, tobacco, gold, silver and cotton. In the United States, southern plantation owners and northern merchants built their wealth

upon the brutal and callous exploitation of chattel-slaves; this practice was abolished only when the economic structure based on labor-intensive slavery was replaced by a more profitable system based on labor-saving machinery.

(2) The sacred Scriptures of the main monotheistic religions sanctified chattel-slavery; they served as the underpinning of the grossest maltreatment and outrages perpetrated by humans against other humans, revealing for all to see and contemplate the grisly underbelly of human nature driven by overriding greed. For if the Deity placed the imprimatur on a social system which countenanced slavery, it was everlasting and unchangeable, a part of the divine design for humanity. No man could condemn as unjust such a social stratification without repudiating the divine purpose. All these God-fearing men who labored hard to rid the world of such flagrant abuse of humans were unwittingly guilty of blasphemy, of questioning the wisdom of the divine intent. Cited in the Scriptures and Koran: Deuteronomy 15:12-13, Ecclesiasticus 7:21, 1 Corinthian 7:21-22, Sura 4:1, 4:24, 5:88, 23:5, 24:33, to mention but a few references to slavery. It demonstrates, as if it were necessary, the utter futility of using the Scriptures and Koran as sole guidelines for man's moral conduct, writings authored by ignorant men corrupted by their self-serving agenda.

Epictetus (ca 55–ca 135 A.D.), a major Stoic moralist, originally a slave, preached that slavery was contrary to Nature. Like all Greek and Roman thinkers of antiquity, he was convinced that the key to orderly human existence was following the rules of Nature and being one with Nature. But Epictetus and other Roman and Greek thinkers of antiquity were mistaken, for they could not have grasped the underlying conflicts and disorder which only became manifestly apparent in the early 19th century with the excesses and social upheavals caused by the changes brought about since the Industrial Revolution. Slavery is not only not contrary to Nature but finds resonance with Nature. The relentless and merciless struggle for existence of all living organisms is fundamental to the natural order of things; it favors the strong, resourceful, and cunning, seeking exploitation of advantages wherever found. Greed and crude self-interest are the hallmark of the successful. Slavery is the vehicle of choice used to extract the maximum economic benefits by exploiting the labor of the poor, ignorant and helpless; they were forcibly, or by stealth, enslaved by enterprising and remorseless slaveholders who understandably showed no apprehension because the practice received endorsement in the Bible and Koran. The latter two sacred writings contain not a word of censure. Christian slaveholders were released from any obligation to grant manumission to their slaves when none other than the most influential Church father, St. Augustine (354–430), declared that the Old Testament injunction of freeing slaves in the seventh year was not binding and not to be observed by Christians. The Church itself employed slaves and justified such conduct by teaching that slavery was the result of Adam's sin. There has always been an oversupply of poor laborers; as long as the supply is abundant, the temptation will persist to enslave and exploit as many as are needed to perform hard labor and menial tasks at minimum costs. We have it on the authority of the Hebrew Scripture that the poor will always be with us. "Of course there will never cease to be poor in the land" (Deuteronomy 15:11).

(3) Men were not the only ones enslaved. Women and children (some as young as five years old) were required to perform slave labor with disastrous consequences on their health; the mortality rate was high and replacements abundant. The price of slaves was cheap, and as long as they performed their assigned labor for at least 18 months, the slaveholder recouped his investment and realized a satisfactory profit. There were minimal maintenance costs: basic food, clothes, and shelter. It was the slaveholders' choice to pay slaves wages since it was cheaper to have slaves pay for their own upkeep as it was always less than the meager upkeep provided by the master. Slavery made economic sense because slaveholders gained an early advantage over their competitors in keeping labor costs to a minimum and had the strenuous and enfeebling tasks performed by forced labor. Adequate free labor, at reasonable costs, could not always be attracted for such back breaking drudgery. But, for example, the typical sugar plantation owner only had a competitive advantage for as long as it took other producers to implement the same system—because demand was great, the selling price of sugar was not affected by any variation of labor costs, and so with other profitable production performed by slave labor. Even as slave labor became an ever greater part of total labor—and of the total population—their consumer demand could be ignored by the elite with impunity since they had no purchasing power; the prevailing economic system was in a highly expansionary mode and could disregard slaves as customers.

(4) Whether as chattel-slaves, serfs, indentured tenant farmers, indentured servants, bondmen, captive laborers working off their debts, or workers whose pay is limited to subsistence wages—they share the following in common:

(a) Their lives are burdened by necessities.

(b) They have no freedom of action; working conditions are harsh and suffer bodily harm as a consequence; their earnings are barely sufficient to provide for meager survival needs.

(c) They have no choice but to keep working and regard the hardships as their allotted burden of existence.

(d) With few exceptions, their economic privations assume the stamp of permanence.

(e) Although their labor is not financially rewarding, there is a constant supply of their services.

(f) The well-being of society depends on their production of an indispensable surplus.

(g) Their onerous working conditions and meager subsistence pay qualifies them as slave laborers.

(h) Since recorded history and up to the present, all well-integrated societies have depended upon the existence of slave labor and the bare subsistence wage-earners.

Because labor-intensive work is performed by segments of the population barely able to satisfy their primary needs, certain more proficient and talented groups of society are energized to pursue secondary and tertiary interests, the foundation of all civilizations, all in contravention of the natural order of things. All civilizations have depended on the existence of human slavery. The well-being of the minority always depended on the privation of the majority. If man possessed the time to pursue noble aspirations, it was because certain segments of the population produced life's basic necessities who had neither the means nor the aptitude to ease the burden of existence. A society in which everyone pursued self-preservation confined by necessity to primary needs and therefore disposed of no discretionary surplus and no freedom of action would be structurally dysfunctional and could not survive as a viable organization. Such societies could not exist in the world as we know it. Every society or association of individuals must have, at the minimum, political leaders and a system of administration; such magistrates could only function if others labored to provide the supply of basic necessities and performed the essential menial services.

(5) The present-day level 4 and 3 employees who receive as compensation subsistence wages, whose energies are wholly consumed by the self-preservation effort, and who are, as a consequence, in bondage to necessities, are wage-slaves. As opposed to conditions prevailing centuries ago

when a chattel-slave could not choose his employer but was coerced to work for his master under threat of physical force and possessed no rights since he was treated as property, the contemporary wage-slave (and the marginally self-employed) can choose his employer, possesses civil rights—in most countries—and his rights are protected by governmental authorities. But as to earning a living-wage sufficient to provide for more than just the bare necessities, he faces, like the chattel-slave before him, employers driven by crude profit-motives and intense market competition, willing to pay no more than is required in order to sustain a profitable enterprise. For any employer, regardless of the level of financial security he managed to achieve, is subject like his employees to the instinct of self-preservation and the preservation of maximum creature comforts. All categories of employers and employees—including those who triumphed by their excellence to satisfy tertiary needs—are motivated to action by the same instinct, by the desire to persevere and achieve maximum affordable creature comforts.

Organized societies have always been compartmentalized into four levels of income earners, whose rewards are dependent upon the capacity of each to bargain for increased compensation by withholding services for a duration long enough to exert an impact by their absence. Societies have a need for a great multitude of services, many of which are performed by workers earning just enough to satisfy necessities; their availability always exceeds demand. As a result, the supply/demand equation sets the compensation at the lowest level necessary to satisfy subsistence needs, subsistence wages, i.e., slave-wages. If the compensation were to be set below these levels, the workers would need to supplement their income from other sources; the strain could affect their performance, all to the detriment of employers. Most of these workers possess a limited education which gives their level of employment a degree of permanence, unless some are driven by ambition to better their qualifications and advance to a higher level of income earners. The lifting of the burden of necessities is in proportion to the procurement of a discretionary surplus, a measure of financial security.

(6) Just as better qualified employees and self-employed manage to attain a level of financial security which not only satisfies basic necessities but leaves disposable funds for discretionary needs, they could also revert to a condition of financial insecurity by incurring excessive debts, business losses, burdensome alimony and child support obligations, gambling losses, uninsured casualty losses—to name a few possible setbacks. Those

affected contributed to their own reverses of fortune in lacking the necessary discipline and foresight. But there are circumstances beyond the
control of the financially secure which could adversely expose them to
the caprice of natural disasters, such as earthquakes, fires, floods, or inca-
pacitating illnesses, suffering crushing financial reverses despite adequate insurance coverage. Such victims of unforeseen circumstances
could be humbled to seek government assistance or support from charities; their plight would confine them, even if temporarily, to satisfy basic
primary needs in an effort to persevere—a predicament akin to slavery.
The super-haves, those belonging to the financial elite disposing of a discretionary surplus to satisfy tertiary needs, feel secure enough in their
circumstances to withstand any onrush of most man-made necessities,
but could, nevertheless, be brought down to humbler circumstances by
the vicissitudes of natural disasters, the natural order of things. Man
must be mindful that the unpredictability of Nature could abruptly nullify any preferments based upon financial security and well-being, and
reduce his standing to that of seeker of subsistence-level necessities, the
imperatives of basic existence, i.e., analogous to the extremities suffered
by slaves.

The upper level two and level one income earners are financially
secure and free from the gravitational pull of necessities. Unless they
stuff their wealth into a mattress, they have to invest their surplus assets
to generate income and/or place them in reputable financial depositories
for safekeeping. But these are man-made institutions functioning in an
economic climate designed by man, given to flaws and not loophole-
proof, beset by shortcomings even under the best of circumstances.
Losses can and do occur, formerly profitable enterprises fail, financial
depositories are weakened because of incompetent and sometimes corrupt management, fortunes are made and lost by the vagaries of a defective system manipulated by shortsighted and unscrupulous speculators.
Even the financial elite, those economically independent, who managed
to reach the pinnacle of success, have reason to be concerned about the
safety of their investments, about their preeminence in the world of
wealth; they have reason to be exercised about their continued well-
being, given the prior history of the financially powerful humbled by
unforeseen and hapless circumstances, not caused by natural phenomena
but by the malfunctioning of a man-managed economic system, defying
planned permanence, a fabled failsafe system falling into disrepair. This
anxiety about the durability of their circumstances gives them the

needed impetus to pile wealth upon wealth in a determined effort to beat the odds against possible debilitating perils. In this resolute pursuit to circumvent a contraction of their fortune they do not differ from the subsistence level strugglers for self-preservation, i.e., slaves.

(7)   The concept of slavery is mired in a mix of ideas about slave ships, manacled captives transported mostly from Africa on long voyages to unfamiliar lands, auctioned off like cattle, and forced to do hard labor often under the most unhealthy conditions and for long hours per day, seven days a week on meager rations, all for an exploitative master, to be sold or discarded when no longer useful, only bare subsistence provided in lieu of pay with just enough time off for sleep and meals. The public is familiar with movies richly portraying the life of Roman slaves, with the strongest and most agile trained for gladiatorial combat to the finish in specially built arenas, all for the amusement of demanding and thrilled spectators. The rapid rise of Christianity in and after the 2nd century A.D. owed its success primarily to the message it preached to slaves of the Roman Empire, who were ready and willing converts to a new faith which declared that all humans, including slaves, are equal before the Christian Deity (yet without encouraging a change in the status quo, i.e., manumission), a message which, understandably, made the greatest impression on the downtrodden. During the Middle Ages in feudal Europe, it was the serf (he replaced the slave, although the serf had some freedoms) who labored on manorial estates under oppressive conditions, producing the supply of food that sustained the nobles. The Black Death (1347-1351) destroyed almost half the population of Europe regardless of rank; it created a scarcity of farm labor, and gave the serfs an opportunity to demand privileges which lightened the burden of their existence (the nobles had to eat), until serfdom gradually disappeared in the 18th century (except in Russia, which abolished it in 1857), though the peasantry was still burdened by old levies and duties, the standby shackles of serfs. Forced labor had become the backbone of the world economy and was not abolished till the 19th century, although pockets still exist chiefly in Brazil, Pakistan and Thailand. Slave labor reappeared in 20th century Europe; millions were sent to forced labor camps (gulags) by the communist regime of the Soviet Union; millions were conscripted for forced labor by Nazi Germany during World War II.

(8)   Since recorded history, slavery and serfdom were convenient vehicles of the privileged segment of society to enhance their economic advantage by legal exploitation of forced labor. The political leadership joined

forces with the privileged factions to pass laws to legalize the use of slave labor until technological improvements in the means of production and the use of constantly upgraded machinery made the need for slaves unprofitable. This degradation of humans was not abolished in observance of moral imperatives or the sudden remorses afflicting exploiters, but pure business calculation made the abandonment inevitable.

Involuntary servitude under which a worker is obliged to perform services for another under conditions of social inferiority is the mark of forced labor, i.e., slavery. All humans are impelled to action by their instinct of self-preservation which involves satisfying hunger, provision for adequate shelter, and clothing for protection against inclement weather. That instinct is the more pronounced the less a human possesses a discretionary surplus and the more so if it is absent, in which case he is burdened to provide for bare necessities. Natural instinct forces such a human to seek gainful employment to provide for his needs; he is without choice in this matter but to follow his inner drive to persevere in existence. His instinct forces him to perform services for others, if necessary, under conditions of social inferiority which is a criterion of his disadvantage in competing with those disposing of a discretionary surplus. Unlike the absence of rights of a chattel-slave who was treated as property, in a contemporary civilized society a worker possesses freedom of speech and assembly, the right to vote, and the political system protects him and his property from physical harm by others. But such rights and freedoms have little meaning to one on the edge of starvation and who suffers other privations. What is paramount in his mind and overshadows everything else is the constant awareness that but for the regular and periodic paychecks, he could not make ends meet and would suffer from hunger and loss of shelter. Such employment does not carry the stigma of "involuntary servitude" but comes close to being identical. His employment is not voluntary since circumstances force him to work for another and differs from servitude because he can seek other employment. But this is a distinction without a difference. Circumstances of need compel him to work and he has no choice in the matter. It is not his employer who compels him to work; it is not his employer who seeks forcibly to bond him; it is the involuntary servitude to natural instincts which makes him a slave, oppressed by anxiety and necessity, without choice but forced into bondage by his survival effort. He differs from the erstwhile slave by exercising freedom of movement and treated not as property but as a human in possession of an assortment of civil rights. But these freedoms are shared by all humans in civilized societies. The involuntary servitude to the instinct of self-preservation, that feeling of being held captive to, and dominated by, the necessity of securing the means of providing for a livelihood, this single-minded purpose of basic existence following the natural order of things, bound by compulsion to secure primary needs—all of these make him a slave to circumstances beyond his control, a slave nevertheless. To this category belong the level four and three income earners, the unskilled and semiskilled; their services are essential for the proper functioning of society.

(9) Those who advanced on the economic scale by earning a discretionary surplus went beyond primary needs and managed to satisfy secondary needs, i.e., needs which are elective by definition. Secondary needs are all wants beyond those necessary to persevere in existence; they improve the quality of man's endurance, i.e., raise his standard of living; he is no longer bound by necessities to live from paycheck to paycheck and depending on the size of his discretionary surplus, gains freedom of action to pursue satisfaction of wants not tied to primary needs. The prudent man would not relent in pursuit of financial security for fear of losing his level of comforts if some reverses caused the surplus to diminish or disappear, in which case he would be hard put to provide for his retirement, medical bills or a cushion for emergencies. The loss of income and changed circumstances would confine his efforts just to satisfy primary needs. The fear of descent into plebeian circumstances is a sufficient spur to greater dependence upon natural instincts. The urge to unceasingly improve the level of comforts to lighten the burden of existence; the stimulus to maintain the desired level of comforts is on a par with the stimulus to exceed primary needs—both stimuli subject man to stressful exertions, a victim to inflated needs, a slave to circumstances beyond his control. The greater the inflated needs, the greater the enslavement to their gratification. These are burdens of the middle class, the haves, the level two income earners.

(10) The wealthiest individuals, those counted among the successful money-makers, belong to the financial elite who managed to inflate their needs far beyond the reach of others. They dispose of sufficient wealth to satisfy tertiary needs known as luxuries and often identified with conspicuous consumption. Unless heirs to fortunes, these achievers of notable financial success climbed to the top by outperforming competitors, investing prudently, making timely savings, and endowed with an above average business acumen. Some of the super-haves who belong to the

dominant class and whose determination for aggrandizement reflects the
intensity of securing privileges display a maturity of vision commensurate with their refusal of submission to Mammon, know when to relax
their quest for accumulating wealth upon wealth, and devote some of the
leisure to ease the burden placed on the less fortunate. Such efforts would
not always exhibit altruism, but more than likely express a determination
to protect their social standing and economic privileges against potential
usurpers. Unless disturbed by political upheaval or revolution changing
the established economic stratification, the standing of the financial elite
is secure in a democratic capitalistic society, unaffected by the less
endowed. Their large discretionary surplus is safe and immune from
untoward encroachments—the police power of the State is the surety.
But such prudent super-haves who possess the maturity of vision are the
exception; most of the others display an arrogance of power and self-
seeking bordering on unbounded zeal to confine their interest exclusively
to their own and unmindful how their zealous wealth-enhancement
affects the less privileged. It is the lack of security of another kind which
strikes an element of apprehension into an otherwise self-assured way of
life. The accumulated wealth has to be invested to return a profit; some
investments are safer than others, some are marginal and the more speculative, if successful, the most profitable. There is a constant competition
for the best placement of capital to generate maximum returns. More
capital is chasing fewer profitable investment possibilities; there is an
inherent tendency to invest in riskier ventures, domestic and foreign, the
latter taking advantage of the globalization of capital, the most speculative of all available investment opportunities despite the age of instant
global communication. The more geographically remote the investment,
the less control can be exercised and the more reliance must be placed on
the advice, honesty, and competence of investment counselors and fund
managers—criteria of possible misplaced trust. Speculation in commodity futures and foreign currencies, for some a preferred road to
riches, for others a dicey playing of the casino market—the potential for
losses is considerable. All the super-haves are gratified to see accretions
to their wealth and apprehensive about any diminutions. Either outcome
would affect their standing in the councils of the privileged—a culture of
cronyism to be treasured at all costs. At times it seems as if these captains
of finance, industry, and wealth, engaged in global competitive capitalism, held on to the tail of an economic tiger and unable to let go for
fear of vitiating the commands of natural instincts to persevere in the

contest of their choice. The constant vacillations between long and short odds, between risk and reward light-years distanced from primary needs, restlessly and without respite, systematically pursuing the path of expanded profits to preserve the privileged lifestyle—by all these actions they betray a servility to the wealth effect, subservient slaves to greed, the most intense of human constants.

(11) Slavery accords with the natural order of things; all humans are compelled, without exception or distinction, to subservience in involuntary bondage to the instinct of self-preservation. To be coerced by any force, natural or human, to follow a specific course of action, precluded from exercising alternate choices, is to be bound to that force and to be a slave to circumstances created by that force. If the concept of slavery were to be dissected into its component parts and all those with an affinity to other predicates removed, the residuum would be "compelled or coerced to act". It is with this understanding that it can be stated that all humans are slaves to their instinct of self-preservation, an unalterable behavioral response, not gained from experience, and to persevere in existence. It conforms to the natural order of things that all humans differ in their physical and mental characteristics—no fingerprints, shape of ears, sensory perception or personality are the same; to the canine super-developed scent, no two humans smell alike. Humans differ in their responses to instincts, from the phlegmatic to the focused, to the changeable. Nature endowed humans with instincts sufficient for their survival, albeit unequally and arbitrarily, for those born deformed, dim-witted or otherwise handicapped are excluded from the natural design, emblematic of Nature's laws but repugnant to man's sense of morality—distressingly exemplified in the animal kingdom where with some species a thousand are born so that one can survive.

Without giving any credence to the doctrine of predestination, the unequal responses of humans to their instincts—the inequality of aptitudes and potential for intelligence, almost invariably an accident of birth and the vivid experiences during the first six years of life—preordain the disparity of individuals in society and their standing on the economic ladder. The well-being of any society is dependent upon the expedient economic stratification of its members, i.e., managers, entrepreneurs, professionals, producers, service and maintenance personnel, all representing different levels of income but all responding of necessity, although variously, to their natural instincts. As a result of the inequality determined by the natural order, all dynamic societies are fragmented into segments according to the economic contribution to the integrated whole, with the market allocating compensation in proportion to the worth of the contribution to private and public enterprises but ignoring the benefits rendered to the social well-being. Although the value of the contribution is determined by market forces, the minimum compensation cannot fall below subsistence levels, the lowest rank on the economic scale, or else the wage earner would not acquiesce to the hardships suffered and cause enough tumult to have the income adjusted. In seeking adjustments to income, life-sustaining wages are the floor, and the wage earner would seek parity between real and nominal wages based on inflation and the consumer price index. The power to demand adjustments above subsistence levels is limited since, lacking savings for support, the wage earner cannot withhold his services to force a settlement to his liking; lacking freedom of action, he is compelled by necessities to remain in strained circumstances. These are the unskilled and semi-skilled laborers whose supply is always in excess of demand, further restricting any economic improvement in their status. Yet these humans living on the edge of poverty perform an indispensable service without which no society could function; they fill a social and economic need essential to the well-being of organized society. These were also the slaves of old who could not shake off their servile circumstances on their own despite occasional attempts at rebellion. All civilizations have depended on the existence of slave labor, for if man possessed the time to pursue noble aspirations it was because forced labor, i.e., slaves, produced a surplus of life's basic necessities. The permanent inequality of humans as determined by Nature is mirrored in the permanent economic division in society. At the lowest rank are the level four and three subsistence wage earners, wholly consumed by the effort of self-preservation, living from paycheck to paycheck, disposing of no discretionary surplus and no freedom of action, subservient slaves to their natural instincts.

Possession of a discretionary surplus marks the economic status of the level two income earners. They are engaged in an uninterrupted effort to increase the discretionary surplus, maintain a steady income stream, and strive without letup to enhance the level of comforts. They possess the financial wherewithal to withhold services to improve their income, but the more likely method utilized would capitalize on better proficiency, greater efficiency, and more marketable experience. Placed between the economic aristocracy and the subsistence wage earners and guided by middle class ethics, they are typically weighed down by obligations such as home mortgage, education of children, business loans, health and retirement plans, life and accident insurance, car loans—just to name the more obvious—which serve as an additional impetus not to moderate efforts to persevere and continuously strive to improve the standard of living. Anxious not to reduce the level of comforts and painfully aware of the instability of achievements, there is little incentive to relax and enjoy the fruits of labor. On the contrary, responsibility for the obligations assumed would dictate constant vigilance to abort potential reverses and maintain adequate reserves should the income stream be interrupted—a condition of bondage to circumstances demanding nothing short of total commitment—slaves to the instinct of perseverance to retain and improve the advantages achieved.

The level one super-haves enjoy the luxury of having numerous choices of placing their investments. As the dominant class of financial aristocrats positioned at the apex of the economic pyramid, these major players are the movers and shakers of a flawed man-made economic system designed to facilitate their empowerment, which thrives on instability and risk-taking, constantly impelled to advance forward and abhorring the thought of standing still. Constantly maneuvering to place their wealth in more profitable ventures, investing, liquidating, and reinvesting often shrewdly and, at times, based on flawed information; placing their trust in the professional know-how of others since they could not adequately analyze the suitability of all possible investments—this cannot help but add to their concern and misgivings. They are deluded into thinking, a peculiar view of human existence, that the target of man's efforts in seeking great wealth is the enjoyment of a life of leisure, leaving work and responsibility to others. Such diversions, however, lead to a life of boredom, giving ample time to reflect upon the fragility and instability of their blessings and all of man's existence. They are determined, without respite, to protect their social standing and economic privileges, proceed in fits and starts to seek lucrative investments in capital markets, whose security and profitability are unpredictable, at best. Held captive to their zeal for aggrandizement, guided in judgment not by principles but sustained by self-interest and determined to persevere—they are slaves to self-preservation of their kind.

(12) The instinct of self-preservation is common to all organisms. To persevere in existence, humans have to satisfy hunger, obtain the cover of shelter and procure adequate clothing. These are the basic necessities for survival, the primary needs. The organization of societies enabled

humans to satisfy more than necessities, i.e., secondary and tertiary needs, by instituting a legal system which protects life and property against encroachment by others. It also enabled humans to systematize the means of securing needs, i.e., the means of procuring earnings based upon the economic utility of services provided. The inequality of aptitudes and education evolved into an inequality of earnings and the economic stratification of society into segments of have-nots and haves, more aptly described as the poor, the haves and super-haves. Each economic segment guards its income stream with tenacity, determined to augment the satisfaction of additional needs and considers the level of attained well-being at any particular time as the minimum targeted degree of accomplishments; any retreat or erosion would be stubbornly resisted.

Although the natural instinct is paramount, some humans are capable of frustrating Nature's scheme of things by intentionally reducing their needs and suppressing the zeal for aggrandizement. Such humans refuse to participate in the drive to constantly improve their level of comforts and, under color of virtue and exercise of stoic resignation, find real happiness in defying Nature's evolutionary process reserved for rapacious seekers of affluence; such humans have attained a level of morality which finds demeaning the besting of fellow humans and the gaining of competitive advantages at the expense of others. Their numbers do not embrace the poor, who are burdened with necessities, but some of the haves and super-haves who are modest enough to attribute their achievements, in great part, to the accident of birth; they derive satisfaction in helping the less advantaged rather than in the constant drives to maximize profits and pile wealth upon wealth in pursuit of capital investment opportunities. By their fierce independence they have proved that some humans can mount the pedestal of high moral values, express satisfaction with the wealth possessed without seeking further accumulations, the sure mark of civilized humans. This sets them distances apart from the rest of money-grabbers, rebels against Nature's design to enslave humans to their natural instincts.

(13) The turbulent and bloody history of man is indicative of the stress and strain of existence; it led him to participate in Nature's ordained principle of survival of the fittest. Despite man's pretensions to be the noblest of Nature's creations, his species is no more than part of the process of natural selection and self-preservation in common with other animal species. Nature is flawed in that its design, the unlimited struggle for existence, i.e., self-preservation, causes conflicts of interest leading to

interminable violence, bloodshed and social instability. The world is a field of discord which will never reach a state of tranquility—insecurity and turmoil are in accord with the natural order. The concept of enlightened self-interest is a myth, a contradiction; self-interest is based upon natural law, the force which impels man to persist without restraints and impediments in the preservation of comforts to make his existence bearable. The term "enlightened" denotes an injection of man's moral values and is contrary to anything natural, such as self-interest. He needs food, shelter and clothing, which he seeks as a matter of natural right; morality does not come into play when satisfying basic primary needs. Man's security rests in constantly striving to civilize societal conduct involving relationship with others in maintaining and improving the standard of living, i.e., the maximum level of comfort for all members of society. For man must recognize that this is the best of all possible worlds where egoism, rapacity and cruelty are rampant; it would be foolhardy to hope that these defects, these emanations from natural instincts, could ever disappear from the scene.

With the rare exceptions noted above, humans are without options but to follow their basic instincts, induced to promote their self-interests in conformity with natural laws dictating compliance with Nature's ordained principle of survival of the fittest, victims of involuntary servitude. For all humans are slaves, though there is a difference in degree but slaves nevertheless, without choice but to follow their instincts in competing for a share of basic needs. Inequality of competence results in a wide disparity of satisfying necessities, with the most capable, the minority, obtaining much more than a basic share and the marginally qualified majority just managing to make the grade, with many failing even in that effort. The level four and three income earners would treat the attribution of slavery to their economic standing as not far off the mark, given their primitive level of comforts and servility to survival needs. But the level two and one income earners would find such attribution absurd. If asked to halt their income activities because competition for money and unrestrained greed bring out the worst in humans and give their less successful neighbors an opportunity to narrow the gap, they would assuredly decline and point out that they are without choice but to vigorously preserve their wealth (obligations, providing an inheritance for family members); that their investments require constant supervision, timely transfers to more profitable outlets, and keeping current with prospective venture opportunities—obliged to carry on income activities. Most of them are not aware that basic natural instincts beyond their control propel them to action to protect and improve their economic standing, nor are they aware that they lack freedom of will (the latter will be discussed in Chapter 15).

(14) Centuries ago, slave-traders organized expeditions into dark Africa to round-up natives to be sold on the slave markets in the United States, South America and the Caribbean, for a time a most profitable business; the Soviets imprisoned millions of their citizens into forced labor camps working under conditions of slavery; Nazi Germany used millions of nationals from occupied territories as slave laborers to sustain their wartime economy: all these forced laborers were brutally exploited and had the following in common:

(a) They were enslaved to exploit labor to maximize profits or other gains.

(b) They could be freed by their slavemasters at any time.

(c) It is possible, but not probable, that the world could ever be free from literal slavery.

This kind of enslavement was an imposed involuntary servitude of humans by other humans, legally authorized by changeable man-made laws; they could be freed as a result of altered conditions or freed by man-made laws which legalized the enslavement in the first place. Some enforced slavery still exists nowadays because of lax law enforcement which strictly prohibit such violations, or sinister entrapment by corrupt scofflaws (Brazil, Pakistan, Thailand). This kind of slavery affects only a minority of the world's population. In contrast to the man-made enslavement—a mere subtext in a much larger natural scheme of things—the involuntary servitude attributable to Nature's instinct of self-preservation embraces all humans without exception, forces them, with minor variations, to submit to the natural order and become virtual slaves in the effort to persevere, an unseen and consummate burden imposed upon mankind by forces having a paramount presence in all human activities. It is the underlying purpose of this Chapter to distinguish man-caused "literal" slavery from the Nature-caused "virtual" slavery, or slavery for short, to better understand the economic and social ramifications motivating man to action, a universal premise from which more conclusions can be drawn than from any other mode of human existence. This has been the underlying motivation of all humans who have ever occupied this planet Earth, i.e., former slavemasters, emperors, royalty, politicians, philosophers, scientists and common people. Likewise, the ancient

Judaean priestly aristocracy, the struggles of the Catholic Bishops of Rome to become Supreme Pontiffs, as well as circumstances surrounding the founding of all other religions, best exemplify this subservience to the overriding and supreme principle of Nature's scheme of things. That same principle applies to communities, societies, nations and States.

If following the instinct of self-preservation—the efficient procurement of primary needs—is considered a virtue, the fulfillment of a paramount duty, and, by extension, the satisfaction of secondary and tertiary needs conforms to the involuntary dictates of perseverance rendering humans slaves to the natural order, then it is understandable why mainstream economists have done so poorly in forecasting economic trends. Economics is said to be the study of the process of earning an income, a profit, based upon free-market capitalism; it presupposes the existence of a level playing field, knowledgeable, enterprising, and ambitious participants, a degree of honesty which enables competing forces to attain some equilibrium based on merit and aptitude. But this is contrary to reality, for natural instincts arouse humans to seek anything but a level playing field and give subterfuge, selfishness, guile, double-dealing, and deception a forum to turn the odds in their favor. Anyone who has gained a working knowledge of the world of profit-seekers cannot help but reach the conclusion that economics institutionalizes greed and graspingness, its design favors the wealthy and powerful, who act in concert to thwart competition, subvert all restrictive regulations and frustrate free enterprise. But this is the essence of capitalism, a grab bag of riches for the beneficiaries of maldistribution. Economists will have to rewrite their fancied script and acknowledge that in a capitalistic free-market economy, honesty, morality, fair dealing are, in the long run, the traits of losers and that the vaunted level playing field is never level—all in accord with the natural order of things.

(15) The total enslavement of humans to their natural instincts and the effort to lighten the burden of existence allow predictability of actions and reactions in all fields of human endeavor, be they economic, social, political, personal or religious. They are the key to the understanding of all manner of human activities throughout history, such as rapacious wars of conquest, enslavement of captives and seizing the wealth of conquered nations, wars of national liberation, rebellions against oppression and emancipation of the exploited, revolts against religious absolutism and persecution, religious wars for economic supremacy and compelled conversions, forced abdication of rulers and enthronement of others, the

grandeur and dignity achieved by artists, inventors and scientists, in many cases against overwhelming odds, and all other manner of giving vent to aggrandizement, greed and power—all manifestations of the natural instinct of self-preservation and the effort to lighten the burden of existence as the ruling principle of all human aspirations and activities.

Nature's design permeates all human endeavors; the political and economic structure of society is a reflection of this underlying principle. Society, the arrangement of humans, is structured upon the inequality of contributions to its well-being, resulting in unequal opportunities for compensation adjusted according to the utility of such contributions. The consequence is the unequal income distribution among members of society—the poor, the haves and the super-haves—constituting the various economic segments. This is the most efficient adaptation to economic realities in a democratic free enterprise system and has the air of stability about it. All members of segments are slaves to natural instincts, but the disproportionate income distribution lightens the burden of existence for the achievers. The effort of self-preservation affects all humans equally regardless of income distribution and places them in bondage to persevere in existence at the level of comforts achieved. Although poverty is a world-shaking problem, the scourge of the majority of humans, and the economic architecture of man's extreme self-indulgent instincts extended beyond the pale, this is still the best of all possible worlds, given the frailty and bondage of man and the flawed design of Nature. Basic human nature is unchangeable, only society's laws change—restraining man and redefining his rights.

CHAPTER 14

CIVILIZATION REDEFINED

Before discussing the subject of civilization, I would like to comment on "Nature", "Ethics and Morality", and "Virtue".

(1) *Nature*

Nature is the sum total of the life giving and life sustaining forces, creative and created, organic and inorganic, which comprise all the phenomena of existence on Earth. The fundamental principle underlying all existence is self-preservation. As far as all organisms are concerned, self-preservation embraces specifically the struggle for existence, the survival of the fittest and the continuation of the species: these are identified as natural laws which give rise to natural rights. The principle of self-preservation applies equally to Nature itself, not as a cosmological principle but one confined to the planet Earth. Nature's nurturing precepts embrace a sustainable ecology and biosphere. In the fulfillment of that function, moral principles and the question of good and bad are irrelevant. Nature's guidelines for the survival of the fittest and the struggle for existence were not designed to serve the best interests of man, who mistakenly believes that the function of Nature is to promote his well-being.

As humans became more numerous, there ignited fierce competition among them to succeed in the struggle for existence, which required, among others, the procurement of ever scarcer resources. Competition provided a decided advantage to the more accomplished, to the stronger, more cunning and aggressive. The lesser endowed was forced to compensate for such shortcomings by becoming proficient in schemes of artifice, cultivating impulses such as deviousness, lying, envy, jealousy, intolerance, hatred and cupidity—all to further intense efforts to succeed in the struggle for existence. The stratagem reflects the primitive nature of man, all in accord with the natural order of things, i.e., Nature. All humans are, to varying degrees, in bondage to their natural instinct of self-preservation to provide for basic necessities, with the more successful creating a surplus, thus gaining some freedom of action and reducing their subservience to the natural order. Man is in constant turmoil, fractious and fragile because:

(a) At best, he can never be totally free from bondage and subservience to Nature's primary instincts: existence involves such subservience.

(b) The creation of a surplus above basic necessities diminishes his bondage to the instinct of self-preservation.

(c) Morality, that exclusive and sublime invention of man, frustrates Nature's principle of the survival of the fittest and interferes with the evolutionary process by opposing the natural order.

(d) Any attempt to alleviate the burden and pain of existence is contrary to the natural order.

(e) Any actions, views or opinions, unless involving moral principles, are influenced, affected and subservient to the natural order. It is an illusion for man to claim total freedom from servility to natural instincts.

(f) The greater his dependence upon basic necessities, the more his activities accord with Nature.

(g) To assure the well-being of society, man must contravene the moral indifference of Nature.

Nature's design is flawed because:

(a) The principle of self-preservation applicable to all living species from microorganisms to man involves the continuous struggle for existence and survival of the fittest, an interminable turmoil and contest for primacy among contenders, wasteful and destabilizing. It could incline evolution toward progress just as toward regression. When the strong die fighting on the battlefields, the weak stay behind to propagate the race.

(b) The instinct of procreation controlled by Nature's stabilizing forces, harmonious and self-adjusting, is applicable to all species except the human. The procreation of the human species is controlled by the condition of the environment and atmosphere.

(c) The propagation of the human species is uncontrollable without sustainable self-adjusting limits, dependent upon Nature's life-sustaining forces.

(d) Nature is without an effective antidote to rectify the havoc caused by progressive contamination of the life-supporting ecosystem, the result of unrestrained human procreation.

(e) The progressive contamination of the environment by technological overexploitation will make it unsuitable for human habitation.

(2) *Ethics and Morality*

There is an invisible line separating the concept of morality from ethics. Thinkers of the past and present have used the terms interchangeably without adding or detracting from either in the effort to describe and promote behavior exclusively human, a big step above animal species and a step above the conduct of humans consumed by the struggle for existence. But the confusion can be cleared up by recognizing that certain behavior which promotes harmony among members of society can be regulated by laws and punishment imposed for violators to act as deterrent. The other behavior is immediately recognizable as praiseworthy and totally voluntary; it cannot be enforced as there are no external guidelines; this only adds to its probity and distances human conduct from the natural order of things. The former enforceable behavior falls under the rubric of "Ethics"; the latter is referred to as "Morality". Examples of ethical conduct: one should not murder, lie, cheat, steal, harm others, mistreat animals, commit perjury or testify falsely, commit adultery. Examples of moral conduct: respect for family life, parents and children; charity toward the poor; protecting the weak and orphans; care for the aged and infirm; respect for neighbors; settling disputes by negotiation; practice fairness in business dealings; avoidance of envy, hatred and showing compassion toward the deserving. Moral behavior embraces ethical conduct. Morality is the more extensive term, the genus, ethics is one of its species. Henceforth, the terms "morality" and "moral" will be used in referring to uplifting human and social values.

Primitive man depended on Nature's abundant gifts for food and shelter; it was bountiful, and the demand for skills and intelligence were minimal since the struggle for existence presented limited demands on his ability to cope with survival. Because competition was mostly non-existent, conflicts among humans were tractable problems; man was in harmony with Nature. But life became more complicated and stressed as the inevitable growth of population caused periodic scarcities of food, competition for space, formation of societies and urbanization, leading to discords among factions demanding more of the fruits of labor than was their due. There were winners and losers, conquerors and conquered, masters and slaves, rulers and ruled. As soon as societies were established, restraints on certain freedoms had to be enforced for the protection of all so that those on the same team would not hurt each other in the procurement of life's necessities. Ethical rules were established and restricted actions of the strong, ruthless, cunning, i.e., the successful, so as to balance the scale somewhat and enable the many less qualified to earn a share of the benefits life could offer. To place restraints on man's actions designed to inhibit the strong and resourceful and promote the weak and irresolute violates the natural order and is in opposition to Nature's scheme of things. This conflict between Nature and man will increase in scope as the man-caused overpopulation and environmental degradation reveal the deepening discord between them. It will result in far-reaching consequences upon every aspect of his economic, social, and political efforts to find remedies and enable him to cope with the problems of his own witting creation, handicaps which could exceed his capacity to overcome.

(3) *Virtue*

Virtue has been variously defined. Socrates taught that knowledge is the highest virtue. Epicurus defined virtue as a means to a happy life. For the Stoics, the virtuous man will content himself with little and accept the difficulties and disappointments of life. To Marcus Aurelius, recognizing man's limitations was a sign of virtue. For Epictetus, virtue is striving for happiness. To Spinoza, virtue was attaining a true peace of mind. Schopenhauer concluded that virtue is happiness involving deliverance from pain and want. Diderot defined virtue as any quality that makes for survival.

The Latin "virtus" meaning bravery, strength, capacity, skill, merit, was derived from "vir", meaning man, virile as in manly, manlike. The sense is that "virtue" meant to describe physical qualities admired in man. It has nothing to do with happy life, limitations or peace of mind. Diderot came closest to the meaning, namely, "any quality that makes for survival", a sign of masculinity, a virile man who is a survivor. I would, therefore, define virtue as the totality of efforts to prevail in the struggle for existence; the virtuous man is one who is successful in that struggle. On the other hand, one need not look far to find the culprit responsible for the corruption and all the pedestrian confusion surrounding the meaning of "virtue". It was the early Christian theologians who defined "virtue" as man's total submission to the will of God—substituting contrition and self-humiliation for masculinity, a total perversion of the meaning.

Man is deemed virtuous because he adequately feeds and provides for his family, prepares for contingencies, and in the process does not violate laws established by society. It is in the nature of all existing things to seek the preservation of their existence, never to let up in this effort but constantly strive to improve their capacity to persist in the struggle for survival and for the enjoyment of maximum benefits existence has to offer. This effort is for maximum achievable power because it facilitates the process. This is basic to all existence and is called the law of Nature. Such endeavors are referred to as "virtue". Every individual aspires to pursue what is pleasurable and avoid pain and hunger; he strives to avoid uncertainty and mitigate fear. If successful, he soon discovers the potential for conflicts between him and Nature, no harmony with the environment, and compelled by necessity to accept suffering and pain as part of the natural order. The requirements of society to restrain and circumscribe his natural instincts point to a planned waste pervading the scene. For man who has satisfied his basic needs, such as hunger, shelter and adequate clothing, all standard benefits life has to offer, would not be motivated to approach secondary needs with the same aggression and persistence utilized to satisfy primary needs. Man will retain his moral "conscience" for as long as his attained comfort level or survival are not threatened. This is the basic law of human nature. He must work within the social system that involves conformity with certain established rules set up so that he—and others like him—may enjoy the fruits of their endeavors. All members of society strive for maximum freedom of action, for casting off the burden of restraints imposed upon them in order to pursue their interests unhindered. The inevitable unequal distribution of benefits due to the disparity of efforts and aptitudes will be the cause of envy, resentment, and unhappiness with the rules governing competition enforced by society; in any contest there must be losers and winners. Nature provided some remedy to restore a balance between opposing forces by imposing, what appears, a law of compensation, which consoles the simple-minded and not overly successful with prosaic pleasures and increases the capacity for suffering by the sophisticated and highly successful, a seeming symmetry which a superficial observer mistakes for coincidence.

To make do with less, to accept with equanimity the fickleness of fortune, to fulfill the responsibility to society by making some contributions to its well-being, and sharing with others the benefits justly gained—this is the highest virtue man can aspire to. For never did man stand so tall as when he stooped to help his neighbor, the weak, infirm, aged, children, the poor and abandoned. In this truly moral and virtuous manner he rebelled against Nature's way of dispensing favors and forcefully expressed his opposition to the natural order.

(4)   There are few words with as divergent and obscure meanings in the language of the cultured as the term "civilization", despite its relatively short history of usage. Originated in France in the middle of the 18th century, it first had to do something with manners and civility, as when used by a French writer in, "Nothing is more apt to civilize a young man than the conversation of ladies". It began to be identified with culture, "Culture or civilization that complex whole which includes knowledge, belief, art, morals, law, custom and any other capabilities acquired by man as a member of society.", or as the aggregate of characteristics displayed in the collective life of an advanced people. The Frenchman Turgot, who coined the word, gave it the following meaning: "Humanity marches through calm and agitation, although slowly toward still higher perfection." Voltaire liked "enlightenment" better when he stated: "Enlightenment gradually resulted in the upward progress of mankind." The French still thought of it as applicable to a particular era, as when De Condercet stated: "The French Revolution was destined to usher in the rights of man and the perfection of the human race." Since the word could be applied to any historical epoch, however ancient, it had to embrace a meaning of some universality that shared a common thread applicable to all situations. Kenneth Clark came closer when he stated that "Civilization requires a modicum of material prosperity—enough to provide a little leisure, it requires confidence." He added that no society based on obedience, repression, and superstition could really be civilized and that individuals who are prepared to join in a corporate effort for the public good can afford to do so because they have some leisure, and they have some leisure because they have money in the bank; he goes on to add that tolerance of human diversity is an attribute of civilized life. It was not till Toynbee declared: "The rise of civilization was a people's response to a challenge in a situation of special difficulty that rouses them to make an unprecedented effort ..." that we are getting closer to a workable definition. He stated more precisely that all human achievements involved challenge and response and that Nature had to present itself as a difficulty to be overcome; if human beings took up the challenge, their response would lay the foundation of civilization.

It was Fernández-Armesto in his book "Civilizations", who came upon the real problem facing the understanding of civilization when he suggests that it depended upon the relationship of man and his environment. He stated that civilization depends upon refashioning the natural environment to suit human uses; that progress is identified with the renunciation of Nature; that civilization is the reformation of Nature and has to be classified according to the degree to which societies modify their natural environment.

The term "civilization" was created during the most modern era and its use should be restricted to peoples of the most modern times when population growth, industrial exploitation of natural resources, and stupendous technological advances revolutionized the structural composition of society, man's relationship with the environment. Within this context, the term civilization cannot be applied to the ancient Greek or Roman periods, nor to the Renaissance, nor to France of the 18th century pre and post-revolutionary period, when Nature represented the paragon to be imitated, as is evident from literature, art and architecture of those periods; when history dealt mostly with the ventures and adventures of the privileged classes who patronized the arts and architecture; when the overwhelming majority of the dispossessed remained unmentioned and were expected to suffer their ordeal of brief existence in silence and obedience, their privations ignored by the ruling aristocracy as unchangeable and ascribed to divine predestination; when religious oppression motivated humans to seek political freedom and self-preservation according to individual merit as a natural right. Mankind was considered part of Nature and in harmony with it, just like all other animal species. But this view was illusory.

The effort which members of a society expend to succeed in the struggle for existence; create a surplus above life's necessities; engage in activities to lighten the burdens of existence; strive for some permanence, order and stability; free some segments of society from the pursuit of primary necessities; promote charity for the poor and weak; care for the orphan and the infirm; show kindness to children; temper the primitive nature of man and teach him respect for authority and law; prepare him for a useful and productive life in society to tolerate diversity and respect for other religious beliefs; foster educational facilities for the general improvement of the mind; build towns and cities, universities, libraries and museums, hospitals, rest homes for the elderly, and an adequate transportation system; empower building and food inspectors to safeguard the safety and health of the public; promote harmony and compatibility among members of society; provide adequate unemployment compensation, universal health-care for those who cannot afford the cost and not deny the needy survival necessities—these efforts expended by members of a society can most assuredly be identified with the existence of a civilized people, civilized societies and civilizations in general. Therefore, the label of civilization could be attached only to the most modern societies which promoted the creation of a sufficient surplus to tame the primitive and aggressive instincts of their members and afford conditions for activities which lighten the burdens of existence of the majority. For a society should be called civilized not because it produced great painters, sculptors, and architects but because a large number of its members were sufficiently dedicated to set aside the natural order of things, working silently and without fanfare or publicity, to mitigate the torment of others. They were well aware that by their actions they had to oppose Nature's aim to entangle man with necessities and make his survival an obstacle course weighed down by greed, envy, cunning, jealousy, avarice and cupidity—all criteria of aiding his self-preservation instinct but hostile to creating a harmonious and forward-moving society, a consequence contrary to the natural order. The thin veneer of civilization can be destabilized and ruptured by Nature's violent acts (volcanic eruptions, tornadoes, earthquakes, hurricanes, floods), which could undo much of man's upward climb to gain some freedom from the natural order of things; so would a protracted mass panic caused by a sudden untreatable infectious epidemic; or a prolonged economic depression causing crushing unemployment and disruption of the financial and market systems; or overpopulation and the consequential environmental damage—these would most assuredly radically affect the tenuous social infrastructure and result in disruptive changes and recidivity of forward achievements, however firmly and meticulously implanted; and finally, all wars and conflicts fought in anger—unless for purely defensive purposes—compromise and fatally impede the development of civilization, that noblest of man's enterprises nurtured with so much exertion, but regrettably, like Sisyphus of Greek mythology, destined to repeatedly fail each time just before reaching the summit of success only to fall back to the starting point by the boldness of his venture and try again. But Nature could just as easily be substituted for Sisyphus and give a touch of stark realism to that profound myth, revealing the travails of civilized man.

(5) When prehistoric man forged for food, leading a nomadic life, hunting and picking plants, he was in harmony with Nature. He obtained nour-

ishment from the renewable bounty of Nature, from its "income" without interfering with its "capital"; when nourishment was exhausted in one location, he wandered to another enabling the former to replenish its stock through the natural process. With the increase in population, he acquired the skill of farming, settled down in one location and he and others like him formed the nucleus of a communal life. With additional population growth, his farming became more intensive as he farmed for more than his own needs and began to extract more from the soil than the natural process had time to restore: he began to delve into Nature's capital. Man ceased to be in harmony with Nature since he interfered with its ecosystem, that natural balance between plants, animals, microorganisms, and the physical environment, by invading the biological and ecological capital built over billions of evolutionary years. As long as he was free and limited only by his power to rob, steal, rape, murder, free to pursue his self-interest and seek only his welfare motivated solely by natural instincts, he was in harmony with Nature. When he employed the services of a shaman, a witch doctor, a magician to cure his diseases, utilize the healing power of natural herbs, and accepted the sickness or death of a clan member as the work of spirits to whom he offered propitiative sacrifices, he was in harmony with Nature. Man was not in harmony with Nature when he began to use artificial means of increasing the yield from land by using chemical fertilizers, pesticides and herbicides: he disturbed the ecosystem. When man determined to alleviate the pain of existence and sought security by agreeing to live in a community under the rule of law and have his rights limited, he was in conflict with Nature. In time, his community set the foundation of a culture which retained the mood of an aggressive optimism for millennia to come. Together with the reassurance religious faith provided, he continued to hope that life on Earth had a definite purpose and was directed to favor the interests of man. This vision was forever tarnished by the ideas of profoundly innovative thinkers (Malthus, Darwin, T. H. Huxley), who exercised an irreversible influence upon subsequent thinking; from that time on (middle of the 19th century) the understanding of the relation between man and Nature was never to be the same. The self-nourished conviction that human living conditions would progressively improve with the aid of scientific and technological innovation was dealt a blow—fear, insecurity and rivalry have to be addressed. Out of sheer concern for the continued endurance of homo sapiens under conditions wherein the growing stratification of society into antagonistic classes with widely dissimilar interests could have plunged it into total chaos, pragmatic political leaders and sociologists had to come up with new concepts of human relationships placing high priority on social legislation, economic opportunity, a safety net for all those unable to compete on equal terms, and reinforced their concepts with a cloak of morality to give it tenacity of purpose—that man's future rests in opposing the natural order of things. This newly defined human relationship gave birth to the concept of civilization.

(6)   Unlimited population increases were kept in check by the limited availability of subsistence. Diseases, pestilence, plagues, wars, brief span of life, stillbirths, lack of hygiene, primitive care of infants and young children, ignorance of the human body and healthcare, and last but not least, the ravages of hunger caused by poverty and uneven distribution of food—all these took their toll and kept population growth within sustainable limits. These were harsh conditions particularly for those who ended up on the short end; but this was the way of Nature: waste without purpose, random and pitiless. But man, endowed by Nature with instincts sufficient for survival, began to exceed the limits imposed on all other animal species. Seeing the unbalanced attrition which characterized the struggle for self-preservation, he opposed Nature—which pitilessly discarded the unfit—when he forged ahead in the science of medicine to discover remedies for the ill and physically afflicted. It was not till the 19th century with the invention of better microscopes and methods of injection that radical changes for the better occurred in the management of healthcare. By saving lives and prolonging the usefulness of the disadvantaged, the science of medicine has been one of the prime catalysts that helped bring about an unsustainable population growth. The consequent erosion of the ecosystem, damage to the biosphere upsetting the balancing limits set by Nature to maintain a self-adjusting environmental equilibrium will inevitably force man to call an abrupt halt to the purposeless and useless overpopulation. He will be forced to interfere with the biological process of reproduction, in opposition to the natural order, to save mankind from the fate of many extinct prehistoric species.

Basic instincts, foundational to man's perseverance, have exposed his habitat to influences never encountered before and gradually changed a beneficial environment into one that has progressively become distressed, hostile and pathogenic. Man must place limits, voluntary or compelled, on the choice to procreate in numbers exceeding a predetermined growth target. In doing so, he would constrain the free exercise of one of his basic natural instincts for the common good of his species. Any action taken by him to mitigate and reverse the process of overpopulation would constitute an act of opposing Nature.

(7) Infectious diseases have existed since the beginning of time, but over-crowded urban centers and the rapidity of global contacts are recent phenomena. Widespread poverty, unsanitary living conditions on a scale never thought possible in the 21st century, and increasing antibiotic resistance have exacerbated the problem of lethal infections. One must view the magnitude of the problem from the increasing tendency for the majority of the world population to gravitate toward cities, creating megalopolises at the rate of 170,000 additional people each day—an inevitable ecological disaster in the making. Mounting pressures have contributed to a siege mentality; the urgency to find solutions to the life-threatening problems that plague man will direct his thoughts away from reliance on the failed natural order. He is forced to reach for a reprieve with the utmost audacity, seeking to amend Nature's evolutionary process and improve and alter the structural elements of the human body cells and tissues—acts of sheer defiance. All these aims will require concerted actions and the mobilization of the scientific community to devise new alternate technologies—to improve upon the natural order—before the problems overwhelm man's ability to counteract. He came up with the proposed solutions, relying on two new disciplines: Biotechnology and Genetic Engineering. The economy of developed countries started in the 19th century with a change from an agrarian to a manufacturing base dominated by ever greater need for untrained factory labor; the consequences were the beginning of a population explosion and environmental pollution. In the latter half of the 20th century, with ecological problems going from bad to worse worldwide, the previously unthinkable notion began to influence man with an ever greater impact, namely, that Nature has certain defects which had to be removed and that man must attempt such corrections; that in order to restore some semblance of order within which mankind can function instead of wasting away under the impact of diminishing resources and an inhospitable environment, man will have to interfere in his evolution by modifying his genetic makeup. That aim is nothing less than an attempt to improve upon Nature and become dominant in affecting his own destiny.

But how much should man interfere? If the present trend continues, Genetic Engineering will soon permeate every aspect of human activity. As knowledge about genes increases, it will become apparent that all human activity is in some way determined by its genetic makeup, including behavior and reasoning. It serves the cause of humanity that genetic scientists ease the physical suffering which is so much part of human experience. It is equally important to do so as much for mental diseases, that invisible curse which affects much of humanity. Is relieving man's physical and mental pain worth the risk of interfering with the process of Nature, as some allege, worth trading away his "humanity"? There is no choice but to interfere with the natural process and possibly assure relief from pain and suffering. If the crowning achievement of uncontrolled Nature is responsible for creating an environment which enabled mankind to reach the present plateau of anguish and distress after millions of years of unhindered evolution and selection, then man must declare the existing natural process unacceptable and attempt to modify the natural order to ensure an environment more conducive to his physical and mental well-being and more in harmony with a truly elevated concept of "humanity". Biotechnology and Genetic Engineering will help create such conditions and environment.

(8) Greed is a strong desire for more than is required to satisfy one's needs. It is a peculiarly human trait and has an affinity with excessive fear and insecurity about one's present or future ability to satisfy survival needs. Certain animal species hoard feed in excess of current needs in order to prepare for winter when such feed would be unavailable. This need for "hoarding" is instinctive with man and is not related to seasonal conditions, perhaps a memory of past privations and similar experiences in the "state of nature", harking back to prehistoric times. Fear and insecurity find expression in man's aggression. This susceptibility to cruelty and related destructiveness are natural characteristics of the human species and must be moderated to harmonize within a social setting. With the advance of organized society, one would have thought that the feeling of fear and insecurity would abate, since one of the prime functions of the State is to provide physical security to its citizens. Whereas fear of physical attacks abated, it transformed into fear of economic insecurity, which feeling is coextensive with man's effort of self-preservation and the preservation of benefits gained, his most basic and motivating instincts calculated to ensure survival of his species. The greater the opportunity to satisfy a multitude of needs, the more vehement the effort to satisfy them. The greater the challenges, the more ruthless the contest becomes. If the contest is not to satisfy primary needs, such as food and shelter, but optional needs, the primary object is lost sight of and becomes a contest for the sake of winning, a matter of pride in achieving the besting of one's opponents.

Within the limits of applicable State laws, an individual is free to pursue his needs to the extent of his ability and do any and all things he deems necessary to accomplish this goal; that his actions, if pursued to the extreme, could be deleterious to the welfare of the community would not deflect him from the single-minded purpose to seek his self-interest. In a free-market economy, the interplay of efforts of individuals creates a competitive economic system with rewards to the successful, making it worthwhile to be a participant in the process. To the degree that the successful collect their rewards, this is the best of all possible worlds. The less successful or unsuccessful have to fend for themselves as best they can. The misfortune of the many is treated as a casualty of the economic system, an unfair world, or attributed to a lack of effort, or initiative, to follow the example of their betters. No thought is given to the possibility that many of them could be genetically handicapped or lack of nutrition precludes them from becoming active participants in the contest, or simply, they are treated as a surplus commodity of no use to the process. The successful continue to overconsume and overproduce, unmindful of the damage to the ecosystem, uncaring about the proliferation of humanity, which to most is just a series of unpleasant blips on an otherwise bright world screen. Man must come face to face with the inescapable realities of his present existence and accept not only primary responsibility for poisoning the environment and encouraging overpopulation but put his house in order by repudiating as morally destructive the much vaunted uninhibited competition, which has brought many blessings but much harmful disruption to mankind. In Western countries, home of most of the developed industrial nations and birthplace of the Industrial Revolution of the 19th century, social thinkers warned of the great harm coming to the life force of any nation that benefited from the blessings of unrestricted competition, but treated the great masses of impoverished workers as an expendable commodity to be used, discarded, replaced and the process repeated.

No matter how much leeway free-market entrepreneurs have gained in pursuing their interests, no matter how many credits they have earned in increasing the wealth of nations, no matter how indispensable their contributions were to the raising of the general standard of living, there will come a time when much larger issues would take precedence over efforts to preserve the comfort-level enjoyed by an advanced segment of population, when the stakes are the dangers of overpopulation and degradation of the ecosystem. The hope is that moral thinkers will rouse the public conscience from apathy by urging the need of throttling down the intensity of the struggle for existence and self-preservation of overzealous and overassertive moneymakers and cease being the witting participants of an evolutionary process of Nature not suited for the overall well-being of humans. Organized society is becoming destabilized as an ever greater segment of population does not benefit from a standard of living sufficient for primary needs, and this privation is gaining an air of permanence. All men are not created equal and any assertion of unalienable rights is without meaning to those to whom the concept "equality of opportunity" is a sham. For it is a consequence of the natural process that genetically impaired parents are most likely to pass on the defective genes to their offspring, who will lack the right combination of physical and mental faculties to participate in the economic process and be reduced to the status of the disadvantaged or permanently dependent.

Since the dawn of history, man aspired to shed the chains of oppressive rules and succeeded in gaining progressively more freedom, be it political, economic or religious—they are aspects of the same struggle—at the cost of uncountable lives and suffering, in a shifting history of successes and failures, advances and retreats, to surface at the top of the heap to secure a high standard of living for the successful achievers. But the very efficiency with which the system produced a cornucopia of consumer goods at prices flattened by competition caused cracks to appear, which cast a pall of gloom and doubt in the adequacy of the natural order to keep pace with the increasing demands of man. It has become apparent that man's needs amplified by overpopulation began to exceed Nature's capacity to accommodate his uncurbed pursuit of self-interest, which brought him to such peaks of achievement, but began to run afoul of the harmonious social progress. Competition to achieve the most rewarding financial success carries with it the baggage of a darker side of man's passions—the incentive for stealing, cheating, greed, lying, trickery, ruthlessness, and an aggressive stance toward his fellowmen—not conducive to anything even remotely qualified as agreeable to the interests of society as a whole. Brutish competition leads to brutish behavior, with the result that fair-minded participants exemplify the maxim that honest competitors always end up last and are forced to adjust to the least scrupulous to achieve better results. The frenzy for money and riches infects, sooner or later, most competitors and leads to antisocial behavior. Man must come to the realization that the struggle for existence and enhancement of comforts—embracing a ruthlessness, aggression and overconsumption unmatched before—must be mitigated, blunted and tempered sufficiently to reverse the antisocial orientation. This will call for a revaluation of values. It is not man's basic self-preservation effort which conflicts with morality and virtue but the uncommon intensity and perversion of passions for winning on any terms, the besting of rivals and the incisive zeal for piling wealth upon wealth as an end in itself which makes a mockery of his natural survival instinct. The profligacy with which man has proceeded to exploit the bounties of Nature, the total contempt he has shown for sustaining the ecological equilibrium and signs of a looming ecocide, the disdain and recklessness he displayed toward any effort to control his reproductive process in light of a soaring population—are clear indications that he is no longer an edifying force but an agent of disintegration and decay. Survival of the fittest, as it applies to man, means the advantage of the most cunning, resourceful, ruthless and egotistic, endowed with a special kind of cupidity and predatory qualities, unmindful of the plight of losers—it is Nature in the raw. The uncurbed pursuit of such advantages served mankind well for now as it was an essential element of an unrestrained competitive system that achieved a previously unmatched standard of living for a particular segment of the world's population. But there are ominous signs that something is amiss with a system of profit-seeking which limits benefits to a narrow elite and leaves more than one-half of the world's population (the unemployed and underemployed) and an additional one-third totally adrift in the economic wilderness, just barely satisfying basic primary needs.

Man and Nature are in conflict, their aims are antithetical and stern stuff is needed to guide the course; he must oppose the moral indifference of Nature and accept that the well-being of society depends in combating Nature and not imitating it. Growth does not necessarily mean improvement and under present conditions could likely result in decay. If the prevailing trend continues, this is far from being the best of all possible worlds.

(9) From the long recorded history of human affairs, certain particulars can be deduced which constitute the bare bone motives, actions and reactions, the fundamental elements of conflict of factions at both sides of the spectrum. The power and wealth of the dominant class and the coterie of hangers-on on one side; the subservience, insecurity, and wanting lifestyle of the ruled commoners on the other side. The rulers used their power to maintain wealth by decree and force of arms; the ruled used any

artifice to reduce their insecurity and wants and were quick to profit from
any sign of weakness of the rulers to gain an advantage at the other's
expense. The rulers felt secure if the commoners were kept in firm subjection; the ruled benefited if the security of the dominant class diminished. The rulers were the wealthy super-haves—the privileged; the
ruled constituted those of moderate means and the poor—the hired
labor. The wealthy would never concede any benefits to the lesser-haves
or the poor if it meant willingly relinquishing any of their preferments.
In the early stages, the privileged were dominant due to ownership of
vast tracts of agricultural land and derived income from tenant farmers—
those of moderate means and the poor, sharecroppers at best. The privileged occupied their time by engaging in chivalrous contests for sport or
waging endless wars of conquest and for enrichment. All aggressive wars
throughout history were waged for loot, enrichment, or commercial
advantage regardless of the stated motive; the aims were base rapacity or
maintenance of the status quo. Business and manufacturing became the
domain of the guilds—the trade and merchant guilds—responsible for
increased economic specialization, supported by bankers who, in time,
exceeded in wealth the privileged rulers. The guilds pushed slowly into
government, for with new wealth came political power, demands for more
freedom and rights to conduct commerce unmolested and unregulated
with special concessions gained at the expense of the privileged. The
bankers were responsible for the rapid growth of commerce not merely
on account of their lending practices but more so for their development
of novel accounting techniques like double-entry bookkeeping and more
sophisticated instruments of credit and exchange (15th century), which
greatly facilitated the growth of foreign trade. In time, power and wealth
of business and manufacturing entrepreneurs were in ascendancy and the
power and wealth of the former privileged were in decline, causing fundamental structural changes, both social and economic, shifting the
mainstay of the economy from agriculture to industry and commerce,
thereafter additionally to technology and communications. The standard
of living of the well-to-do minority was increasing faster than that of the
majority earning a living wage; the wealth-gap between them kept
expanding as did the cause for conflict. Countries became known as
developed and undeveloped, depending on the extent of surplus wealth,
industrialization, and commercial activities generated by them. History is
the chronicle depicting shifting balances of power and wealth between
the privileged and commoners, the haves and those of moderate means,

with alternate gains and losses not only reflecting individual merit and blunder respectively but the working of a causal chain beyond the capacity of humans to understand.

(10) Conspicuously absent from this abridged version of history is the influence of religions, particularly Christian. Unperturbed by the questionable authenticity and incongruity of their ideas, leaders and theologians of Christian religions, the Roman Catholic in particular (they split, in time, into many sects), totally dominated the minds of their congregants into believing that man was sinful and destined to burn in hell but could be redeemed through salvation by the grace of Christ, the Savior, and spend eternity in heaven united with progenitors, immediate family and descendants. What an impact such a belief must have had on humans. How simple and convenient! No matter what cruelties and abuses were perpetrated by Christian upon Christian or others, the simple expedient of accepting Christ as Savior sufficed for salvation. A heavy layer of dogmatic air drifted above human habitats perverting the mind of all who breathed it, subservient to priests who promised absolution and salvation for all crimes and misdeeds committed at their behest. The priesthood made comfortable by obligatory tithes of their flock and testamentary dispositions in their favor, justified and were responsible for innumerable sectarian bloodsheds, misery, and desolation resulting from instigated conflicts serving chiefly to buttress their security and venal interests. The first overt resistance against religious oppression occurred (in Europe) during the Renaissance; thereafter the best minds engaged, at first, in reconciling the contradictions of religious dogma with humanism and, failing to do so, gradually freed philosophy from theological casuistry. All this was done at great risk to their person, for the powerful tentacles of the Roman Church, their spies and secret informers demonized all who attempted to breathe the fresh air of personal freedom and espoused the rights of man—but excommunications and fagots were losing their power to silence recusants and apostates. The Roman Church of old was losing its mastery with the rise of dominant nation-States, to be replaced by a more contrite, deferential, and quasi-apologetic hierarchy, abjuring all violence and intolerance, intent on confining its ministry to the care of the soul of congregants—as was the case with most other religions the world over. This trend continued till the latter part of the 20th century when, like the proverbial phoenix of Egyptian mythology, incoherent religious fundamentalisms inimical to each other arose from the forgotten past, founded upon the literal interpretation of the Bible and

Koran, restricted to certain geographic areas but influential on a global basis. Each combined religious orthodoxy with extreme nationalism, resolved to influence political affairs of States within its sway, explosive combinations which cannot help but have adverse consequences; for Christians, a retreat from cherished accomplishments paid for with so much blood and sacrifice in prior centuries; for Islam, a revival of its energies which lay dormant for seven centuries; for Judaism, an incongruous marriage of Diaspora messianism with political Zionism.

The steady rise of commerce and merchant banking commencing in the 16th century was unstoppable and gradually shifted wealth and power to a new class of enlightened and proud entrepreneurs, who pioneered the idea that no problem was too difficult for man to solve and that reliance on intelligence and aptitude were adequate instruments to justify such optimism. They patronized the arts and financially assisted painters, sculptors, poets, musical composers and architects. We are primarily indebted to them for the great artistic treasures created by a galaxy of artists whose works epitomized the zenith of man's creativity, liberated from spiritual chains of religious intolerance and the bondage of primary needs.

Throughout recorded history, some exceptional men managed to penetrate the blanket of natural obstacles weighed down, as if, by gravitation to rise above common events and for a brief moment become masters of their destiny to leave a permanent elevating imprint to benefit posterity. But before the middle of the 19th century, these benefits assisted almost exclusively the privileged and moneyed well-to-do minority and nothing worth recording trickled down to the common people to lighten the burden of existence. The latter had to be comforted by the divine embrace of absolution and salvation as preached to them by priesthoods since the earliest of times, but especially since the founding of what claimed to be monotheistic religions. Unlike ancient beliefs, which are cynically denigrated as pagan and animistic, the three monotheistic faiths have certain guidelines in common, although thankfully somewhat muted in practice since the 19th century only to rediscover their ignoble roots in the latter part of the 20th century and apply them vigorously in many countries (the next Chapter will discuss the post-19th century impact). The orthodoxy of each is against free speech and free thought; condemns apostasy although each welcomes converts; treats the followers of the others as infidels; intolerant and hostile to each other; each claims exclusivity of divine blessings and sole possession of the true faith to the exclusion of the others; only followers of one faith are entitled to grace and salvation; non-followers can expect the worst in afterlife notwithstanding a life of probity. Historically speaking, the worst offender against human dignity was the Catholic Church, the oldest of the Christian religions and the faith of "resplendent love". From the darkest recesses of the mind giving cunning and duplicity a bad name, contemptuous of Christ's teaching, drunk with power, and scornful of human suffering, a papacy and priesthood emerged that instigated the worst excesses and crimes ostensibly to protect the faith and salvation of believers but in reality to maintain and increase power, wealth, and supremacy of a Church which regarded itself as the divinely ordained sovereign over all Christian potentates and nations, all this pursuant to a document known as the "Donation of Constantine", the 8th century forgery of first impression not exposed till the 15th century when all the fictions have long since taken root, and possessing the self-declared divine duty to intrude in the innermost lives of Christians. Fearful of apostasy and seeing heresy behind the slightest deviation from dogma, the Church felt threatened—and for good reason—by any expression of skepticism which it answered with the utmost terror and violence. Between the 5th and 18th century in particular, the history of Europe— and everywhere else the Church set foot—is blackened by the most violent misdeeds and treachery, exercise of pure Machiavellian power politics that would lift the spirit of the most perfidious secular potentate. The suffering inflicted on fellow-Catholics, Jews and Muslims is without equal. The Crusades (11th–13th century); the Albigensian Heresy (13th century); the elimination of the Knights of Templar (14th century); the many massacres of Jews by the Christian populace incensed and abetted by the Church's fabricated charges of deicide, ritual murders, desecration of the consecrated Host (11th–17th century); St. Bartholomew's Day Massacre (16th century); the Roman and Spanish Inquisitions (13th–19th century); the Thirty Years' War (17th century); the burning of witches (15th–18th century)—just to name some of the murderous episodes. Millions upon millions of humans died in Church-sponsored and Church-instigated wars, persecutions and massacres, in the vain effort to regenerate a faith that was corrupted by the papacy and its minions. Yet the spirit of Man could not be vanquished. During the zenith of Vatican power and influence, the undaunted spirit of man yielded such luminaries as Dante, Erasmus and Montaigne; Raphael, Leonardo da Vinci and Rembrandt; Copernicus, Brahe and Galileo; Descartes, Spinoza and Leibniz—a complete list would fill several pages.

(11) All these turbulent activities brought on the insolvency of most States; they could have dumped their gold hoardings into the ocean and been better off for it—no need to keep rebuilding the devastated cities, countryside, bridges, churches, and government buildings. The treasuries were empty; exorbitant taxes had to be levied; the wealth of losers was totally expropriated and the wealth of winners recklessly dissipated on senseless religious conflicts. Colonies had to be conquered and exploited to repay debts incurred in fighting wars; the common people were kept in varying degrees of poverty by oppressive exactions so that the small minority of the privileged circles and their cohorts could live in comfort.

The Church was powerful as long as the ruling nobility, its confederate, was powerful. They supported each other, fully convinced that a decline of one would doom the power of the other. Throughout the dark period during which the Church held sway, dispensing its brand of suffocating spirituality, intolerance, and persecution choked off any budding aspirations of recusants to lay the foundation of a liberating enlightenment, a seeming civilization, to rid society of a priesthood gone mad. That the spark which could have ignited a civilizing awakening was submerged during the first 18 centuries of the common era and emerged, albeit only briefly, not till the outbreak of the French Revolution, can be laid at the doorstep of various anti-humanist forces, principally the Catholic Church.

What were the humanizing conditions that one could applaud? With the passage of all these centuries up to the middle of the 19th, how was the burden of existence lightened for the common man? Fear of religious terror was only matched by fear of poverty, disease, and the inexplicable natural death at a relatively young age; panics caused by an armed enemy suddenly appearing at the city gates and known to take no prisoners; reluctance to express any thoughts or criticism for fear it could be misinterpreted and the benighted culprit hauled before the Inquisition; or the trepidations suffered by wives of all ages who feared displeasing their husbands who could, without provocation, accuse them of witchcraft and denounce them to the authorities—guilt was foreordained and punishment death by burning. In vain does one search for anything even distantly corresponding to the concept of civilization. There was nothing even remotely resembling that concept as I partly defined it in Par. 5 of this Chapter and will more fully do so in the next paragraph. There was culture in abundance as well as great art and science, even humanism shared the spotlight at times, but no traces of civilization. For the latter requires, at the minimum, ennobling social legislation; economic opportunities for the ambitious; a safety net for those failing to provide for their primary needs; a fiscal surplus to fund, regulate and enforce these amenities; and a political system which guarantees freedom of speech, personal safety and equality before the law. Even had religious intolerance and terror been absent from the scene, there was no nation or State within the epoch of this discussion to which the label "civilization" could apply. There were most assuredly some civilized individuals who practiced tolerance toward diverse views and beliefs, showed considerations for those in need, did not cheat or steal from others, and managed to suppress their primitive nature—they were civilized, but even their numbers, however large, combined within a society could not be called a civilization without adding other essential characteristics broadly mentioned in this Chapter. It was only after the middle of the 19th century, when the Industrial Revolution was in full swing and created a surplus for nation-States and great wealth for many entrepreneurs, that nation-States had the wherewithal to raise the standards sufficiently high to be called a civilization. But this potential was thwarted then and later by men blinded by their newly discovered prosperity and power. The next Chapter will examine the claimed "civilization" of the Greeks and Romans of antiquity and of the post-middle 19th century nation-States.

(12) "Civilization", a relatively new term (18th century), has been loosely applied to cultures, to historical periods when great art, architecture, poetry and music were created by exceptionally gifted men; to nation-States which built great cities and the essential infrastructures; had stable governments, an adequate judiciary and law enforcement to maintain tranquility. But the concept of civilization is primarily tied to human conduct; how they interrelate in society under competitive economic conditions; how they manage to control their instinct of self-preservation in order to create a harmonious community and who possess sufficient education and experience to know that all humans are not equal; that there must be winners and losers and that it serves the interest of winners not to humiliate losers and make them suffer unnecessarily—in short, to lighten the burden of their existence. For the losers could one day be winners and return the slight, only to create greater friction and disharmony. Civilization is not about paintings, sculptures, or magnificent buildings but about the capacity of humans to make life collectively an endurable experience by taming their aggressive and rapacious nature, creating an orderly and tolerant society, adequate educational and medical facilities, gainful employ-

ment opportunities for the greatest number, and, most importantly, progressively improved living conditions with the passage of time.

Civilization, the realization of the highest of man's morality and aspirations, the apex of his social achievements, must embrace that solemnity of purpose to be a light unto nations. It necessarily comprises civilized men and women who constitute a society, a State, which possesses an adequate disposable surplus to fund various projects of benefit to its citizens and contributes to making their lives a gratifying and ennobling experience. The traditional term "civilization", purporting to describe what was regarded as the crowning sophistication of various nation-States, is a corruption of language. When reference is made in this book to civilizations as dependent upon the existence of slavery, the term was used in the traditional meaning of the word. For a nation-State could not be called "civilized" if it were dependent upon the existence of slavery. To be labeled a civilization, the citizenry and State (society) must, at a minimum, embody the following attributes:

(a) *The Citizenry*

Oppose the natural order which demands an unrelenting and uncompromising struggle for self-preservation.

- Acknowledge that man and Nature are in conflict and their aims are antithetical.
- Recognize that a disposable surplus is essential to gain some freedom of action and pursue activities not tied to basic needs.
- Understand that all humans are in bondage to survival instincts and slaves to circumstances beyond their control.
- Humans must compensate for the moral indifference of Nature.
- A high degree of morality is the essence of civilizations.

(b) *The State (Society)*

- Man's excessive aggression in pursuit of needs must be moderated to make his conduct socially acceptable.
- Oppose the natural order which demands the elimination of the weak, unfit, and simple-minded and promotes the survival of the strong, cunning and ruthless.
- It should be unacceptable for man to gain freedom from entanglements and improvement of his well-being by causing others to be abused and humiliated.
- Freedom of speech, beliefs and toleration of diversity and divers views must be unconditionally guaranteed.
- Overpopulation and degradation of the environment are an attack on

the vital ecosystem, thereby endangering man's survival. Restraint must be placed on both to assure sustainable development.

- Judicious rules and laws must be established to make social life as harmonious as possible.
- Social legislation and a safety net should be promoted to assist underachievers and those unable to provide for their primary needs; responsibility must be assumed to create employment opportunities for the greatest number.
- Aggressive wars, religious intolerance and hostility, or the institution of slavery (literal), each signify the repudiation of civilization.
- Blind reliance, unquestioned and uncritical obedience to the leadership of a State cannot be part of civilization.
- The well-being of society demands combating the way of Nature and not imitating it.
- The State (society) must have enough wealth to create a sufficient surplus to fund infrastructural needs, take care of emergencies such as natural disasters; provide for an adequate school system, hospital and retirement home facilities, universal healthcare, unemployment benefits, mandatory retirement and disability pensions to provide for basic needs to bring about conditions of permanence, order and stability.
- Promote harmony and compatibility among its inhabitants to ensure conditions conducive to a forward-oriented standard of living.
- Subscribe to participation in international cooperation based on international law.
- A civilization cannot be firmly established when the minority prospers and the majority endures privation, insecurity, bare existence and the gap between them keeps increasing.

The prior use of the term "civilization" in some parts of this book, although in accord with convention and tradition to determine society's appreciation of art, scientific progress in all disciplines, advanced infrastructures and urbanization, a forum for the playground of the well-to-do to display their talents in a frenzy of self-seeking and uninhibited aggrandizement—must be treated as a pseudo-civilization, more properly referred to as a period culture or period enlightenment and not as the pinnacle of human achievement, a civilization redefined as critically illustrated in this Chapter.

CHAPTER 15

CIVILIZATION
The Doubts

(1)   Morality and an adequate economic surplus are the necessary preconditions of a state of civilization; the former to oppose the natural order and the latter to enable segments of society to manage better than satisfying basic primary needs. Man, as a member of society, promotes its well-being by following ethical rules set up to make social intercourse a functionally harmonious experience. Society can operate harmoniously without members following a moral code, but cannot attain, in its absence, the potential of being counted among civilizations. An adequate economic surplus is essential for a society's well-being, for the wealth effect on some of the affluent privileged. Total absence of a surplus would render society inoperable; the possession of a considerable surplus would make it prosperous, but prosperity by itself could not elevate society to be part of a civilization.

The concept of civilization is the creation of moral minds, contemplating a world at peace, harmony among nations maneuvering for advantages but expected to solve their problems by negotiation; powers that be are reconciled to enabling every gainfully employed to earn a living wage and secure some creature comforts even in times of keen competition, without discomfiting or threatening the status of the economically privileged. These moral minds must have despised wars and armed conflicts as violent manifestations of greed and rapacity (unless fought in self-defense) and totally destructive of civilized conduct by lowering humanity to the level of savages; regarded any and all religious persecutions and intolerance as madness gone astray in search of victims to torture or murder. These moral minds gave man's resourcefulness too much credit for finding solutions to human ills, such as starvation and poverty in the midst of plenty; denying medical relief to the ailing underclass while dispensing therapy to the advantaged; tolerating and profiting from an oppressive and degrading system of human slavery (children in particular) existing in one form or another throughout history up to the very present. These humans of high moral standing labored hard to civilize mankind, but could not have foreseen that cultured societies were not motivated to control a worldwide population sprawl in order to restore some sanity to sustainable growth; that capital resources of advanced countries were wholly insufficient to integrate and absorb into the world economy such annual additions to humanity which will inevitably lead to more unemployment, more poverty, more starvation, more diseases, more crime and violence—conditions impeding any measure of civilization; that enlightened societies would recklessly countenance, despite repeated warnings, the progressive environmental degradation and pollution of the atmosphere, which cannot but escalate the deterioration of everyone's lifestyle and, in the long run, adversely affect the physical health and sanity of mankind—none would be spared—a plight of critical significance, socially destabilizing and foreshadowing a period of long darkness for the forces of civilization.

(2)   The incremental steps toward a civilization would require, de minimis, the reallocation of resources to prevent shortages; income redistribution to dispense with concentrated and disproportionate distribution of wealth of more benefit to charitable organizations or family charitable trusts than to the economy; the achievement of a stable, permanent, tranquil, business-friendly society based on an economy following democratic capitalism; placing a hold on the periodicity of wars and rearmament which antediluvian minds deem necessary (under a conspiratorial cloak of secrecy) to boost a sluggish economy; regulation of business activities to promote public health and safety—all these are necessary attributes of a moral standing to reach the highest plateau of human achievement: the attainment of a civilization. This is a progressive effort, incremental in stages toward the supreme goal, elusive, and placing a continuous burden on future generations not to slacken but move forward. There has been some progress within the conceptual framework, benefits of the surplus were extended beyond the narrow elite, but

despite the tenacity of purpose the desired goal has always eluded man's grasp. It could not be otherwise: there is an inherent conflict between morality and the procurement of an economic surplus.

(3) In the struggle for man's basic existence and the preservation of desired creature comforts, morality has always taken a back seat; the instinct of self-preservation is the strongest motivation. Man's uninhibited competitive effort and aggressive self-seeking extending beyond the satisfaction of primary needs—driven by greed peculiar to humans—places his needs in conflict with morality. For some degree of moral behavior is only achievable if his competitive effort is sufficiently inhibited and his aggressive self-seeking mitigated to promote harmonious social interactions. Possession of morality is a luxury. Divorced from pressures of earning more than a basic living; detached from the competitive urge of besting opponents for the sake of winning; separated from the wealth-effect in earning an income not for increased perquisites of success but to be free from entanglements and possess freedom of choice; knowing when the accumulated discretionary surplus is sufficient to slow the profit-seeking, even if only briefly, and cease being a slave to Nature's ordained circumstances and in bondage to the instinct of self-preservation—these are indicative of some basic conditions that would enable morality to ripen and bear fruit. That is why the process is so difficult and attaining the state of civilization so full of obstacles. There are civilized humans possessing all the proper attributes, but a company of them would not suffice to be called a civilization. To complete the circle, a political State is necessary, a free enterprise democratic republic preferably, whose elected legislators are morally competent to dispose of the national surplus to benefit all citizens, qualified to enact laws and regulations to promote the highest prosperity for the greatest part of the citizenry. But most elected legislators, even if sufficiently competent to comprehend the complexities of the task facing them, are themselves not free from entanglements and subservience to the instinct of self-preservation motivated by greed, envy, and cupidity solely to advance their self-seeking, in conformity with the natural order of things, particularly if exposed to the corrupt lures of special interest groups. An aristocratic, oligarchic or plutocratic form of government would eliminate most of the noted failings of elected officials only to bring on greater shortcomings. It is Nature's design for man to persevere in existence, to be entangled with necessities, to constantly strive to augment his financial standing and improve the level of comforts, never to be satisfied with the

results achieved, and to continuously view events with pure self-interest. A man with an above average aptitude would manage to advance, in time, beyond basic needs. His flawed design does not regulate aspirations or comfort levels and is not programmed to signal a state of overindulgence. It takes uncommon introspection to temper the conatus when the desired level of financial security is reached. It is more the rule, in accordance with the natural order, to pursue self-gratification as if it were a constantly elusive target, without regard to the sufficiency of results achieved. More wealth for the sake of greater wealth, more power for the sake of greater power. Such an addict is a stranger to morality, incapable of grasping its profound meaning: that there is a great assortment of human values which are not meant to be measured in economic terms, cannot be bought or sold at any price, whose promotion and advocacy lighten the burden of human existence.

Returning to the elected legislators, most of whom entangled with necessities, in bondage to the instinct of self-preservation and additionally troubled with periodic reelections, the inevitable subservience to self-seeking precludes them from following the public calling with a moral sense of service. For to enact laws and appropriate funds not exclusively of benefit to constituents or special interest groups but for the public good in general require wisdom and selfless dedication, i.e., an infusion of morality to guide them in their calling. Without an environment suitable for morality to sink its roots, most of the State's legislators are incapable of discharging their responsibilities with justice regardless of the availability of a satisfactory economic surplus; a state of civilization, as defined, would forever prove elusive. One would be inclined to caution the amoral legislators, particularly those who managed to be rid of entanglements, gained freedom of action and freedom from the gravitational pull of necessities unable to dissimulate their predilection for the privileged classes, all to the detriment of the general welfare, who lack the moral orientation and courage required to avert their eyes from the pandemic of greed to ponder the majestic words of an Isaiah, an Israelite prophet, whose exhortations retain the moral validity as when they were fearlessly pronounced 28 centuries ago: "Woe to legislators of infamous laws, to those who issue tyrannical decrees, who refuse justice to the unfortunate ..." Is. 9:1-2; "Woe to those who for a bribe acquit the guilty and cheat the good man of his due." Is. 5:23; "Cease to do evil, learn to do good, search for justice, help the oppressed, be just to the orphan, plead for the widow." Is. 1:16-17. These moral pronouncements are free of any religious connotation—they reflect humanism at its best and put to deserved rest any claims by theists that religious beliefs are a precondition of morality.

(4) A state of civilization has proved to be an elusive goal throughout human history. There have been civilized individuals and associations of small civilized groups of quasi-fraternal orders sharing a culture and morality in common, whose programs and philosophy of communal life place them among the noblest of mankind. Certain nations managed to approach that goal by incremental steps—with some measure of success—only to be thwarted in the final stages by internal contradictions, making the attainment of civilization a seemingly insurmountable endeavor. Civilization is contrary to the natural order and would entail arduous work by selfless and stimulated humans; it would benefit most segments of society dedicated to lighten the burden of existence of the great majority, making them more secure in terms of satisfying basic needs. But this is exactly what the ruling elites of nations wanted to avoid ever since antiquity. In order for the affluent elites to feel physically and financially secure, the rest of society had to be made insecure and wholly consumed with the struggle for self-preservation; attaining the level of comforts was not an option. It served the elites to keep the rest of society in constant turmoil and financially vulnerable, docile and passive, for if they felt subdued they would not likely complain about their unstable circumstances, contrive complots to express grievances, and perhaps even destabilize the comfort level of the privileged. In the past, the wealthy ruling circles depended on a closely regulated system of slavery (literal) to retain and expand their well-being to make the design of their structured society function. Much merit was claimed when slavery was abolished and slaves emancipated. But only the form changed. It was replaced by the modern kind of wage-slaves, seemingly docile, working as employees for profit and non-profit enterprises, earning barely enough to cover basic needs but freed from other legal disabilities formerly associated with literal slavery. They comprise the level four and level three employees, living on subsistence wages which, by design, have about them a kind of structured permanence, i.e., no degree of upward mobility. Their uninterrupted services are essential for modern societies to survive as viable organizations. The level two and one employees (and entrepreneurs) form the better compensated segments who share kindred interests with ruling circles and together make-up a social minority. This system resulting in grossly disparate compensation and level of comforts was designed by those

responsible for the propagation and acceptance of a new philosophy of wealth, flourishing on inequality and vested interests, a culture of insatiable acquisitiveness and overemphasis on moneymaking as the foremost aim of existence. Such economic configuration of society would apply regardless what form of government is in existence, be it free enterprise democracy, socialism, corporate fascism or communism. Regardless which system of government is in power, the economic fragmentation of society is structured so that the well-being of the minority depends on the privation of the majority; that if some are free to ponder on speculative subjects, possess the time to pursue noble aspirations, or while away the time in happy enjoyment of personal comforts it is because subsistence wage earners, the majority, produced the essential goods and services and a surplus of life's basic necessities; that it served the interest of those designers who primarily benefited from the system to keep the majority from earning more than subsistence wages, to work as wage-slaves, economically reminiscent of former slaves benignly renamed as earners of living wages, so as not to offend their sensibilities and at the same time create the appearance of normalcy. Without the newly recast minimum-wage workers, no society, or nation, could survive as an economically functioning entity.

Some sensitive observers might be appalled by the unfairness of such a social design, its seeming permanence and lack of potential for reform. They should be even more appalled at a system of economics designed to justify the complexities of commercial intercourse among profit-seekers— be they individuals, corporations or nations—serving primarily the interests of the successful to safeguard and perpetuate their wealth and economic dominance, while totally ignoring the existence and plight of the poor who constitute over 50% of the world's population, the one billion who suffer from chronic hunger, and the 600 million children who live in impoverished circumstances. The disadvantaged most assuredly have reason to rail against a man-designed system which provides no place for their existence, finds them irrelevant, and wishes they somehow disappeared from the scene. The patient observer would be further chagrined to note the cynical regard for self-interest to the detriment of the underclass; the obsession with the importance of the bottom line to the exclusion of all else; the shortages of food artificially created by profiteers to maintain stable prices despite conditions of worldwide starvation; that some knowingly sell food contaminated with traces of PBC and mercury to unsuspecting consumers causing irreparable damage to children's brains; that

250 million children between ages 5 to 15 work every day somewhere in the world producing goods eagerly marketed in developed countries; that millions of children are born every year brain-damaged or physically crippled due to diet-deficient parents and will grow up of no use to society and swell the number of the destitute; that more than one-half of the world's population is not needed for the others to function effectively—all these can be attributed to man's insatiable greed, unrestricted acquisitiveness and the drive for unlimited accumulation of wealth.

(5) Man, that insecure, fractious and self-centered product of Nature's flawed design, whose existence is not planned or purposeful other than seeking freedom from entanglements and freedom of action by pursuing satisfaction of wants, a victim of self-inflated needs, subservient in involuntary bondage to the instinct of self-preservation, precluded from exercising alternate choices, a slave to anxiety and necessity—circumstances which are beyond his control. Man must be mindful that despite efforts to progress beyond satisfying primary needs and achieving a comfort level of choice, the unpredictability of circumstances could abruptly nullify preferments vouchsafing his security and well-being. Man's grievous defect is the absence of any cautionary signal to cease or slow the forward momentum and recognize the limitation of needs, since a prudent man should not like to spend his productive life interminably engaged in self-enrichment to the exclusion of other stimulating activities. The natural order provided no marker or signal for man when enough enrichment and accumulation are adequate, as it did for the animal kingdom. The excessive aggression and frenzy of self-seeking in satisfying needs lead to conflicts, frictions, to a collision of diverse interests, behavior considered socially destabilizing.

In the international field, unresolved frictions involving major commercial interests were settled in the past, as last resort, by military conflicts at great cost in lives and resources. Most countries are dependent for their economic sufficiency on exports of one kind or another. Having recognized the sheer madness of past violent strifes, the international community of nations hammered out an agreement after much wrangling calling for the establishment of a supranational agency with powers to arbitrate and settle international commercial disputes, and do so with finality; the ultimate decision is not appealable. The World Trade Organization (WTO) was established in 1955 with a membership comprising most of the world's trading countries. Its chief function is to foster suitable trade relations among member countries. In the end, however, the success of the WTO depends on members following established rules and keeping bilateral agreements honorably. Adherence to such conduct would reveal moral qualities which are conducive to civilized behavior. The problem greed poses domestically is only magnified on the international scene; national governments look for ways to run interference for major domestic corporations and their underhanded schemes to gain undue export or import advantages; becoming witting accessories to the unilateral bending of rules; dissembling while granting hidden export subsidies; establishing requested protective import tariffs, quotas, import duties, or if need be, declaring specific highly competitive imports in violation of anti-dumping laws, all to protect inefficient domestic exporters or marginal domestic businesses against more efficient importers, in violation of the spirit and rules previously solemnly affirmed. But then governments, no less than private entrepreneurs, distort or override with impunity bilateral agreements if the need arises to prevail over a competitor. The oversight of the WTO notwithstanding, the financially stronger members take advantage of the weaker ones; the powerful bypass the WTO by threatening costly retaliations against the non-accommodating party. Free-market capitalism started with a bang to expand profits by corporate globalization, expecting miracles from cheap labor and the absence of governmental oversight, but miscalculated badly in making projections. They abused the trust of host countries; their high-handedness earned them nothing but contempt; behaved in a conspiratorial manner assisted by intrigues of the IMF and the World Bank; by practicing corporate colonialism unwittingly contributed to a broadbased worldwide recession (2000). They flooded the international markets with goods but failed to consider whether consumer demand would keep up with the supply; overconfidence caused the largest corporations to invest more than 40% of their capital in global enterprises, weakening their capital base in times of economic contraction. The global economic experiment will prove to be a blunder of far-reaching consequences. But greed is a human constant not exempting corporations from its clutches. By using subterfuge to circumvent solemn agreements, they radicalized developing and emerging countries in their opposition to the free-market system. Developed countries are guilty of the same imprudence in dealing with weaker trading partners. Multinational corporations could pay dearly for gaining what amounts to a temporary advantage: friction, hostility, disputes, hatred and more poverty are the inevitable consequences of conduct light-years removed from moral dealings. It is a further demonstration of the inherent conflict between morality and aggressive and uninhibited seeking of an economic surplus, removing traces of civilized conduct and thwarting prospects of moving closer to civilization.

(6) Man is in bondage to his instinct of self-preservation, a slave to necessities, a victim of circumstances beyond his control. He possesses no natural rights but one, the right to persevere in existence, i.e., self-preservation, but this right is meaningless unless guaranteed by the laws of society. In the state of Nature, his right was coextensive with his might. Therefore, most humans had limited rights since they were subservient to the stronger, more cunning and more resourceful who possessed supreme rights. Other natural rights are not human rights; the latter are the design of man. No humans are born equal—the concept of tabula rasa is a myth. All humans remain in bondage to the instinct of self-preservation throughout their existence, the only modification is the degree of outright dependence which will vary according to the capacity of satisfying primary and non-basic needs. The principal human motive to action is the desire for self-preservation. The survival of the burgeoning human species requires opposition to the natural order of things. The maintenance and improvement of man's standard of living depend on his success in opposing Nature's design. All species, except man, are totally subject to Nature's design throughout their existence. Man's idea of order contravenes Nature's design, which requires an unlimited and unceasing struggle for existence, the survival of the fittest—obstacles to his effort to progress to a civilized status. The successful man managed to acquire a discretionary surplus to satisfy secondary, even tertiary needs; completed the steps needed to mitigate his slavery to necessities; gained some control over his circumstances; secured some freedom of action to devote time to activities not tied to the preservation of existence. Such a man would be capable of overcoming his innate insecurity and fractiousness to lessen the effects of Nature's turmoil, ease resentment of his exclusion from participating in another's preferments, and take part in easing the burden of existence of the less advantaged. Such a man could be touched by morality and advance several steps on the ladder of civilized conduct. Although he is part of a mere minority, society counting him among its members is better off for it because his activities are bound to encourage positive responses from others and contribute to the enhancement of the general well-being.

(7) In a rare moment of introspection, a man mature in age and experience is apt to question the meaning and purpose of existence. Is it ever repe-

titious procreation from generation to generation until the burgeoning population becomes unsustainable? After that climactic stage has been reached, then what? Is it Nature's way of weaning out the less fit to improve the gene pool of subsequent generations? The experience of humans argues against it—the degradation of the ecosystem and poisoning of the atmosphere, just to name the most harmful developments, will more than cancel any improvement in the genetic make-up. That modern medicine would prolong the human life span? Of what benefit to society is a substantial increase in retirement homes and increased drain on healthcare for the nonproductive? Or improving the health of humans? Such problems could be minimized if man managed to keep toxins out of food. Is it progress of science and rocketry to populate Mars and other planets? Man polluted and almost devastated the planet Earth in less than 150 years, what hopes are there for other planets? If the purpose of existence is for mankind to perfect weapons of mass destruction with which to exterminate obstructionists, recusants, or other obstinate nonconformists, it succeeded beyond all expectations. If the purpose of existence is to improve the morals of some segments of mankind and lead to a state of civilization, it failed beyond the most modest expectations. The religious will find the purpose of existence a preparation for afterlife; the ultra-religious as the crowning opportunity in experiencing rapture by witnessing the anticipated Apocalypse. But in the final analysis, no matter how esoteric and profound the purpose, man is without choice but to persevere in existence, follow his instinct of self-preservation, satisfy needs, avoid pain, lighten the burden of existence, and seek a level of comforts and enjoyment commensurate with his aptitude. He is without independent choice in seeking these goals—there is no freedom of will (the latter is discussed in Par. 8 of this Chapter).

A long step toward civilized conduct is in the direction of repressing impulses and mitigating gratifications in order to place limits on excessive profit-seeking, which tempt man to pursue undue competitive advantages by lying, deceit and fraud, to maintain harmony in the conduct of business, social order, and avoid disruptive economic turmoil. But such an attempt at civilized behavior would be contrary to the natural order which impels man to pursue, without respite or interruption, the augmentation of wealth with no limits and without regard to the destabilizing consequences to other humans or society. For Nature favors, by design, the strong, cunning and competent; it treats those below the marginally successful as consigned to an existence burdened by pain, insecu rity and anxiety, a life of unceasing toil to make ends meet, limited to basic survival needs. A long step toward civilized conduct would result in defying the natural order, opposing Nature's design and evolutionary process—the rule of the survival of the fittest. The human mind may not be capable of solving all the problems and removing all the obstacle courses Nature placed in the path of man. But preserving the four level economic infrastructure is essential for a free enterprise society to function, utilized throughout history and the mainstay of human economic design. The human mind should be capable of loosening its attachments to the prison of classical economics and declare that the configuration of the general pricing system be restructured to provide every workingman and workingwoman with a truly living-wage, sufficient to cover expanded primary needs (including health insurance and retirement benefits) and a minimum level of creature comforts life can offer. No human deserves to be treated harshly and without pity just because he is not clever enough to stay on par with the well-to-do: none should have to live like an animal. The economic system will have to make accommodations to the earners of poverty-level wages with some reduction of income insupportably disproportionate at the opposite end of the spectrum; extend the potential of upward mobility for all that is presently reserved for the privileged few and reduce the growing gap between the rich and poor. For the pricing system in a free enterprise capitalism, the distribution of income and consumer spending are interdependent, interlinked and relative, totally implicated with one another. A redistribution of income would permanently influence the wealth effect of all the gainfully employed, i.e., the income level would shift in favor of the lowest paid and their new increased spending power would stabilize relative to prices. A program of some upward mobility for the lower-level employees must be instituted to prevent the social order from becoming increasingly class-ridden. In the final analysis, it is in the interest of the elites to keep control of their concentrated wealth, retain the achieved security and freedom of action; all economic strata of society would benefit from a general upward mobility: the well-to-do would enjoy the perquisites of success; the former wage-slaves would enjoy a minimum level of creature comforts.

It is well recognized that a prosperous economy depends on strong consumer spending. It is in the interest of all the income segments that some discretionary surplus be permanently placed at the disposal of the largest segment, i.e., the earners of low wages, by raising their income

level to increase their purchasing power to keep the wheels of the
economy turning. This would not only benefit the economy in general
but radiate a powerful civilizing effect throughout the whole community.
Absent any change in the present lopsided income distribution and
absent any permanent improvement in the lot of subsistence wage
earners, not only would any progress toward a civilized society fail but
the underachievers' poverty would conspire against free-market capitalism—none could feel safe while so many are doing without.

(8)   Humans should be relieved to know that they are guided in their decisions necessarily determined by causes, external and internal. They
should be additionally relieved to know that their ideas, inclinations,
motivations, likes and dislikes, talents, and aptitudes are not the result of
whims or caprices born in a vacuum, floating about to be picked up ran-
domly by the mind without some design. But design there is, for it must
be taken as axiomatic that a man in command of his wits will not choose
a lesser good over a better good, or a worse bad over a lesser bad. This
inclination is tied to the principle of determinism, i.e., that free choice
and free will are non-existent. This is consistent with man being subservient and in bondage to his instinct of self-preservation. But these
concepts are anathema to protagonists of organized religion, for if good
or bad deeds are not the result of volition, the result of choices freely
made, it would undermine the doctrine of divine reward and punishment
in afterlife, prayer, and the Day of Judgment. It was the Greek philosopher Protagoras (5th century B.C.) who stated that man is the measure of
all things. It must also be taken as axiomatic that good and bad are relative terms and that man considers something as "good" if it aids his self-
preservation and "bad" if it hinders it, i.e., man does not choose something because it is good but is good because he chooses it; he does not
reject something because it is bad but treats it as bad because he rejects
it. The notion that man can make choices freely, i.e., that he could choose
whatever comes to his mind at any particular moment without reference
to past choices is a myth; that he could pick and choose without rhyme
or reason, totally at random and against all his instincts, a course of action
without following any pattern can be attributed to the flawed perception
of the mind. It is due to the imperfection of the mind that man suffers
from such delusions in the mistaken belief that he possesses freedom of
choice, of will. For man has no more freedom of will to deflect from his
virtue than to prefer what is damaging, bitter, tasteless, hateful and
repugnant. He feels free to choose because he is ignorant of the causes

which determine his actions. Nothing exists in Nature without being part of the chain of causation affecting all things. All changes, without exception, have their causes and this is a universal principle. An uncaused event is a vacuum in Nature, without antecedents and incapable of existence. All events are coextensive with their causes as all existence is determined by its causes. There is no "chance" or "coincidence" in the order of things, for only ignorance prevents the mind from recognizing the necessary sequences. All laws of Nature are permanent and the same set of antecedents is followed uniformly and invariably by the same set of consequents; all phenomena are causally dependent on other phenomena; everything that happens has its causes and is, in turn, followed by necessary effects. The mind's reasoning process and its sanity depend on the necessary causation of events. There are no values independent of man, and they are determined by his innermost instincts, environment, education, social standing, physical and mental capacity and economic status, i.e., by the confluence of causes acting out their scheme of things. The skeptic who is convinced that he possesses freedom of will could be inclined, by ignorance, to choose what is not in his best interest, or what is damaging to his self-preservation, or move a finger to the left or right, or lift his foot up or down, but these are acts of no possible consequence and not affecting his innermost personality, out of spite to prove his point—but even his poor judgment or levity are subject to the same universal principle.

(9) A civilization could only mature by the necessary confluence of morality and an adequate economic surplus within the framework of a stable society. The progress toward a state of civilization proceeds in incremental steps from which freedom of choice or will are absent. Opposing the natural order is a necessary precondition of morality. The procurement of an adequate economic surplus is the necessary consequent of following the natural order. Moderating self-interest and the effort of self-preservation, if they lead to the procurement of an adequate economic surplus, are the necessary antecedents of morality. Giving free rein to self-interest and self-preservation are in accord with the natural order and obstacles which conflict with morality—they inhibit its emergence. Since the attainment of morality, and by inference civilization, is conditioned on mitigating the effort of procuring a satisfactory economic surplus, freedom of choice being absent from this interaction, the attainment of morality under these circumstances can be accomplished only by a minority of society; it is foreclosed to the majority unable to procure a

satisfactory economic surplus even in the best of circumstances, but facing prohibitive odds if required to mitigate efforts. The viability of society is predicated on the four level income infrastructure which precludes the majority from gaining an adequate economic surplus. The natural order and man's bondage to the instinct of self-preservation are antithetical to the creation of a state of civilization other than approaching by incremental steps man's highest aspirations, but ever precluded from reaching that goal. Most of the well-to-do segments of society are instinctively opposed to any semblance of civilization for fear that its rules or mores would place their economic privileges in jeopardy and inhibit the process of uncontrolled enrichment. For the same reason they are opposed to political equality for everyone and prefer an authoritarian rather than a democratic regime. The utopia, the hidden paradise, the Shangri-La as depicted in James Hilton's novel, that perfect state of civilization, is destined to remain an exercise in creative writing.

There are people, content to limit self-preservation to basic primary needs, who managed to distance themselves from the hustle and bustle of the coarse and crude competition of humans and who, from feelings of deep piety or belief in evolutionary humanism, retained a pristine sense of morality. No economic surplus is in play, or needed. The secluded, culturally semi-isolated and self-supporting communities nestled in the Alpine villages of Austria, Bavaria and Switzerland come to mind, where simple folks live out their lives from generation to generation in harmony, mutual respect, and lending a friendly helping hand when necessary, far removed from the irreverent goings on in cynical urban societies. No murders, no shootings, no pushing to the front of the line. But as soon as city influences or growth intrude, the curtain drops on this Garden of Eden and man reverts to his accustomed conduct. These are isolated interruptions of the natural order, beautiful to behold, but of no significance in the struggle for self-preservation.

(10) Most traditional high schools in cultured countries acquaint impressionable young minds with the glories of classical Athens and the Roman Empire; their poetry and literature; the schools of philosophy; the imposing architectural and engineering achievements; the unsurpassed beauty of their sculptures; the large and disciplined armies and famous generals; the many land and sea battles and exploits; the passion for symmetry, law and order; the absolute power of rulers—in short, during the pinnacle of their glories, Athens (the Golden Age under Pericles, 480–399 B.C.) and the Roman Empire (during the Principate, 30

B.C.–192 A.D.), were described in unmistakable terms as the apex of civilization which man has tried to emulate ever since. This uncritical and incomplete concept became indelibly frozen in the minds of students who in their mature years compared later pseudo-civilizations with the splendor of classical antiquity. From generation to generation, scholars, historians, students, and the educated public contemplated with awe the grandeur of the Athenian Acropolis, the statues of Laocoon and Aphrodite, the aqueducts near Nimes, the amphitheatre at Arles, the Roman Forum, the Temple of Castor and Pollux, the Arches of Trajan and Titus, the Colosseum, and the culture of peoples who brought such masterpieces to life. But such exuberance is guilty of omitting defects in letting rightful esteem overshadow less pleasing aspects, or worse, judging creators of this magnificence to be incapable of conduct standing in complete contrast with the more pleasing and memorable achievements. For the misdeeds and transgressions (only partially outlined below) committed in their name by elitist oligarchies, who among other offenses prevailed upon their peoples to adopt and approve a lifestyle of insupportable brutality and callousness toward opponents, enemies and subjugated nations, crediting such conduct for the triumphs and successes of their long-lasting hegemony. This kind of conduct practiced long enough against subject nations could not help but become part of their nature, the stern, uncompromising and pitiless behavior toward one another played a great part in their notorious military discipline. But either by design or necessity, such discipline was needed to live on loot and retain control of conquered provinces. Any rebellion was mercilessly crushed by the army.

In cataloguing the dark side of these pseudo-civilizations, brevity requires the citing of only the most egregious wrongdoings (excerpts are summarized from various historical sources, including Will Durant's "The History of Civilizations").

(a) *Athens*
- Intermittent wars between neighboring cities was the rule.
- Old age was feared, for the elderly were mistreated and exposed to boorish insolence—they ceased to be of use to society.
- During the rule of Pericles, Athens exercised dominion over an empire of oppressed subjects held down by force to thwart constant attempts at rebellion.
- Class wars raged most of the time between the rich and poor, the oligarchs and populists; the victor executed surviving prisoners; the con-

quered city was sacked; the wounded combatants killed and noncombatants enslaved.

- Thucydides, the Greek 5th century B.C. historian, described the class wars with vivid realism: " ... sons were killed by their fathers ... Revolution thus ran its course from city to city ... carried to still greater excess ... the atrocity of their reprisal ... the revenge exacted by the governed ... the savage and pitiless excesses into which men ... were hurled by their passions ... The cause of all these evils was the lust for power arising from greed and ambition ... Religion was in honor with neither party ... society was divided into camps in which no man trusted his fellow ... The whole Hellenic world was convulsed."
- Labor was brutally extracted from slaves who replaced free laborers reduced to destitution; manual labor was a sign of bondage, unworthy of freemen. When testimony was obtained from slaves, it was admitted only when elicited by torture—relying on a peculiar validity of testimony.
- Most tillers of land made do on borrowed money; if unable to repay the debts, they were forced to work as serfs for their creditors.
- No legal marriage was permitted between a citizen and noncitizen.
- They felt no obligation towards foreigners.
- A citizen could avoid the death penalty by going into exile before trial and forfeit all his property. In case of slaves, they were either hurled over a cliff or clubbed to death.

(b)   *The Roman Empire*
This is the essence that made Rome great:

- Huge armies and good commanders; conquest of nations; pacify them and make them clients of Rome, paying sizeable taxes and tributes which kept Rome prosperous. Roman armies brutally subdued uprisings and revolts, exacting even larger tributes as punishment. Roman leaders paid huge bribes to influential members of the Senate and Assembly, keeping the Roman army well paid and the populace docile and occupied with profuse amusements, games and lotteries. When necessary, the State distributed free corn to the poor, kept the price of corn low for buyers, and distributed money gifts to all citizens who applied for it.
- The captives, men, women and children, were sold to slave merchants of Italy.
- To be Rome's leader, Emperor, Consul, or dictator was so lucrative that constant intrigues, assassinations, coups, bribes, and conspiracies cov-

ered the political scene. Constant maneuvering for position, political conflict among conservatives, aristocrats, populares, and the proletariat kept the population in turmoil.

- Political factions were busy engaging in bribery of votes, intimidation of juries, occasional murder when it suited a political advantage. Offices were sold to the highest bidder.
- The Principate (30 B.C.–192 A.D.), a dictatorship, was made possible since Roman citizens no longer desired freedom but security and order. The powers of the Prince were at once legislative, executive and judicial; there was no freedom.
- The rights of the plebs, the lower class, to hold offices was restricted to men having a fortune of 400,000 sesterces, or more.
- Rome maintained an aggressive expansionary policy on every frontier.
- Applying only to Roman citizens, the father retained the right to kill an adulterous daughter and her accomplice as soon as he discovered them.
- A Roman law was aimed at retarding the dilution of Roman with alien blood.
- Lex julia de maiestate (law of treason) was a convenient vehicle of those in power to get rid of enemies by falsely accusing them. If the accused was condemned, the informer was awarded one-quarter of his estate; the State confiscated the rest. Men were accused of treason, exiled or killed, because the State's treasury was exhausted and needed replenishment by confiscated wealth.
- Constant plots and counterplots, betrayals, sale of offices, assassinations in high places made reliance on stability a folly—this condition permeated the Roman political scene during the glory of the Empire.
- Rome was doomed when she could not force her possessions to send food and soldiers for the Roman army.
- The staged gladiatorial fights to the death fought by specially trained slaves were the most popular entertainment of all classes, as well as battles to the death fought by condemned prisoners. The spectators were titillated to no end by the gruesome spectacle of dying men breathing out their last to the cheers and applause of sadistic-minded brutes. These combats, conducted in the specially designed Colosseum, were the craze of Romans.
- Slaves performed most of the manual and household work. The slave had no legal rights; he could not own, inherit or bequeath; his children were regarded as illegal; children of a slave woman were classed as slaves even if the father was a freeman; male or female slaves could be seduced by

their master without legal redress. If a slave ran away and was caught, he could be branded or crucified. If a slave killed his master, the law required that all slaves of the murdered man be put to death.

The above outline describes societies in constant turmoil which endured by exacting large tributes from subjugated provinces; relied heavily on forced labor of slaves; engaged in interminable wars of conquest and plunder by armies led by competent commanders; their citizens, the privileged in particular, lived in constant fear for their lives due to frequent intrigues, plots, counterplots, and the whims of Emperors. Despite the universally admired accomplishments in art, engineering, architecture and humanities, this veneer of positive attributes is totally overshadowed and dwarfed by a culture of witting savagery which cannot be, by any charitable stretch, identified with civilization as traditionally defined or redefined. To do so would only be at variance with known facts and mock the memory of the many millions of humans slaughtered in cold blood, the terrible suffering needlessly inflicted, and the forcible enslavement of millions by venal military commanders. Never before, or since, have ordinary citizens been so brutally assaulted if they clamored for relief from oppressive conditions, and yet the same oppressors made every effort to keep them docile with bribes and gladiatorial games. Most had no freedoms, only few the right to criticize and complain with impunity.

Classical Athens under Pericles and the Roman Empire during the Principate maintained their hegemony by the force of brutal might. They could have never reached the pinnacle of power had they been part of a civilization.

(11) The rapid change in the method of production, the massive amounts of goods produced, and the opportunity to realize great profits involved a transition from making things by hand with the aid of simple tools to their production by increasingly complicated machines. The domestic system preceded the factory stage of industry. This great transformation called the Industrial Revolution—which initially occurred in England but later spread to other countries—began in the second half of the 18th century, but quickened dramatically in the 19th century as a result of certain inventions by Englishmen such as Hargraves (the spinning jenny), Watt (the steam engine and locomotive), Cartwright (the power loom), Arkwright (spinning machine), Crompton (the mule, which made possible the manufacture of fine cotton cloths and muslins). Power-driven machinery created new wealthy employers, the captains of industry, who replaced the agricultural economy of landowners with the rapid growth

of factory manufacturing. The machinery speeded up production and the accumulation of capital at a rate never experienced before. The factory system introduced industrialization to the world with the result that economic activity underwent radical changes. The large-scale production of wealth revolutionized the social order, resulting in concentration of humanity in major urban centers filled with job seekers dependent on work in factories. Most of them found employment, but the conditions were brutal.

It is revealing to find a concordance of free-market capitalism at its very inception with the system that is dominating the economic scene of industrial nations at present. They share basic fundamental similarities essential for a free-market economy: production efficiency and low factory wages. The conduct of the rich and super-rich made prosperous by the new system of production and free-markets was consumed by greed and unbridled profit-seeking. The English entrepreneurs, a cultured and mostly church going people with a long tradition in commerce, backed by a Parliament then notorious for its support of unimpeded trade and the moneyed classes, soon gained a considerable discretionary surplus for themselves and for their country. The conditions were ripe for a confluence of morality and an adequate economic surplus to lead them and their nation several steps closer toward civilization. This required moderating self-interest as a prerequisite of morality, but this was a price the fiercely competitive and self-seeking entrepreneurs were unwilling to pay for fear of endangering their privileged status and desired security. Natural laws keep all men in bondage, especially the fiercely ambitious captains of industry; this was aptly illustrated in England in the 19th century and up to the present as well as in all other industrial countries. The pursuit of wealth as an end in itself may accord with natural law, but it is destructive of morality because it leads to uninhibited competition and unrestrained acquisitiveness, i.e., it creates greed mongers blinded by their passions to ignore the distress inflicted on their low-level employees by what can only be described as Malthusian institutionalized neglect (Malthus, 1766–1834, an English political economist, came to the conclusion that population explosion, especially among the poor, would ultimately outstrip available food resources and therefore championed any means, however cruel, to reduce the likelihood of that happening. Incredibly, although a clergyman by training, he defended slavery, child murder, abolition of poor relief, opposed housing projects for the working classes and soup kitchens). In 19th century England (and elsewhere), the new factory entrepreneurs urged the government not to regulate or interfere with their profit-seeking activities since, so they alleged, competition and free-market capitalism would, in time, resolve all shortcomings. By the middle of the 19th century, England was the foremost industrial nation in the world. Proponents of laissez-faire economics argued as they do today that regulations instead of promoting progress actually retarded it and that industry owners were the best judges of what was likely to promote the country's economic success. But history proved them wrong, then and now, for a free enterprise economy must be regulated in order to be socially principled and not abusive.

The working conditions in the factories were appalling. Lack of proper means of ventilation and sanitation; numerous accidents due to cleaning of machines while their moving parts were exposed; employment of children at an early age of 6 (sometimes even younger), working alongside with men and women from 5 AM to 9 PM—it was a case from bed to work and from work to bed. Pauper children were apprenticed to factory owners and lived entirely under their control; in many cases beds were never unoccupied due to two shifts, one group of children leaving work taking the place of others going to work; epidemics due to poor nourishment, overwork, and unhealthy surroundings resulted in numerous deaths; insufficient time was allowed for meals, which usually had to be taken in the dust-laden and stuffy atmosphere of the factory; the health of all workers, particularly that of women and children, was greatly impaired and they suffered from many physical deformities.

Conditions were partly corrected by the pressure of public opinion and governmental action. No doubt, the English novelist Charles Dickens (who in his childhood labored in a factory) was eminently motivated to publicize these deplorable conditions in his writings. Who were the social reformers? No economists or clergymen were among them. To the most prominent reformers belonged Robert Owen (a wealthy capitalist and factory owner) and the Earl of Shaftesbury (a wealthy aristocrat), whose wealth endowed them sufficiently to recognize that there are moral values which cannot be bargained away. The horrors they observed motivated them to make it their lifework to deny men driven by such unrestrained greed and aggressive accumulation the opportunity to oppress and exploit the ordinary wage earners and take part in easing their abused existence. What noble conduct, what civilized men, but so few. Yet they and their colleagues exercised sufficient influence to make a difference. It will always be that way. A few moral humans struggling against the tide of indifference to keep the idea of civilized conduct alive and in the forefront.

(12) Despite sanctimonious professions to the contrary, there are still some visible remnants of those ugly bygone times. In the year 2002, 250 million children between the ages 5–15 are working long hours every day somewhere in the world producing low-priced goods eagerly sought by uncaring customers; there is no murmur, outcry or protest but total indifference. Some countries wishing to be counted among the respected still turn a blind eye to the use of slaves (literal) and permit their exploitation (Brazil, Pakistan, India, Thailand, Saudi Arabia), not snatched by raiding armies but hoodwinked into servitude by crafty fast-talkers. No outrage is voiced by economists, clergymen or anyone else. It should be a matter of grievous concern to prosperous countries that 12 million children die each year from poverty associated causes; that 100 million children are homeless; that one billion people are suffering from hunger most of the time; that 50 million people are dying yearly from starvation. Apart from token aid and expression of regrets, few are willing to get involved.

(13) Post-middle 19th century economies of industrial nations outstripped all predictions in wealth accumulation, riches for the efficient entrepreneurs not seen before, praises for free-market capitalism which proved its worth to this day. The climate was ripe for a confluence of morality and an economic surplus to stimulate progress toward the establishment of a state of civilization not experienced before. A degree of civilization means the preservation of security and minimal comforts for most segments of society enjoying an air of permanence. But economic man was not cool and calculating, or else he would have grasped the wisdom of slowing profit-seeking after accumulating an adequate surplus to assure his desired level of comforts and security, enabling (or assist by various means) those of moderate means to gain upward mobility. He was most assuredly able to mitigate his bondage to the instinct of self-preservation and realize that his security and preservation of the fruits of his labor depended on most segments of society sharing, albeit to a lesser extent, some of the personal comforts. Such a mitigation on his part (a minority) would be richly rewarded since the insecurity of the majority of the less endowed meant insecurity for all. For discords, disputes, conflicts, hostility, and dissensions destabilizing the advantages of free-market capitalism are a steep price to pay. In an all-out defense of their prerogatives, the economic elites have the means and wherewithal to affect political and economic legislation to favor and protect their special interests, be

they efficient lobbyists or submissive legislators. If they could have matters in hand, an autocratic political system coupled with unregulated free-market capitalism are most to their liking. But the affluent elites of the prosperous industrial nations have not chosen the path of mitigation and so far successfully prevailed (with some exceptions) in the adverse contest with those of moderate means (the majority) for the extension of prerogatives. In such a contentious economic climate of concentrated wealth morality could not sink its roots despite a high degree of enlightenment and, as a consequence, civilization did not maintain a forward momentum among the many industrial nations. The successful underhanded and crafty tactics of the privileged economic elite, never a secret to those schooled in economics, are gaining an air of transparency and publicity particularly in times of lackluster economic performance and in reaction to the global financial architecture. The guardians of democratic capitalism endorsing the legitimacy and rectitude of a wealth-gap getting ever more outrageously disproportionate will have to answer, sooner or later, to a cynical and suspicious public no longer easily fobbed off by specious play on words and free-trade rhetoric that the profit-making game is not rigged in favor of the affluent privileged. Aggressive aggrandizement and unrestrained greed following the natural order may ultimately arouse the by now more aware disadvantaged majority to force a change in the socio-economic arrangement. If neither segment relents, a radical collision seems inevitable. This bodes ill for a civilized society to gain the needed permanence since, as is apparent, the affluent elite decided long ago that civilized conduct does not favor the interests of the privileged but is conducive instead to improved circumstances for the majority of moderate means. The rich seek culture but spurn a civilized society; those of moderate means seek the establishment of a civilized society but are indifferent about culture.

The repudiation and scuttling by the affluent of prospects for the progressive establishment of a civilized society ultimately to lead prosperous nations to a state of civilization may prove to be fatuously misguided and a momentous blunder.

CHAPTER 16

CIVILIZATION

The Impediment of Monotheism

(1) Of the many religions surviving to the present, Judaism, Christianity, Confucianism, Shintoism, Brahmanism, Buddhism, Hinduism and Islam, only the first two and the last named played a significant role in the history and culture of Western nations; the others were indigenous to and mainly localized in India, China and Japan. Only Judaism, Christianity and Islam claim to possess a theology based on monotheism; each proclaiming to be in possession of the true faith that can offer salvation exclusively to its followers; each declaring to be in possession of sacred Scriptures vouchsafing their divine message, and each denying the authenticity of the other. All three are guilty of preaching an ugly genre of intolerance, animus toward the non-believer, forced proselytizing under pain of death during some periods of their history—these are the peculiar traits of monotheism—and all three are culpable of a fanatical militancy during crucial periods of their history, an inevitable consequence when religions harbored political designs to pursue expansionary aims or silence an inconvenient competitor. Of the three monotheisms, Christianity, Roman Catholicism especially, was by far the most blameworthy offender. But all three were guilty of attempts to methodically and irreversibly subjugate the mind of believers to the doctrines of their faith, especially during the past centuries when they reigned supreme, when the only choice available to man was salvation or damnation, and the skeptic treated as a social outcast, or worse. It must be remembered

that in those long gone terrible days when religion was an all-powerful institution, the choice of belief was not an option, and the non-believer, however justified in his doubts, was treated as an apostate and accorded treatment reserved for heretics. For man is born into a religion; he did not suddenly decide to profess it and converting to another faith could have ugly consequences even if the choice was another sect within the same theology. Anyone born into a particular faith was expected to profess it with tenacity until his death, for it was taken for granted that it was natural for all humans to profess a belief in a particular Deity. Missing an obligatory attendance in the synagogue, church, or mosque was a sufficient reason to come under suspicion of clerical disciplinary councils, and if the lapse was recurrent or the offender was known to question some article of faith, the full weight of the condemnatory power of the religious authorities was applied—they were experts in detecting a budding apostate and most efficient in dealing with the danger. It was incumbent upon rabbis, priests and mullahs to gain converts for their congregations and not let schismatics gain a foothold. The character, deeds, and misdeeds of a religious movement can best be judged when it was at its most powerful—at its zenith—unrestricted and unhindered in the treatment of congregants, how it dealt with apostates, schismatics, heretics, and how it defended its supremacy against usurpers and other enemies, real or imagined. For all ancient religions were contrived:

(a) for political purposes, to ensure the security and stability of the ruler or rulers and ensure the loyalty of the governed.

(b) for the maintenance and enrichment of the priestly order or its equivalents.

The historical development of monotheistic religious organizations are best understood if viewed as commercial monopolies exercising total control of markets, ruthless in combating competition; scrutinizing market violations; top echelon executives jealously guarding the conferred privileges and financial rewards, constantly seeking expansion by corporate acquisitions to increase profitability, prestige and power.

I made a considerable effort in Chapter 4 (Part One to Part Six) to critically analyse the development of religious thoughts; the foundation of the three monotheisms; their spurious claims to divine revelation; the logical invalidity of the terms used to describe attributes of the Deity; some of the methods used in defining creeds and the tenuous foundation on which they are based; the absence of originality; the blatant plagiarisms and the danger that revival of ultra-orthodoxy and the rise of fundamentalism pose. I subjected Catholicism, by far the worst offender in all fields of inquiry, to greater scrutiny in my firm belief, backed up by historical evidence, that it deliberately retarded and frustrated man's advances toward a civilized society, toward a state of civilization, in that it considered all the following as anathema and the work of Satan: free speech, free thought, criticism of dogma, forbidding the reading of books it placed in the Index, scientific inquiries in disciplines bringing into question the biblical text or its creed, the democratic form of government. Its power and influence diminished within the democratic political framework but found comfort and affinity with authoritarian regimes. Although most of these are the characteristics of all monotheisms, the Catholic hierarchy displayed a greater ingenuity and willful contempt for the laity that was beyond the pale.

Despite all the critique and skepticism warranted by the flawed creeds and lack of originality, religion is a serious subject of inquiry because most humans are fragile, lacking the stamina and the wherewithal to withstand the stresses and strains of everyday living without the spiritual reliance and calming reassurance provided by a belief in a just and approachable Deity. Pain, suffering, and tragedies play a daunting role in human existence, just as insecurity, fear of the unknown, pessimism, lack of purpose, and loneliness have played a part in all human lives. Most humans need the consolation of a firm underpinning to help them cope with the drama of reality: religious faith provides such a floor. My interest is to determine whether man-made monotheisms are capable of exerting any civilizing influence on the conduct of believers, their traditions and cultures, and whether such influence contributed to the promotion of amity among nations progressively advancing the cause of civilization.

(2) All the violent natural phenomena, such as thunder, floods, earthquake, hail, etc., which people in antiquity could not understand, became associated with mysteries and attributed to all-powerful unseen and hostile spirits whose anger had to be propitiated by the most treasured offerings, principally items of food and the sacrifice of children, which later included prisoners of war, favored adult sons and daughters, bulls, goats, sheep and other animals. In the cultures of ancient peoples, the spirits developed into tribal gods serving various functions, such as the god of thunder, of earthquake, of fertility, of good harvest, of victory over enemies. The propitiations were not always effective, which made room for a class of intercessors possessing skills in assuaging the anger of gods and whose function was to mediate between the gods and worshippers. This

was the beginning of the priestly order that demanded a status separate from worshippers, privileges which would enable them to enjoy a life of comfort befitting interpreters of divine oracles and transmitters to the gods of the entreaties of supplicants. The newly formed priestly orders, secure in their calling, living in comfort and freed from procuring life's necessities, set about compiling a host of rules governing sacrifices (that part of the flesh of animals not consumed by fire belonged to the priests as their share to enjoy), regulations, and divine commandments to enmesh the worshippers in complex rituals and observances which only they could interpret and declare pleasing to the gods. The belief in after-life was a necessity for earthly existence to make any sense, and ancient primitive creeds showed, especially in burial rites, a vague understanding of immortality but no conception of heaven or hell. A moral life and sal-vation of the soul did not influence the gods (it had no meaning), but improper or inadequate sacrifices brought out their anger. Only a priest could offer sacrifices according to strict rituals acceptable to the gods (the priests devised them) and used an open air altar on which to perform the rites. Trees, large stones, rivers, and mountains were worshipped as sacred manifestations of the presence of gods, until Temples, the dwelling place of gods and priests, limited sacrificial rites to a specific location. These Temples were also used as sacred depositories of trea-sures both of priests and the lay community.

The above represents an outline of a typical priestly administered belief in gods, which predates the establishment of monotheistic reli-gions.

(3) These primitive beliefs in gods and the efficacy of priesthoods embell-ished with rituals, sacrifices, oracles, and divinations were the creations of ancient primitive peoples to fill a distressing and destabilizing void in their lives. The fear of malevolent spirits was driven by total ignorance of the natural order of things; they compensated for the darkness of the mind by inventing childlike fantasies about the power of the priests to calm the anger of gods and placed every detail of their lives under the domination of a tithing priesthood, who schemed to make themselves indispensable by inventing complex rituals only they could monitor and approve as acceptable to the gods.

From human reaction to the fear of the unknown and the need to assuage the anger of hostile spirits, the ancient primitive peoples who lived several thousands of years ago in total ignorance about the Earth and the Universe lacked the most rudimentary knowledge about their natural surrounding and whose lives were spent struggling for survival, a belief arose in gods embellished with a panoply of complex rituals and ceremonies that served as the foundation for the religious creeds of subsequent generations. From the foundation of simplistic beliefs of ancient guileless and ingenuous peoples, an unforgiving, overly demanding, and coercive monotheism emerged incorporating a multiplicity of accretions, emendations and modifications. An excessively ritualistic creed came into existence, immersed in complexities and invoking for additional credibility the assurance of divine revelations. The religion of the Israelites (called Hebrews up to the Exodus from Egypt, Israelites up to the Babylonian Exile, and Jews thereafter) emerged as the first of this genre, followed by Christianity, and later by Islam. Despite the subsequent man-made variations, some of them fundamental, all of them necessarily bear the traces of their ancient provenance. It will come as a shock to the adherents of the three faiths that their religions were not the result of sudden divine revelations but developed by stages from the humblest of superstitious beginnings of ancient primitive peoples. It should come as a rude awakening to the proud and prejudiced worshippers of contemporary monotheisms that despite the tremendous advances made in every discipline of knowledge and culture since ancient primitive tribes roamed the world, the fear of the unknown and the urge to propitiate the anger of the Deity are still the basic motivations of present-day theists as they were in ancient times, and that the quest for salvation of the soul so eagerly sought by the devout did not matter to the ancients, nor did they harbor any hostility toward competing tribal beliefs and gods, as is in vogue nowadays. Since ancient times and up to the present, even though the overall knowledge and cultures progressed immeasurably, the inter-faith harmony and tolerance suffered disconcerting regressions. When fasting on the Day of Atonement, or celebrating the sacrament of High Mass, or setting out on the obligatory pilgrimage to Mecca, the present-day follower of his preferred religion, proud of the ancestral heritage handed down by his forefathers, would falter in total disbelief upon learning that the inspirational religion of his choice evolved from beliefs practiced in the very ancient times and that primitive idolatry, fetishism and polytheism formed the foundation from which his religion evolved. Such a revelation could help dispel the preached hostility toward other religions and dismiss any claims of exclusive possession of the true faith.

(4)   Although the credal affirmations contained in the Old Testament, New

Testament and Koran could not withstand a serious inquiry into their theological foundation if exposed to a critical analysis, they nevertheless had authors who preached a message not only of great importance but exercised a most lasting influence upon the outlook of humans contemplating their relationship with the supernatural. Judaism, as presented in the Torah (the five books of Moses), claimed to be the result of divine revelation, appropriated much from the religions of Babylonians, Canaanites and Egyptians; Christianity took much as its own from Judaism, Mithraism and Egyptian religions; Islam, as made known in the Koran, borrowed much of its teaching and doctrines from Judaism and Christianity. All these religions plagiarized freely from each other without restraints or scruples in a determined effort to achieve primacy, and each claimed to be in possession of the only true faith. It apparently did not occur to the doctrinal framers that since so much was plainly appropriated from others and hence could not entertain any claim to originality, it followed that if any one religion was false, all had to be false. A religion could not plagiarize mistaken or inaccurate notions and still lay claim to divine revelation—traits of a true and original faith.

Any religious system which demands conformity from its adherents and prohibits dissent betrays insecurity. It will use any means commensurate with its power to enforce such decrees. For dissent leads to doubt and apostasy. All monotheisms were guilty of taking stringent measures to avoid defections, but Catholicism was the most forceful; during the zenith of its power from the 11th to the 18th centuries, it treated renunciations, skepticisms, and vacillations on the part of followers with utmost vehemence, particularly since the 16th century rise of Protestantism, which caused its power to drift and brought forth the most determined effort (Counter Reformation) to avoid decline. The firm posture was pure self-preservation, for it was not its creed or sacred Scripture which prescribed countermeasures against defectors, as was the case with the Torah and Koran, but politically conceived steps by the Vatican and clergymen to preserve the nucleus of power. The severity of the treatment of apostates was proportionate to the wielding of power. The latter was achieved by joining in unholy alliances with political potentates who not only furnished support and carried out the mandated punishments but disposed of armies to wage wars against the perceived enemies of the Church.

(5)   In the early centuries of Christianity when the scriptural canon was in the process of compilation, it was a highly proselytizing faith which gained many converts among Greeks, Romans, slaves and Jews wherever

its relentless evangelists set foot; apostasy was not a problem and there was no need to provide for canonical sanctions to secure fidelity. There were differences early on among Bishops and clerics in the formulation of the creed, but excommunication, banishment, murder and the burning of controversial manuscripts (over 35 Gospels written before 150 A.D. by different authors were burned) sufficed to remove doctrinal heterodoxies. In subsequent centuries, the Roman Church feared more the influence of sectarians and critics of the immorality of Popes and Cardinals, who professed an uncorrupted version of Christianity (John Hus, de Molay, Savonarola and Arnold of Brescia paid the supreme price for speaking out) than converts to Judaism and Islam. Since the original Christians and Christian teachings were of Jewish origin, the early Bishops and Church Fathers were concerned about the Judaization of their creed (the Ebionites, Nazarenes, Galileans, the Brethren) and proceeded to unleash the demonization of Jews (who were, by then, considered a rebellious nation by the Roman Emperors) with a vehemence and ferocity unknown in the annals of religions. In contrast, the sacred writings of Judaism and Islam provided for unsparing treatment of deviants, backsliders and apostates. A few excerpts from the sacred writings of the three monotheisms will illustrate these points.

(a) *Judaism (The Torah)*
- "Any man or woman who is a necromancer or magician must be put to death by stoning ..." (LEV. 20:27).
- "You shall not allow a sorceress to live" (EX. 22:17).
- "You must keep the Sabbaths ... The man who profanes it must be put to death" (EX. 31:12-14).
- "Any man who curses his God ... The one who blasphemes the name of Yahweh must die; stranger or native, if he blasphemes the name, he dies" (LEV. 24:16-17).
- "A human being laid under ban cannot be redeemed, he must be put to death" (LEV. 27:29).
- "If anyone presumes to disobey ... the priest ... that man must die" (DEUT. 17:12).
- "But the prophet who presumes to say in my name a thing I have not commanded him to say ... that prophet shall die" (DEUT. 18:20).
- "That prophet ... must be put to death, (if) he has preached apostasy from Yahweh your God" (DEUT. 13:6).
- "If there us anyone, man or woman, ... who goes and serves other gods ... you must stone that man or woman to death" (DEUT. 17:26).

We do not know what ravages these priestly ordained punishments inflicted upon Jews, but we do know that after the destruction of Jerusalem and the Second Commonwealth by the Romans in 70 A.D., the priesthood and Temple sacrifices were abolished, politics was divorced from religion, and the rabbis undertook the spiritual leadership of the Jews. When all was lost after the total collapse of the Bar Kokhba rebellion in 135 A.D. and most Jews forced into slavery or exile, it was thanks to the rabbis, who abjured all future political involvements with the consequent loss of power, that the core of Judaism survived to become a spiritual force.

(b)   *Islam (The Koran)*
  • "The unbelievers are your inveterate enemies" (Sura 4:101).
  • "... do not befriend your fathers or your brothers if they choose unbelief in preference to faith" (Sura 9:23).
  • "Never think that the unbelievers can escape their fate in this world" (Sura 24:57).
  • "Those that deny our revelations we will burn them in fire" (Sura 4:56).
  • "Let the believers not make friends with infidels" (Sura 3:28).
  • "As for unbelievers, neither their riches nor their children will in the least save them from God's wrath" (Sura 3:9)
  • "Those that deny God's revelations shall be sternly punished, God is mighty and capable of revenge" (Sura 3:5).
  • "Slay them wherever you find them ... Idolatry is more grievous than bloodshed" (Sura 2:191).
  • "Never think that the unbelievers can escape their fate in this world. The fire shall be their home ..." (Sura 24:57).
  • "Believers, take neither the Jews nor Christians for your friends ... God does not guide the wrongdoers" (Sura 5:51).

The Koran accuses the Jews of corrupting the Scriptures and the Christians of worshipping Jesus, yet were taught to worship God only; it teaches that there is but one God and Mohammed is his prophet; that God misleads and guides whom he will. Predestination is one of the primary teachings in that nothing can happen but what God has fixed. The indoctrination of followers at a young age, the method of teaching the message of the Koran, their great numbers and dedication without opposition built them into a powerful political force to be reckoned with.

(c)   *Christianity (The Gospels, Paul, Acts)*
  • "... the people (Jews) who put the Lord Jesus to death, and the prophets too. And now they have been persecuting us, and acting in a

way that cannot please God and makes them the enemies of the whole human race ..." (1 Th).

- " ... and those who reject me (Jesus) reject the one who sent me (God)" (Lk 10:16).
- "Alas for you, scribes and Pharisees, you hypocrites!" (Mt 23:13).
- "Serpents, brood of vipers, how can you escape being condemned to hell? ..." (Mt 23:33).
- "Jerusalem, Jerusalem, you that kill the prophets and stone those who are sent to you! ..." (Mt 23:37).
- "They will expel you (Christians) from the synagogues, and indeed the hour is coming when anyone who kills you will think he is doing a holy duty for God" (Jn 16:2).
- "The Jews are enemies of God ... " (Rm 11:28).
- "You stubborn people, with your pagan hearts and pagan ears. You are always resisting the Holy Spirit, just as your ancestors used to do. Can you name a single prophet your ancestors never persecuted? In the past they killed those who foretold the coming of the Just One, and now you have become his betrayers, his murderers" (Ac 7:51-53).

(6) The vilification of Jews as Christ-killers, the murderers of the Lord, served the Christian cause well; the Crucifixion, Resurrection and Ascension of Jesus became the central unifying dogma of Christianity. Whenever it suited the Church or its dignitaries to strengthen their cause, deflect attention from some embarrassment, or restore the devotion of congregants, a call went out to the faithful to avenge the killing of Christ and such repeated accusations sufficed to rouse the anger and blood-lust of the faithful with predictable results. It proved a convenient vehicle for the Church to assert itself without fear of contradiction, or test the veracity of the accusation, for in those days it was all-powerful; none so much as dared to vacillate from the orthodox beliefs. But doubts there were; the internal and historical contradictions could not be resolved. The Gospels of Luke and John stated that Jesus' death sentence was carried out by Jews; the Gospels of Mark and Matthew blamed the Romans. Most puzzling was the silence of Paul, a contemporary of Jesus—they never met. Paul, the earliest of the New Testament writers, knew nothing about Jesus' life on Earth, nothing of his Passion, the arrest at night, the trials by the High Priest and the Sanhedrin, the sentencing by Pontius Pilate, about Golgotha and the burial—all these events were said to have occurred in Jerusalem, a confined area where news traveled fast. Had Paul known any of these episodes, his silence is inexplicable, particularly since

his claimed employment by the High Priest as a persecutor of the followers of Jesus shortly after these events were said to have taken place.
Christian hostility and persecution of Jews as the murderers of the Lord
may have been intentionally misdirected. Yet it was responsible for rivers
of Jewish blood since its inception up to the 20th century; they were
treated as pariahs to be trampled on and abused. But Jews were an easy
target—visible, outnumbered, defenseless, a small minority living in hostile surroundings. It will be shown below that the Roman Church, in
defense of its primacy, motivated its followers to apply the same kind of
hostility and persecution against deviant Christians and fellow-Christian
sectarians, such as Huguenots, Albigenses, Cathari and others.

(7)   Like all monotheisms, but decidedly more so, the Catholic Church
became intolerant and brutal in its struggle for supremacy, continuously
in search of converts by any means, however corrupt and violent. When
it acquired the right to own real estate and became prosperous, the
Catholic Church raised armies like any secular State; fought wars for
enrichment and extermination of schismatics; hired mercenaries and all
the time invoked the blessings of God; persecuted and treated with violence anyone who dared question its authority of doctrinal interpretation
even though embellished and skewed to justify its own deviations; ruled,
in time, as an absolutist imperium as it brooked no opposition to its hegemony and proceeded with utter ruthlessness to eliminate all resistance
and interference. The Church displayed an uncommon rapacity, greed,
venality and engaged in Machiavellian plots typical of secular monarchs.
The Popes and Curia took part in political intrigues, assassinations, murders and false imprisonments; raised money from the sale of ecclesiastical
preferments, bishoprics and indulgences—the latter was the most profitable; forged documents to suit the agenda; unleashed the horrors of the
Crusades and Inquisitions; enriched the purses of the Church by confis-
cating properties of innocent victims forced to confess heresies. The
preservation of the papacy, episcopal and priestly orders, their welfare,
comfortable lifestyle, and satisfaction of inflated needs were the be-all
and end-all of their vision of organized religion.

The Catholic Church claimed to be in possession of the "truth", the
true religion to the exclusion of all others; it claimed sole possession of
the key to salvation. It hounded its own followers for the slightest infraction, deviation, or infringement of the prescribed rules not using persuasion but the threat of torture chambers of the Inquisition and the fiery
stake. It cleverly hid behind the secular arm of the State not to take

responsibility for carrying out the punishment. It trampled on the rights of believers and terrorized them into submission; condemned free speech and thought it the work of the devil; for a time, forbade the laity possession of the Bible under penalty of death by burning, fearing its content would lead to heresy for not sanctioning all the imagery and special adorations imposed by the Church. The Albigenses were condemned for heresy in 1163 for reading the Bible and refusal to worship images, saints, angels and the Virgin. The sectarians became the target of a ruthless Crusade instigated by Pope Innocent III and led by his minion Simon de Montfort, whose army slew 20,000 men, women and children; blinded or otherwise mutilated all prisoners (all Christians); devastated the whole countryside and instructed his marauders not to make any distinction between the hunted and true Catholics who lived among them peacefully. In the end, all the Albigenses were exterminated, but not in vain; their refusal to toe the line became the first spark which lit the fuse of resistance. Since the dawn of the faith over 200 million Christians died in Christian-instigated wars over dissenting theological ideologies. In addition to the deviant Christian sects already mentioned against whom the venom of the Church was directed and which were mercilessly persecuted, were: Arians, Gnostics, Manicheans, Jansenists, Bogomiles, Nestorians, Valentinians. The fires of dissent were slowly spreading, but the Church had the mercenaries. The historian Gibbon declared that the Church of Rome defended by violence what it had acquired by fraud.

Witchcraft is defined as the practice of sorcery and association with the devil to commit acts of evil, engage in sexual intercourse with the devil and cast evil spells on innocent humans. It strains one's credulity to contemplate whether the death-dealing witch-hunters and Inquisitors really believed their accusations and treated the accused as heretics or whether it was a convenient means of terrorizing the congregants into silence. When Pope Innocent VIII (1482-1492) issued his Bull against witches in 1484 and ordered the Inquisition to investigate the accused, he placed the stamp of approval of the Catholic Church on the validity of witchcraft. As a result, two Dominicans wrote a commentary on witchcraft (Hammer of Witches) in 1487 to serve as a guide in recognizing witches. The guide refuted all skepticism by asserting that anyone who admitted the slightest doubt of the existence of witches was guilty of heresy and hauled before the Inquisition to answer charges; that women were more inclined to be witches than men; that female witches could cause impotence in men, barrenness in women, hailstorms and crop failures. Those once accused confessed under torture and faced the inevitable fate: death by fire. None was safe from the horrors of this madness. This witch-mania was a European (later also a limited American) phenomenon; the 15th and 16th centuries were the most active in pursuing the unfortunates. In 1623, Pope Gregory XV (1621-1623) commanded that anyone who made a pact with the devil should be given the death penalty. The Protestant Martin Luther also thought that witches should be burnt for making a pact with the devil. Resistance to pain under torture was taken as proof of alliance with the devil and the accused suffered the same fate as witches. Even women over 90 years old and girls as young as 9 were not safe. This papal insanity was terminated after the last witch-burning in 1793, but not before about 300,000 totally innocent victims died a horrible death after they were brutalized by torture, protesting their innocence to the last.

By the 13th century, the Catholic Church felt threatened when nonbelievers and skeptics increased in number as a result of the failed Crusades and decided that Christians diverging from orthodoxy merited harsher punishment than excommunication; they deserved to be treated as heretics and given the capital punishment. Pope Gregory IX (1227-1241) in 1231 established the Inquisition as a papal Tribunal and published its procedural constitution. Extended to Aragon in 1232, the Inquisition became general in 1233; the Spanish Inquisition began its operation in 1481 and was not permanently suppressed until 1834. The Italian Inquisition (the Holy Office) was active up to the 19th century and finally abolished in 1965. For centuries, nothing was permitted to be written about it to keep the proceedings out of public view. The powers of the Inquisition were unlimited; the accused was guilty until proven innocent and was ignorant of the charges until the day of sentencing; never faced his accuser nor informed of his or her identity; was not familiar with the legal proceedings which were conducted in Latin; could not be defended by a lawyer nor call a witness, who was liable to be accused by the Inquisition for testifying; was jailed (in chains) and kept incommunicado; his property was impounded and in most cases with finality, depending on the severity of the charges; when examined, he had to take an oath to answer all questions truthfully and therefore be his own accuser; obliged under oath to reveal to the Court the names of other heretics known to him; when confession could not be obtained, torture was applied and the accused was broken in body and spirit. No mercy was shown by the Inquisitors, their sentences were harsh and pitiless; they had a vested interest in death sentences and life imprisonments, for under the rules they benefited from the confiscation of the accused's property. There were no appeals and the Court's decisions were final. For those judged "obstinate" heretics the penalty was death by burning. The condemned was turned over to secular authorities for the execution of the sentence.

The Thirty Years War (1618-1648) was a religious conflict pitting Catholics, Protestants and Calvinists in a war involving most of Europe's powers in an enormous and bloody conflict for Germany. After thirty years, most of Germany and much of Western Europe lay in ruins, the towns devastated, their industries destroyed. One-third of the German population had died in war-related catastrophes. Armies of mercenaries subjected Germany to slaughter and plunder, all in the name of religion; the carnage and devastation took centuries to rehabilitate. The Catholic Church was on the defensive trying to prevent the secularization of ecclesiastical property. The war marked the end of the Counter Reformation, which was the Church's response to Luther's Protestant Reformation.

In the middle of the 16th century, Protestants were persecuted as heretics in Catholic France. The new faith was increasingly feared by the established religion due to the success achieved in drawing converts to its ranks, despite the panic spread across France by officials ordered to report all suspicious proselytizing activities. Catherine de Medici, the widow of King Henry II and a fervent Catholic, was regent during the minority of Charles IX—in fact, exercised control that title bestowed during his entire reign (1560-1574). In that capacity, she stirred up wars between Catholics and Protestants (Huguenots) and was a witting participant in the instigation of the St. Bartholomew's Day Massacre (August 24, 1572). In this brutal slaughter, 30,000 Protestants were mercilessly murdered in a failed attempt to remove all vestiges of the new faith from Catholic France.

(8) If an effect is said to be caused by a specific group of antecedents and some other antecedent is added to the specific group without changing the effect, it can be said that the added antecedent had no relevance in influencing the outcome. For we learn from history that the bloody conflicts of the human race caused by greed, rapacity, and covetousness in uncurbed pursuit of self-interest, in bondage to the instinct of self-preservation, slaves to circumstances beyond control, have never abated but continued unaffected and unmitigated by any infusion of religious scruples, considerations or influences. On the contrary, not only did the presence on this planet of religions preaching monotheism administered

by an arrogant clergy embroil humanity in innumerable bloody conflicts, but a new kind of hatred, animosity, and fanaticism entered the scene of human relations, disruptive and destabilizing to social tranquility, unsettling the order of natural thinking by deprecating the worth of cognition as useless for salvation, and elevating blind faith and belief in a supernatural Deity as the ultimate goal of man's existence.

All three monotheistic religions share a similarity of design in what constitutes the basics of morality, a world outlook that is hostile to the progress of civilization, to basic human ideals, to freedom of expression and tolerance of dissent: that morality is dependent upon a belief in God; that the highest good is following the laws of God; that all the problems of man are attributable to his lack of belief, and that their respective creeds contain all the answers to his problems. It follows, therefore, that non-believers must of necessity lack morality, cannot be trusted and associated with. A new kind of hostility made its entry, one that was not encountered before, namely, religious persecution, forcible conversion under penalty of death for refusal to submit; trials and punishments by religious courts following their own rules of procedure tilted entirely in favor of the accuser. Their kind of morality, no matter how ennobled by the passage of time, that preaches hostility and hatred of other beliefs as a religious duty can be quickly dismissed: a morality worthy of that name must have universal application and cannot be selective; moral behavior doctrinally restricted to coreligionists is unworthy of that label. The claim they assert of being the sole source of a divinely revealed morality is unfounded and false. A high level of morality existed before the three religions received their claimed revelations and before the enlightened prophets of the Israelites had their visions. As far back as 2000 B.C., the rulers of the Mesopotamian peoples spoke of establishing justice in the land and although they had their gods, the moral system was not identified with or depended upon any particular religious doctrines. The standards of conduct prescribed by the rulers were based on laws totally detached from anything divine. Or the sublime teachings of the Upanishads, a segment of literature of the Veda followed by the Vedanta, about 3,000 years in existence, which arose on the Indian subcontinent. It admonished man to be tolerant of other religions, subdue the passions of the senses, be charitable to the neighbor, pity those who deserve pity, and stressed the following precepts as fundamental to a compatible social life: generosity, benevolence, cooperation, courtesy, sympathy and honesty. It claimed no divine revelation, offered no mystical salvation or forgiveness of sins but asserted that meditation alone can secure salvation, which it identified with immortality; demanded a strict moral discipline of all before they were allowed to study the Vedanta. This is an eternity distanced from the crude anthropomorphism of monotheistic religions.

The principles of conduct taught by the three central religions are harsh, uncompromising and cruel; threaten violators with severe divine punishment, even eternal damnation to induce compliance. The nature of punishment prescribed by their holy books inspired religious leaders to assume an attitude of rancor toward the faithful, which in due time bred the seeds of reforms. Clerical vindictiveness (especially as practiced by the Catholic clergy) in all its fury brought out, in time, revulsion and doubts even in ardent believers whose faith was shaken by the harsh treatment meted out to those accused of heresy, and who observed with profound trepidation the more than occasional upright morality and devout belief of the condemned heretics.

(9) Man's principal motivation to action is the instinct of self-preservation, which prompts the satisfaction of primary and other needs; he is without options in pursuing that effort, except when the needs are secondary (or tertiary) he may mitigate that endeavor motivated by considerations of morality. Such mitigation is in opposition to the natural order, praiseworthy and unselfish, induced by causes beyond his control, leading to civilized conduct. A man who is unable of earning a discretionary surplus, not able to achieve a level of desired comfort and freedom of action would be fearful to risk exposure to life's hazards without blaming selected mundane causes beyond his control to relieve his anxiety and explanation for failure. But there is another kind of fear unsettling man, that fragile and vulnerable creation of a flawed Nature: fear of the unknown, a natural instinct like self-preservation and sexual desire. Needing the stamina to face the pain and anxieties of existence compounded by the fear of the unknown, unaffected by satisfying natural needs, man found the belief in powerful invisible tribal gods, later replaced by a stern but approachable Deity, a relief to his tensions. For nothing calms human anxieties as surely as the sustained faith in salvation, immortality of the soul, rewards in this life and the hereafter. From the varied catalogue of cunning, clever and scheming, ambitious for power and the life of comfort, seizing the opportunity that presented itself, a group of shrewd and skillful men turned the primal instinctive fear tormenting humans to their advantage by claiming to possess the mystic keys to appeasing the anger of the gods (or the Deity). A new pro-

fession was born, an aristocratic, secretive, and exclusive priesthood that burdened the life of followers by devising complex rituals and ceremonies, ordinances and commandments. The priesthood, a select group of people who grew wealthy and worldly on account of the power wielded, of necessity jealously guarded their prerogatives against usurpers. By imposing elaborate and time-consuming rituals and ceremonies declared necessary to appease and win the favor of the Deity, they managed to preempt the spare moments of the errant pious to entrap them into transgressions. Dispensing the doctrines needed for salvation and heavenly immortality, the priests hijacked the path to morality open to humans and substituted a new form of bondage: total obedience and submission to the preached theology to be assured of a meaning to life. To prevent their flock from succumbing to the blandishments of other religions, the priesthoods of monotheisms preached enmity toward other faiths, forbade associating with non-believers, devised brutal punishments for backsliders and apostates, declared other religions false and cursed, which could not help but arouse the hostile passions of adherents, attitudes totally disruptive of social harmony and human fellowship. The priests prosper the more their followers are exposed to dissensions, hostility and intolerance.

Humans do foolish things when driven by fanaticism, i.e., unreasonable zeal in conflict with self-preservation, for some passionate religious zealots prefer to gain the favor of the Deity to the cares of humdrum everyday existence, generated by a different kind of self-interest and self-seeking divorced from material gains; they are unaware to have relapsed into a new kind of bondage, willing to sacrifice life's comforts, freedom of action, even life itself, convinced in the truth of religious beliefs taken on faith alone as opposed to the concrete bread and butter realities of worldly existence. Priestly pretensions filled the void caused by fear of the unknown and provided belief in the supernatural as a remedy to be taken on blind faith. When pleasing the Deity, hope for salvation and expectation of immortality become part of self-preservation. They affect the conduct of humans to the point where a lesser good is preferred to a greater good, the mind is said to be perverted. The mundane is eclipsed by the celestial. The history of religious bigotry and atrocities chronicled in this Chapter not only presents the dismal failure of the civilizing power of monotheisms but clearly demonstrates the bitter misfortunes that can afflict mankind if humans of perverted minds dominate the scene.

(10) Any faith that claims to be the exclusive dispenser of truth, salvation lim-

ited for its own and damnation for others, demands absolute submission to its tenets and hatred for others as a religious duty, reserves severe punishment for the nonconformist, requires its ordinances to be treated as eternal and immutable, and warns that any relapse or backsliding would invite divine retribution, but uncritically tolerates unbridled savagery committed for its greater glory—such a faith is antithetical to any concept civilization stands for. The need to believe in the supernatural and occult by the majority of humans as a way of combating primal fear, ignores and totally overlooks the internal contradictions of religious teachings. The faithful seek no consistency or harmony, on the contrary, the lack of these only magnifies the mysteries and increases the attraction of the symbolisms.

The need to believe in salvation, the immortality of the soul and the afterlife give a purpose to an otherwise inexplicable human existence. Considering the tremendous progress achieved by science and technology since antiquity in making the life of man a more enduring experience, an existence made immeasurably more enjoyable and less burdensome, one would be justified in assuming that his mind would focus less on fearing the unknown, less affected by the attraction of priestly machinations, and more absorbed by the culture of greed and aggressive self-aggrandizement made possible by modern free-market capitalism. But the need to believe in a caring Deity is just as strong today, even stronger by the language of religious zealots, than it was when primitive man engaged in hunting or when Judaism, Christianity or Islam were founded. The fear of the unknown was compounded by the suffering and brutality inflicted on mankind by countless wars growing ever more savage using more death-dealing weaponry and greater armies of warriors. More widows, orphans, parents losing sons, diseased and disabled soldiers, more massive destruction of property than ever before (the World Wars I and II) left millions upon millions of troubled men and women searching for a reason to go on. Most chose to place their trust in a protective Providence to comfort their grief.

(11) Religious Fundamentalism

(a) *Islam*

In the past terrible days, a great number of dedicated men and women sacrificed their lives in opposing the powers exercised by religious leaders of monotheisms in imposing doctrinal obligations of their choosing on compliant followers, devising brutal punishments for nonconformists. The rise of sectarian activists and reformers allowed

a variety of doctrinal interpretations, a trend which aimed at simplifying the faith, moderate ritual and ceremonial demands, inject a
degree of tolerance of unorthodox reverence and abjure bigotry.
Although some progress was made—Reform Judaism, Christian Unitarianism and Moslem Sufism—the hardcore orthodoxy remained
unchanged since their halcyon days, albeit shorn of political power,
except in the case of Islam. The latest addition to monotheism, Islam
has never distinguished between the secular and spiritual. Believers
are beholden to the ulema (clergy), who constitute a spiritual hierarchy of despotic power, more powerful politically than most temporal rulers of Moslem countries; regard Islam and the Koran as perfect and permitting no changes. The ulema and mullahs, caliphs
(Mohammed's successors as secular and religious heads of Islam),
imams, and muftis accept nothing short of an absolutist theocracy,
effectively ruling by decree based upon the Shariah—the basic religious concept of Islam, which makes no distinction between religious
and secular law. Islamic leaders abhor the concept of democracy; consider as heretical the rule of men over men, violating the control of
the Deity over all things, and reject the Western way of life as the
curse of infidels. The creation of the State of Israel in the midst of 350
million devoted Moslems was the catalyst which provoked a virulent
religious fanaticism. It culminated in Islamic jihadism, a powerful fundamentalist force not only dedicated to the destruction of the State of
Israel but harboring ambitions of spreading Islam to all infidels. The
intolerance, fundamentalist religious self-righteousness, the authoritarian theocracy, hatred of unbelievers, the sanctioning of the murder
of idolaters, the preached certitude of the dogma—all these combined
to pervert the mind of the faithful in total subservience to the ulema.
In such a climate, it is inconceivable that universal morality, civilized
conduct and civilization could ever find an acceptance.

(b) *Judaism*

The excessive adherence to the literal interpretation of the Tanak, the
Hebrew Bible (the Old Testament), a mark of religious fundamentalism, has been the badge of Orthodox Jews since the Exile from
Judea in the 1st and 2nd centuries A.D., became even more uncompromising, dedicated and separatist thanks to the addition of Tal-
mudic and Mishnaic commentaries and interpretations of scriptural
ordinances and the introspection of the esoteric and occult Kabala.
But the creation of the State of Israel in 1948 gave the impetus for a

new efflorescence of a narrow-minded fundamentalism, since the Orthodox—by then designated by the prefix "ultra"—gained some political power by forming various splinter groups under the fractionalized political party system of the coalition government. The ultra-Orthodox proudly state that only Jews are endowed with divine blessing; reject the definition of a "Jew" as one born of a Jewish mother without professing acceptance of the Torah and the laws of halacha (the whole legal system of Judaism embracing all the detailed laws and observances); uncompromisingly reject democratic values and aim to establish a theocratic State of Israel, with the Torah replacing the present system of laws and judged only by ultra-Orthodox rabbinical courts; they are active in enforcing the Sabbath-rest by any means, including violence; view secular and less observant Jews as beyond the pale of redemption; regard the laws of the State of Israel as "Gentile" and equate secular outlook with blasphemy; they do not care for nor wish to recognize pluralism in Judaism; affirm the rabbinical halacha as the source of answers to all questions; are mandated to follow the 613 commandments contained in the Torah; made it their creed to stay a people apart following the divine commandments; strongly disavow any attempt to be like other nations. The ultra-Orthodox go even so far as to warn Reform and Conservative worshippers that their prayers on High Holidays are not acceptable to God—the spirit of fanaticism and intolerance is here to stay. The ultra-Orthodox, with their unshakeable faith in the Torah, Talmud and the strictures of the halacha, are without question the bedrock of Judaism, who chose isolation as a way of life and who view self-imposed segregation as a blessing. They bear the calamities and misfortunes suffered since Exile as part of a providential plan and there is never any question about steadfastness. The fundamentalist faith they follow, the separateness from others it involves is not feasible without the "others" shouldering the responsibilities and necessities demanded of a functioning balanced society. The State of Israel would cease to exist if the ultra-Orthodox were the only inhabitants. Their uncompromising religious zeal made them slaves to an unyielding creed interfering with the instinct of self-preservation, unfit to share with mankind the responsibilities of a communal life. Their perverted mind made them prisoners of their self-imposed apartness; follow a culture opposed to the recognition of the merits of civilized conduct, and unqualified to contribute anything to the tenets of civilization.

(c) *Christianity*

Evangelical Christians, also known as Christian Fundamentalists, a part of a group of theologically conservative Protestant Churches, a religious movement that arose early in the 20th century but gained prominence from the 1960s, principally an American phenomenon, maintain the belief in the full inspiration and authenticity of the Bible and its complete authority over matters of faith. They contend that the Bible possesses complete infallibility and must therefore be defended against Modernists, those willing to concede some of the biblical criticism of the 19th century. Thoroughly uncompromising and convinced in the religious certainty of their interpretation of the Bible, they maintain that the Second Coming of Christ is imminent; vehemently condemn the theory of Darwinian evolution; call for the elimination of Modernism and all its associated iniquities; tolerate no diversity of opinions (they are alarmed by the growth of Liberalism); express anxiety over communist subversion, which they believe undermines Christianity; preach that eternal punishment in hell awaits non-believers and convey assurance of salvation for the faithful. Disturbed over the symptoms of social degeneracy, they accept the total depravity of man as attributable to the abandonment of Christian fundamentalist beliefs as well as responsible for the frequent break-up of marriages, the general immorality and juvenile delinquency, requiring a recommitment to the fundamentalist faith and becoming born-again Christians. They stress as a paramount tenet that salvation is achieved by conversion to faith in the atonement of Christ and pray for, and with eagerness anticipate, the Second Coming of Christ who, according to the prophecy contained in the Book of Revelation and their apocalyptic theology, will return in all his glory to decree the Day of Judgment, punish the persecutors of the faithful, and establish the kingdom of perfect happiness for the followers when death itself has been destroyed. The language of the apocalyptic writing in the Book of Revelation is richly symbolic, the imagery and allegories convey ideas susceptible to various interpretations and have, in fact, been variously expounded.

Evangelical fundamentalists/Conservative Evangelicals number approximately 60 million adherents in the United States (particularly in the South, called the Bible-belt, where fundamentalist clergymen are especially influential), have become active politically to espouse Evangelical-backed policies in their fight against communism, feminism, homosexuality, legalized abortion, secular humanism, and are especially vocal against the ban on school prayer. They care not the least about the dangers of overpopulation, pollution and degradation of the environment, nor do they work for improvement of social conditions, since, according to their beliefs, the biblical end-of-days is near and will culminate in the cataclysmic battle of Armageddon, the fight of the powers of evil against the powers of good.

Messianic expectations and the Second Coming of Christ have been the subjects of frequent prophecies throughout history only to end in frustration and disappointments. Christianity itself came into existence as a separate faith because Jesus' prophecy about the coming Kingdom of God and Paul's expectation in the imminence of the Kingdom of God on Earth during the lifetime of each were mistaken. It is one thing to entertain such spiritual beliefs and uplift the vision of man during critical times in his life. It is another thing to close one's mind to progress and the betterment of mankind's conditions in expectation of the fulfillment of a prophecy, however blessed, rather than show concern for his and his neighbor's well-being. Evangelical fundamentalists are not in favor of a pluralistic society; closed their mind to change, social improvement, and tolerance of religious diversity; they do not believe in the democratic political system and the rule of majority; they are seized with paralyzing frenzy when confronted with aborted fetuses but appear unmoved by worldwide children's homelessness, slavery and forced prostitution; despise secularists and consider them enemies. Unshaken by obvious biblical contradictions and anachronisms, belief in the certainty of their faith and the prophecies of the Book of Revelation perverted their mind to reserve salvation for their own at the apocalyptic end-of-days and eternal punishment in hell for freethinkers. Their aspirations, intolerance, and avowed purpose make them unfit to participate in improving moral behavior toward all and incapable of making any contribution to civilized conduct.

(12) *Conclusion*

Most humans succeed in alleviating the primal fear of the unknown by seeking spiritual consolation from a Deity, a supernatural father-figure, who fills a need created by the natural order. This need is common to all as is evident from the colorful history of mankind where a specific system of belief and worship of supernatural powers bound people together to form a particular culture, a particular religion, under the guidance of self-styled and self-promoting priests as intercessors between the divinity and the faithful. It manifests clearly the fragility of man that he requires priestly designs to calm his fears. The idea of a divine father-figure monitoring the goings-on in the life of humans is implanted early in childhood and the mythologies remain imbedded for most throughout life. It is the self-assured whose mind is given to restlessness, those discontented possessing sufficient lucidity, who hold that the religion of an adult cannot be the same as the one taught to a child; that what was meant to satisfy a child's needs for security would be inadequate to nourish the mind of a grown-up; that the impressive rituals and dreamy mythologies so pleasing to an impressionable young mind would discourage an adult wizened by life's experiences. For to see through the intrigues and contrivances of a power-hungry priesthood requires no more wisdom than to recognize the profit motive of an entrepreneur. But religious monotheism is a serious matter. It may fascinate the imagination of a child without delving into doctrines and dogma, but an adult exposed to religious commandments and ordinances cannot help but have his conduct and social outlooks affected by the teaching of intolerance, hatred, jealousy, exclusivity, oppression, contempt for diversity—the history of religious bigotry and atrocities are but the consequences of such persuasion.

Monotheism is in conflict with the instinct of self-preservation (which is concerned with the mundane aspects of life) since it appeals to otherworldly interests, such as salvation, rewards in afterlife, immortality, and gaining the favor of the Deity, which, for some humans, are more captivating than transitory earthly needs. For piety is a luxury affordable only after basic material needs are met. But for most faithful, monotheism encourages religious feelings that go beyond piety, prompted by unthinking fear and submissive obedience akin to bondage; they are vulnerable to the corrupting effects of an intolerant faith preaching a crude form of self-interest, exclusivity, preference, revenge and violence—all antithetical to the concepts propounded by civilization. Intolerance of diversity and dissent; abhorrence of liberal democratic ideals and freedom of speech; the preference for an authoritarian theocracy; the claim to be in possession of the only true faith and restricting salvation exclusively to its own followers—all these not only project a vastly inflated sense of self-importance causing resentment in adherents of other monotheisms but make religions propagating such invidious doctrinal precepts unfit to provide any contributions to civilized conduct and to the progress of civilization. Additionally, all three monotheisms share a similarity of design in the resurgence of a zeal-driven religious fundamentalism, radicalized to bigotize the mind of the faithful to treat with contempt and hostility essential human values, such as freedom of thought and expression, respect for another's culture and religion, the worth of all beneficial pain-relieving scientific progress, tolerance of diverse opinions, beliefs and divergent political sentiments. They are contemptuous of working to improve the lot of all humans, profess no interest in creating a climate conducive to social harmony and take delight in fostering an apartness from others as an expression of superiority to promote conditions appealing to their own zealots. The contempt and hostility directed against basic human values place fundamentalist monotheisms beyond the pale of making any contribution toward civilized principles, civilized behavior, and progress leading to a stable state of civilization.

This compendium on the subject of religious monotheism exposed the frailty of human understanding and how easily Nature-given fears of the unknown can be hijacked by unsophisticated schemes, whose design turns adherents into hatemongers perpetuating a never-ending fragmentation of mankind into multi-religious camps of intolerance. Monotheists do not unite but divide; do not stabilize but disrupt; do not befriend but alienate; possess but do not share; do not promote harmony but impede human aspirations to achieve it. Monotheisms, in the full display of all their colors, constitute an impediment to human dignity, to human enlightenment, to civilized conduct, to civilization.

CHAPTER 17

RECAPITULATION AND PERORATION

(1) It was my aim to strip man of the anthropological impediments, cut through the emotions such as the likes, dislikes, happiness, sorrow, love and hatred, which have obscured a clear understanding of him and discover a rather uncomplicated being reacting to basic survival instincts in common with all humans, be they savage, primitive, modern, cultured, poor or well-to-do; whether his is subject to any teleological design, i.e., if he has the potential of progressing toward definite end, a purpose, elevating his conduct from that of a crude hunter to one capable of living harmoniously in a social setting, gradually acquiring moral inculcation to reach the peaks of civilized conduct—the highest moral plateau attainable by man during his brief sojourn among the living.

It was my further aim to strip the term "civilization" from all the baggage it has acquired over the few centuries of its existence and whether it was not simply confused, by default, with culture and enlightenment by artful dilettantes aiming to wrap their field of expertise and predilections in the aura of preeminence. If so, they surely erred in the worst possible way for civilization is not about the achievements of gloriously endowed artists and master architects while the majority of mankind was brutalized by poverty, suffering from malnutrition, and dying helplessly from the consequent diseases without the lovers of art as much as muttering a muffled gasp. But civilization is about creating a social environment for humans conducive to easing the pain of existence, moderating the excessive greed which caused so much disorder, and assuring the majority of humans the benefits of some creature comforts.

It was my further aim to establish as undisputable that for civilized man, civilized society, and a state of civilization to come into being collectively or individually, man must not only oppose the natural order, exercise some discipline over his natural instinct of self-preservation, but also procure a discretionary surplus beyond satisfying basic needs as a precondition of attaining a measure of morality since man is inclined to be considerate to others and curb his greed if he feels financially secure and his enjoyment of comforts is not threatened by being tolerant, indulgent or charitable.

It was my further aim to establish that the discipline of economics (as structured at present) is flawed and unreliable in forecasting results of economic activities based on statistical significance and economic models, describing in mathematical terms the relationship of key economic forces such as labor, capital, interest rate and government policies. Relevant statistics are improperly used by deliberately repressing some features and emphasizing others, imposing order on a world that appears disorderly and arriving eventually at some predictions of limited significance. What is wrong with such predictions based on economic models is that human responses are unpredictable, incalculable, and their economic behavior lacks any degree of expected probability. But there is no need to be mired in econometrics to explain some basic principles of economic activities, such as that central bankers are most concerned with the well-being of bondholders; that volatility is induced in price movements to generate greater profits; that stock market indices have no necessary relation with the health of the economy; that a certain amount of poverty is necessary for the economic process to function; that the foundation of economics are affordable wants and scarcity because they constitute the basic elements of demand; that slumps follow booms because booms cause slumps; and finally, that private enterprise is not immune to inefficiency and corruption, which is to be found in all human activities, public or private. Economic models are not necessary to determine that economies cannot long endure within a Darwinian environment, ignoring the need of fair-dealing, espousing the maximizing of short-term corporate profits and neglecting long-term planning and needs, corporate and individual excessive greed, uncontrolled unemployment and grinding poverty. Based on unreliable government statistics (using a peculiar manner of compilation), which, strangely, are never challenged by the private sector as if sacrosanct, such as gross domestic product (GDP), consumer price index (CPI), producer price index (PPI), the unemployment rate, trends in productivity and consumer confidence, the business elite and the movers and shakers have a made-to-order conduit to use any combination of statistics in conjunction with selective economic theories to advance their agenda without fear of being questioned or opposed, since an adept sophist could justify any economic course of action or conclusion. But as such an endeavor is meant to dissemble and simulate, it is objectionable on moral grounds, socially unacceptable and repugnant to civilized conduct, for real progress must be based on factual footing to succeed and not on triviality or obfuscation, given the challenging economic, social and ecological problems facing mankind.

It was my further aim to inquire what contribution religions, especially monotheisms, could render toward the establishment of a civilization; whether anything that happened in their dynamic past could shape events and influence the minds of the faithful to make progress to a state of civilization possible. The conclusion is not encouraging since all religions were man-originated and hence susceptible to corruption and abuse. None of them can lay claim to divine revelation. Imposed on receptive humans at a tender age to calm and control the instinctive fear of the unknown, thrust upon believers to enslave them to an aristocratic self-appointed priesthood so that the latter could live in comfort and have their needs taken care of. The 20th century diminished the long-lasting euphoria concerning matters of faith due to religious institutions losing the protection of political powers. But because of the rise of religious zealotry and fundamentalism, a new kind of fanaticism is making its presence felt nowadays by spreading hatred, contempt for non-believers and competing religions, claiming exclusivity of their faith, abjuring free speech, freedom of thought, and denigrating the democratic process as being contrary to their sacred writings. By their teaching and preaching, the priests perverted the minds of believers to place their trust of blind faith in the dogma of divine benediction and beneficence, vouchsafing salvation and eternal life to the submissive faithful, a persuasion banishing any thoughts of tolerance and charity toward non-believers—attitudes not conducive to moral and civilized behavior.

It was my foremost aim to determine whether the natural order placed obstacles in man's path undermining his efforts to progress toward a state of civilization and whether even a group of moral men could ever exercise sufficient influence to civilize a society, a community, a State.

The natural order is flawed and passed on some of the defects to man, a fragile and fractious being in that he possesses the natural instincts basic to his existence which may prove, in time, incompatible with his well-being; and whether there is not something amiss in Nature's design of man satisfying his needs when the minority (the affluent prestige class) is positioned to preclude the majority (the wage workers and moderate income earners) from ever attaining the moral ground necessary for a civilized existence. Man's self-preservation places him in bondage to survival instincts, making him a virtual slave to circumstances beyond his control, giving rise to excessive greed, cupidity and unlimited aggrandizement. The efforts of the economic elites are not directed to structuring an economic system benefiting the best interests of society as a whole, but serving the most advantaged, capable, and ambitious, leaving the rest confined to make ends meet (some managing somewhat better), contributing to social strife and unrest, conditions not disposed towards the creation of a civilized society.

(2) Man must be humbled and awed contemplating the immensity of the Universe, the billions of galaxies, some of which contain trillions of suns, the planet Earth, which is part of a solar system on the edge of a peripheral galaxy located on the edge of a supercluster of galaxies, one of a billion of such systems, and wonder about the insignificance of his existence, how secure it is and what his relationship might be with the natural order. He is aware that the planet Earth was formed about 4.5 billions of years ago, a process involving trial and error, and by the time conditions were favorable for the appearance of man (the right temperature, an oxygen atmosphere, adequate potable water) under circumstances akin to a chance event, an accident, 99.998% of its natural evolution was over. Man marvelled at the seeming perfection of Nature, its grand design, its superior excellence, its unfailing symmetry and regularity, and wondered whether it was fashioned by a super-natural and all-knowing creator, a Deity. The ancient Greek thinkers apparently thought so. Benefiting from their astounding mathematical and astronomical calculations performed without the crucial visual instruments by just applying common sense, they came amazingly close in anticipating the findings of modern astronomers. These profound thinkers also admired Nature as something to be imitated, counselled its study in order to discover its hidden wisdom and apply the results to guide human conduct. But in the latter conclusion they were mistaken despite their other intellectual achievements, for Nature has to be studied so man can oppose it. The rational Greeks were

totally ignorant, or could not have known of Nature's ordained struggle for existence and survival of the fittest, of the human havoc caused by microbes, viruses and germs causing deadly diseases; the fatal illnesses spread by mosquitos and the immunodeficient conditions afflicting mankind; the genetic make-up of man affecting his character and mental faculties; the congenital diseases causing children to be born crippled, defective or brain-damaged; that natural disasters like earthquakes, floods, droughts and hailstorms bring desolation to humans; that trial and error were the rules in the evolution of animal species and not the seeming perfection of design in that a thousand were born so that one could survive—in fact, 99% of the species have died out not finding the natural order accommodating. Nature is flawed, defective and impaired—it favors the strong and ruthless, its process of evolution is pitiless in sanctioning the struggle for survival of the fittest, casting the losers aside. The implacable struggle for existence is the rule of Nature; any deviation is contrary to the natural order and in conflict with it. Human resistance is mandated by defying as morally unacceptable Nature's ordained struggle for survival of the fittest and the harsh natural evolutionary process by mitigating the rigorous competition, to level the playing field somewhat and abate the struggle for existence, making life more bearable by reducing the burden of pain and suffering—all these are acts in opposition to Nature, the natural order of things.

(3) Equipping man with an uncontrollable instinct of procreation resulting in the consequent environmental degradation present criteria of Nature's flawed design, placing formidable obstacles to his well-being, possibly endangering his survival. Man will have to accept the thought-provoking conclusion that his existence, no more than that of other animal species, is not central to Nature's scheme of things, which are guided by laws not relevant to man's interests. He must be modest enough to admit that his presence is of no benefit to Nature, animal life, and the ecosystem and that matters would be more harmonious within the natural order if he were to disappear from the scene. But therein lies the challenge. For man to create his own bearable existence within a social setting, he must oppose and find a substitute for the discord within Nature's scheme of things. That calls for the creation of a moral order, a civilized society, a state of civilization.

Human population increases by about 100 million per annum, requiring more land to live on and more food grown on less acreage, fortified by chemical fertilizers, pesticides and herbicides—all detracting

from the wholesomeness of the product and in addition poisoning the
aquifers. More people than the environment can accommodate will
degrade the ecosystem, burning more fossil fuel, causing global warming,
harming the life-essential green-house effect, impair the ozone layer, but
most importantly, damaging the reproductive process by giving birth to
defective and disfigured offspring—perhaps Nature's way of restoring a
sustainable population balance and letting man know that there are limits
which he cannot exceed with impunity. Man's instinct of procreation is
flawed in that it exceeds the absorption capacity of the environment,
which points to Nature's defective symmetry—not indicative of superior
excellence and intelligent design.

(4) The rules of Nature demand conformity with its most fundamental
imperative applicable to living species: self-preservation, an instinctive
response common to all organisms. Health, physical strength, and cunning gained from experience are the preferred attributes in accord with
the natural order. There are no acts, however devious, crafty, insidious,
dishonest, cruel, and perfidious that are barred from employment which
further the interests of self-preservation, in conformity with Nature's
design. Man's rules of ethical conduct and morality find no resonance
with Nature and are opposed to the natural order; such rules benefit the
feeble and inept, those unable to compete or falling behind. Prehistoric
man was unrestricted in his struggle for existence by any man-made or
artificial obstacles—he was in harmony with Nature. With the increase in
population, the prudent man needed to gain some stability and protection from exploitation by the strong, proceeded to create artificial political societies with rules and laws that invalidated the advantages of the
strong and dishonest to benefit the less competitive majority, heal the
ailing, care for the old, widows and orphans. For his protection and from
fear for his safety, man transformed his existence from one in harmony
with the natural order to one observing ethical laws of a new social order,
undergoing a revaluation of values, enabling moral conduct—superior to
ethical laws—to gain a foothold. By seeking protection and the benefit of
a judicial system from a society, a social setting, man declared his defiance for the natural order.

(5) Some members of the social group rose to pre-eminence by virtue of
their organizing talents and superior leadership. They were the minority
who, in time, became the leaders of the rest, the majority. It was incumbent upon the leaders to plan for the well-being of the social group and
were exempt, on that account, from performing the menial labor-inten-

sive work demanded of the majority. The leaders gained in power and influence, allocated duties and benefits, and sought to make their advantages permanent and hereditary. The governing groups were the administrators and the working group the hunters, food-gatherers and soldiers. This brought about the first division of labor. The administrators gained freedom of action within an aristocracy of common interests—they were free men. The majority, the working group, had limited or no freedom of action as their work was all-consuming and never-ending—they became unrecognizable from virtual slaves.

(6) The essence of all living things is the effort of self-preservation, which involves the struggle for existence. For humans, the most important components in the struggle are the procurement of food and shelter to protect against the elements (added much later were healthcare and provision for old age) referred to as primary needs or basic needs. All other than basic needs are referred to as secondary (and tertiary), such as enjoyment of creature comforts above those necessary to persevere in existence. Confined to satisfying primary needs only, man is said to lack freedom of action whereas in satisfying secondary (or tertiary) needs, he is free to be selective about his needs and possesses freedom of action. Man disposes of a surplus when he satisfies more than basic needs. Animals have only primary needs, i.e., those essential for survival. Man rises above the natural order by pursuing secondary (or tertiary) needs. Reduced to satisfying primary needs only, man is in bondage to his survival instincts, a virtual slave to circumstances beyond his control, Nature's design to keep him entangled with necessities; this has always been the condition of the majority of mankind. The man not weighed down by the demands of his conatus (the effort to persevere), i.e., the well-to-do who preserves freedom of action in satisfying secondary needs, not driven by the perverse zeal for power and wealth, can contribute, if so minded, to alleviating the burden of existence of his fellowmen. Some of them contributed selflessly toward the betterment of human conditions to make progress toward a state of civilization a reality. But for most of the haves and super-haves, the privileged who have always comprised a minority, the gained advantages and benefits have to be perpetuated by stealth, cunning, subterfuge, mystique, and an aura of the supernatural, for their privileges hung by the thinnest threads and would have easily ruptured by the sustained drive of the majority, had they been minded to do so. But the majority had to keep their nose to the grindstone in an all-consuming effort to earn a decent livelihood, bur-

dened by necessities and take care of responsibilities in an exhausting and time-consuming effort that left little stamina for the level of thinking required to gain a clear understanding of the foundation upon which the system of privileges is based. Fearing loss of their favored status, the haves and super-haves invented artificial props of pretended gravity, profound on the surface but shallow beneath, to remove their activities from the comprehension of the uninitiated and tilt the playing field in their favor. To that scheme belong: (1) The establishment of revealed religions. (2) The economic theory of capitalism. (3) The concept of gold as a store of value. This is the way of Nature, for man's self-preservation impedes the voluntary alienation of advantages unless confronted by a more powerful and resourceful adversary.

(7) Man must make it his mission to defy Nature's design to keep him entangled in turmoil and with necessities. If man's time is fully absorbed in satisfying primary needs solely, the creation of a discretionary surplus will almost always elude his grasp. It is the existence of a discretionary surplus that frees a segment of society from the entanglements with necessities to partake in the more elevated form of existence, variously described as the moral order. But no matter how large the discretionary surplus, there has never been a time in the known history of man when he was totally free from turmoil and friction on account of his cupidity and graspingness, striving constantly to enlarge his surplus to the detriment of others and thus create conflicts with his fellowmen. Human aspirations are invariably in search of more advantages and diminished disadvantages, for betterment of their status at the expense of competitors or adversaries, drawing on innate impulses, such as, greed, envy, avarice and self-promotion. Man must strive to overcome obstacles placed in his path by the natural order; to the extent he succeeded, he can be said to have opened the gate on the road to a state of civilization. When the struggle to persevere in existence concerns primary needs essential for survival, appeal is made instinctively to the natural order; when secondary needs and discretionary creature comforts are pursued, the call is made for law and order, protection of property and civil rights, a degree of security and permanence, a civilized conduct. Any man who disposes of a discretionary surplus is well aware of the impermanence of his good fortune, how transitory and ephemeral the conditions are which brought it about and the danger that conditions beyond his control—natural, political or economic—could rupture the bond which keeps his estate under control. An earthquake, hurricane, flood, or tornado could

endanger his estate—such is the unpredictable play of human privileges, which, like any of man's achievements, are not on solid foundation. In the struggle for economic supremacy there are no principles, no stability, no rest for the sated, and no future for losers—all these demonstrate the fragility and impermanence of a man-made system which permits no one to stand still in the world of competition. The availability of a discretionary surplus should create stability conducive to a civilized conduct but for the frailty of man who is unable to keep free from entanglements and turmoil. He regards as just the use of any means without restrictions as long as they serve his quest for survival and the preservation of the desired level of creature comforts.

(8) Morality and Nature are in conflict. Nature favors the relentless and merciless struggle for existence of all living species advancing the cause of the strong, ruthless, cunning and provides no quarter for the weak, ailing, dim-witted and compassionate. As far as moral man is concerned, Nature does not favor his survival—it is his objective to frustrate Nature's efforts to maintain him at the level of animal species, to entangle him with necessities in order to make his survival an obstacle course. The conduct of the "haves", the minority, is paramount in setting the standard of morality. It is the treatment of the majority of the less advantaged by the minority (the haves) that elevates or denigrates the standard of morality, which in turn depends on the level of intensity of the minority's efforts of self-preservation. A high degree of morality is most profitable to those who achieved success, who enjoy the fruits of a discretionary surplus which also provides them sufficient leisure to pursue activities not directly connected with the effort of earning a living—the standard of morality has always been defined by the privileged, for they have the most to lose by its absence.

(9) Immune to the rules of consumption spending, enjoying an autonomy reserved for the elect, and living in a surrounding of their own making by managing to defy gravity, the super-haves, an elite class, are capable of satisfying any wants without limitations, i.e., tertiary needs. They dispose of an excessively large discretionary surplus sufficient to handle all practical contingencies—their struggle for existence cannot be measured in financial terms. The super-haves constitute a small minority (1%–2%) of modern society, yet by exercising their vast financial powers they succeeded in inducing the governing chieftains to bend many of the economic rules in their favor. Such rules are of questionable benefit to the less advantaged. In the intense interplay of the various economic groups

comprising modern society, the interests of the have-nots, the haves and the super-haves are on a collision course. The economic standing of the super-haves is dependent upon the existence of the have-nots—the wage-slaves—by far the great majority, whose continued perseverance should, therefore, be a matter of their unceasing self-interest. Yet they have acted unreasonably throughout history in that they treated any gain achieved by the have-nots as an unwelcome intrusion into their own prosperity—a threat to their secure standing, a cynical regard for self-interest to the detriment of others, a denial of progress for the sake of preserving tertiary benefits. Most of the have-nots survive by greed as a necessary tool of self-interest—as applied to them, greed is a virtue. The super-haves who pile possession upon possession giving free reign to their predatory instincts are also guilty of excessive greed—as applied to them, greed is a vice, a defect.

(10) Nature is guided by forces which promote the struggle for self-preservation and the survival of the fittest; no place is provided for the unfit in its scheme of things. The planet Earth in all its natural outbursts which appear to the human eye as unplanned upheavals, are the normal working of the natural process adapted to its own evolution and rhythm of existence. Such violence presents no design for humans who are guided by rules contravening the natural order, few places permanently adaptable as their habitat, and few forces at work to provide a human-friendly environment. By populating the Earth, humans assumed the role of squatters and interlopers, forced to seek habitats whose environment is conducive to their survival. They began to form social units, established ethical rules of conduct to facilitate communal living, and undertook to reduce the natural impediments to their safe existence by creating and adapting to the environment accommodating their needs. But these were acts opposed to the natural order, for Nature's design does not acclimatize to human aspirations. Ethical rules are enforceable and violators punished. Morality, unlike ethical rules, cannot be legislated but held forth as a standard of civilized conduct, the proudest achievement of man in his effort to defy the natural order. By overpopulating, man is determined to follow a course that may drive him to his inevitable doom. For he cannot comprehend that the planet Earth is not adapted for his exclusive exploitation, abuse, and corruption without suffering the consequences of his misdeeds. The cause of this mischief is his insatiable greed and drive for unlimited growth, believing that "more is better and most is best", which led him far beyond satisfying needs and providing for creature comforts.

(11) Those who are financially well-off and dispose of a large enough discretionary surplus to assure them stability in the face of any foreseeable exigency, have they not gained enough security to defy the natural order of things? Does the instinctive compulsion to pursue the dictates of financial gains to the exclusion of moral imperatives obscure and confound the perception of their long-term interests, even though self-preservation is no longer an overriding motive? Defiance of the natural order elevates man from the pursuit of instincts in common with the animal species to want to mitigate the plight of the less fortunate—a sign of moral purpose, a manifestation of morality. For a society is called civilized not because it produced great artists, architects, or poets but because a large number of selfless and motivated citizenry possessed enough strength of character to set aside Nature's imperatives and refused, for whatever reason, to overlook the torment of others, banding together with those similarly minded to mitigate the plight of their less favored neighbors. To act in this manner is to reach the highest level of moral conduct and join the true forces of civilization.

(12) Because the labor-intensive work is performed by segments of society barely able to satisfy primary needs, the more proficient and talented groups are energized to pursue secondary and tertiary interests, a prerequisite of civilization. All cultures and pseudo-civilizations have depended on the existence of human slavery, literal and virtual, for the well-being of the minority has always depended on the privation of the majority. If man possessed the time to pursue noble aspirations it was because the labor-intensive segments of society, who had neither the means nor aptitude to ease the burden of their existence, produced a surplus of life's basic necessities. A society in which everyone pursued necessities confined to primary needs and therefore disposed of no discretionary surplus and possessed no freedom of action would be structurally dysfunctional and could not endure as a viable organization. It could only function if the disadvantaged labored to provide the supply of basic necessities and performed the essential menial services. The permanent inequality of humans as determined by Nature is mirrored in the enduring economic stratification of society.

(13) All humans are without options but to follow their basic instincts, induced to promote self-interests in conformity with natural laws dictating compliance with Nature's ordained principle of survival of the fittest, victims of involuntary servitude. For all humans are virtual slaves—though there are differences in degree, but slaves nevertheless—

without choice but to compete for a share of necessities. Inequality of competence results in a wide disparity of satisfying needs, with the most capable, the minority, obtaining much more than the required share, and the marginally qualified majority just managing to make the grade, with many failing even in that. Most are not aware that basic natural instincts beyond their control propel them to action to protect and improve their standard of living, nor are they aware that they lack freedom of will, as conventionally understood. The involuntary servitude attributable to Nature's instincts of self-preservation embraces all humans without exception, forces them to become virtual slaves to perseverance, an unseen and consummate bond imposed upon mankind by forces having a permanent presence in all human activities.

(14) With ecological problems going worldwide from bad to worse due to overpopulation, the previously unthinkable notion began to influence man with an ever greater impact, namely, that Nature has certain defects which had to be overcome and that he must attempt such corrections; that in order to restore some semblance of order within which mankind could function instead of wasting away from the impact of contaminants and a degraded environment, man will have to interfere in the natural evolution by modifying his genetic makeup. This aim is nothing less than an attempt in improving upon Nature and become a participant in affecting his own destiny. It serves the cause of an improved humanity that genetic scientists ease the physical suffering which is so much part of human existence. It is equally important to do as much for mental diseases, that invisible curse affecting much of mankind. Man must declare the existing natural process unacceptable and attempt its modification to ensure an environment more conducive to his physical and mental well-being and more in harmony with a truly elevated concept of morality, a step forward to a state of civilization.

(15) In the effort to satisfy basic needs and the preservation of minimum creature comforts, morality has always taken a back seat. Man's uninhibited competitive effort and aggressive self-seeking extending far beyond the satisfaction of primary needs—driven by a greed peculiar to humans—places such enterprise, if unchecked, in conflict with morality. For some degree of moral behavior is only achievable if his competitive effort is sufficiently inhibited and the aggressive self-seeking mitigated to promote a more harmonious social interaction—there is an inherent conflict between morality and the uninhibited procurement of an excessive economic surplus.

(16) Man is in bondage to the instinct of self-preservation, a virtual slave to necessities, a victim of circumstances beyond his control, seeking freedom from entanglements and freedom of action by pursuing satisfaction of wants, distracted by self-inflated needs, and precluded from exercising alternate choices. He possesses no natural rights but one, the right to persevere in existence, i.e., self-preservation, but this right is meaningless unless guaranteed by the laws of society. In the state of Nature, right was coextensive with might. The procurement of a satisfactory standard of living for most depends on their success in opposing Nature's design. Man's idea of order and security contravene Nature's design, which requires an unlimited and unceasing struggle for existence, the survival of the fittest—obstacles in his effort to progress to a civilized status.

(17) To be civilized means to temper the primitive nature of man, teach him principles that will accommodate and prepare him for harmonious living in a social setting; achieve some permanence, order and stability; procure sufficient means to free him from the pursuit of primary necessities in order to gain freedom of action, to make life more secure and enduring; to lighten the burdens of existence in order to provide sufficient time to attend to interests not tied to the instinct of self-preservation. A civilized man will treat his fellowman fairly, with respect and kindness; abjure settling differences or arguments by force; show tolerance for the diversity of opinions, beliefs and religions; insist on the compassionate treatment of the poor, weak, helpless and ailing; deal with the aged, widows, orphans, and children with consideration and understanding; be moved to action by the suffering of humanity, be it from hunger, diseases or catastrophic acts of Nature. Civilized conduct entails respect for parents and family life, practice of fairness in business dealings, avoidance of hatred, and showing compassion toward the deserving.

(18) Out of sheer concern for the continued endurance of humanity under conditions in which the growing stratification of society into classes with hostile interests could have plunged it into total chaos, political leaders came up with new concepts of human relationships, placing high priority on social legislation, economic opportunity, and a safety net for all those unable to compete on equal terms, proclaiming that man's future rests in opposing the natural order. This newly proposed social order gave birth to an elevated state of morality and to the concept of civilization. Civilization is about the aspiration of humans making life an endurable experience by taming their aggressive and grasping nature, creating an orderly and tolerant society, gainful employment opportunities for the greatest

number resulting in incrementally improved living standards with the passage of time.

(19) The concept of civilization is the creation of moral minds contemplating social harmony, rapport among nations and a world at peace. For nothing is as destructive to civilized conduct as wars and violent conflicts in pursuit of greed and rapacity, lowering humanity to the level of savages. Nor can civilization come to terms with religious intolerance, hatred or bigotry, not to mention the sprouting fanaticism dominating a new pedigree of fundamentalism, concocted by self-righteous spiritual leaders of uncommon arrogance agitating brain-damaged followers who do not care one whit about freedom of speech and thought, respect for other beliefs, nor do they tolerate the slightest deviations. They seek to usurp political power by exercising total control over congregants and are most anxious to gain new adherents by any means, using guile, if necessary. Humanity could not survive a return to the Dark Ages of priestly despotism, given the overwhelming destructive power of modern technology. The brutality exhibited by the Inquisition and its functionaries of the past and other numerous sordid crimes—that work product befitting the Catholic mind warped by theological inbreeding, making a mockery of judicial procedure, cynically foisting invented religious fables upon frightened victims caught in their dragnet—plunged humanity for centuries to the lowest depth of suffering. The lies, guile, connivance, cunning and duplicity necessary to maintain that fraud in defense of a corrupt apparatus of power perpetuated by the Catholic hierarchy indicate the depth to which educated men can sink in pursuit of self-preservation and the perpetuation of the level of comforts. Humans must make certain that these monstrous aberrations would never again see the light of day, for the sanity of homo sapiens could not overcome a repeat of such an onslaught. And all this in furtherance of a specious faith which had almost no affinity with the written prototype. Nor can civilization come to terms with the huge disparity of incomes between the super-haves and earners of subsistence wages; that flawed design of men where the well-to-do keep piling wealth upon wealth, never to be satisfied with the results achieved, unable to regulate aspirations since the pursuit of self-gratification is a constantly elusive target, whereas the wage-slaves barely keep progressing beyond inflation and beyond necessities, possessing little upward mobility; that it serves the interest of the financial elites, a distinct minority, to keep the rest of society insecure, in turmoil, subdued, and financially vulnerable—crossing the line of oppression—in

the hope their privileged comfort level would not be affected; that the well-being of the secure and privileged minority depends on the privation of the majority—and finally, that the pursuit of wealth is not to be inhibited by any moral considerations, especially for those who managed to gain a considerable advantage. These guidelines keep society destabilized and of no use for moral conduct which would only interfere with their aggressive and acquisitive pursuits.

(20) Economics stripped of its esoteric language, its misleading statistics, weighty mathematical equations, and unreliable predictions could still emerge if restructured to conform with present-day challenges as an observational discipline dealing with man's efforts in earning a living within a social setting. The claim that economic models are simplified representations of reality is false, for it is based on the assumption of "other things being equal", which is a myth. Economics cannot endure if concerned mainly with factors of production, setting price levels and equilibriums of the market. It cannot endure ignoring morality, corporate greed, value preferences, unemployment and poverty, global overpopulation, environmental degradation and global warming. It cannot endure by holding the false views that the ups and downs of the stock market are indications of the soundness of the economy; that Wall Street is an investment market for serious-minded profit seekers instead of a gambling casino, where insiders and friends of top traders reap the largest profits; that falling wages are good for the economy since they reduce costs and are anti-inflationary, but ignore the consumer factor; that economic indicators published by governmental agencies are trustworthy instead of based on unreliable compilations mixed with guesswork. The well-being of a nation cannot be measured by the volume of capital investments and production; foreign aid or loans are not necessarily charity or altruism but subsidies for domestic business; reliance on monetary policy is a myth since the velocity of money turnover is not computable; Central Banks are not capable of controlling the economy. Overpopulation is bound to cause a radical income redistribution with the greatest share allocated to necessities at the expense of non-essentials. Food, shelter, utilities, and healthcare will experience the largest price increases not only due to greater consumer demand but because of the rise of intrinsic costs.

(21) Effective demand is the driving force of any economy and is dependent on the purchasing power of consumers. Demand of the unemployed is limited to bare necessities. When an enterprise moves its production facil-

ities to a foreign country, the resultant unemployment will reduce demand regardless of cheaper global imports; job replacement at reduced wages would cause slumping consumer spending, which, in turn, would lead to further downsizing. Globalization is of temporary economic benefit because a point of market-saturation is reached due to the increased supply of goods and there are no further horizons to exploit. Economic slowdowns and stagnation are the inevitable results. Innovative products would energize the markets, provided there is adequate consumer spendable income. The capitalist system is dependent upon a steady increase of the consumer base, i.e., penetrating new markets, because maximum utilization of production capacity reduces unit cost of products, leading to greater return on investment; that is why a sustainable population growth, or a zero-population increase, is anathema to global free-traders. But global population increases of about 100 million per annum occur primarily in the poor developing countries—of little benefit to producers. Population increases in developed countries are minimal, hence a liberal immigration policy is tried in an attempt to draw skilled workers from other developed countries, the young in particular, and employable immigrants from developing regions are the choices to pursue in increasing the consumer base. Additionally, such steps are favored to increase competition among wage earners. But such a policy cannot be applied by all developed countries and only the potentially wealthiest stand to profit from such an approach to the detriment of the less successful—some will enjoy growth, others will experience economic decline. Growth would occur mainly in those segments of the economy that provide basic necessities. When over 40% of the capital of multinationals is invested overseas, the domestic employment base is reduced and the consequent unemployment assumes a mode of permanence, made even more so as part-time jobs proliferate and liberal immigration aggravates the problem. Contemporary production methods are just too efficient and the discretionary spending too marginalized for the economic system to employ all the willing workers—realistically speaking, one-half of the world's skilled and unskilled workers are redundant, not needed for the other half to function. But these paragons of efficiency only externalize the problem, i.e., pass on to the State the care of the impoverished unemployed, straining social welfare finances. Perhaps too much efficiency in downsizing employment is not socially desirable if overall greater unemployment is the result—the multiplier effect on related businesses, the financial hardships caused to suppliers and humans, the demoralizing idleness, the burden placed on State human service agencies, are a steep price to pay for reducing unit costs. Sectors of the economy are not autonomous spheres of activity but are implicated with one another to form an economic climate affecting all. More farsighted thinking and a mandate to internalize social costs would go a long way in curbing the fascination with efficiency. Yet these super-efficient multinationals move their facilities overseas to benefit from the $1.00 per hour wages, profit from cost efficiency, and help the bottom line by moving their corporate situs offshore and manage to legally avoid paying income taxes—to the detriment of the community and State which made their success possible. No matter which profit-seeking avenues an entrepreneur pursues, no matter how efficient his organization and production facilities, there is a limit to growth because spendable income is limited and there are too many supplies and too few consumers.

(22) Sustainable growth will have to give way to sustainable development, i.e., more technologically improved production and distribution, more urgency in achieving greater product utility, more advances in improving product quality. There may not be any limits to individual wealth accumulation, but a sustainable economy based on intensive development would require a more equitable income distribution. People with limited means do not make desirable customers. Producers and merchants could finally reach the conclusion that the foundation of healthy and viable economies is an effective demand and consumer confidence—that the products offered are of highest quality. Lack of foresight of entrepreneurs in failing to match output with consumer demand is the main cause of persistent business cycles.

(23) Industrialized countries cannot passively countenance the plight of the major part of humanity sinking into the morass of poverty. Even if sufficiently aroused, it is beyond the competence of any group of men, however knowledgeable, to find a total solution to the problem, given the present distortion of the free-market system. The massive global unemployment, below minimum-wage workers, and poverty-wages give the concept of civilization a black eye, particularly if placed alongside of unrestrained consumption and conspicuous wealth. The movers and shakers of the business world betray no tinge of remorse for wittingly contributing to the problem. No voice is heard, no hand lifted, no regret is shown—the elites keep silent, totally distanced, beneficiaries of a dysfunctional economic design tilted in their favor. The poverty-related suffering and humiliation of more than 50% of the global population and

the despair of the dispossessed is a ticking time bomb which should give
the well-to-do pause to reflect about their own lasting security and continued enjoyment of their privileged standard of living. No one can feel
safe while so many suffer the pain of existence. For the present, democratic capitalism is not blooming; it has been destabilized by a culture of
unrestrained greed and uninhibited competition for a maximum market-
share, a practice which could not help but corrupt the political system
and abort any effort to exercise restraint of the raw power of aggrandizement—forces antithetical to the promotion of a civilizing influence.
Lacking any practical and workable solutions to the problems of massive
global poverty, the political and business elites could be expected to rely
on the unthinkable, namely, natural attrition resulting in untimely deaths
due to lack of medical care, undernourished diet, primitive hygiene and
other deficient health habits, decimating a population enfeebled by lack
of care and abandoned to its fate. To leave one half of the world's population fending for itself, suffer the ravages of untreatable diseases, and
defenseless against man-caused environmental toxins suppressing the
immune system is to invite the merciless process of Nature's awesome
power to force a resolution of a long-standing institutionalized neglect of
a troubled society becoming increasingly class-ridden. The intended
solution could backfire since the foreshadowed calamity recognizes no
borders. Not excluding any segments of society from harm could likely
devastate the fabric of society. In any case, the contemplation of such an
execrable solution is morally repugnant and would remove any possibility of civilizing social interaction. The unintended consequences
could be the destructive radicalization of human relationships. Man must
recognize the limitations of benign neglect in resolving problems unemployment and poverty pose, since the intended solution could only be
temporary, given the unchangeable human nature and the failed economic system.

(24) Society is becoming increasingly class-ridden and economically unstable.
The inequality of humans as set by Nature and the determinism of circumstance limit superior benefits to a narrow elite who, blessed with
good fortune and the perquisites of success, continue to rig the privileges
of their own class. Most are the possessors of wealth admittedly disproportionate to their merits and talents, positions of privilege as if occasioned by the roll of dice. They perpetuate their own economic preferences by insider domination of the government and, if need be, defend
their interests at the expense of the less advantaged citizenry and at the

sacrifice of the well-being of the country as a whole. Recognizing the fragility of their own good fortune, they are determined to censure any upward mobility of economic climbers as a threat to their preferred standing and motivated to maintain the achieved status quo—ranking politically as the intransigent conservative hard-liners. They denigrate and oppose as godless socialism the safety net for the less fortunate, government sponsored universal healthcare, welfare programs, job training, social security and child care, yet are quick to seek relief from the risks free-market capitalism poses, such as devaluation of the currency to aid exports, subsidies for agribusiness, tariffs on imports, foreign loan guarantees, protection from expropriations of foreign investments, bail out of troubled banks and other large financial institutions, i.e., they seek a benign system that does not pose awkward risks. These fortuitous possessors of wealth, guarding their good fortune with tenacity, would not be the likely participants in modifying the economy, curbing the cycles of unemployment and mitigate the plight of the impoverished. It is the proud entrepreneurs, the industrious self-starters who managed to climb the pyramid of financial success, secure and brimming with confidence, who could be called to set aside sufficient time from their busy schedule to ignite a mass movement for social justice, find a way to restructure and stimulate the economy in order to alleviate the unemployment problem and the plight of the impoverished. There is no one else, no other institution capable of following through. Being responsible for self-made fortunes and attuned to the exercise of moral principles, they are not simply motivated by altruism but by the instinct of self-preservation, for they are sufficiently enlightened to understand the problems facing the current impaired economy—that they cannot continue to prosper nor can society survive as a functioning entity if so many of their fellowmen fail to earn a living and unable to make ends meet. They grasp that the key to economic relief can come primarily from adequate consumers' disposable income and sustained demand. Being the dominant class of financial aristocrats, they don't feel threatened by narrowing the gap between the rich and poor, nor are they alarmed by lifting the incomes of millions to free men from the burden of basic necessities and gain some freedom of action—all humans are entitled to some levels of comfort. These proud self-made men of wealth grasp the implication of their action as assuring the preservation of their own preferred status. By these acts they most assuredly could advance the cause of civilized conduct and come closer to a state of civilization.

(25) It is a consequence of Nature's design to bond man to his natural instincts, a captive to the zeal for aggrandizement. Nature is flawed in that its design for the unceasing struggle for existence leads to interminable violence, strife, bloodshed, instability and antisocial behavior. The world is filled with discords of competing interests which, if unopposed, can never reach a state of reduced tensions since insecurity and turmoil are in accord with the natural order. A victim of self-inflated needs, man is in bondage to the instinct of self-preservation, a virtual slave to circumstances beyond control, precluded from exercising alternate choices. The effect of this design, which applies to any and all of man's activities is permanent, but the intensity could be abated, less grating and less unsparing, sufficiently modified to turn ruthless and callous behavior into one of indulgence and probity, a scrupulous engagement in human interaction—fairness is contagious. The blunting and softening of the impact of Nature's harsh design are attributes of morality—the expression of man's defiance of the natural order. His progress, the orderly and judicious functioning of social intercourse, requires the rejection as destructive and unacceptable Nature's uninhibited and unceasing competition, the rigors of blind natural selection and attempt to improve, however moderately, the natural order based upon his ennobling values known as the code of morality. But the inclination to comply with the man-made moral order is dependent upon his ability to satisfy more than basic primary needs, for a virtual slave to circumstances beyond control is not likely to mitigate efforts to be relieved of burdensome necessities, using instead any and all means at his disposal, including greed, lies, dishonesty, and rank selfishness to get the better of his competitor, his neighbor, in the effort to persevere—it is his natural right and virtue to do so. Only one who achieved some security in his standing and managed to acquire—thanks to his efforts and aptitude—sufficient means to break the chains of subjection to life's necessities could gain enough freedom of action to oppose the natural order and recognize the benefits a moral disposition bestows, making living more people-friendly and the enjoyment of creature comforts more pleasurable. Morality, an assured passage to civilized behavior, is predicated on freedom of discretionary spending, possession of a disposable surplus. But there are exceptions. As with anything that concerns human conduct, people belonging to religious Orders, especially of Eastern affiliations, who are provided with life's necessities in exchange for vows of obedience to the rules of their Order, however modest and humble their needs, project an uncommon serenity

and peace of mind, circumstances predisposing votaries to moral and civilized behavior—their lifestyle freed from Nature's ordained struggle for existence. They managed in their unpretentious manner to defy the gravitational impediments of the natural order.

(26) That part of human activity which deals with the effort to provide for self-preservation is the subject of economics, i.e., the study of the process of earning an income, a profit, based on free-market designs. A free-market economy exists if prices are determined by the unregulated interchange of supply, demand and the allocation of resources, the effects of unfettered competition being pivotal in setting the level of prices. Economics accepts as foundational the centrality of competition in guiding the market economy. It presupposes that competitors act rationally and honestly, being equally knowledgeable about market conditions, desire equal opportunities and a level playing field. But as anyone who has a working knowledge of the world of business must know, such assumptions are illusory. It is a false pretense of competitors to claim that they desire a level playing field when most of them conspire to win an undue advantage and seek to exploit unequal opportunities to gain the upper hand. It is the essence of free-market competition that no two individuals are equally rational and knowledgeable. Besides, impulse, emotion, and intuition create a distinct advantage. The rational and knowledgeable competitor would have to be capable of analyzing and grasping all possible permutations of production, demand, supply, employment, governmental budget surplus or deficit, population growth, interest rates and savings, a task far too complex for any human mind to comprehend in order to determine the effect that an increase or decrease of each one will have on the other—that is, if there is any measurable correlation between them, a matter of pure speculation and hypothesis. No sooner do businessmen engage in intense competition than one tries to get the better of the other by employing underhanded tactics. Morality is almost never a consideration—self-preservation is paramount and reciprocity of fair dealing an obstacle. Classical economics ignores the corrupting influence upon man's integrity of high-powered pursuits of an inordinate desire for wealth since its protagonists hold forth that to be persuasive one has to be amoral, a matter of great concern for intense competition tends to slide into immorality. Greed, deception, guile, double-dealing, and rapacity escalate the aggressive pursuit of besting one's opponent, traits consistent with the natural order, exacerbating tension and turmoil among contestants and leading to social instability. Economics institutionalizes unin-

hibited self-seeking and graspingness, its design places the crude pursuit
of wealth within the framework of presumed probity, favors the wealthy
and powerful who tend to act in concert to thwart the role of competition, subvert regulations considered restrictive and frustrate free enterprise. Man must repudiate unrestricted competition as morally destructive and self-defeating for it has brought much harm and disruption to
mankind. Economists will have to rewrite their fancy theories and
acknowledge that in a free-market economy as presently constituted—
with inequality among competitors becoming more pronounced—honesty, morality and fair dealing are the traits of losers. Economics denigrates the process of earning a living to the level of amoral pursuits, providing a cover for the unscrupulous intriguers and speculators to do their
scheming. As long as the economic infrastructure of any well-functioning
society requires the poor and middle class to embrace an overwhelming
majority, their struggle for existence, unlike that of many of the super-
rich, will be consumed with relentless and increasing efforts to succeed
in the competitive world, endeavors pursued with unyielding vigor
thanks to the prevailing deception of playing fields being level with
rewards belonging to the most zealous and unrestrained. The message is
clear: classical economics and its subsequent variations provide no room
for morality, for civilized conduct, for civilized man—most competitors
are destined to yield to unscrupulous self-seeking.

(27) The soundness of business judgment is overrated since it is based upon
short-term results as contrasted with long-term outcomes. Short-term
results are easier to ascertain because consideration need be given only to
extant opportunities and knowable circumstances. Long-term planning is
complex, beset with contingencies and undetermined variables which
could favor or abort the projected results. Three such variables of undetermined consequences affecting the long-term outcomes of a balanced
or retreating economy are:
(a) Overpopulation
(b) Environmental disequilibrium
(c) Chronic unemployment
Neither the much vaunted business acumen nor the much maligned
ineptitude of the public sector seem capable of critically analyzing, much
less reacting, to the long-term repercussions of these festering defects. Or
so it seems. But the inability of the private sector is contrived, it must, at
the least, be capable of analysis—the elites of the business world have no
intention of confronting such vexing problems for they claim they are

outside the conceptual framework of the market based system, which is focused on achieving the maximum market share and bring about the most profitable operation. In calculating optimum solutions, the three variables are ignored. The elected public representatives, the public sector, charged with the responsibility of addressing the concerns of all the governed, are mostly too beholden financially to the interests of the influential business community to discharge their public duties—for them, as for others, self-seeking is the results of self-preservation.

(a) Overpopulation is one of the causes of surplus labor, chronic unemployment, and the existence of a permanent underclass of workers. Overpopulation can only be impeded by drastic governmental interventions to institute strict policies of zero-population growth, involving, among other tested measures, limiting offsprings to two per family. The success of such a radical policy rests upon the dedication of public authorities to employ such autocratic deterrents—these extreme steps are, as yet, unthinkable in a democracy. Therefore, achieving population stability at optimum levels will have to await Nature's imposed limitations—measures much more drastic and intimidating than any democratic government would dare imposing.

(b) Environmental disequilibrium, also known as environmental degradation, will make life most unpleasant for mankind. Its chief coefficients are unlimited procreation, inordinate quest for wealth in complete disregard for the consequential damage caused, the drive for continued growth and the intensity of competition. It is inevitable that mankind will persist in abusing the environment since the struggle for existence is paramount. Global warming, the pollution of the atmosphere, the presence of toxic substances in potable water and food supplies will have far-reaching consequences for the physical health of humans, their sanity and life on Earth. The more the environment is violated, the more will humans experience degradation. The private and public sectors are incapable of recognizing the dangers posed and all efforts to mitigate the menace are irresolute—Nature will exact a steep price for the abuses inflicted upon the ecological equilibrium.

(c) Chronic unemployment is the equivalent of a Darwinian economy. Selective cost-cutting in the name of business efficiency bears a heavy responsibility in making over one-half of the world's population unwanted and redundant—their services are not needed to make the other one-half function. The surplus unemployed, largely the result of overpopulation and parallel cost-cutting, require the maintenance of

an elaborate safety net for the most needy, a cost to governments getting progressively larger, resulting in transfers of wealth within and
without developed economies. Unrestricted competition is morally
destructive whether pursued for profits or jobs. Work provides dignity
for the employed, rich or poor; unless people have work and a prospect
of a tolerable quality of life, the primary function of present-day governments must be revised to add the pursuit of an employment
economy to the protection of wealth. It is the unwritten policy among
large producers to protect the profit margin by keeping unemployment at artificially high levels. Such an economic experiment ignores
slumping consumer spending which could only aggravate the profitability of enterprises. The privileged should be concerned and
cannot feel secure in a dysfunctional society which is forced to provide
basic necessities to the disadvantaged for fear that the day could come
when the unemployed and poor would explode out of their misery
and bring on sufficient chaos to menace the standing of the well-to-do
class. Nature could provide a solution to the problem—but absent
that, man must set his sights on the establishment of an employment
economy. Any rise in joblessness or chronic unemployment would hit
consumer spending and inevitably put downward pressure on the
economy, a fact of life that should give pause to the moneyed class.
Modern economics perpetuates a host of outworn ideas, one of which
maintains that there is a correlation between a certain level of unemployment and stable prices—a false concept whose use, like so many
others, brought much unnecessary hardship.

Overpopulation, environmental disequilibrium and chronic unemployment carry the hallmarks of ultimate social disorder and instability. In
so far as these social defects are the result of a permissive economy necessarily tolerant of abuses, injuries caused will forcefully exacerbate relations
among affected humans and abort any civilizing upclimb buried beneath
the surface. Man's natural aggression and primitive lack of restraint will be
further provoked by the feuds over suitable living space, scuffles for scarce
anti-pollution medication and clashes over employment—any mitigation
of his quests opposes the struggle for perseverance and is a non-starter.
The myopia of the private and public sectors let the three variables fester
unchecked, convinced that the dangers were exaggerated and alarmist. But
the strife and conflicts set in motion could only be resolved by the survival
of the fittest—the principle of the natural order—supplanting the forces
of morality and banishing civilization into shadowy oblivion.

CHAPTER 18

CONCLUSION

(1) Prior to mid-19th century, after which advances in science, technology, and medicine began to impact mankind with ever greater intensity, the great majority of humans experienced a painful existence, one of overwhelming privation, distress and grief. Life was harsh for the common people, unsuited for the inept and frail. Husbands toiled to provide the basic necessities for their families; wives were preoccupied with giving birth to numerous children—few survived the early rigors of life; births had to stay ahead of infant and adolescent mortality—burdened with never ending chores from sunrise to sunset, feeding the family unit, and caring for the household. Leisure for the non-wealthy was the rare respite from all-consuming drudgery—the obligatory Sunday church attendance where the priest assured the faithful of divine grace and salvation and eternal damnation for the depraved; the colorful religious festivals; getting together with friends satisfying the thirst for gossip; the occasional communal festivities and carnivals to drive away evil spirits and marked by merry eating and drinking to excess; celebrating the marriage of kin and friends; attending the inevitable funerals of family members and fellow companions—most solemn occasions graced by praying for the departed to receive their eternal reward. Public hangings and burnings of criminals or saints presented the jaded with diverting spectacles. Tormented by diseases which were not understood and attributed to divine retribution; plagued by recurring epidemics, for the importance of

hygiene and cleanliness were unknown; harassed by recurrent wars of religious, political or frivolous origin—usually no prisoners were taken; armies burned villages and ravaged fields; the sword, dagger, or pike inflicted lingering agonies on victims before succumbing to the inevitable—the hardships of such existence were mercifully cut short at a relatively young age (40 years was the average lifespan). Religious beliefs, of necessity, pervaded the scene and life on Earth treated as a preparation for salvation beyond the grave and hope for a more merciful afterlife. The poor and frail were mostly abandoned to their fate, which meant starvation and a slow death; beggars, thieves, robbers, and rapists made the streets unsafe; crimes of murder and arson pervaded the scene; demobilized soldiers begged or robbed to survive; cruelty and corruption were endemic; in most cases armies were not paid and gathered their rewards by plunder; charitable institutions, such as there were, managed by the Church including orphanages, hospitals, schools, and almshouses were too few to relieve the crises caused by massive social problems of the helpless, especially the paupers. Internationally, treaties between countries were solemnly made and just as solemnly violated with impunity.

(2) Life of the well-to-do and privileged was strikingly less stressful and more enjoyable. Financial success was the standard by which men were judged, the same as now. Morality was treated as weakness and a premium placed on deceit, betrayal, cunning, and bribery in business as in politics. Their lives were made more bearable by countless servants; they engaged in various sports, hunting and gambling; jousting tournaments kept the chivalrous busy and the spectators thrilled; lived in roomy houses, well adorned and furnished; dressed and ate well to distinguish them from the lower classes; fear of diminished standing made them intolerant and cruel toward the less advantaged, which was amply manifested in the harsh punishments meted out for the slightest infringement of laws designed to protect the wealthy and privileged.

(3) Punishment for violators of civil, criminal, and religious laws were excessively harsh and reflected not only the cruelty of the times and the severity of retaliations but the fears and insecurity of the Establishment and religious authorities. The police powers were insufficient to keep offenders under control, therefore an example had to be made by the brutality of punishment to discourage potential culprits, in most cases totally out of proportion to the severity of the charges, such as, flogging, mutilation (cutting off limbs, tongue or gouging out an eye, branding as a permanent stigma), hanging, drowning, use of the wheel to break limbs,

burning alive at the stake, flaying, boiling alive in oil or water. When guilt was in doubt, recourse was had to trial by combat or ordeal, invoking the Deity's intervention in resolving the shabby disputes of man. In cases of treason, treated as the most serious crime, the culprit's limbs were tied to four horses pulling in four directions. Yet despite the brutality of punishment, crime was a constant problem, reflecting the hardships suffered by the disadvantaged and the easy recompense of scofflaws, as avoidance of detection and the rebellious spirit of the times encouraged temptation.

(4) Throughout most of this period, the world, but especially Europe, was ravaged by incessant wars of a political or religious nature, insurrections, rebellions, massacres, adventurisms, revolutions, military occupations, assassinations, political and religious murders, violent regime and dynastic changes, which compounded the misery and suffering of an age exhausted by violence, destruction and insecurity. Selecting Europe as a microcosm representative of more than its share of the global turbulent history, the below catalogued episodes are confined to post-11th century to the mid-19th century conflicts which molded the character, thoughts, and beliefs of the affected population. The constant political and military alliances, counter-alliances, and renewed alliances of the royalty, States, and their religious proxies representing the crudest forms of shifting Machiavellian cynical power plays, though affecting the historical development of nations, were omitted wherever possible as not contributing to the emancipation of man from the naked political and religious oppression, nor easing the burden of his existence, nor enhancing the general well-being of the social setting. The millions upon millions of combatants who perished or were maimed in interminable hostile encounters satisfying the whim of this or that monarch, military commander or government—their sacrifices were mostly of momentary gains and vanished, in time, into the thin air of nothingness—are vivid testimony to what extent hollow ambition, insatiable rapacity, and religious fanaticism perverted the conduct of man, light years removed from any vestiges of morality and civilization.

(5) The following historical events, mostly selected from the "Chronicle of the World", ECAM Publications (Published in 1990 in the USA), are catalogued as bearing upon the subject:

• Pope Gregory VII bids to curb the power of princes (1075).
• Pope Urban II organizes 1st Crusade (1095).
• Pope Eugenius III calls for 2nd Crusade (1146).
• Arnold of Brescia, a priest who preached poverty, burned for heresy (1155).

- Thomas Becket murdered at Canterbury (1170).
- Richard Lionheart organizes the 3rd Crusade (1189).
- Anti-Semitic riots spread in England as 500 Jews die at York (1190).
- Constantinople looted by Crusaders of the 4th Crusade (1204).
- English King John forced to sign the Magna Carta—The Great Charter of Liberties for the nobles (1215).
- Pope Innocent III in major attack against Jews and heresy (1215).
- Khan Ogodei's death saves Europe from Mongol horde (1242).
- Catholic Church approves use of torture in hunt for heretics (1255).
- Thomas Aquinas died at the papal court at the age of 48 (1274).
- England expelled Jews to boost the royal coffers (1290).
- Black powder invented in China revolutionized the nature of warfare (1300).
- Philip the Fair of France banishes the Jews and confiscates their property (1306).
- A general council at Vienne, France, abolishes the Order of the Templars (1312).
- Edward III repudiates his debts and bankrupts Italian banks (1346).
- Black Death claims a third of European population (1347-1351).
- Bands of hooded flagellants seek to appease angry God (1349).
- The 100 Years War ignited between England and France (1337).
- The nobles of France crushed the Jacquerie, the peasant revolt with savage ferocity (1358).
- Two Popes, Clement VII and Urban VI split the Catholic Church (1378).
- John Wycliff and his "Lollards" challenge papal power (1379).
- Workers take over the city of Florence from wealthy magnates (1378).
- Revolt of English peasants led by Wat Tyler (1381).
- High taxes provoke uprising in France (1382).
- Spanish mobs set Jewish ghettoes ablaze in Seville and Toledo, forcibly baptizing Jews (1391).
- Freebooting mercenaries roam and plunder Europe (1391).
- A statute is passed in England handing over obdurate heretics to the secular authorities to be burnt (1401).
- Church schism enables three Popes (Benedict XIII, Gregory XII, Alexander V) to claim sole authority (1409).
- Jan Hus, Czech Church reformer, convicted of heresy before Council of Constance and burnt (1415).
- Joan of Arc is condemned by the Inquisition and burnt at Rouen (1431).

- The Hussites (followers of Jan Hus) win a series of victories against Catholic German armies sent to oppose them in Bohemia (1431).
- Cosimo de Medici seizes power in Florence (1434).
- Peasant rebellion prompts King Eric to flee Denmark (1438).
- France defeats England at Castillon, ending the 100 Years War (1453).
- Germans (Gutenberg) print the Bible (1483).
- Lorenzo (the Magnificent) and his brother Guiliano succeed their father Piero de Medici, as rulers of Florence (1468).
- Isabella of Castille marries Ferdinand, heir to the throne of Aragon (1469).
- Ferdinand and Isabella unite Spain (1479).
- Pope Innocent VIII issues a bull deploring the spread of witchcraft and heresy in Germany; he authorized the Dominican Inquisitors to deal with it (1484).
- For well over a century Dominican friars have been burning witches (1486).
- A royal decree orders all Jews out of Spain (1492).
- Columbus proves the world is round (1492).
- Armies with "French pox" (a genital disease) infect Europe (1494).
- Spain and Portugal divide between them all the new lands discovered in the recent voyages of exploration (1494).
- All Jews are expelled from Portugal (1498).
- Spain's Catholic Kings obtained consent of Pope Sixtus IV to appoint Inquisitors (1478).
- German peasants' rebellion breaks out in Speyer (1502).
- Spanish settlers (Santo Domingo) make slaves of Indians (1508).
- The importation of slaves into America is given authorization by Spain (1510).
- The Fuggers bank (German) is asked to sell indulgences to finance the work on the basilica of St. Peter (1513).
- Ulrich Zwingli, a Zurich priest, denounces the morals of the monks and condemns the luxury of the Church (1516).
- The Augustinian monk Martin Luther publishes 95 theses against the sale of indulgences (1517).
- Martin Luther refuses to retract his theses on indulgences (1518).
- Martin Luther implied that the Pope is fallible and is summoned to Rome to answer a charge of heresy (1519).
- Zwingli bans the sale of indulgences in Zurich (1519).
- After publicly burning the papal bull condemning his theses, Luther is excommunicated (1521).

- Charles V sets up a state-run Inquisition in the Netherlands to supplement the long-established papal Inquisition (1522).
- Luther translates Bible into German for the common people (1522).
- Peasants in southern Germany revolt and demand abolition of feudal dues, serfdom and tithes (1524); revolt crushed by German princes, revolt leader beheaded (1525).
- First bibles appear in English language (1525).
- Charles V prohibits the adoption of Protestant doctrines in the Netherlands (1531).
- Henry VIII defies the Pope and marries Anne Boleyn (1533); King becomes head of English Church in final break with Rome (1534).
- Anti-Catholic posters criticizing the Mass posted in Paris (1534).
- The German town of Munster, the stronghold of Anabaptists, is taken by an alliance of Protestant and Catholic troops; its inhabitants massacred (1535).
- Henry VIII seizes monastic wealth (1536).
- Waldensian Protestants who live in Provence, France, massacred (1545).
- Sparked by rising prices, a rebellion breaks out in various parts of England (1549).
- The Peace of Augsburg (Germany) advocates that the religion of a prince should determine the faith of his subjects (1555).
- The manufacture of firearms begins in Austria (1558).
- Attempts by the regent Mary of Guise to suppress Protestant reformers in Scotland provoke them into open rebellion (1559).
- The Scottish Parliament accepts a Protestant confession drafted by John Knox which forbids the saying of Mass and renounces the Pope's authority in Scotland (1560).
- Elizabeth I (Queen of England), in the wake of anti-Roman demonstrations in London, firmly repudiates papal authority (1559).
- Ivan the Terrible orders the drowning of Jews in the Dvina river (1563).
- In London more than 17,000 people (one quarter of the population) have died of the plague (the sixth attack this century) (1563).
- A bad harvest, an increase in the price of bread and resentment against the Inquisition caused Netherland rebels to sack and loot churches (1566).
- Spanish Duke of Alba crushes revolt in Netherlands and reimposes the Inquisition (1568).
- Massacre of Huguenots in Paris on St. Bartholomew's Day instigated by the Catholic Catherine de Medici (1572).

- Imperial Spain goes bankrupt for the second time—costly wars against the Netherlands and England drained the royal treasury (1575).
- Catherine of Medici orders suppression of peasant revolt who rebelled against crushing taxes (1580).
- Catholic Church bans book by Jesuit detailing horrors of the Inquisition (1581).
- The Spanish Armada is defeated in its attempt to invade England (1588).
- Amsterdam, a city of religious toleration, is becoming refugee capital of Europe (1589).
- A violent peasant rebellion breaks out in south-western France in protest at heavy taxes, is met with savage repression (1592).
- Germany torn by a series of witch-hunts, followed by extraction of confession under torture and execution by burning (1595).
- Giordano Bruno is burnt to death as a heretic for advocating pantheism and the idea of an infinite universe (1600).
- The Counter-Reformation gathers force with the persecution of Protestants in Hungary and Bohemia (1602).
- London suffers a serious outbreak of the plague (1603).
- 205 people convicted of witchcraft have been burnt in the last two years at the abbey of Fulda, Germany (1605).
- Since the policy of forced conversion failed, the Spanish king decided to expel converted Moslems from Spain (1609).
- Since 1611, the ecclesiastical officials of Ellwangen, Germany, have some 390 people burnt for witchcraft (1618).
- Lucillo Vanini, an Italian ex-Carmelite monk, was strangled at the stake, then burnt to ashes for his blasphemous view of miracles (1619).
- A band of 35 religious dissenters sets sail in the Mayflower for Virginia, jubilant at the prospect of practicing their brand of worship in the New World (1620).
- Pope Urban III, angered by tobacco imports from the American colonies, pledges to excommunicate all those who take the snuff (1624).
- Peasants in the province of Quercy, France, oppressed by heavy taxation and ravages of continuing wars, rebel (1624).
- London is ravaged by an attack of plague (1625).
- Food shortages in northern France cause much unrest. Exportation of wheat is forbidden in attempt to improve the situation (1626).
- The Bubonic plague hit northern Italy. A million feared dead (1630).
- 274 people accused of witchcraft are executed in the prince-bishopric of Eichstatt, Germany (1629).

- Bishop von Ehrenberg ordered the execution of 900 people for witch-craft at Würzburg, Germany (1630).
- After the Protestant town of Magdeburg (Germany) was sacked by a coalition of Catholic troops, 25,000 of its inhabitants were slaughtered (1631).
- Galileo tried by the Inquisition in Rome, found guilty of teaching the banned Copernican doctrine (1633).
- A serious peasant revolt broke out in Normandy due to increasing demands for taxes to pay for the war against Spain (1639).
- Irish rebels massacred some 10,000 colonists in Ulster and drove the English from the province (1642).
- Conferences throughout Europe brought peace; the Thirty Years War which ravaged Europe ended (1648).
- The English King Charles was beheaded, brought to trial by the Rump parliament. Thomas Pride signed the death warrant. Parliament abolished the monarchy and the House of Lords (1649).
- War, plague and famine ravaged Europe. Death decimated the population. Spain and the German states devastated. The plague is the worst since the 14th century (1650).
- One in two Poles dies of war and plague; invasions, plagues, slave raids and mass murders are the causes of the disasters (1657).
- London gripped by the worst attack of the plague since the Black Death. The death toll reached 100,000 (1665).
- After four days and nights, a fire devastated London (1666).
- In spite of Charles II's opposition, the Act of Habeas Corpus passed making it impossible for anyone in England to be imprisoned without a court appearance (1679).
- Thousands of Huguenots all over France forced to give up their Protestant religion; the King wishes to have a unified Catholic France with one religion (1681).
- Following a revolt, the Praetorian guard of nobles founded by Ivan the Terrible—a thousand of their number were publicly executed on orders of Peter the Great (1698).
- The English invention of a seed-sowing machine causes fear to farm laborers of job losses (1701).
- A Swedish invasion force of 10,000 warriors lured into the depth of the worst winter that even Russia has known, is massively defeated (1709).
- Frederick William of Prussia abolished serfdom on crown property (1719).

- Shuttle inventor (textiles) fled to Paris after narrowly escaping from violent mob that stormed his house in Bury, England. The rioters blame his labor-saving invention, which halved manpower requirements for putting their jobs in jeopardy (1753).
- An earthquake lasting nine minutes devastated Lisbon; more than 10,000 people were killed. A completely new city is to be designed (1755).
- A statement of militant atheism by the French philosopher Helvetius is denounced by the Sorbonne and publicly burnt on the orders of the parliament of Paris (1758).
- Rousseau published "The Social Contract", which outraged the church and state with its unorthodox views on monarchy and religion. The author fled to Switzerland (1762).
- As many as 200,000 people died in three weeks of bitter fighting, which followed a Russian crackdown on Polish moves for greater political and religious freedom (1768).
- An army deserter who stirred up a Russian rebellion of serfs, whose condition worsened under Catherine the Great of Russia, was captured and executed (1775).
- Bread shortages and poor harvest caused violent unrest to break-out in some French regions (1775).
- A series of sweeping legal reforms including the abolition of the death penalty, torture, and the crime of witchcraft were promulgated by Austrian Emperor Joseph II (1776).
- The French King Louis XVI abolished serfdom and torture (1780).
- Anti-Catholic rioters devastated London (1780).
- Catherine II of Russia officially introduced slavery into the Ukraine (1783).
- Peasant revolt broke out in Bohemia following land reforms (1783).
- After the performance of Beaumarchais' play "The Marriage of Figaro" (ordered banned by Louis XVI), he is the object of violent attacks and incarcerated. It was banned because in the play a valet outwits his master (1784).
- Austrian Emperor Joseph II's latest edict promoted religious tolerance and freedom of worship. Priests no longer permitted to publish papal bulls without his consent. Jews no longer barred from the university (1784).
- Leopold, the grand duke of Tuscany, abolished torture and the death sentence (1786).

- France is heading for bankruptcy unless a universal land tax, payable by everyone, is legislated immediately (1786). Parliament refused to approve a new land tax (1787). Louis XVI decreed the parliament's exile (1787).
- Emperor Joseph II (Austria) guaranteed the equality of all his subjects before the law (1787).
- French financial reforms blocked by the entrenched interests of the aristocracy and provincial parliaments (1787).
- The French Assembly approved the "Declaration of the Rights of Man". The document is based on the American "Declaration of Independence" (1789). The Assembly abrogated the feudal rights of the old regime (1789). Peasants revolted against their landlords (1787).
- Influenced by the events in France, peasants in the Rhineland revolted against the nobles' privileges (1789).
- French churches' property is nationalized (1790). The Assembly passed a law abolishing hereditary nobility (1790). The Marquis Condorcet proposed giving civil rights to women (1790).
- Revolution fever spread to Geneva involving the poor townspeople and peasants (1790).
- Jews in France granted French citizenship (1791).
- At the first public meeting of the French National Convention, the monarchy was abolished and the republic declared (1792).
- Louis XVI is guillotined (1793).
- Napoleon Bonaparte and his family exiled from Corsica and forced to seek refuge in France (1793).
- Marie Antoinette was guillotined (1793).
- 21 moderate Girondin leaders executed despite the plea of Robespierre (1793).
- Citizens of France are equal as long as they are not women (1793).
- European monarchs unite against France (1793).
- The Convention issued a decree abolishing slavery throughout the French colonies (1794).
- Napoleon Bonaparte appointed a general in the French army (1794).
- Robespierre and 21 of his companions are guillotined (1794).
- Smallpox—which killed millions over the centuries—could be eradicated, thanks to the work of an English doctor E. Jenner (1795).
- Mutiny broke out in the Royal Navy, refused to put to sea, demanding better pay, better food and better medical treatment. The House of Commons conceded to the men's demands (1796).

- Bonaparte's army conquered Egypt. An uprising by the people of Cairo brutally suppressed by French soldiers of occupation (1798).
- A Belgian peasants' revolt against conscription into the French army is suppressed (1798).
- Napoleon captures Jaffa when his men massacre more than 2,000 Albanian prisoners. French garrison at Jaffa dying of bubonic plague at the rate of 30 a day (1799).
- The Combination Act passed in Britain forbidding the forming of an association by two or more people for the purpose of obtaining wage increases or improved working conditions (1799).
- Royalist uprising broke out across France (1799).
- Bonaparte ousted the French government and seized power (1799).
- Slavery and slave trade restored by the French in the colonies (1802).
- Concerned that pauper children sent to factories are exploited and made to work at night, the British Parliament banned pauper apprentices to work more than 12 hours per day (1802).
- Britain abolished slave trade (1807).
- Shattered by Napoleon's defeat of his army, the Prussian king abolished serfdom, all class distinctions in State employment and the privileges of nobility (1807).
- With the country in the grip of economic crisis, the British government is forced to adopt paper money as currency (1811).
- Napoleon begins his invasion of Russia (1812).
- After failing to persuade Czar Alexander to come to terms, Napoleon begins a retreat from Moscow (1812).
- The Allies (Austria, Russia, Prussia and Britain) enter Paris. Napoleon is exiled to Elba (1814).
- Returning from Elba, Napoleon enters Paris and after a crushing defeat at Waterloo, exiled to the island St. Helena (1815).
- Catholic royalists in southern France began a campaign of reprisals against Bonapartists; part of the garrison at Nimes is massacred (1815).
- Austria's Prince Metternich persuaded ministers of the German States to ban political meetings, impose press censorship, and investigate the educational system in an effort to check revolutionary and liberal movements in Germany (1819).
- Britain recognized workers' right to strike (1824).
- The Northern Society (Russia) which campaigned for representative government, the abolition of serfdom and social reforms launched a revolt which is crushed by Czar Nicholas (1825).

- Greeks gained independence from the Ottoman Empire (1829).
- Violent riots by farmworkers in the south of England harshly repressed by the army (1830).
- The Italian republican Mazzini founded a revolutionary society that aims in uniting Italy through a general uprising (1831).
- A bill of parliamentary reform is passed in England giving the vote to men of substantial property (1832).
- A liberal student uprising against Frankfurt (Germany) police is brutally suppressed (1833).
- Papal bull condemned freedom of the press, abolition of censorship, freedom of education, and freedom of worship; the Pope declared that the church did not need reforming (1832).
- Republican uprising against the Bourbon monarch crushed in France (1834).
- Slavery abolished throughout the British Empire (1834).
- The League of the Just (Germany) is founded which brought together apprentices and journeymen aiming to free Germany from oppression and humankind from slavery (1836).
- "Peoples Charter" (London) demanded "one man, one vote" elections, secret ballots and the right of workingmen becoming MPs (1838). The threat of an armed working-class revolt organized by the Chartists suppressed following army intervention (1839).
- Riots and strikes broke out in northern England, protesting against reduction in wages (1842).
- Weavers in Silesia rebelled in protest against lower wages due to use of mechanical weaving. The revolt is bloodily suppressed (1844).
- Blight struck the potato, the staple food of 4 million people in Ireland who live almost wholly on potatoes; a serious famine looms; Irish families are emigrating in the tens of thousands (1845).
- During a period of severe depression and unemployment, disturbances broke out among agricultural workers in central France provoked by food shortages (1847).
- An act passed in Britain that limits the working day of women and children aged 13 to 18 to 10 hours (1847).
- Marx called Europe's workers to revolt. Flames of revolution burned capitalistic power bases. French monarchy dissolved, republic declared. Austrian rulers expelled from Italy. Prince Metternich resigned following demonstrations in Vienna. With the outbreak of revolt in Berlin, the Prussian king granted a constitution. Venetians proclaimed

their independence. Hungary proclaimed its independence of Austria. Prussian troops suppress Warsaw uprising. The revolt in Naples collapses (1848).

- Austrian emperor forced to abdicate. The Pope fled from the Vatican alarmed by the activities of revolutionary clubs. Prussian king dissolved the National Assembly. The Austrian army invaded Hungary forcing Budapest to surrender. Mazzini proclaimed the Roman republic (1848).
- Russia aided Austria and crushed Hungarian uprising (1849).
- College is founded for women in London giving them the opportunity of a university education (1849).

(6) Throughout the period covered there was frequent hunger due to poor harvests, even occasional instances of starvation; shortages of bread which always caused riots or open expressions of discontent, perhaps the sumptuous lifestyle of the nobility was only too visible; increased taxes levied against the less affluent classes repeatedly caused civil unrest since raising the level of taxes is not only never popular but the discriminatory imposition most irritating because of the exemption granted to the favored nobility; the same for price increases of staples since the underclass, the majority, was most affected and the causes laid at the doorstep of arbitrary greed and transparent speculation. All the foregoing rebellions, revolts, riots, civil unrest, and the intermittent conflicts between the property owner/entrepreneur and the tenant farmer/employee/peasant were mercilessly crushed by the armed forces in the employ of the Establishment since they were rightfully viewed as undermining the privileges of the ruling classes. The elites, the ruling circles, maintained their dominant power in league with religious authorities, Catholic and later also Protestant Churches, so that any aspirations to reduce the oppressive yoke and gain some freedom were directed against the more menacing, invasive, and more readily culpable Church hierarchy, who defended their privileged lifestyle with uncommon intrigues, connivance and ruthlessness. If there is a common thread permeating the narrated episodes, it is the gradual, persistent, and unrelenting struggle of the common people against the suffocating and inflexible oppression maintained by the Church priesthood, yielding grudgingly in the least installments only when forced to do so until the French Revolution abruptly swept away, albeit in France only for a few fleeting years, the last vestiges of that grim experience. Likewise, as if operating in tandem with the Church, the political Establishment of the privileged yielded political rights and par-

ticipation to the common people under duress only and when faced with no alternatives, revoking concessions granted, from time to time, in seemingly desperate rear guard actions to postpone the inevitable. But the seal was broken, the way shown, the liberties once experienced spread like wildfire and could not be erased or retracted without arousing hostile resentment. That is, until the 20th century when communism, fascism, Nazism, totalitarianism and autocratic regimes made a mockery of the revolutionary freedom-loving spirit which energized the optimism and sacrifices of prior generations.

(7)   Throughout the period covered art in all its forms flourished, sponsored by wealthy patrons (sometimes even by the Vatican) who unstintingly supported painters, sculptors, architects, musical composers, and others to create masterpieces of lasting glory to be enjoyed by contemporary and future generations of well-sated admirers. Yet throughout most of this period, the fagots of the Inquisitions lit up the sky, millions of innocents were massacred or rotted in dungeons, victims of man's cruelty and contempt for others, crushing anyone who dared express aspirations for a less oppressive existence. Throughout most of this period, Nature's various plagues and epidemics seemingly selected victims at random, claiming the lives of tens of millions and terrorized the survivors by fear of an agonizing and abrupt demise, the havoc caused as yet medically inexplicable and totally irreconcilable with the preached beneficence of Providence.

These were harsh times for humans. Their grim existence presented too few occasions for morality to sink its roots and exercise any effect upon human conduct. Civilization was non-existent by any standards or definitions and most assuredly not by the standard defined at great length by the author. The corruption of the term would be a crude affront to the memory of countless humans who experienced the suffering and indignities inflicted on them by man's uncontrolled and uninhibited natural instinct of self-preservation run amok, who made the existence and life's experiment for so many something akin to hell on Earth.

(8)   Some pundits tell us that Western civilization is in decline. They enlarge on the causes: that the majority of present and future generations will be increasingly more dependent on a drug culture, exposed to submarginal education deficient in basic skills required of a responsible and productive citizenry; that the influence of loosened sexual mores discourage traditional marriages and raising of children; the marked increase in what is commonly referred to as moral depravity, lamenting the social impact of

homosexuality, lesbianism, gay marriages and gay parents; that the rise of dissolute and licentious content and language in public entertainment expose viewers to corrupt influences; that the absence of thought-provoking reading of any kind leads to paucity of vocabulary, inability to formulate ideas, lack of simple writing ability, and absence of spatial thinking; last but not least, that the absence of religious content and values account for the lack of compass in guiding the morally perplexed in times of stress and anguish.

This litany of jeremiads can be readily applied to any segment of man's history as representing the criteria of a subculture of contempt for normative attitudes, a rebellion against the unattainable and missed opportunities, a mistaken critique of something seemingly unique when, in fact, it has been commonplace and a transparent feature of organized societies in all historical periods. All these defects bemoaned by pundits have nothing to do with civilization. A study of the various social settings throughout history would lead to the realization that they all experienced temporary "declines", a natural consequence of systematic and persistent benign neglect, of unalterable social fragmentation and deplored as such by each generation.

(9) A state of affairs in which the majority of mankind observe a conduct that is truly moral; where humans strive to lighten the burden of existence of their fellowmen and satisfaction of primary needs mandate the requisite restraint of the aggressive instinct of self-preservation; where freedom of speech, thought, assembly, redress of grievances, religious tolerance, and equal justice are guaranteed to all by a truly democratic system in which voters retain the primary political power and not yield any to lobbyists who, acting for special interest groups, distort the will of the electorate; where a genuinely free enterprise system presents unlimited opportunities to the qualified, but does not abandon or discard the disadvantaged; where the State is obligated to pursue a full employment economy (any economy that does not pursue maximum employment as a means of preserving social tranquility is a fake economy) and retain sufficient of the accumulated surplus to provide a safety net for those too old, ailing, or otherwise unable to provide for themselves; where healthcare, education, old-age pension benefits, and retirement homes are not treated as privileges but State responsibilities to safeguard social order and harmony; where international trade or political disputes and conflicts are settled by bilateral or multilateral negotiations given the horror and destruction the latest technological weaponry pose to all combatants—these are truly the

hallmarks of civilization deserving of that appellation, a conjunction of the better attributes of humankind, a coalescence of mutually compatible values which could not but promote harmony, tranquility and the necessary symmetry of permanence.

Civilized societies could not countenance with equanimity and be guilty of apathy bordering on indifference when the following are made manifest:

(a) Where undernourishment, starvation, poverty, diseases caused by polluted food or water, insect-borne infections, and sexually transmitted contagions especially AIDS, malaria and tuberculosis, devastate the lives of large segments of population inhabiting underdeveloped and developing countries.

(b) Where goods and services are exported to be sold in developed countries and produced by literal slave labor, particularly when children of school age are forced to work long hours under the most primitive conditions.

(c) Where young girls and women are forced into prostitution by means of deception and traded like commodities among procurers.

(d) Where faith-based beliefs are permitted to interfere with, or even halt, scientific advances in genetic engineering and thus deprive humanity of modifying its own evolution by designing replacement of diseased body parts and preventing physical and mental infirmities by altering the genetic make-up of man.

(e) Where producers, distributors and users, but especially the auto, oil and utilities industries are permitted to degrade the environment, unbalance the ecosystem and cause global warming, all to the detriment of the physical and mental well-being of the present and future generations of mankind.

(f) Where religious groups and cynical entrepreneurs are permitted to interfere with, nay even abort, any efforts to impede unlimited population procreation and thus contribute to the many hazards overpopulation poses to mankind.

(10) It must be taken for granted that every human of sound mind would wish for civilized society to become a permanent fixture and the culmination of the historical development, shedding the innumerable detours and handicaps of the past, the peaks and valleys, in order to arrive and settle on an elevated plateau conducive to social harmony. Most humans wish to avoid tension and stress which lead to disharmony and dissension, making existence a less pleasurable experience. In the past, civilization

was subdued in the contest of opposing forces, political, military and religious, contests for the domination of one kind or another given the simplicity and immaturity of man harboring the vain conviction that supremacy was attainable and that he could impose his will and perspective on others with finality and permanence, a singular world crafted as a reflection of his deemed superiority and sense of order. But the world and mankind were not amenable. Man failed in the past because his aims were ahead of technological developments; he will fail in the future because technological developments have overtaken his capacity to cope with the advances achieved and will retain their primacy for the foreseeable future. Man's sense of order is transitory and artificial, imposed upon others till the momentary advantages are exhausted only to have the process repeated by another's sense of order. There have always been social and economic forces, contradictory in purpose and pulling in conflicting directions, sometimes openly antagonistic and at times keeping the lid on and biding time for an opportune moment to manifest the latent resentment. A state of civilization was beyond mankind's reach in the past and will remain so in the future because of the permanent and unchangeable economic fragmentation of society, a necessary appendage of human intercourse, with the privileged segment resisting the usurpation of their benefits by the less advantaged. Greed and self-seeking have ever been human constants. In the past, the machinations of the privileged, always a mere minority, succeeded in preserving its hegemony by the expedient use of obscure facades of pious flimflams only to gain at present an uncommon transparency revealing the crudity of purpose. As a consequence, the minority is coerced to fortify its claims by masking its objectives behind pretensions which, in plain language, are nothing short of fraud, deception, cunning, duplicity, obfuscation and subtle smokescreen, attitudes of the natural order, man's unbridled instinct of self-preservation. As long as the majority remains cowed by such craftiness, the balance of power will remain with the privileged and the status quo unchangeable.

(11) But if the self-seeking of the privileged and wealthy is not sufficiently abated in the future to narrow the gap between the advantaged and disadvantaged and thus achieve more acceptable levels—and all signs point to the contrary—then the turmoil and agitation will keep on festering even though some segments achieve sufficient gains by whatever means only to face a repeat of future discontent. Such ongoing and deep-seated dissentions would not permit morality to sink its roots, nor permit civi-

lization to brighten man's future. The instincts of self-preservation are Nature's superior design to provide man with the means of survival in a competitive environment. But by their very design they are unsuited to promote harmony, rapport and communal cooperation toward a common goal. Man structured the economic and faith-based systems—the two main engines that drive mankind—the former to satisfy survival needs, the latter to vanquish fears of the unknown, all in accordance with Nature's scheme since competition is basic to both systems, competition which involves winners and losers in the former, salvation and damnation in the latter; the preservation of the privileges and wealth status in the former, life's comforts and security provided for the religious priestly orders in the latter. The privileged and wealthy seek imbalance, turmoil and undemocratic means to maintain their standing—a state of civilization is not an option. The religious priestly orders disdain freedom of speech and thought, treat their beliefs as preeminent, unique and exclusive, dogmatize about their teaching and use undemocratic means to maintain their standing—a state of civilization is not an option.

The finding is inevitable and unavoidable: Nature's engines that drive mankind failed to make a state of civilization feasible in the past. They will make it unattainable in the future.

BIBLIOGRAPHY

(1) Civilization—Kenneth Clark (Harper & Row—1969)

(2) A History of Civilization—Fernand Braudel (Penguin Books—1995)

(3) The Civilization of Europe in the Renaissance—John Hale (Atheneum—1993)

(4) The Story of Civilization—Will Durant (Simon and Schuster, Inc.—1963 to 1975)

(5) Civilization Before Greece and Rome—H. W. F. Saggs (Yale University Press—1989)

(6) The Vices of Economics—Deidre N. McCloskey (Amsterdam University Press—1996)

(7) Money—John Kenneth Galbraith (Houghton Mifflin Company (Revised ed. 1995)

(8) Economics at Bay—Robert Lekachman (McGraw-Hill Book Company—1976)

(9) Economics Explained—Robert Heilbroner and Lester Thurow (Simon and Schuster—1998)

(10) Turbo Capitalism—Edward Luttwak (Harper Collins Publishers, Inc.—1999)

(11) The Crisis of Global Capitalism—George Sokos (Public Affairs—1998)

(12) The Case Against the Global Economy—Edited by Jerry Mander and Edward Goldsmith (The Sierra Book Club—1996)

(13) Money and the Nation State—Edited by Kevin Dowd and Richard H. Timberlake, Jr. (Transaction Publishers—1998)

(14) Economics of a Pure Gold Standard—Mark Skousen (The Foundation for Economic Education, Inc.—1977)

(15) The Zero-Sum Society—Lester C. Thurow (Basic Books, N.Y.—1980)

(16) Environmental Economics—R. Kerry Turner David Pearce and Ian Bateman (The Johns Hopkins University Press)

(17) The Critics of Keynesian Economics—Henry Hazlitt (The Foundation for Economic Education, Inc.—1995)

(18) Globalizing Capital—Barry Eichengreen (Princeton University Press—1996)

(19) Capital Flows and Financial Crises—Edited by Miles Kahler (Cornell University Press—1998)

(20) Disposable People—Kevin Bales (University of California Press—1999)

(21) Secrets of the Temple—William Greider (Simon and Schuster, Inc.—1987)

(22) The Age of Economists—The Ludwig Von Mises Lecture Series, Volume 26 (Hillsdale College Press—1999)

(23) The History of Money—Jack Weatherford (Three River Press—1997)

(24) Winner Take All—William R. Gallacher (McGraw-Hill—1994)

(25) Principals of Economics—Lewis A. Froman (Richard D. Irwin, Inc.—1947)

(26) Money and Banking—Charles L. Prather (Richard D. Irwin, Inc.—1947)

(27) The Wordly Philosophers—Robert L. Heilbroner (Simon and Schuster, Inc.—1986)

(28) Classical Economics Reconsidered—Thomas Sowell (Princeton University Press—1974)

(29) The Money Lenders—Anthony Sampson (The Viking Press—1982)

(30) Trading for a Living—Dr. Alexander Elder (John Wiley & Sons, Inc.—1993)

INDEX